War Stories
Lived by a L.A. Cop

ROBERT E REYNOLDS

To Family and Students

Without the inspiration of my family and former students, I would not have sat down and relived my stories on paper. And a special thank you to my daughter-in-law, Anna Porter, for putting it all in motion.

Contents

Chapter 1

Harbor Division Patrol—Morning Watch

November 1960–October 1961

It is the middle of November, the year 1960; I am sitting in the kitchen of my new apartment, just rented in the beach city of San Pedro, California. Just a month earlier, I graduated from the Los Angeles Police Academy, and tonight I will be starting my first assignment attached to the Harbor Division of the Los Angeles Police Department.

Getting ready to start my first shift as a LAPD police officer, first night on the job, I have just finished laying out my police uniform and my police equipment,. My shift is to start at midnight. I am rechecking my uniform and equipment to make sure it was ready to go. My leather gear, known as a Sam Brown belt—which will hold my nightstick, the holster for my .38-caliber weapon, ammo pouch, and handcuffs—was spit-shined. I check my weapon, which is a Colt .38 six-inch revolver, to assure it is as clean as possible. I double-check that my Peerless key works my handcuffs perfectly. My ammo pouch is loaded full of backup .38-caliber rounds. I check the leather strap on my nightstick to assure it's securely attached to the stick. My new police-blue uniform is sharply pressed and my shoes are polished. I am ready to go.

Can you believe this? Am I ready for this? They told us at the academy that we would be on probation for one year. One year to prove to the department and to myself that I can and will perform as a competent police officer. After that first year, I will be reviewed and could be let go! Have I made the right decision in my life? I can only hope that I will be able to perform to the standards set for me.

• • •

I had only been in Los Angeles for less than a year, moving out from Ohio. I had been attending Kent State University in Ohio on a football scholarship. Prior to my second season of football, it was revealed to me that I would not be eligible to play football for the university. After having several brain concussions of various degrees, the team doctors would not allow me to play, ending my career. I could continue my education, but no more sports. At home, trying to decide if the classroom was where I wanted to be, I noticed a request in the local paper from my high school English teacher's husband, looking for someone to help him drive to California. I went back to college that weekend, dropped out, and left for California.

When I got to California, I stayed in the LA area and found a job at a manufacturing company in El Segundo. An ad in the *TV Guide* recruiting officers for the Los Angeles police department caught my eye. The ad featured a Los Angeles police officer in uniform, and stated you could be your own boss and make $489 a month working for the Los Angeles Police Department. At the time that seemed like a lot of money. I also liked the idea of being my own boss. So I applied for the job in June of 1960, made it into the police academy in August, and graduated in October.

So here I was, sitting in my new apartment in San Pedro, getting ready to go to work for the Los Angeles Police Department in the Harbor Division. I had just had my twenty-first birthday in May of that year. In looking back, it was hard to realize that in the last year and a half I had came to California at the age of nineteen, and here I was: a Los Angeles police officer about to go to work for the city of Los Angeles.

"OK, let's do it. It's time to go to work. It's eleven at night, and I have to be at roll call at midnight," I told myself. My shift was going to be from 12:30 a.m. until 8:30 a.m. After carefully gathering up my uniform and police equipment, I drove to work. It took only seven minutes to get to the station, but took another fifteen minutes to find a parking place—the whole time I was looking, I was laughing at myself, thinking I would be late my first night! Finally I found a parking place and walked up a dozen steps to the front-door entrance. I worked myself through the station to the locker room, where I began to change out of my street clothes into my uniform. As I was changing , I was approached by a huge police officer. He must have been six foot four inches tall and weighed about 260 pounds.

"So you are the new police officer. My name is Carl Weems. You'll be working with me tonight. Get your gear on and meet me in the coffee room. I will introduce you to some of the other police officers who will be working this shift. You need to get to know them, as they could save your life someday." With that he walks off and leaves me to get ready for work.

I finished putting on my uniform and equipment and proceeded to walk down the hall to the coffee room, adjacent to the roll-call room. Entering the coffee room, I saw Weems sitting at a table with several other officers. Most of these officers were sporting hash marks on their uniform sleeves that indicated they had been on the job for fifteen years or more: each hash mark indicated five years of service. I was sure that most of the officers working this division had prior military duty; a lot of police officers hired on after World War Two.

After getting my coffee, I approached the table and asked if I could sit down. Weems spoke up: "Pull up a chair, and I'll introduce you to my friends and fellow officers. This officer sitting to my left is Wes Parker, referred to as The Groaner. This officer sitting to my right is Dominic Pizza—he answers to Dom—and this officer sitting across from me is Henry 'Hank' Trotter. You will be working with all of us on this morning watch, and as long as you follow our lead, you'll get through your probation just fine. Do what we say and you will be OK. We all have been here a long time and know these streets. Some rookies listen to us and do OK and others, who don't listen, don't make it."

Next to speak was Wes, the groaner. He was shorter, bald-headed, and as big a round as he was tall.

"Welcome to Sleepy Hollow, my friend. We will be working together when Weems is on days off, so we'll get to know each other. Weems will take good care of you."

4

"I'm looking forward to working with you and will try and do a good job," I said.

"Yeah, that's what they all say," replied Hank. He was a tall, skinny guy, and looked like the wind could blow him away.

"Leave the kid alone, Hank; you're always trying to put someone down," said Dominic. "Don't let him bother you, kid, he's just a traffic officer. Any time you need good advice, you come to me and I'll square you away." Dominic then got up and went to the roll-call room.

The rest of us got up and followed Dominic into the roll-call room. I noticed that the watch commander was already there, at the front of the room, waiting on us. The roll-call room was filled with long tables and benches to sit on, arranged on the right and left side of the room with a walkway up the middle. There were other officers already seated at the tables. Once we sat down, the watch commander started roll call by calling off the assigned units and who was manning each. My unit tonight was going to be five *A* five.

"I want you all to recognize our new probation officer who's been assigned our division and will be working with all of you on morning watch for the next six months. Officer Reynolds, stand up and let everyone see you," the watch commander stated.

I stood up, and, as I did, everyone in the room turned and looked at me. I heard someone say "the city is going to be well protected tonight." This was followed by several officers laughing and clapping. When things quieted down, the watch commander began to conduct the roll call again. As he was giving the vacation checks and administrative instructions, I looked around the roll-call room. I noticed that all of the officers (with the exception of two) were veteran officers. They all appeared to be bigger than my height of six feet and weight of 175 pounds. I considered myself in good shape, having just come out of Academy. In the academy, physical conditioning was stressed strongly, and I had continued my conditioning by working out and running on the beach.

After finishing the roll call, the watch commander dismissed us, and we all left the roll-call room, taking our gear with us and proceeding downstairs to go to work. We all walked out the front of the building and down the steps to the street level. I was told that the preceding watch would be coming in with the vehicles, and we were to swap out the cars and go to work. As the cars would pull up in front of the station, the corresponding officers would swap out with the incoming officers and drive off for their adventure of the night. Officer Weems signaled to me that our car had arrived. He stated that he would be the one to drive and I would be the passenger officer, responsible for taking care of the book-work. He further informed me that I would not be driving for at least a week or until I familiarized myself with the area.

As we approached our car, I noted that the car was a 1958 Chevrolet; some of the other cars there were 1959 Fords. All of the cars were four-door sedans, painted black and white, with light bars on the rooftop, and they all had the LAPD logo on their doors: To Protect and Serve. When I sat myself in the front passenger seat, I noticed that the car had no heater or air conditioning. The car had a radio in the center of the dash that had the LAPD frequencies. There was a lighted display in the center of the dash that contained what was called a hot sheet. This was a list of the most recently stolen cars. The car also had a plug-in spotlight that was lying on the front seat. Officer Weems approached the car on the driver side, opened the rear driver-side door, placed a briefcase on the backseat, and took out a packet of papers. He asked me to give him my "nightstick" (which is a baton two feet long and one inch in diameter). I handed my baton to him over the top of the front seat, and, explaining "We keep them there pointed out, so we can grab them as we get out of the car, when we need them," he shoved it into the space between the top and bottom of the backseat. Weems closed the back door, opened the front door, and got in behind the wheel. Handing me the notebook containing the packet of papers, he turned to me.

"OK, kid, you can take this notebook and keep it with you during our shift. It has a daily log inside, as well as the typical reports that we may be using during the shift. You are going to be in charge of filling out any and all paperwork. We use the daily log to list the activities that we engage in over the next eight hours. We list them by the time of occurrence and how long they each take us. So you can make the first entry from midnight until twelve thirty, showing that we attended roll call." He started the car, and we drove off for my first of many nights patrolling the streets of LA.

As we drove down the street, I took the notebook and put it on the floor between my feet. In 1960 seatbelts were not yet a fixed safety option, so there was no need to buckle up—there were no seatbelts. Officer Weems instructed me to use the radio to inform the dispatcher that we were in service—that translated to police jargon as "unit five A five is clear." I picked up the radio mike to make this notification. The mike looked like a snake about to bite me. After I stated "Unit five A five is clear," a woman's voice responded "I am showing unit five Adam five clear." At this time the realization hit me that I was actually on patrol in the city of Los Angeles.

As we started driving the area, Officer Weems began to explain the makeup of the different cities we would be patrolling. It seems that all the towns—San Pedro, Harbor City and Wilmington—are made up of many different cultures. "Harbor City and San Pedro have a lot of intermixed cultures as well. Wilmington is predominantly Hispanic. So you're going to encounter people from many different cultures, including Somali, Hispanic, Scandinavian, Grecian, Italian, and Caucasian. You will need to learn how to interpret each culture's background and adjust your approach to respect the nationality of the person you're dealing with. You need to forget any forethought conclusions you might have had about any other culture. You're going to learn to treat each situation objectively and not judge other people's lifestyles or beliefs. The first thing to know about police work is that we cannot bring any prejudices to work with us about people and how they live. If you can learn your job is to enforce the laws as they are written and not to let your own beliefs become the laws, you will be a hell of a cop."

I chose not to answer Weems about what he had just told me until I grasped the meaning of it. He continued to drive the car, and in about ten minutes told me we were entering our area of responsibility. I observed that we were in a residential area and that the houses were middle class. The streets we were driving on were two-lane roadways as were the intersecting streets. We drove by various businesses including markets, liquor stores, and gas stations. Since it was almost one in the morning, the only places open were liquor stores, gas stations, and occasional bars. The traffic on the streets was minimal, and there were very few people on the sidewalks. The radio spoke only on occasion.

After patrolling the area for about an hour, we received our first radio call. "Unit five Adam five, see the man about a physical assault. He is at the Harbor Medical Center's emergency room." I answered the call by stating, "Unit five Adam five, roger." This was going to be the first radio call for service I would answer.

Officer Weems drove the car to the Harbor Medical Center and upon arrival instructed me to bring the notebook with the reports into the facility with us. He also reminded me not to forget to log the call on our officer's log and list the time that we had received it. We went into the emergency room of the medical center; there an on-duty nurse met us. She informed us that the person we needed to interview was receiving emergency medical care, but we could interview him. The nurse led us to the room where the patient was being treated. Officer Weems informed me that I was to go into the room and take a report from the patient; Weems was going to remain in the lobby. He indicated it was my job to take the reports, and to just rely on my academy training to get it done.

I carried my notebook with me into the emergency room. I noted that the patient was lying on a table and that a doctor was standing alongside the patient. The patient's right arm was stretched away from his body, revealing a cut to the forearm on the inside of the arm. The cut was approximately six inches long. The skin on either side of this cut had been laid back to the bone. The wound was bleeding superficially. It appeared that no major blood vessels had been cut. The doctor was in the process of sewing up the wound.

I stood there for a minute, allowing my stomach to settle, and then asked the doctor if I could talk to the patient. The doctor informed me it was OK to speak with the patient while he sewed up the wound. I noted that the patient's chart listed him as Somalian descent. I asked him what had happened to his arm, and he refused to talk to me. Upon asking him if he had called us to make a report, he stated no. After several attempts to get the information from the patient about what led to his being cut and ending up at the medical facility, with no results, I left the room.

I met up with Officer Weems in the lobby. "Well, looks like you passed your first test, Kid. You were able to walk, not run, out of that room after seeing that nasty wound, with all the blood. Some recruits I worked with would have come running out of there sick to their stomach! Did you get the report?"

"No, I didn't," I replied. "He wouldn't tell me what had happened to him or where it had happened. But I was able to get his name, address, birth date, and social security number from the receptionist at the desk. Her entry into his file showed he came in by ambulance from the No Knock bar. Do you want to follow up and go to that location to see what we can find out?"

"That won't be necessary," Officer Weems replied. "If he doesn't want to make a report and feels he will take care of this himself, we can't get involved. It would be a waste of paper, anyhow, because he wouldn't appear in court to testify against whoever cut him. The lesson learned is that some cases aren't worth the effort to pursue, when we have no cooperation. We try to persuade them to work with us, but if they won't, we can't make them; besides, there are plenty of cases we can win."

As we were walking into the parking lot to get into the car, I began thinking about what Weems had said about my passing the test of blood. Yes, I had been able to, but it was not so easy; I have to admit that my stomach did turn while watching that doctor sewing up that wound. For some bizarre reason, while watching the stitching of the arm, I imagined that the person was a cow! I have no idea why a cow came to mind for me—maybe because cows are cut for meat all the time, and we have all seen cow blood. By being able to transpose a person into a cow I was able to not feel any sorrow for the person. (From this day on I was able to handle any injured person by thinking of them as a cow.)

We got into the car, and I logged in the call that we had just completed. It was now 2:00 a.m. Weems turned to me and said, "We have to talk about something."

"OK."

"I know they taught you a lot about departmental policies while you were in the police academy. You are going to have to make some decisions about how you will handle some of these policies. Did you notice the officer in roll call wearing glasses and writing in a notebook the whole time? His name is Phil Smith."

"Yes, I saw him. I noticed that he didn't have any hash marks on his sleeve."

"He's been on the job for four years. He transferred into Harbor Division about a year ago. Most officers I work with do not care to work with him. He's a strict 'by the book' officer. He writes everything down in that notebook of his. Someday you will probably be working for him, if you are assigned to work with him, make sure you go by the book."

"OK. Is that what you wanted to talk about?"

"No, it's about our hats. I know they told you at the academy that you are to wear your hat at all times you are out in the public. That includes while you're sitting in this car. So far I have worn my hat continually since the first time you first saw me tonight, including at the station, where wearing the hat is not necessary. I am aware you have done the same. Now this is one of the policies you can make your own choice about. I'm going to take my hat off and lay it down in the back seat. Most of the guys don't wear their hats while in the car. In my case it hits the headliner all the time. I just have to remember to get my hat and put it on when I get out of the car. Some will say that's out of policy, so if my comfort comes before policy, I'm going to be comfortable. You make your own decisions as to wearing your hat. You can keep it on or take it off. Now, Phil Smith would leave it on."

Weems took off his hat and reached across the back of the front seat and laid it on the backseat. I looked at him and was shocked to see he had a full head of hair that was solid white. This gave him the appearance of a movie star. I would classify him as a ladies' man. Weems started up the car and pulled out of the parking lot. As he did this, I took my hat off, reached across the back of the front seat, and laid my hat on the back-seat.

"You need to get on the radio and clear of us from that call," Weems said.

I picked up the radio mike, keyed it, and stated, "Five Adam five clear." The dispatcher came back stating we were clear. I took out my pocket notebook and opened it up to review the radio codes; I had a cheat sheet in my notebook. Upon examining them I saw that a code two meant we would proceed to a call in all haste, not using our siren. Code three meant to proceed in all haste with the siren. Code four was used for telling other units no response to our call was needed by them. Code six was used to tell communications that we were going to be out of our car. The most important code was code seven. We used this code when we were requesting permission to stop and eat. We had to get clearance from communications in order to take our half-hour lunch break. This was done so not all units were out of the field (division) at the same time. I put my notebook back in my pocket and realized, since I had been reading about code seven, that I was hungry.

"Officer Weems, when are we going to eat?"

"Lay off of that 'officer' stuff. Just Weems is fine. We are going to meet up with The Groaner and his partner at around three o'clock. We have a special coffee spot that we meet at. They are working the San Pedro unit, and since we patrol both San Pedro and Harbor City, we can eat in either place. In the future you need to remember you only eat in that area you are patrolling. Can you wait until then?"

"That is fine with me. What kind of place are we going to be eating at?"

"It's an all-night restaurant that serves a variety of food. I'm sure you will find something on the menu that you'll like. Now if you were Phil Smith, you would be brown-bagging it and not eating in the public's eye. We have some time before we go eat, so let's look for a couple of traffic tickets. I don't know if they told you, but we have an unwritten policy that we each write two traffic tickets per watch. I guess they figure we are out here eight hours, and we should be able to write

WAR STORIES LIVED BY A L.A. COP

two tickets apiece. As I said, it's not a written policy, but if you want to get a good rating report, you will write the two tickets. If we don't find two tickets before we go to eat, we can find them during rush hour later in the morning."

We were able to find our two traffic violations, and we each wrote a ticket. This was the first ticket that I had written as an active police officer. We practiced writing tickets at the academy, so I was able to complete the ticket form properly. I did not get any satisfaction from writing the ticket, which was for speeding, and I knew that in the future, I would most likely not be a traffic cop.

At the time that I issued the citation, Weems had told me that the traffic units wrote tickets all night; in fact, they had to write ten tickets a shift. He stated that their responsibility was traffic enforcement and the investigation of traffic accidents. I instinctively knew I would not make a good traffic officer. The importance of traffic officers is crucial, but I already felt it was not the path I would take. It would be necessary for me to write citations, and I would do what it takes to perform my job—it just wouldn't be my path.

It was now about three in the morning, so we went for something to eat. We pulled into a Norm's Restaurant on Western Avenue and parked the car in the parking lot. I noticed that another police car was already parked there. I picked up the mike and requested code seven at this location. The dispatcher came back on the radio and told us it was OK to take code seven, and added that the current time was 3:00 a.m. We had a half hour to eat. As we enter the restaurant, I noticed that there were very few people in the place. Of course, it was three o'clock in the morning, and the few people that were in the restaurant had shut down the local bars. After looking around, I saw Wes, The Groaner, and his partner sitting at a table near the back of the restaurant. They were both sitting at the table facing the front door. As we approached the table, Weems told me to sit at the side of the table as he sat down at the other side.

"Here is another thing for you to learn on your first night." Weems continued, "You never sit at a table with your back to the door. You always want to be able to see who is coming into the place. As we sit here we can all watch the door. Just a little habit you want to get into. You are no longer a citizen; you are a police officer. That will draw attention to you, some good and some bad."

"Weems, how did the kid handle that call you got at Harbor Medical?" Groaner asked.

"He handled it just fine; we also got two of our tickets written, and you don't have to worry about his *hat*. It found a home on the rear seat, and he can handle the radio OK."

We ordered our food and ate it. After paying for our meals, the four of us went back out into the parking lot, got into our cars, and drove off. I took out the log and logged in our code seven. It was now around quarter to four in the morning, and we were back on patrol.

For the next two hours we drove around Harbor City and San Pedro. Weems pointed out various locations that were heavy crime areas and areas that were low crime areas. He showed me the quickest way to get from one area to the other. The radio was not busy, and only a few radio calls were assigned to other units. We did not receive any radio calls during this time, and it was not necessary for us to back up other units. Weems told me to log in this time and show that we were on patrol. In a short time the sun came up, and the streets became filled with traffic. In the business districts, people showed up on the sidewalk. Weems said that "the day people" were showing up and "the night people" were going inside. With time on the job, I would learn the difference between the two.

Between five and six we were able to write two other traffic tickets. We also stopped several people walking on the sidewalk. These people looked out of place to Weems, and we wrote FI (field interview) cards on these people. None of the persons were up to anything wrong. The field interview cards would be filed at the station for later reference if anything of interest showed up later in that area. Over time I learned that these files are very important to the detectives.

At six thirty that morning, we received our second radio call. We were to go to a business in San Pedro that had been broken into that morning. Upon arrival at the location, we soon realized the business was a clothing store, and a lot of inventory had been taken. The burglars had broken into the building by way of the roof. They had bypassed the burglar alarm and had exited back out the roof. I was able to choose the correct report and fill in the needed information without any problems. There were no known suspects to list on the report, and no one had been seen at the location. Weems told me that this report, and any reports we took during our watch, would be turned over to the detectives for further investigation. I learned that patrol officers were not responsible for the follow-up investigation of criminal reports. Patrol officers do the preliminary investigation, and the only time patrol officers get involved in investigations is if the activity occurred in their presence.

After finishing the report, we left the location and drove out to the ocean, which bordered the South end of San Pedro. We drove down into an area called Cabrillo Beach. There was a beautiful park and a marina for some really nice boats. It had a sandy beach and picnic tables scattered around in a grassy area. I learned that at night this was a Lover's Lane area, and that in the future I would patrol this area. Cabrillo Beach was close to where I was living, and this beach became a hangout for me when not on duty.

After driving around the beach, we headed back to the station. It was now a quarter after eight in the morning. Our shift was to end at eight thirty. As we approached the station, the oncoming shift was standing in front of the station. Weems drove up in front of the station and parked the car. Taking our nightsticks and notebooks from the car, we got out, and Weems gave the car keys to the officers who came up to our car. We started to walk up the steps to go end-of-watch (EOW).

"Kid, don't forget to turn in our daily log to the watch commander before you go up and change clothes. It was good working with you, and I'll enjoy working with you again. You did a good job for your first patrol. Take care of yourself, and I'll see you later."

With that Weems walked up the steps and into the station, and I followed him. When we got inside, he went to the locker room, and I went into the watch commander's office. I gave the watch commander our daily log, and he signed off on it. I then went to the locker room and changed out from my uniform to my street clothes. I had just finished my first day on the job. I felt good about it and knew that I was going to enjoy this job. I left the station, walked to the parking lot where my car was, and drove home.

• • •

I was in the locker room, changing out of my uniform into my street clothes, and it was several weeks later. I had been working unit five Adam five for the last five days and had been working with Weems. We had made several arrests during that time. The arrests had been for family disputes (where there were injuries), for theft of a car that we had stopped and found to be stolen, and for a couple of persons who we had stopped and found to have warrants out on them. I was learning a lot about police work, and Harbor Division, by working with Weems. Some of the things that I learned were necessary in order to do the job properly. For instance:

A police officer working in the field has a lot of discretion, as I had learned from Weems. An officer decides when to arrest and when not to, who to arrest and who not to, who to cite for a traffic violation and who to let go, and where to go and what to do while he is on patrol Only radio calls would cause you to go to a specific location. That ad I saw that caused me to apply for this job was right. An officer really is his own boss and does what he wants to while working the streets. Your main concern when you are working with a partner is that you are not jeopardizing your partner in any way by what it is you choose to do.

As I was leaving the locker room, another officer approached and told me that the watch commander would like to see me in his office. As I was walking to the watch commander's office, I was trying to think of anything that I might have done wrong. I had been working several weeks and knew of nothing that I had done wrong. I was going to be on two days off and planned on going back to Manhattan Beach to see some friends. As I entered the watch commander's office, I was wondering if I would be turning in my gear.

"Come on in and take a seat," Sgt. Sam Wilson said. "I just want to let you know that when you come back to work after your days off, I am assigning you to the foot beat. You will be working the foot beat for the next week. The hours of the foot beat are from eight at night until four in the morning. The first night you come to work, I suggest you come in a little early and meet with Murphy, who is the regular beat officer, and he will show you the ropes. His normal partner is going to be on vacation, so I want you to fill in while he's gone. Any questions?"

"No, sir, that will be fine with me. I am looking forward to working with officer Murphy on the foot beat. I will make sure I come in an hour early so that we can talk about the responsibilities of working the foot beat. I appreciate getting the opportunity to work assignments that I have not worked before. Thank you, sir." I left the office and felt relieved that I had not been fired.

• • •

I came back to the station on a Wednesday night at seven. I was coming back to work from my two days off. After going to the locker room and changing into my uniform, I went into the coffee room. There was one officer sitting at one of the coffee tables. Since the foot-beat hours ran from 8:00 p.m. until 4:00 a.m., it was in between the night watch and the morning watch shifts. Therefore the coffee room did not have other officers around. I walked up to the officer sitting there and asked him if he was officer Murphy. He had three hash marks on his shirtsleeve, indicating he had over fifteen years' service. He was my height, weighing around two hundred pounds, and unremarkable in appearance.

"Yes, I am Murphy. That's Tom Murphy. Are you Officer Reynolds?"

"Yes I am. I have been assigned to work with you the next week. I understand your partner is on vacation. The watch commander has told me to meet with you early so that you can explain our responsibilities to me."

"It will probably be better if we go on out to the street, and, as we are walking the beat, I can show you the area and what we will be doing. I see you have your nightstick with you. Just make sure that you don't go down on the beat without it. If you're ready, we can go."

After my telling Officer Murphy that I was ready, we walked out of the front of the station onto Beacon Street.

I was amazed at what I was seeing on Beacon. It looked like a mini Las Vegas, without casinos, to me. The area was lit up like a candlelit birthday cake. Neon signs were everywhere. The sidewalks were full of people. It was four blocks long, and almost every establishment was a bar. The only exception to this was restaurants. There were some tattoo parlors, liquor stores, mini markets, and merchandise stores. I asked Officer Murphy if it got busier on the weekends, and he told me that every night was the weekend.

Officer Murphy said that it was time for us to go to Tommy Good Fellows. Tommy Good Fellows was one of the bars that had an opening onto Harbor Boulevard. We walked up Beacon from Third Street ,and I found that Tommy Good Fellows was on the police-station side of Bacon at Fifth Street. We entered Tommy Good Fellows from Beacon. Upon entering I noted that we were in an area that appeared to be a hotel reception desk. Beyond this area was the bar area. The bar was humongous. It ran down one side all the way to the back wall. This back wall contained doors that opened out onto Harbor Boulevard. The bar was essentially one block long. The area to the right of the bar was loaded with tables and booths. There was a dance floor with an area for a band. It appeared to me that this bar could accommodate over three hundred people. We stood at the area that appeared to be a desk. Soon a bartender approached us, coming up to the desk from the bar area.

"Hello, Murphy. Who is this you got with you?"

"Tommy, I'd like you to meet my partner. This is Officer Reynolds; we call him The Kid. He's going to be working the beat with me for the next week. Kid, I want you to meet Tommy. Tommy is the owner of this place. Any problems you have on the beat, you want to come to Tommy, and he will take care of it."

"Glad to meet you, Tommy," I said. "Quite the place you have here. I noticed that you almost have a full house. Business must be good."

"Actually, it's a slow night. Some of the navy ships must be out. We don't have as much navy in here as we have most nights. Most nights there's more navy in here than army. Tonight we have more army, but the locals are making up for the lack of navy."

"Tommy, can we come behind the desk and use the landline?" Murphy asked. "It's time I called into the station to let them know things are OK. Kid, for your information, we have a landline phone behind the desk. It's linked with the station. We call in about every two hours to let the station know we are still living. The only communications we have with the station is this landline. We got it here because Tommy is a good friend, and he will call the station if he thinks we're in trouble or need assistance."

"Sure, come on back in and use the phone. I have to get back to tending the bar. It was nice meeting you, Reynolds; be sure and stop in and see me again."

"And the same to you, Tommy," I said. "By the way, my first name is Bob. Feel free to call me that. All of the officers I've met so far call me The Kid. If it sounds better to you to call me that, it won't offend me. With all these old-timers I'm working with, I feel comfortable with being known as The Kid. I've been called a lot of worse things. I'm sure I'll be seeing you again."

"Let me see—Officer Kid, Officer Bob, Officer Reynolds; I think I like Officer Bob the best."

"How about just calling me Bob?"

"That will work. Be seeing you around, Bob. Take care of Murphy while you're working with him. Or if the truth be known, he will probably be taking care of you." With that said, Tommy walked back into the bar area and began to take orders.

Murphy and I went behind the desk, and he took a phone out from underneath and placed it on the desk. He picked it up, and I noticed there is no dialing on the phone. This was because it was a direct line to the police desk. Murphy talked to someone on the phone and reported that we were having no problems down on the beat, and that he will call in again in a couple of hours. I checked my watch and noticed that it was 10:30 p.m. We had been out on the beat for about three hours.

We walked through the bar, to the back doors and through them, and then we were on Harbor Boulevard. Murphy told me that anyone using the foot ferry came out this way because it was quicker to get to the ferry. He further said that most people who did this were the sailors going back to Terminal Island. He also stated if there was any trouble with the sailors, we would use a landline, the station would notify the shore patrol on Terminal Island, and they would come over to pick up the sailors. Most of the time the sailors were just drunk, and, rather than put them in jail, we would turn them over to the shore patrol. The same goes for the army. We called the MPs at Fort MacArthur, and they would come down and pick up the soldiers. Murphy told me that about the only people we put in jail were the locals, mostly Hispanics. It seemed the Hispanics living in San Pedro did not get along with the Hispanics living in Wilmington. When they got together down here on Beacon Street, there was usually trouble.

We walked back into Tommy Good Fellows bar and walked through the bar back to Beacon, where we exited the bar. As we were walking through the bar, I noticed that the band had begun to play and the bar had filled up. The people in the bar consisted of sailors, soldiers, Hispanics, Caucasians, and Somalians. There were as many women in the bar as there were males, and all appeared to be having a good time.

"Murphy, what is that desk area inside the bar used for? It's good to know that we have a landline inside there, I don't really see the need for a 'hotel desk' inside a bar."

"Well, Kid, there's a downstairs to the bar that is as big as the bar itself. There are about thirty rooms down there that are not used as hotel rooms would be used. Tommy's girls use them all. In order to go down there and meet one of the girls, you have to check at the desk. At the time you check in, you're given a photo book that has all the pictures of the girls. You pick out which one you want to see, and, after paying the amount of money it takes to see her, you are allowed to go downstairs. You are given a room number that the girl will be in, and you pay the going rate. You also leave a deposit or item of yours at the desk that you pick up on your way out. That way they know that you have exited the downstairs. It seems to work for Tommy."

"Have you ever been downstairs, Murphy?"

"I refuse to answer that on the grounds that it might incriminate me."

We spent the next couple of hours going in and out of various bars, and Murphy introduced me to either the owners or the bartenders. All of the bars seemed to be orderly, and there didn't seem to be any unsavory persons or undesirable activity going on in any of them. Everyone seemed to be enjoying themselves, and again I am reminded of downtown Las Vegas. Around midnight Murphy takes me into a very small Mexican restaurant located on Third Street. This restaurant had only two booths and a dozen seats at a counter. Murphy introduced me to the waitress, who is a Hispanic woman named Lisa; I judged her to be in her forties. She cooked us up a meal on the grill and added the rice and beans. It was the best Mexican food I had eaten since I had been in California.

After we finished eating, we went back out on the street and back to Tommy Good Fellows. Here Murphy again used the landline and called the station to let them know that everything was fine out here on the street. We spent the next couple of hours walking the sidewalks and talking to various people.

We made out FI cards on all these people, which would later be put into a file. At no time did we encounter someone who was doing something wrong that would necessitate us taking them to the station. Murphy had told me that if we needed to take someone to the station or make an arrest, we had two choices. The first choice would be to walk them up to the station and take them into the garage. From the garage we would use the elevator to take them up to "seventh heaven"—the jail. The second choice would be to use the landline at Tommy's and have a car meet us to transport the person. Murphy said that the second choice was only used if it was felt we could not handle the person. It was not good to have a radio car have to take time to come down and do this for us. After explaining this to me, Murphy said it was time for us to go EOW. I noticed after looking at my watch that it was a quarter till four in the morning. Time sure goes by fast when you're having fun. With that we walked to the station, entering through the front doors from Beacon. We went into the watch commander's office and let him know that we are going end of watch. We went back to the locker room and changed out of our uniforms.

"OK, Kid, that was a good night's work. I'll be seeing you later on today. It's time to go home and sack out."

"Thanks for the tour, Murphy. I enjoyed that. See you later on tonight. Take care!"

I was back at the station that night around eight o'clock. I had gone home and gotten some sleep, and, after doing some shopping and going to the beach, I had returned to the station to go back to work. After I changed into my uniform, I met Murphy in the coffee room, and we informed the watch commander we were going out on the beat. We went back out on Beacon and walked the beat, as we had done the previous evening. Everything was a repeat performance until around one in the morning. We had walked into a bar called the Shangri-La. The bartender had pointed out two Hispanic persons sitting at one of the tables and stated that they were giving him a hard time. They were drunk and being obnoxious and were hitting on all the women in the bar. He asked us if we would speak to them and, if nothing else, remove them from his bar.

After having the bartender point the two individuals out to us, we walked over to their table and sat down with them. The table was in the main seating area, and we had several people at tables around us. As we sat down, the people around us got up and moved away from the area. Both of the individuals were of the same size, which was approximately five foot eight in height and a hundred and fifty pounds in weight. They both appeared to be in their early twenties. They gave the appearance of the local Hispanics, as noted by their white tee shirts, kaki pants, hair styles and manorisms. They definitely were not military personnel. As we sat down, they became very irate and clearly did not want us sitting with them. Murphy was the first to speak.

"We are going to ask you gentlemen to leave the bar. It appears to us that you both are inebriated and do not need to drink anymore. If you don't leave the bar, you are going to have to come with us."

"We are not going to leave this bar. We have as much right here as anyone has. Why are you picking on us? We haven't did anything wrong. If anyone needs to leave this bar it's you," one of the Hispanics said.

"You don't understand," Murphy said. "I'm telling you what to do, you are not telling me. Now get your shit together, and let's leave this bar together."

"You aren't taking us anyplace. *We will kick your ass!*"

At this time I saw Mrphy bend over in his chair and reach underneath the suspect's chair he was talking to. Murphy sat up, placed his hand on the table, and opened it up. Inside his hand was a marijuana cigarette, better known as a roach. He then reached into the shirt pocket of the Hispanic who had been talking, and when he removed his hand and opened it up, it held another roach.

"It seems that you are in possession of marijuana. The roach I found on the floor under your chair was in plain sight. This gave me probable cause to believe it was yours. That gave me the right to search you, and in so doing I find you in possession of a roach. Now, because I can't say whose roach it was that was on the floor, I am going to place you both under arrest for possession of a narcotic substance. Kid, you take control of the other individual and I will take control of this guy."

I got up from the table, pulled the individual closest to me out of his chair, spun him around, and pulled his arms behind him. I took my handcuffs out of their case and handcuffed his hands behind his back. As I did this, he didn't offer any resistance.

Officer Murphy did the same to the other individual, but had to fight him to the floor in order to get it done. All the time this was happening, the individual was cussing Murphy and attempting to pull away from him. All of his struggling was to no avail, because Murphy was a bigger man and was able to control him. Once Murphy got control of him and got him handcuffed, we left the bar with the two individuals in tow.

We walked them up to the station, took them into the garage area, and put them on the elevator. Murphy pushed the seventh-floor button and told the individuals that they were going to be placed into the jail. As the elevator was going up to the seventh floor the man with Murphy began to struggle again. He began to cuss Murphy out and attempted to kick him.

Murphy stopped the elevator between the sixth and seventh floors, took a SAP (leather strap with a ball bearing sewed inside of it) out of his uniform pants pocket, and hit the individual on the kneecap. This caused the man to fall to the floor in pain.

"Kid, another lesson learned. The jailers upstairs do not like us bringing a combative person into the jail. So if we have a person that is combative, we take care of it on the elevator before we get to the seventh floor."

When we reached the seventh floor and the elevator doors opened, I walked off the elevator with the man I had in custody. Murphy dragged his individual off the elevator, from the elevator floor, and up to the booking desk. At this time we completed the booking process on both men and put them in jail, charged with possession of a controlled substance, which was a felony. After booking them into the jail and getting our cuffs back from the jailer, we went back down to the garage by way of the elevator.

"Hey Kid. What do you think about getting something to eat? That sort of made me hungry."

"Don't we have to fill out arrest reports on these two guys? We need to go upstairs and fill out the reports and book the evidence. Our probable cause might not be very strong. As I see it the search and seizure is going to be weak."

"As I see it, we do not need to fill out any reports. These cases are not going to be filed, and no one is going to end up in court. I did not plan on this going to court from the get-go. All we needed to do was get them out of that bar. And we did that. Besides, why would I want to book into evidence roaches and try and prove who they belong to? All that's going to happen is that they will sit in jail for forty-eight hours, and then they'll be kicked out. It's what's called a 'cooling off.' "Murphy concluded.

I learned that these types of arrests were called "humbug" arrests. A crime had been committed, and the arrest was justified, but it was not worth the effort to take it to court. As long as we solved a problem by putting the person in jail for forty-eight hours, the end justified the means.

"You know, I always wondered what these little pockets on the side of my uniform pants were for. After seeing where you got that SAP from, now I know. I have been carrying my cigarettes in one of those pockets. I think getting something to eat is a good idea." (I soon bought a SAP and carried it after this incident. They are illegal to carry now.)

• • •

Two nights later, I came into work anticipating working the beat with Murphy. Instead the watch commander informed me that Murphy had called in sick, and I was going to be working the beat by myself. The watch commander reminded me to call in every two hours, and he felt I was capable of working the beat by myself. He told me that they were short-handed and that if he could, he would have put someone with me. He asked me if I had any problem with that, and I told him I did not. After leaving the watch commander's office, I walked down onto Beacon Street on my own. I wondered at the time if I was going to be able to handle this.

For the first couple of hours I did the same thing that I had done with Murphy, which was going into the various bars along the street and walking through them. I would talk to the bartenders and check out the activity to ensure there were no problems. Things seem to be working out for me until I approached a bar that was on Fifth Street, up the street and away from Beacon Street. As I approached this bar, I saw that there was what appeared to be a drunken soldier on the side-walk in front of the bar. I approached this individual and at the time noted that he had on a soldier's uniform with captain's bars on his shoulders. He was in a full khaki uniform. He was stumbling around and leaning up against the front part of the bar. When I got close enough to touch him, I grabbed his shoulders and turned him around and placed him against the wall of the bar. I patted him down for weapons and found that he did not have a weapon on his person. I asked him to show me identification, and at that time he handed me a military ID card. This card indicated that he was in fact a captain in the US Army. I asked him if he was stationed at Fort MacArthur, and he said he was. I noted that there were taxi loading zones a short way from the bar and there was a taxi in one of these spaces. I informed him that he was too drunk to be out on the street and that he should use the available taxi to get back to the fort. I told him that I was going to leave, and I would be back in about a half hour, and I did not want to see him at the bar when I came back. With that I walked off down the street.

An hour later I came back by the bar and again saw a person outside of the bar on the sidewalk. He was stumbling around and gave all the appearance of being drunk. I walked up to him and recognized that he was the same army captain I had seen previously.

"Did I not tell you to catch a cab and go back to your base? Apparently you decided to stay here at the bar and not take my advice. In my opinion, you've had enough to drink, and you need to go back to the base and sleep it off." After I said this to him, I pointed toward a cab that was parked at the curb. I told him to go over and get in the cab and go back to the base.

He replied, "I'm not going anywhere. I have a right to be at this bar, and I'm going to go back inside. You have no right to not let me go into this bar."

"Captain, you are causing a commotion here on my beat. I'm here to assure that the people coming and going can do so in a safe manner. It is my opinion that you are interfering with others' rights to enjoy their evening. I'm going to insist that you get into a cab and go back to the base and not return to the bar."

"It is my opinion that you are a rookie police officer attempting to tell a captain in the U.S. Army what he can and can't do. If you don't let me go into this bar, I will be getting hold of your captain and telling him what I think of you."

At this time the captain took out his wallet and removed a fifty-dollar bill and threw it down on the sidewalk. After doing this, he started to walk toward the front door of the bar.

"Captain, you have just dropped some of your money on the sidewalk—you need to pick it up, take it over to that cab, and tell the cabbie to take you back to the base. If you do not do this, I am going to do it for you, so I suggest you do as I am asking you to do."

The captain replied, "I did not drop any money. Therefore I do not have to pick up any money. I am going back in this bar and continue what I started before you interfered with my activity."

Upon saying this, the captain again made an attempt to enter the bar. I quickly picked up the fifty-dollar bill, took the captain by the arm, and took him over to the cab parked at the curb. I opened the rear door and placed the captain in the backseat of the cab. I then handed the fifty-dollar bill to the cabbie and told him to take the captain back to Fort MacArthur. I also told the cabbie that the fifty-dollar bill was the captain's, and he was to give the captain the change after taking out his fare. I then closed the rear door and told the captain to go back to the base and sleep it off. After my saying this, the cabbie drove off with the captain.

After finishing my shift, I returned to the station and went into the watch commander's office to inform him that I was going end of watch. After I did this, I was walking down the hallway that led to the locker room. As I passed the detective room, I looked into the room through the windows and saw the same captain that I had encountered at the bar in the detective room. He was drinking coffee and talking to two detectives who were sitting with him. I continued on into the locker room to change my clothes. As I was changing my clothes, I thought to myself that I had just passed another test. It was my opinion that I had been set up to take a bribe. Had I taken the fifty dollars that the captain had thrown down on the sidewalk, I probably would have given up my job.

The next night I was walking the beat again by myself. It was around one in the morning, and I was going into Tommy Good Fellows to use the landline phone and call in. As I approached the desk, Tommy came up to me in a hurry.

"Two sailors just beat up two of my girls. They just left out the rear door onto Harbor Boulevard. The girls are hurt pretty bad. You go after the sailors, and I'll call the station and get you backup." With that Tommy got the landline phone and began to make the call.

I ran through the bar and out the back door onto Harbor Boulevard. When I reached the sidewalk, I looked to the right, toward Sixth Street. I saw two sailors walking up the sidewalk in the direction of the foot ferry. They were shoulder to shoulder and talking to each other. At that time I hollered at them and told them to stop.

Both of the sailors turned around and looked at me but did not stop walking. At this point I began to run toward them in an effort to catch up with them. I got to within fifteen or twenty feet of them when the sailor on the street side turned around and aimed a firearm at me and pulled the trigger. The gun did not go off. Removing my nightstick, I ran up to them and hit the sailor with the weapon in the kneecap with my nightstick, as I had seen Murphy do several evenings ago. When I hit him, he fell to the sidewalk, and the gun came out of his hand and slid down the sidewalk. I turned to the other sailor, and, raising his hands, he stepped back and told me not to hit him.

At this time a patrol unit drove up to my location. It stopped in the street, and the two officers jumped out of the car and ran over toward me. I hollered at them: "These two sailors just assaulted two girls in Tommy Good Fellows bar. I ran up to take them into custody, and as I attempted to, this one here tried to shoot me with that gun laying over there on the sidewalk. Help me take them into custody. I want to arrest them for the assaults on the girls and an assault on me."

Each officer took a sailor into custody, and they handcuffed them. I walked over to where the gun was laying, picked it up, and examined it. The gun was a .45 caliber automatic. It was a Colt firearm and appeared to be a military weapon. I released the clip in the weapon, and, as it came out, I noted that it was fully loaded. Further examination of the weapon revealed that the safety had been on, and there was not a round in the chamber. This explained why the weapon had not fired. It wasn't until after I had done this that I realized I could have been shot.

With the other two officers' help, we put the suspects in their car, drove down to the station, took them upstairs to seventh heaven by way of the elevator, and booked them for felony assault on the girls at Tommy's and felony assault on a police officer. After booking them I went into the station and made my reports. I then went back to Tommy Good Fellows and located the two girls that had been assaulted by the sailors. The girls told me that the sailors had beaten them in their rooms downstairs in Tommy's. It was their opinion that the sailor's intent had been to rob them. I asked the girls if they wanted medical treatment, and both of the girls refused.

I had each of the girls fill out crime reports for felony assault and robbery. After doing this I went back to the jail and added additional charges for robbery against the two sailors. After filling out the reports, I noted that it was 5:00 a.m. and my tour of duty had ended two hours ago. This was the first time that I had been in a position to be shot, but it would not be the last.

It was two-thirty in the morning, and I was working my sixth month on the morning watch. One more month to go, and I would be reassigned to the night watch. I was working with Dominic, and we were working the San Pedro unit. We received a radio call directing us to a traffic accident on the Wilmington-San Pedro Road at the railroad tracks. We had been informed by communications that all the traffic units were tied up, and we were to handle the call. We were further informed that there were fatalities, and that we were to proceed to the call code two.

"Dominic, I haven't worked a traffic accident yet. This will be my first one. I'm sure I'll be able to help you on this. I can remember handling traffic accidents at the academy. I know that it's important for us to determine the point of impact. This will also be the first dead body that I've handled."

"Kid, we have worked a lot of mornings together over the past several months. I'm confident in your ability to do the necessary job to handle this. No sweat. I've handled quite a few traffic accidents in my time. If it is a fatal traffic accident, downtown administrative traffic division will come out and pick up a follow-up investigation after we've completed the preliminary. All we're going to have to do is the initial reports."

When we arrived I noted that the location of the traffic accident was on the Wilmington-San Pedro Road where the railroad tracks ran across the road, as reported. The traffic crossing lights were on, blinking red. The fire department was at the location with their fire truck, and the paramedics were also there, along with the field sergeant. The sergeant had used his car to block off the eastbound traffic. I noted that on the other side of the railroad tracks were barricades set up to block the westbound traffic. All of the traffic was being diverted around the accident site.

The accident itself consisted of a flatbed eighteen-wheeler and what appeared to be a '50s-model Ford car. As we approached the scene of the accident on foot, I noted that the Ford had run into the back of the eighteen-wheeler. About half of the Ford's front hood was under the bed of the truck. At this point it appeared that the eighteen-wheeler had been stopped at the crossing, and that the Ford had run into the back of it. The truck had been loaded with twelve-foot sections of rebar approximately one inch in diameter. The impact of the Ford on the rear of the eighteen-wheeler had caused the load of rebar to break loose and shoot back in the direction of the Ford. Around ten pieces of twelve-foot rebar had shot off the truck, as an arrow would have been shot off a bow. The velocity of this rebar was so great that six pieces of it shot through the windshield of the Ford, three of which went through a sailor who was sitting in the passenger seat and pinned him to the back of the front seat. The other three pieces had also gone through the window and did the same thing to the sailor who was driving the Ford. Looking into the Ford, we saw that both sailors obviously were deceased.

The Ford had been turned off, as was the truck. The driver of the eighteen-wheeler was sitting in the sergeant's police car. The paramedics approached us and informed us that they had examined both sailors, and that they were in fact deceased. The paramedics also informed us that the coroner had been contacted and was en route.

We talked to the fire department and were informed that they had called a truck from public works to come out with special equipment to enable them to disengage the rebar from the Ford. This would be necessary in order to remove the two sailors.

"Well, the point of impact won't be hard to figure out," Dom said. "It's where that Ford struck that eighteen-wheeler. When you run into an eighteen-wheeler, it does not move. I'm sure we're going to find out the sailors had been drinking. They probably were down on Beacon Street and were returning to their base on Terminal Island. I'll take care of the removing and identifying the sailors when the coroner gets here, and you can start diagramming the scene and taking all the required measurements. If we work this together, we *will* get through it. You OK with that?"

"Yeah, I'm OK with that. We have a kit in the trunk of our car, and I can get all the tools of the trade that I need to do the measurements with. There is also a camera in the trunk that I can use to photograph the scene. Based on the training I got at the academy, I'm sure I can handle this scene."

"You sure picked a real tragedy to be your first traffic accident. If you need to go back and sit in our car, I *can* handle the whole thing. When we get back to the station, I'll get Henry"—a traffic officer—"to come in and make sure all our reports are done properly."

"I appreciate that Dom, but I *am* OK. One of the first things I learned while working down here was to disassociate myself from people who have been injured—by thinking of them as being only cows. As long as I keep that frame of mind, I can deal with injuries I've seen—and now even death."

The public works truck arrived, and, between that truck driver and the firefighters from the fire truck, they removed the rebar from the Ford. The coroner had arrived, and the two sailors were removed from the Ford and placed in his vehicle. The driver of the eighteen-wheeler was allowed to leave the location in his truck. A tow truck had responded to the location, and this truck removed the Ford.

I finished up my diagram, and when Dom finished with the coroner, we returned to the police station. I met up with Henry, who went over all our reports with us. After the reports were completed, he informed us that they would be turned over to administrative traffic that morning, and they would complete the follow-up investigation. The preliminary investigation attributed the cause of the accident to the fact that that the sailors were speeding and were unable to stop prior to slamming into the eighteen-wheeler. Probable cause was attributed to the sailor driving the car being too drunk to drive safely. I looked at my watch and saw that it was a little after six in the morning. Administrative traffic would be taking over this investigation in less than two hours, at which time they would notify the navy as to the deaths of the sailors. At the time I was glad that I did not have to make these notifications. I suddenly realized that I was tired and ready to go home.

• • •

It was my last morning of the morning watch. I was working with Weems. We were working the San Pedro car and were driving to Cabrillo Beach. It was four on a Friday morning. We both had Saturday and Sunday off. The wind was blowing pretty well, and it was a very dark night. It felt as if it were going to rain. Weems had told me that he wanted to drive down to the beach and see the breakwater that separated the ocean from the outer LA harbor. He said that when the wind kicked up like this, it really crashed the waves into the breakwater. It was quite a sight to see all that water crashing. He wanted me to see this sight.

As we were driving down the entrance road to the harbor, Weems quickly slammed on the brakes, and I felt the car strike something. When Weems got the car stopped (approximately fifteen feet beyond where the impact occurred), I asked him what he had hit.

"I think it was a possum. It could have been a cat, but if it was a cat, it was a damn big cat. I'm looking in the rearview mirror, and it's laying there in the road. I'm sure it's dead. Let's get out and pick it up. I have just the place for it in mind."

We got out of the car and walked back to where the animal was lying in the road. Upon examining it, we found that it was in fact a possum. Now it was a dead possum.

"Kid, you pick that possum up, and I'm going to go open the trunk of our car, and I want you to put the possum in the trunk."

"Why do you want me to do that? Why don't we just throw it in the Dumpster down by the beach?"

"I have better plans for that possum. Just put it in the trunk like I told you, and after we go look at the breakwater, I'll tell you what we're going to do with that possum."

"OK, Weems. It's your play. I can do that."

As Weems walked back to the car and opened the trunk, I picked up the possum. It was a good-sized animal. It must've weighed twelve or thirteen pounds. I had never seen a possum down here at the beach before. I carried it down to the car and put it in the trunk. Weems closed the trunk, and we got back in the car and drove out to the breakwater. We watched the water breaking across the breakwater for about twenty minutes. The breakers were breaking at least ten feet high. The sound that they were making was very loud. It turned out that it was something to see, and I would come down here a lot in the future, just to watch this when the wind was blowing.

"Now what we are going to do, Kid, is go back to the station," Weems said as we were driving out of Cabrillo beach. "Do you know about that ticket meter maid who has been writing us all tickets around the station when we park our cars to go to court? That damn parking meter maid only lets you park for two hours. Every time we get tied up in court and come out, we find a ticket on our car. We have talked to the watch commander about this, but there is nothing he can do for us. We *have* talked to her about this, and she will *not* listen to us. She is a civilian and is hired by the city to write tickets. Good or bad, she insists that we are no exception. As you know, parking is at a premium. If we don't park around the station, the only other place to park is across Harbor Boulevard, in the parking area by the foot ferry. Do you know about this?"

"I *have* heard about it," I responded. "I've been to court a couple of times on some tickets I wrote since I've worked here, but I *have* been parking over by the foot ferry. I didn't want to get any tickets, since I'm on probation."

"Well, the plans I have for this possum are going to be what I call payback. It's my plan, so if you don't want to go along with it, I'll drop you off at the station while I go around to the garage."

"No problem, partner; what it is, is what it is."

We drove down into the garage of the police station, and Weems parked the car at the elevator. Inside the garage I saw the three-wheel vehicle that the ticket maid uses. Weems got out of the car and opened the trunk. He took the possum out of the trunk and carried it over to the three-wheeler. He opened up it's back compartment and put the possum inside. He closed the compartment and came back to the car, and we drove out of the garage.

"Now, Kid, what's going to happen is that dead possum will stay in there until Monday morning when she comes back to work. She doesn't work on the weekend. When she gets into that compartment to get her supplies, she will be surprised not only by the possum but by the smell. I just wish I could be there when she finds that possum. You'll find out about it before I will, since you're going to come back Monday to work the night watch. I just want to let you know that Dom, The Groaner, and I have enjoyed this last six months working with you. We don't go to the night watch or day watch. Since we have seniority we are able to stay on the morning watch. We're going to miss working with you, and you've been a good sport. You will have no trouble making your probation. You're halfway there, and you can do the next six months in the same fashion that you have done these six months. It's time to go end of watch, so I'll drive us back to the station, and we can say good-bye there."

"I am going to miss working with you guys. You all have taught me a lot. I could not have worked with any better partners. I only hope the guys I will be working with on the night watch will be as good a partner as you guys have been."

We drove back up Beacon to the station and changed out the watch. We both went into the locker room and changed our clothes. We shook hands and say our good-byes, both of us knowing that we will talk again.

1961 Harbor Patrol Night Watch

It is Monday afternoon, and I am sitting in my apartment getting ready to go to work. I had last worked the morning watch on Friday. I had been off Saturday and Sunday. It's around three o'clock, and I will go to work from four o'clock until twelve-thirty in the morning. This will be my first night to work the night watch, which contains a half-hour off for code seven, eating. That means roll call from four to four thirtyis part of the work shift. This is why this shift actually contains eight hours. I have completed the first six months of my probation. I have six additional months to work yet to finish my probation. I am looking forward to working nights and not having to go to work at midnight. I had checked in at the station over the weekend and found out that I had been assigned to the San Pedro car for the first month. I found that I was working a ten-day stretch before I had two days off. Two senior officers were assigned to the unit I was to work. They always scheduled three officers to a unit in order to cover days off on the part of each officer. I knew both officers that I would be working with, having met them at the change of watch between the night watch cars and the morning watch cars. This was true with respect to most of the night-watch officers. Coming on watch while working the morning watch, I would always take time to meet the night-watch officers going end of watch. I knew that I would be working nights after finishing my first six months on the morning watch. This way I would be able to go to work tonight and not feel apprehensive about working with new officers.

I got to the police station a round three thirty. After changing into my uniform, I went into the coffee room. The coffee room had five tables, with four chairs at each table. The coffee room was filled with police officers. This was different from the morning watch. The night watch was made up of four additional cars. This meant that we had nine cars in the field on the night watch. It appeared that most of the officers going on shift were here in the coffee room. Most of the officers were talking to each other about the same subject. I heard several comments being made about an attempted escape last Saturday.

"Wasn't that something? I don't believe anyone would try to escape from this station. What do you think he was thinking?"

"It takes a lot of guts to run down the street like that. You wouldn't put it past me if he had been shot."

"Yeah, that was the great escape. I always thought we should not have trustees. Just goes to show you, you can't trust anyone."

"I don't know, man; I would have probably done the same thing. I hate rats or possums too. If I had seen what he saw I would have gotten out of there too."

This was just part of the conversation I was hearing. Everyone, it appeared, in the coffee room was talking about this incident. I saw Tony Allison sitting at one of the tables. I knew that I was assigned to work with him tonight. I went over to the table and said hi to Tony. Tony said hi back to me and asked me if I wanted to sit down with them. I sat down, and at that time asked Tony what was everyone talking about. I told Tony that I had been off-duty over the weekend and had not heard anything about an attempted escape.

"You don't know the story about what happened on Saturday morning? Let me tell you all about it, before we go to roll call. We have about fifteen minutes before we have to go into the roll-call room. Well, to start out with, you know that we have trustees here at the station. The trustees are mainly convicted drunks that are doing thirty days' time upstairs in seventh heaven. They are what you call short-timers. Some of them are in and out of jail all the time. They are glad to be trustees because they get out of their cells every day for at least eight hours. They clean up various areas of this building, including all our police areas," Tony said.

"Yes, I've seen the trustees around the building when I would get off the morning watch. I didn't know they worked on the weekend, because I never noticed them on a weekend," I said.

"They haven't been working on the weekends, but there was a lot of work that needed taken care of in the police garage this weekend. So the watch commander had requested the jailer to allow some trustees to come down into the police garage on Saturday to take care of the cleanup work that needed to be done. It seems part of the work to be done was cleaning the three-wheeler vehicle that the meter maid uses when she checks for parking violations. Do you know what I'm talking about?"

"I'm very familiar with that three-wheeler. Does this story have something to do with that?" I asked.

"Yes, it does," Tony replied. "You see, when the trustee was cleaning that three-wheeler, he opened up the rear compartment, slammed it back down, and took off running out the back door of the garage onto Harbor Boulevard. He ran all the way down to Third Street before the jailer, who was supervising the trustees in the garage, could catch up with him. Now check this out. That trustee was an old guy. He is a regular around here—you know, an alcoholic, in and out of the jail all the time. In fact, I think seventh heaven is his real home. He's all of five foot ten and 140 pounds. Can you imagine him trying to escape? I mean, the first person that has ever attempted escape from this jail is an old alcoholic?"

"Did he explain to the jailer why he tried to escape?" I asked.

"When the jailer brought him back to the garage, the trustee did not want to go into the garage and pleaded with the jailer to take him in around to the front of the building and enter that way. When the jailer asked him why, he told the jailer he did not want to stay in the garage, that's why he ran off. He explained that while he was cleaning the three-wheeler, he opened up the rear compartment and started to reach in to clean the inside. At that time, he saw what he believed to be a rat. That rat was two feet long and probably weighed ten to twelve pounds, in his estimation. When he saw that rat he took off out the back door. He told the jailer that if the jail and the building the jail were housed in had rats that big, he could not sleep that night. Also he said that after seeing that rat, he just panicked and took off. He was not trying to escape."

"Was there a rat in that three-wheeler vehicle?" I asked.

"Well, as I heard the story, the jailer, after taking the trustee up to the jail, came back down to the garage, went to the three-wheeler, and opened up the rear compartment. Inside the compartment he found a dead possum. So the truth of the matter is, it was not a rat, it was a possum. Now what everyone is trying to figure out is, how did a dead possum get into that three-wheeler? No one I talked to has an answer."

"I guess you can't blame the trustee from running away from the garage. It does make a good story though, don't it? I said." I wonder what would have happened had the meter maid found that possum this morning." With that being said, we all got up and went in to the roll-call room.

I had been working the night watch for about two weeks when I met another officer working the night watch. His name was Art Hansen. He also was on probation and had just come down to the Harbor Division from Seventy-seventh Division. He was the same age I was and about the same height and weight. He was from Little Rock, Arkansas. He told me that he was looking for a place to stay and that he wanted to find a place to live in San Pedro. I told him that he could stay with me and that we would look for a place to rent together. It turned out that another police officer had just moved out of his house into a new place. The police officer was looking for someone to rent his old house. This worked out fine for Art and me. We ended up renting the police officer's house and moving in together. The house was located about ten blocks west of where I had been living. It also was within a few blocks of Fort MacArthur. It was located in a residential area where most of the houses were occupied by Fort MacArthur soldiers and their families. The house was a two-bedroom up and down duplex. When you walked in the front door, you walked into the living room. At the rear of the living room there was a door to the right that went into a small hallway.

One bedroom was off to the right, and one bedroom was off to the left. There was a bathroom off of the small hallway too. The bathroom was to the left. The kitchen was behind the front room and was entered by way of a doorway on the rear left side of the front room. There was also a back door that went out into a yard from the kitchen. There was a two-car garage adjacent to the backyard that opened into the alley.

After moving into the house, I took the bedroom to the right, and Art took the bedroom to the left. We both decided that the house would work out just fine. It would work out to be able to come home at night while working and eat our code seven at the house. We would be able to park our police cars in the garage so that no one would notice that we were home during our shift of work.

One night, not long after we had moved in, I came home while working to do just that. I had left my partner at the station while I came home to eat. It was around eleven o'clock at night, and all of the neighbors appeared to either be gone or in bed. As I drove the police car into the garage, I noticed that there was another police car in the garage. At the time, I felt that this meant that Art had also come home to eat. I got out of the police car, closed the garage door, and walked into the backyard. The lights were on inside our house. I remembered that we had cooked up a batch of spaghetti earlier that day. I was thinking that Art had come home also to get some of that spaghetti. I went up to the back door of the kitchen and, as I began to enter the kitchen through the door, I heard a gunshot go off from inside the house. Immediately after I heard the gunshot I felt the bullet fly by my head and smash into a window that was to my right, inside the kitchen. I ran into the kitchen, and, through the door to the front room, I entered the small hallway and looked into Art's bedroom, to the left. I saw Art standing there with his drawn gun in his right hand. He had a sheepish look on his face. His dresser was in front of him, along the wall that connected to the bathroom. The mirror of the dresser was shattered.

"I was practicing my quick draw into the mirror," Art said. "The gun went off."

"It not only went off," I said, "the bullet went through the dresser mirror, through the wall, through the bathroom, through another wall. It then went through the kitchen and out the window on the other side. And if the truth be known, had I been one step earlier, it would have gone through my head."

"Damn, I'm sorry. I've practiced this quick draw many times in front of this mirror, and the gun has never gone off before. That's going to be the last time I practice my quick draw inside the house. If it gets out that this happened, I probably won't make my probation."

"When I came in I noticed all the neighbors were either sleeping or not home," I said. "I'm sure the noise was muffled somewhat by being inside the house. I'll go outside and make sure no one heard the noise or came out to see what happened. You clean up the glass in your room and the kitchen. As long as no questions are asked by anyone, no one will know about this. I'm just glad that shot missed me. We will keep this between you and me."

Upon checking the neighborhood I found that no one was aware of what had happened, and no one had been awakened or had came out as a result of the gunshot. Both Art and I then went back to work, and the incident was forgotten. Later on we patched up the holes in the walls. We never did find the spent round outside the house.

• • •

It was several days later, and I was on patrol, working the San Pedro car. I did not know it at the time, but I was about to have my first traffic accident while driving a police car. I was working with my normal partner, Tony Allison. It was around eleven thirty that evening when we received the following radio call.

"Unit five-A-seven, see the man about four-five-nine suspects there now at two-zero-one-five West Callow Street, code two."

I was driving the car at the time and turned to Tony and asked him if he knew where Callow Street was. I told him I knew 459 suspects were burglars, but I did not know where Callow Street was. Tony told me that Callow Street was over in Wilmington. He told me to take the Wilmington–San Pedro Road, and when we got into Wilmington he would direct me to Callow Street. Code two meant that we were to proceed to that location as quickly as possible, without using the siren. Following Tony's directions, I drove to Callow Street. At the time of arrival at Callow Street, I noted that it was a residential street. The street was dark, with no streetlights. Cars were parked up and down Callow Street, on both sides of the street, and there was no place to park. We had to use our car spotlight in an attempt to locate the address. As we were looking for an address, I noticed that there was a police car double-parked in the street, heading away from us. It was about a block away from where we were. I pulled up behind this police car, and at the time I noted that the car was our patrol sergeant's (Sergeant Davis) car. I further noted that Sgt. Davis was not in the car.

Tony shone the spotlight on the building directly to his right that was parallel to the sergeant's police car. He told me that the building was 2015 W. Callow Street, and it was the building that we were looking for. We noted that the building was a two-story motel. From past experience I knew that these types of motels were used by sailors from Terminal Island. The sailors would use the motel rooms to have a residence off base. The rooms were also used by local prostitutes to turn tricks in. These types of motels had the slang name *flophouses*.

"Should I park the car here behind the sergeant's car? We are double-parked in the street," I asked Tony.

"We were told to get here code two. Plus the sergeant double-parked, and we don't know where he's at. I assume he's inside the motel. Let's leave the car here and get in that damn motel. If the sergeant is in the motel, he will probably need our help," Tony replied.

We both got out of our car, taking our nightsticks with us and putting our hats on. We ran up the steps of the motel and through the front door. Once we got inside, we noticed that we were in the motel lobby. We observed Sgt. Davis talking to the motel manager at the desk. He immediately informed us that the manager had told him that the suspects, who were two drunken Hispanics, were in a back room down the hallway. The manager had said that the two suspects were attempting to steal the TV from the room. Sgt. Davis told us to go back and locate the suspects while he remained with the motel manager to get additional information.

Tony and I then ran down the hallway to the back room. Upon arriving at the room, we found that the door to the room was standing open. We heard voices coming from the room, and it appeared that two people were arguing. We entered the room and found it to be a combination living room/ bedroom. We observed the two suspects arguing with each other as they were attempting to pry a TV off of a wall-mounted bracket. We noted that the two suspects were male Hispanics, and that they were each approximately five foot six, 140 pounds, and of slender build. Both of them gave the appearance of being in their twenties and drunk.

Tony ran up to one of the suspects and began to take him into custody. I ran up to the other suspect and did the same. Both of the suspects began to struggle, and it was necessary for us to take them down to the floor. While on the floor, I was struggling with my suspect, and I was able to get his hands behind him and handcuff his wrists. I looked over to see if Tony needed any help. I saw that his suspect was getting up off of the floor and stumbling toward the door, but Tony was no longer in the room. I jumped up immediately and hit the second suspect on the knees with my nightstick.. This caused him to fall to the floor in close proximity to where I was with my suspect. I got on top of him and dragged him over to where my suspect was. I then removed one of the handcuffs from my suspect and handcuffed my suspect to the second suspect. I now had both suspects lying on the floor face down handcuffed together. I stood up pondering what I would do next.

At this time Tony reentered the room.

"Where did you go?" I shouted at Tony. "You left me with both of the suspects!"

"Didn't you hear that crash! I heard it. When I heard it, I got up off of my suspect and ran out of the room and down the hallway to the front of the building. I thought that something might have happened to the sergeant. I knew that you could handle these two drunks and that the sergeant might need my help more than you would."

"OK, partner, tell me about the crash."

"We need to pick up these two suspects and take them out front of the building. When we get out in front of the building, you'll see what I'm talking about."

"If it's not too much trouble for you, I can handle my suspect, but you will have to handle yours."

We each picked up a suspect off the floor and left the room. We walked down the hallway and out the front door to the front steps. Sgt. Davis was standing there on the steps.

"Well, the great train wrecker has arrived," the sergeant said. He pointed out into the street toward where our police cars were sitting.

I looked out into the street and saw that a freight train's engine was sitting in the trunk of my car. The train was hissing steam as it sat there. The back end of my car was sitting under the cowcatcher in front of the train. The train cars attached to the engine ran all the way down the street and out of sight. The crash of the train into my car had pushed my car forward, but not enough forward to strike the sergeant's car. The operator of the train was examining the damage to his engine.

We took our suspects and put them into the sergeant's car. The sergeant told us to take his car and take the suspects to this station and book them. He stated that he would stay at the location and deal with the train wreck. He further told us that he had talked to the train operator and had learned that the train was pulling one hundred freight cars. The operator had also said that a main steam line that was necessary to run the engine had been broken. In his estimation it was going to take several hours to fix the train in order for it to move on. Sgt. Davis further stated that he had called for the traffic unit to come to the location and complete a traffic accident report.

As we left the location, I noted that the railroad tracks ran right down the center of the street. It had been so dark at the time I parked my car that I did not see the railroad tracks. As I drove down the street I followed the train. I found that the train cars were blocking traffic on the two main thoroughfares through Wilmington. I was lucky in that I was on the station side of the train. It was obvious that soon people would be coming to work and they would be unable to get from one side of the train to the other without detouring around the train. *What a mess!*

It was two days later when I had my inquiry. I was called into the watch commander's office. Upon entering his office, I observed that the watch commander, Sgt. Davis, and a traffic supervisor were present. I was told by the watch commander that the review of my accident would either show I was negligent in parking the car where I had, or I was justified because of the police action that was necessary at the time.

After I had given my explanation as to why I parked where I did, which included the facts I have previously stated, I rested my case.

Sgt. Davis then gave a statement. He stated that he had arrived at the location prior to my arrival and that he had double-parked in the street at the location as had I. He further stated that he had arrived first, and I had arrived second. In conclusion, he stated that had I not parked where I did, the train would have struck his vehicle instead of mine.

Fortunately for me the traffic review board found in my favor—it was felt I was justified in parking my car where I did and could not have anticipated it being struck by a train. Since the call I was on was a code two call, I had only done what would have been expected in acting expediently.

"Kid, thanks for keeping my car from being hit," Sgt. Davis stated. "Just remember in the future you are to do as I say, not as I do. Lesson learned is a sergeant can make mistakes as well as police officers. So you need to judge for yourself in the future on this job, what is best to do for you. You're a good police officer, and this traffic accident will not put you in jeopardy with respect to your probation. I am proud to have officers of your caliber work for me."

I guess you could say this experience stayed with me throughout my career in that I challenged the actions on the part of supervisors in cases where I felt I was right, in the future.

• • •

And then there was the story of "my new car."

I had just bought a 1960 T Bird from another police officer. The 1960 T Bird was a two-door vehicle with both front and back seats. I had bought the car as a birthday present to myself. It was in May of 1961, and my birthday was May 9. I had just turned twenty-two . I had gotten rid of my 1955 Mercury convertible.

Let me tell you about the '55 Mercury. I had bought it right after I had come to California. I was living in Manhattan Beach at the time. As you know, everyone has to have a convertible while living at the beach. I had bought the Mercury convertible for $999. It was the first time I had bought anything on time payments. I put $55 down and was to pay $55 a month until the car was paid off. About three months after making payments, I had checked my balance and found out that I owed more money for the car than when I bought it. I went to the dealer who sold me the car to find out why my balance was more than what the car had cost. I was told that I was paying compound interest, and that the interest was computed daily. My $55-a-month payment was not enough to cover the interest owed each month. Therefore the unpaid interest was added to the principal balance of the loan. Can you believe that? Needless to say, I saved my money until I was able to pay off the balance.

Now let's get back to the 1960 T Bird. I was really proud of this car. It was red, with white sidewall tires and a leather interior. I felt like anyone feels driving a new car. It was my pride and joy. I had had the car only about one week when I was driving to work one night, and the following incident took place. I was driving down Seventh Street, from Pacific Avenue, in the business district of San Pedro. I was about three blocks away from the police station at Seventh Street and Bacon Boulevard. As I was driving down Seventh Street, I noted that in front of me, about a block away, was a 1949 Chevy Coupe. The Chevy was double-parked in the street. It was blocking my way. As I approached the back of the Chevy, I noticed three male Hispanics running down the sidewalk on the passenger side of my car. I had my front windows down, so I yelled out at the running persons, who at this time were running toward the Chevy.

"Move your car. It is blocking my way," I said. "I am a police officer, and you are double-parked." After saying this, I displayed my police badge and showed it to them out of my car window.

They all looked at me, as they were running, and one of them, who was carrying a six pack of beer, took out one of the beer cans and threw it at me. I assumed they were trying to throw it inside the open passenger window. Instead, the can hit my passenger-side door and fell into the street. I heard it clunk against my door, and all I could think of was it had dented my door. I got out of my car and ran down the street toward the Chevy, which, at this time, the three Hispanics were trying to get into. One of them had run to the driver's side of the car, and the other two ran to the passenger-side door. I ran to the passenger side of the Chevy and grabbed one of the Hispanics as he attempted to get in the front seat. He had just gotten the door open when I grabbed him. He fell to the floorboard and began kicking at me with his feet. He had on combat boots and was kicking me in the chest. I began to hit him in the face with my fists. As I was doing this, the second man came at me from the rear. I noticed him raise his left hand in an attempt to hit me. I could see that he had an object in his left hand, and it appeared to be a knife. I turned to my right and spun around, grabbing him, and threw him into the car. He landed on top of the first man. At the time that I did this, he dropped the item in his hand onto the seat. I noticed that the object was a church key or beer-can and bottle opener. By this time, the individual on the driver's side of the car had gotten into the car and started it up. He was yelling at the other two to get all the way into the car. As the car drove off down the street, the other two Hispanics crawled up into the front seat. I was not able to pull them back out of the car, so I ran back to my car, but before I could pursue the Chevy, it drove out of sight.

As I got into my car, an individual approached me and said that he owned the market up the street. He told me that the three Hispanics had been in his store and had ripped off a couple of six-packs of beer, and ran out.

I told him that I was a police officer, and that I would be going to the station to report the incident, and that I would see that a police car came to a store to take a report from him. I then drove down to the police station. I told the desk police officer what had happened and asked him to put a broadcast out on the three Hispanics and their car. I said that at this time, they were wanted for an assault on a police officer and a theft. After giving him a description of the three suspects and their car, I went to change into my uniform for the start of my shift.

After roll call the desk officer told me that the three suspects and their car had been located in Wilmington, and that they had been taken into custody and were being transported back to the police station. The watch commander had asked that I make out a crime report on the assaults that occurred to my person, so that the suspects could be booked on that assault. He also wanted me to stand by to identify the suspects and their car when they arrived. After I made out the paperwork, I was to meet him in his office.

After completing the reports, I went to the watch commander's office. Upon entering, I met with the watch commander,

Lieut. Jones. Lieut. Jones asked to see the reports that I had just completed and told me to have a seat. I gave him my reports and sat down and waited for him to read them. When he was through, he turned to me and stated he had a few questions to clear up the incident in his mind.

"I really have only one question to ask you, after reading your reports," Lieut. Jones said. "Where was your gun during this incident?"

"My gun was in the glove compartment of my car," I replied. "I always keep my gun in my car glove compartment when I'm on my way to work."

"In the future you will keep your gun on your person," Lieut. Jones replied. "We should have three wounded Hispanics out there at the scene. It would have saved us from looking for them."

Another lesson learned. From this point on, I would carry my weapon on my person at all times, whether I was going to work, working, or coming home from work. I came to realize again that a police officer is a police officer twenty-four hours a day, seven days a week.

Within the next month, two other incidents occurred in which I could have been shot with a gun. These incidents showed me how vulnerable a police officer can be and that at any time you can be shot on this job.

• • •

At twenty-two years of age, a person still feels that they are invincible. This carries over from your teenage years when you do not care what you do or how you do it. You never consider the danger of your actions.

The first incident in which I could have been shot occurred while I was working the San Pedro car; it was late at night, and I was getting ready to go end of watch. I was working with Tony again. At the time we had just received a call that had been assigned to us in the Wilmington area. The dispatcher had informed us that the Wilmington cars were tied up, and we were to handle the call. The call was "Four-five-nine suspect there now." After giving us the address, the dispatcher asked us to roll on the call code two. I was driving our car, and knew where the location was. I proceeded there without delay. Upon arrival, we noticed that it was in a residential area, and the house in question was a two-story house that sat back from the street. I parked the police car in front of the house, and we got out of the car and approached the house. The house had a front porch with a front door leading to the interior of the house. We decided to set up a two-man perimeter at the house. Tony went to the rear of the house and positioned himself so that he could observe the rear and the left side of the house. I went to the right front corner of the house so I could observe the front of and the right side of the house. Once we arrived at these locations, we agreed to wait for the backup we had requested before we got out of our car.

In about five minutes a backup car arrived. The two officers approached my location and asked me if I knew what we had. I told them at this time I did not. and that my partner was at the back of the house. I asked them to cover my location and told them that I was going to go around to the back of the house and hook up with my partner. I further stated that when I hooked up with him I would give them a signal, and we would see if the back door opened, and they could see if the front door opened. That way, either two-officer team could enter the house, and whichever of us did not enter the house could maintain the perimeter.

As I was going down the right side of the house, about half-way down I noticed an open window. I pointed the window out to the two officers who were standing at the front corner of the house. I motioned that I was going to go into the open window. After doing this I boosted myself up to the open window and began going through the window. At this time, a gunshot went off from inside the house. The noise of the gun-shot deafened me, and I had seen the flash of the gun in front of my eyes. I fell back out of the window onto the ground At this time, we heard someone saying from within the house, "Don't shoot me. I have thrown the gun away. I don't want to get shot. I did not mean for the gun to go off. I am going to come out the back door with my hands up. Please don't shoot me when I come out. I did not try to shoot you coming in the window. The gun wasn't mine. I was stealing it from the house. I don't know anything about the gun and it was an accident."

I had discovered that I had not been shot. I did not know how the bullet that had been fired had not hit me, but it hadn't. We three ran to the rear of the house, joining my partner Tony at that location. While we were at the rear of the house, the sus-pect from within the house came out the back door with his hands over his head. We took the suspect into custody, hand-cuffed him, and took him out to our police car and placed him in the back seat. While Tony and I were doing this, the other two officers went through the house and found the gun that the suspect had fired, underneath the window. The gun turned out to be a .25-caliber automatic. The clip to the gun was empty. They found the spent casing from the fired round in the room that the gun had been found in. They gave the gun to us, and, after reporting that the location was clear, they left.

Tony and I talked to the suspect, and he admitted that he was burglarizing the house. He stated that he had found the .25-caliber automatic in the house as he was searching the house for valuables. He had entered the house through the open window that I had attempted to go through. He stated when he arrived at the house, the window had been closed but unlocked. He had opened the window and entered the house through it. He left the window open in order to leave the house through it. While he was in the house, he observed us pull up in front of the house. He had run back to the window to exit the house, but had seen us outside and knew he could not come out unnoticed. He had seen me walk back along the side of the house and find the open window. He immediately lay down beneath the window. He placed his back against the wall and drew his legs up under his chin. He was holding the gun when he got into this position. When he saw me coming through the window, he started to raise the gun, and as he was doing this, it went off. He had not gotten the gun up into a position that would have caused the gunshot to strike me. He further stated that he was not attempting to shoot me when the gun went off. He was trying to throw the gun across the room so that he would not have it when he was caught. He stated that he had never had any experience in the past with an automatic weapon.

Our investigation revealed that the .25-caliber automatic was loaded only with a round in the chamber. The clip of the weapon was empty. The chambered round was the round that had gone off, and the direction of flight was out away from the window into the wall on the opposite side of the room. Also, in talking to the owner of the house, I found out that he had used up all of the ammunition for the gun with the exception of the chambered round. The owner had stated that he kept the one round in the chamber in case he had to use the gun for protection. The owner also stated that he kept the gun in the house for protection and only took the gun out when he went to the range and target-practiced with it. He was in the process of buying ammunition for the gun, but had not done so yet.

In completing our investigation, I felt that the suspect had not tried to shoot me. I believed his story, and we arrested the suspect for burglary and for firing a weapon in the city limits. I got my hearing back shortly after the incident. I had learned not to go into a house through an open window until I was assured it was of little danger to me.

• • •

The second incident also occurred while I was working with Tony. It was about a week after the first incident. We were working the Wilmington car, and it was around midnight. We had received a radio call to respond to an assault that was in progress at a motel. Upon arrival at the motel, we noted that it was being used by sailors from Terminal Island. We went into the motel and met with the manager. The manager informed us that the assaults were occurring in one of the back rooms on the first floor. He gave us the room number and pointed out the direction down the hallway to the room. He stated that the room was being rented by a navy chief and that the navy chief had a girlfriend staying with him in the room. About five minutes ago he heard the girlfriend screaming from within the room and screaming that she needed help. He had not gone back to the room to see what was wrong and had just called the police. At the time he was telling this, we could hear a female's voice screaming, *"Help me! Help me!"*

We ran down the hallway and approached the room in question. When we reached the door of the room, we continued to hear the woman screaming from inside the room. We also heard a male's voice hollering. We could not make out what the male was saying from inside the room. We both hollered ourselves, announcing that we were police officers and they were to let us into the room. After not getting a response, we tried to open the door and found it was locked. I told Tony that I was going to kick the door in, and for him to be ready to go into the room. At that point I threw myself against the door, and it gave way. As the door opened, we looked into the room and immediately observed a white male standing inside the room in his underwear. The male appeared to be holding a .22-caliber rifle. At the same time, we noticed a woman sitting on a couch with another male lying on the couch with his head in her lap. He was bleeding profusely from wounds he had received to his head. A wastebasket was on the floor underneath his head and was catching the blood that was coming from it. The male holding the rifle immediately pointed it at me as I entered the room and pulled the trigger. The weapon did not discharge, and I ran up to the man and hit him across the head with my nightstick. This caused him to fall to the floor, and I jerked the weapon out of his hands and threw it across the room. I got down on top of the man and was able to get him handcuffed. Tony went back out to the desk to call for an ambulance. While Tony was doing this, I tried to calm the woman down by telling her that we would take care of the situation.

Within a short time, the ambulance arrived, and the male who had been lying on the couch was transported to the emergency hospital for medical treatment. We took the female and the male that had the rifle to the station for further investigation. We also confiscated the rifle as evidence.

Our investigation into the incident revealed the following set of facts. The female was living at the location with the male who had had the rifle. He was a chief in the navy. He paid for the room at the motel and allowed the female to live there. They had been living with each other for about a month. She was providing him with sexual favors for the free rent. On this particular night, the chief was on duty and away from the motel room. She had been out and around for a period of time barhopping. She had met the other male, who was a petty officer in the navy. She had brought him home to party, thinking that the chief would not be back there until the next morning. As she and the petty officer were having sex on the couch, the chief came back and discovered the two of them having sex on the couch. He had gotten the .22 rifle from the closet and hit the petty officer over the head with it, twice. Then he had stated to the woman that he was going to finish the job with her. At the time she thought he was going to kill both of them with the rifle. That is when she started hollering for help. She further stated that instead of shooting them with the rifle, the chief began to undress and stated that he was going to finish the job sexually with her. While the chief was undressing, she had run into the kitchen and gotten the wastebasket. She returned to the couch and was holding the petty officer's head and allowing the blood to flow into the wastebasket. At the time we came through the door, the chief had undressed down to his underwear and was attempting to get on top of the female on the couch.

Our investigation further revealed that the rifle did have a live round in the chamber. Examination of the rifle showed that the firing pin was unable to strike the primer of the round, which would have caused it to go off. The reason for this was that the barrel of the rifle had bent away from the stock at the time that the chief had used the rifle to beat the petty officer in the head. The rifle barrel's bending had caused it to not line up with the firing pin. So when the trigger was pulled, the firing pin had not struck the primer of the bullet.

Further investigation showed that the petty officer had received serious wounds and was being admitted to the hospital for further treatment. The wounds he had received were not life-threatening wounds, and he would recover. We arrested and booked the chief for assault with a deadly weapon on both the petty officer and myself. We booked the rifle into evidence. After completing the statement from the female, we wrapped up the investigation.

We were in the coffee room at the police station and were drinking coffee. It was now around four the next morning, and we were relaxing as best we could. Tony turned to me and, after looking me over and forming some sort of an opinion, he said, "You know, I don't know if working with you is unlucky or lucky. Within the last week I've been with you on two occasions where you could have been shot. Let's just say you were lucky!"

"Let's just say I'll consider it being lucky. You know, you never think about what is going on when it's going on. It's not until after it happens, and we are sitting here like this, that it hits you. But you know, rather than pondering on what could have happened, and going through all the scenarios of what could have been, I find myself better off not thinking about the what-for-alls. It's like that guy who almost shot me inside that house last week. He was just a normal guy, in my opinion. He was my size and weight and height. I could have taken him in a fair fight. The only difference between him and me at the time was that he fired his gun, and I didn't fire my gun. And if you look at that navy chief we just dealt with—he was a typical career navy chief. Shacked up with a girlfriend and drinking his self into an early grave. He was short and very fat with a beer gut. He had tattoos up and down both his arms. He had aged himself beyond his years. He probably only thought about where his next drink was going to come from, and when would be the next time he had sex with his girlfriend. And take that petty officer! Whereas the chief was in his late forties, the petty officer was in his early twenties. He was just the opposite: tall, skinny, and young. And that girlfriend! Can you believe anyone would put themselves in jail behind her? She reminds me of a candy wrapper that you take off the candy and throw away. I suppose earlier in life she was the candy and not the wrapper. I had a friend back home in high school who joined the navy; he quit high school when he was seventeen. He said he was eighteen. He joined the navy because he heard sailors had a girl in every port. You know, I bet that all of those girls are candy wrappers.

"That is what I like about police work. You never know what the next day is going to bring. Jobs I've had in the past were the same every day. I just keep looking forward to the next day at work and realize that each day will bring new challenges. Each challenge that you face adds to your experience to be able to do this job and not spend a whole lot of time trying to rationalize why people do the things they do. I just want to do the job to the best of my ability and help people along the way; I will be helping someone out in some fashion. What it is, is what it is. One thing I can say, Tony, is that you and I work good together. I always know that you will watch my back, and you know I will watch yours."

On the way home that night, I began thinking about what I had been told at the police academy. I had been told that I would have to be making a lot of split-second decisions. I had been taught that a police officer uses his discretion as to when to arrest, when to shoot, when to issue tickets, and when to stop a person. These decisions have to be based on training and experience so that the right decisions are made. So far on the job, I had made decisions and then acted on those decisions, right or wrong. After my decision had been made, I was willing to live with it. And thus far I felt my decisions were sound. I was not a person to either prejudge a decision on my part or think about what could have, should have, or would have, after the decision has been made. In looking at my personality, I felt that I could make decisions and live with them without worrying about what a wrong decision would lead to. Thus far I hadn't shot anyone or seriously hurt anyone. I felt all my arrests were sound, based on probable cause, at the time. I had no trouble treating everyone fairly regardless of who they were. I was not a person to sit around and gossip with the other officers about things that I had done and people I had put in jail.

The one thing about police work I did not enjoy was writing traffic citations. We did have an unwritten quota on the night watch as we had on the morning watch: we would write two tickets per shift. Don't get me wrong, if I saw a serious violation under the traffic code, I had no problem writing a ticket for it. It's just the writing tickets to write tickets to meet a quota that bothered me. But I had learned that I could utilize my eight hours on shift to make good arrests. The average time involved in a good arrest was four hours. My thinking was, if I could make two good arrests per shift, I could justify not writing tickets. As long as I could detect criminal activity on patrol I could do this. Radio calls also allowed arrests to be made as a result of whatever activity had taken place. Patrol police work was based on reacting to incidents. Those incidents would follow either radio calls for service or my detecting criminal activity. Since the radio calls for service were minimal, in the harbor division, a lot of patrol time was used for "shake, rattle, and roll." This term came from *shake* the bushes, *rattle* the doors, and *roll* or turn over the rocks. I was learning that the best way to shake, rattle, and roll was to patrol the alleys and the out-of-way areas. Criminal activity was more prevalent in these areas than on the regular streets that were patrolled. Thus, by patrolling in the alleys, I came across more criminal activity than I did on the regular streets. Patrol functions were reactionary activities. We would react to the crime after it had taken place.

• • •

I was sitting in the front room of my apartment, and it was Friday morning. I had just come from the station. I had been there cleaning out my locker and saying good-bye to a lot of my friends. It was the first week in November 1961. The police department had notified me that I was to transfer to the Seventy-seventh Division patrol. I would be reporting in to them in a few days. I had contacted the watch commander there, and he had informed me that I was being assigned to the morning watch patrol. The hours that I would be working were from midnight until 8:30 a.m.

I started to reminisce about my past year, living and working in San Pedro. The Harbor Division captain had given me my certificate of completion of probation. It felt good to know that I was now off probation. This meant I was a full-fledged Los Angeles police department officer. I would be going to my new assignment not having to worry about probation. Seventy-seventh Division was about a half hour drive up the Harbor Freeway. I decided to still live down here in San Pedro. That way, I would not have to move. I did love it, in San Pedro. I probably would stay in San Pedro as long as I was able to drive to work in a reasonable amount of time.

In the year that I had been living in San Pedro, I was able to learn a lot of new things and benefit from them. One of the best things I learned was how to deep-sea fish. I had learned to love fishing in the ocean. A lot of the sports-fishing boats fished out of Norms Landing. Norms Landing was right across Harbor Boulevard, behind the police station. Working the night watch turned out to be ideal for fishing. I would go end of watch at 12:30 a.m. and go across Harbor Boulevard and get on one of the fishing boats. I would sleep on the boat as it traveled over to Catalina Island. The boat would reach the island at daylight, and we would fish until noon. Then the boat would come back to Norms Landing, arriving at around three in the afternoon. I would then go back to the station and get ready to go to work. I got so I became very good at fishing in that I was fishing at least two days a week. I was catching a multitude of fish, everything from yellowfin tuna to black sea bass. I could also make extra money while fishing by working as a deckhand on the boat. I also would get into the jackpots and would win them a fair amount of the time. The jackpots were worth from fifty to a hundred dollars, depending on how many fishermen went out on the boat. I guess next to being a cop, fishing was my second love.

Chapter 2

Seventy-Seventh Division Patrol— Morning Watch

November 1961–July 1962

I was in my 1960 Ford T Bird and was driving up the Harbor Freeway on my way to work at Seventy-seventh Division. It was around eleven o'clock at night, and I had been working at Seventy-seventh for about six weeks. It was the first week in January, 1962. As I was driving to work, I was reflecting on what the last six weeks had been like in Seventy-seventh Division. In those six weeks I had learned that working that division was as different from the Harbor Division as day was from night.

I was wearing my new black leather jacket. I had bought the jacket from a motorcycle officer several days ago. When I first got to Seventy-seventh Division, I noticed that several officers on the morning watch were wearing leather jackets. I also became aware of the fact that all of the motorcycle officers wore leather jackets. These jackets were especially made for police officers. They had a place on the left breast of the jacket to fasten your badge to. They also had snaps around the waist of the jacket to snap your Sam Brown (gun belt) to. This enabled you to take the jacket off and your gun belt, with all of your equipment, would come off with the jacket. In that it was also a little chilly on the morning watch, it provided more warmth than a cloth jacket would. The jacket was the type I had always wanted to own. In some ways it gave me more confidence in my abilities and my self esteem. Over the next several months I would learn how fortunate it was to have that leather jacket. It would save me some serious injuries.

When I first arrived at Seventy-seventh Division, I was assigned to one of the two patrol cars that patrolled the Watts area of Seventy-seventh. The Watts area made up around a fourth of the total area in Seventy-seventh Division. There were two main project areas in Watts. One of these areas was called Jordan Downs. It was located off of 103rd Street, between Central Avenue and Lou Dillon Street.

The other project area was called Imperial Courts. Imperial Courts bordered Imperial Highway. Most of our radio calls came as a result of activity in these two projects. They were like little cities within the city of Watts. All of the residences in the projects were in apartment-style buildings. Each building contained from five to six separate residences. The residences were two-story and were connected to each other by common walls. There were over one hundred of these apartment-style buildings in each of the project areas. In my opinion, the living was similar to apartment-style living that I had experienced in the past. I have seen tenement-style living in high-rise buildings in cities like Pittsburgh, New York, and Chicago. The projects did not appear to me to be all that bad of a place to live.

There were a total of twelve cars out on the morning watch. All twelve of these cars were two-man patrol cars. This was twice the number of cars that were on the morning watch in Harbor Division. All traffic enforcement in Seventy-seventh Division was handled by traffic units and motorcycle officers out of Central Division. There was no time to do that as well. The patrol units were continuously getting radio calls. The radio calls would even get backed up. A unit could get two or three radio calls at the same time. All of the main streets were always busy with both car traffic and foot traffic. There were always traffic accidents, robberies, burglaries, assaults, and murders occurring. I had spent a year in the Harbor Division and had never been to the scene of a homicide. Here I was at the scene of a homicide at least once a week. The criminal activity in Seventy-seventh Division was constantly occurring. It seemed to me that crime never went to sleep or took a vacation in this division. It was easy to see why this division was said to be the busiest one in the city, and it was easy to see why they called the Harbor Division "Sleepy Hollow."

Fortunately for me, as in the Harbor, I was working with seasoned officers that were showing me the ropes in Seventy-seventh. All the officers I was working with were very energetic and enthused about the job they were doing. I guess you could call it dedication to duty. I noticed that we only had one African American officer on our watch. This struck me as odd, since 90 percent of the population in Seventy-seventh Division was African American. The other 10 percent was mostly made up of Hispanic and elderly Caucasians.

All of the officers were called by their last names. So I lost my nickname of Kid and was known as Reynolds. There were only a few officers who I knew by their first name. One of these officers was Chuck Williams, who was my regular partner. The units were manned the same as they were in the Harbor. There were three officers assigned to each car so that days off were covered. Our patrol cars had shotgun mounts for shotguns between the driver and passenger officer. We were issued shotguns out of roll call and put them in these mounts. The shotguns were the only additional equipment that we had, compared to the Harbor. The area in Seventy-seventh Division was all one big area that bordered two other LA divisions, three other cities, and the LA county sheriff's jurisdiction.

I had, in fact, quit my part-time job at Woolworth's working as a security agent, I had picked up on the side while working at Harbor Div. I found between driving to work, working, driving home, and going to court, I had no time for a second job. It seemed that I would come to work, work, get off and go to court, then go home and sleep. A few hours later I was back at work.

I had been able to make a lot of arrests in the short time I had been there. Most of the arrests were coming from radio calls that I had answered, but I still found time to shake, rattle, and roll. For whatever reason, I was able to detect criminal activity. It just seemed like I knew what and where to look for it. I became good at spotting rolling stolen cars. I could read a stolen car's license plate as the car would be coming toward me down the street. I could also talk to the people I was dealing with and get them to tell me what I wanted to know.

In this area of Los Angeles, there was what appeared to be a liquor store on every corner. A liquor store was the most prevalent business in Watts. In contrast, there was not one grocery store in Watts Everyone, day or night, hung out at the liquor stores. A lot of dope dealing took place in the parking lots and the alleys behind these liquor stores. I soon learned to be knowledgeable about activity in Watts and who was doing what. A police officer had to develop informants in order to be successful in making arrests. I found out that the people hanging out at liquor stores were the best source of information. So I made it a point to fraternize with anyone hanging out at a liquor store. I also got to know the owners of the stores and in becoming friends with them gained valuable information. At this time, in 1962, we had no organized gang activity in Watts. That would come later. What we had was neighborhood kids hanging out in these liquor store parking lots, and they would align themselves with each other, in order to commit criminal activity. There were also neighborhood gangs in the projects. But the organized gangs that were known as the Bloods and the Cripps would not become prevalent until 1968.

Crime was not preventable, nor controllable, in Seventy-seventh Division. All we could do was handle what criminal activity we could in the eight hours we worked each shift, and let the rest go. There was no way that we could protect and serve the citizens with just twelve units on patrol. The only way to do that was to have a cop on every corner. All we could do was set priorities and handle the most serious crime. The most serious crimes occurring were crimes against persons, such as assaults, robbery and murder. As a result, burglars were almost never caught. Most of the burglars were narcotic addicts, feeding their habit with the money they made from their stolen property. When I worked the Harbor Division, I had to look hard for criminal activity. In Seventy-seventh Division crime looked for you. Everyone on the street paid attention to the patrol units, as the units came into their area. It was a combination of being afraid of the police, because of being up to no good, or having the feeling that the police presence was based on harassment and not allowing a person to do what they wanted to do.

Well, that's enough of that. Let's get back to some war stories. When I went to work that night I was patrolling the back alleys in Watts with my partner. We were getting a lot of pressure from the captain to solve several rashes of burglaries that were occurring in the division. The captain had stated that if these burglars did not get caught shortly, he would be fielding two felony cars. The felony cars were plain cars that looked like any other car on the street. I guess you could call them undercover cars. The officers working the felony cars would be in uniform. They also would not have to answer any radio calls for service. Their sole responsibility would be uncovering who was responsible for the rash of burglaries. The captain had stated that he would be assigning officers to these cars who had made the most felony arrests over the past several months. Chuck and I wanted to work the felony cars, so we were making as many felony arrests as we could.

As we were driving down the alley in our car with our lights out, we observed a car parked in the alley. The alley we were in was running behind businesses that fronted the street. As we approached the parked vehicle, we noted that it was a pickup truck, and it was parked in the same direction that we were heading. The truck was parked next to a Dumpster that was located behind a TV repair shop. Two persons were removing TV cabinets from the Dumpster and placing them in the back of the truck. We approached the individuals in an attempt to determine what they were doing. Upon observing them placing the TV cabinets in the pickup bed, we noted that the cabinets were minus the TVs.

I went up to one of the individuals and began to question him about what he was doing. "What are you doing with those cabinets that you're taking out of that Dumpster? You are not committing a crime by removing the thrown-away items that were put in that Dumpster. I'm not going to arrest you for what you're doing; I would just like to know, why you are taking those cabinets?"

"Am beats Nam," he replied.

"What does *Am beats Nam* mean?" I asked.

"It means that when we came into this alley we did not have anything. When we leave this alley we are going to have something. Something is better than nothing," he replied.

"Whatever," I said.

The two individuals got into the pickup truck and drove out of the alley. Chuck and I got back into our patrol car and left the alley as well. About a week later, I saw the pickup truck driving down the streets as I was on patrol. I decided to stop the truck and talk to the driver. After stopping the truck, I walked up to the driver's side and found that the driver was one of the individuals who I had talked to in the alley. I asked him what he had ended up doing with the cabinets he had taken that night.

The driver of the truck told me that he had taken the cabinet's home and put them in his house. His wife complained about them being in the house. So last weekend he tried to sell them, but could not find anyone interested in buying them. His wife had told him not to bring them back home. So he had taken the cabinets to the dump and it had cost him twenty dollars to get rid of them.

I asked the driver of the truck if that Am was better than that Nam, to which he replied that it damn sure wasn't. Taking those cabinets had cost him money.

• • •

Chuck and I continued our patrolling of the alleys, looking for felony arrests. Over the next week or so, we were making arrests for the stripping of stolen cars, possession of narcotics, and assaults. We felt that our chances were going to be good if the captain fielded felony cars in the next couple of months. Neither one of us cared much for answering radio calls because most of the calls dealt with family disputes, better known these days as domestic violence.

For instance, a couple days ago we had picked up a couple on a family dispute. The wife was complaining about the husband physically abusing her. She stated that she wanted him arrested for this abuse. In investigating the incident, there was no sign of physical abuse to her person. We took the couple into the station for further investigation. While interviewing the woman, we found that the couple had come to Los Angeles from Louisiana. They had caught what was called a freedom bus. This bus had given them a free trip to Los Angeles to start a new life. We asked the woman if she was on welfare, to which she replied that she was. She showed us several welfare receipts that she had removed from her purse. She further stated that she had changed her mind about having her husband arrested and that she did not want him put in jail.

While we were interviewing the husband about the complaint his wife was filing against him, we found that he had pay stubs in his wallet from Douglas North American. We told him that we would not arrest him if he could explain how he had work stubs showing that he was working, and she had welfare receipts showing she was drawing welfare.

He then told us the following story: They had come to Los Angeles from Louisiana. He had rented a house and had gotten a job working in a gas station. While he was at work one day, his wife went to a neighbor to borrow some eggs. While in the neighbor's house, she noted that several men were playing poker in the kitchen. The neighbor introduced her to the men sitting at the table. It turned out all the men lived in the neighborhood. His wife had asked the neighbor how all the men were able to sit around the table in the kitchen and play cards and drink beer. ""My wife did not understand why they were not working. The neighbor then asked if she did not know about the welfare. My wife stated, no, she did not know about welfare. My wife told the neighbor that I worked at a gas station and that the children were being taken care of. My wife did not see any need to have welfare.

"The neighbor lady then told my wife that if she wanted to get on welfare, the easiest way was to apply for it, because her husband had left her and gone back to Louisiana. She said that the welfare worker would come out to her house to see if her husband had left. The welfare worker would then canvass the neighborhood to find out if the neighbors knew about her husband leaving. The neighbor lady had said that all the neighbors would say that they saw her husband leave and that he had not been around over the last couple of weeks. My wife would then be eligible for welfare, and, because we had two kids she would qualify for around two hundred and fifty dollars a month, for the support of the children.

"My wife had told the neighbor lady that she did not want me leaving, and it was not worth it to her to get on welfare. The neighbor lady told my wife that I did not actually have to leave her. All I had to do was move in with a neighbor for a week or two, and after that time, the welfare worker would discontinue coming out to the house. After that, each month, my wife would have to go into the welfare office and assure them that her husband had not returned to the house.

"After about a month of working in that gas station, we applied for the welfare. I took all my clothes out of the house and moved in with a neighbor down the street. After calling the welfare and telling them I had left, things happened just like the neighbors said they would. My wife qualified for the two hundred and fifty a month for the support of the children. A couple of months later, I bought the house we were living in. I raised the rent a hundred dollars. By this time I was back living with my wife. My wife went back to the welfare and informed them that the landlord had raised her rent. She qualified for a rental allowance, which was a hundred and fifty dollars a month. So now, my wife was getting four hundred a month. My house payment was only two hundred dollars a month, so I had the welfare paying my house payment. By that time I had got the job at Douglas North American and had quit the gas station.

"I saved up enough money over the next several months to buy a duplex. I got hold of some of my family down in Louisiana and had them come out and live in the duplex. After they arrived, within a short time they did the same thing that we had been doing in qualifying for welfare. So now I am buying the house I live in and renting out the two apartments in the duplex. The families in the duplex are paying me the rent, most of which comes from the welfare. At this time I'm getting ready to quit Douglas North American and go to my neighbor's house and get into that poker game, and kick back and drink beer."

Needless to say, we did not arrest the husband for assault. His wife would not prosecute, and therefore it would be a waste of our time to put him in jail. Most family disputes were handled in this fashion. Arrests were based on injuries received on the part of the victim. If there were no injuries, it was felt that a crime had not occurred. Most victims of family disputes were told that unless they received injuries, the suspect of the dispute would not be put in jail, and to call us back if they received any injuries as a result of the dispute. Unfortunately, in some cases when we were called back, it was to the scene of a homicide.

One early morning at around one forty-five in the morning, Chuck and I were again patrolling an alley, and I was driving. We again observed a vehicle parked in the alley ahead of us and heading in the same direction that we were. The vehicle was running, and its lights were out. We also had our lights out, and as I approached the vehicle we noted that a person was sitting in the front passenger seat. We had gotten to within four car lengths between our car and the car sitting in the alley when we noticed an individual run out into the alley and up to the car from between the buildings. We also noted that the building from which the individual had run from was the back of a liquor store. When the person reached the vehicle, he jumped in behind the steering wheel and took off, driving the car at a high rate of speed down the alley.

"I think that guy just robbed that liquor store," Chuck said. "Let's go get them."

"I think you are right," I said. "Hang on; this might end up being a good chase."

The car we were chasing was an old Ford. I estimated the year of the car to be 1955. When the car left the alley, it made a left turn on the street and headed westbound. Within a half of a block, it came to the cross street. The cross street had speed bumps on either side of it for the traffic coming down the street the car we were chasing was on. The car we were chasing bottomed out on the street it was crossing after it had hit the speed bump. As the car bottomed out, the passenger door came open, and the passenger bailed out into the street.

I had just made my left turn out of the alley and was approaching the fleeing vehicle at the time this happened. I immediately slowed down, and Chuck jumped out of our vehicle to deal with the guy who had bailed out of the car. I kept chasing the car in question. I put out a broadcast that I was in pursuit of a possible 211 (robbery) suspect. I also put out a broadcast on the description of the car I was chasing. Now the chase was on. It was between me and the driver of the fleeing car.

I ended up chasing the car for twenty minutes. We crisscrossed the streets in the area going back and forth and up and down. The car I was chasing hit several parked cars in the process. It also had left the roadway, on occasion, and ended up on the sidewalk. I was having trouble chasing the car and, at the same time, catching the names of the streets I was on from the street signs. I also had trouble keeping the microphone's cord out of the steering wheel as I was broadcasting. We finally ended up heading eastbound on Century Boulevard toward the Los Angeles Airport. We had been up onto the Harbor Freeway and back off of the freeway twice. I had at least three other patrol cars following me during this chase.

Finally, on Century Boulevard, the vehicle I was pursuing spun out and hit a parked car and became disabled. The driver of the car bailed out of the car, ran across the street, and ran into the houses. I noticed at the time the suspect bailed out of his car there were two highway patrolmen in their vehicles and approaching my location from the opposite direction. As the suspect bailed out of his car, the two patrolman bailed out of their cars and immediately pursued the suspect. At the time this was happening I was putting out a radio broadcast, telling communications that the pursuit had ended and the suspect was fleeing the scene.

When I finished my broadcast and was about to pursue the suspect, the two highway patrol officers I had seen go after the suspect reappeared from between the houses. I noticed that they were dragging a person toward the street. They dragged a person out into the street and up to where I was standing next to my car. They released the person at my feet and told me that this was my suspect and that they had found him between the houses. I noted that the suspect had been hit several times by the highway patrolman with their nightsticks. That being said, the two highway patrolman went back to their cars and left the location. I asked the person if he was the person that had been driving the car that had wrecked at the location, and he stated that he was. He also informed me that the next time I chased him, he would have a car with a bigger engine, and that I would not be able to catch him.

Some of the other officers who had been following me in the pursuit came up and stated that they would take care of the traffic accident scene and that I was free to transport my suspect to the station. They further stated that they would get a traffic unit to the location to take the traffic report. I thanked them for their assistance, placed the suspect in my vehicle, and returned to the station. At the station, while I was booking the suspect into the jail, a couple of officers came up and asked me where my partner was.

Can you believe that! I was chasing that suspect for about twenty to thirty minutes. I was going up and down streets, on the freeway, off of the freeway, and out Century Boulevard. After the suspect had crashed his car and was caught by the highway patrol officers, I had returned to the station with the suspect and was booking him into the jail. All this time I had no thought of or for my partner. I asked the officers to finish booking the suspect for me, and immediately ran out to my car and went back to the location where my partner had bailed out of our car. As I approached the area, I saw my partner sitting on a fire hydrant along the sidewalk across the street from the liquor store. He had the person who had bailed out of the car in the intersection. This person was handcuffed and sitting on the curb next to where my partner was sitting. I pulled up and stopped my car in front of where my partner was sitting.

"Where in the hell have you been?" Chuck asked me. "I have been sitting here, and police cars have been racing up and down the street, including yours. I would holler at the police cars, including yours, and no one would stop. Why didn't you send a unit to pick me up a half hour ago? Look at my uniform pants. I tore both knees out bailing out into that damn street, and would you believe it! This guy here, sitting on the curb, was just a hitchhiker. He got picked up by the guy you chased about five minutes before the guy robbed that liquor store."

"Well, Chuck, the least I can do is buy you a new pair of uniform pants. I was so involved in that pursuit that I have to admit I forgot all about you. I'll tell you all about the pursuit when we get back to the station. You won't believe it. I had that suspect I chased take a breathalyzer test before I was booking him. He blew a 3.8 on the breathalyzer. Do you realize he should have been dead, but he sure could drive that car! I had to chase him a long time before I caught them. He did admit to robbing the liquor store, but he told me the next time I would not be able to catch him. I don't know if the next time is going to involve me, but I'm sure there will be a next time."

Chuck told me that he had gone over to the liquor store and taken a robbery report from the clerk. He stated that the clerk had told him that only one suspect had came into the store and robbed him. Chuck had taken the guy he had in custody to the liquor store, and the clerk had told him he was not the person that had robbed him and that he had never seen him before. Chuck and I returned to the station and completed the arrest report on the suspect who had been booked. The suspect had been treated for his injuries and was sleeping it off in the jail. We went back and got him and completed an interview with him, and he admitted robbing the liquor store. The money he had taken from the liquor store had been placed into his property at the time he was booked. We retrieved the money and booked it as evidence. The suspect told us that he had simulated a gun and that he had not had a weapon when he robbed the liquor store. We also got the suspect to confess to additional liquor-store robberies. He told us that he got drunk in order to have the courage to rob the liquor stores, and that he was an alcoholic and stayed drunk most of the time.

We found out the second guy that Chuck had taken into custody was not involved in the robbery. The suspect admitted that he had just picked him up hitchhiking prior to the robbery. The suspect had stated that he did not know the person that he had picked up, and that the person did not know that our suspect was going to rob a liquor store. After we put the suspect back in jail, we found out where the other person lived. It turned out he lived about a mile from the liquor store, on the same street that the liquor store was on. After we drove that person home, we told him that he would be better off catching a bus to get home, in the future, instead of hitchhiking. Now it was time for us to get something to eat, and that's just what we did.

• • •

It wasn't too long after we had caught that suspect that we got involved with another robbery suspect, under the same set of circumstances. This occurrence led to my first time being wrote up in the *Los Angeles Times*. At the time it went down I had not thought that it would be worthy of an *LA Times* story.

The occurrence came about as a result of a radio call, "A two-one-one [robbery] suspect is there now. Unit one-two-A-two-seven, handle the call. Any unit in the area assist unit one-two-A-two-seven."

Chuck and I were unit 12A27, so we took the call and immediately drove to the location. We did not use our red lights and siren. We arrived at the location and drove into the alley behind it. The alley ran parallel to the location, which was a liquor store. Chuck dropped me off in the alley and drove down the alley and around to the front of the location. It was our habit to do this so that we would have the location covered from the front and the rear. This way, if the suspect was leaving or had left prior to our arrival, we had a better chance of catching the suspect at the location. As I was approaching the liquor store from the rear, I noticed that there was an alcove off the alley behind the liquor store. I assumed that this alcove was used for delivery trucks to offload into the back of the liquor store. There were what appeared to be garages on both sides of this alcove. I noticed that there was a car parked in the alcove and facing out toward the alley. As I drew near to the alcove, I saw a suspect run into the alcove from the side of the liquor store and jump into the car. I ran up to the driver's side of the car, and, at the same time, the suspect in the car was starting the car. The cars driver's side window was down. When I got to the car, I stuck my gun in the suspect's left ear and told him to shut off the car. The suspect looked at me and then immediately lay down on the front seat toward the passenger side of the car. The suspect kept his hands on the steering wheel as he did this. I reached my gun further into the car and again ordered the suspect to shut off the car. The suspect immediately hit the accelerator of the car, and, at the same time, turned the steering wheel as he came up off the seat. The car struck me and knocked me off my feet with such force that it tore my badge off my jacket. The suspect lost control of the car, coming out of the alcove, and was backing up in order to go down the alley when he rammed into another police car that was coming down the alley. I got to my feet, and, as the car was correcting itself and proceeding southbound in the alley, I ran into the alley and began firing my weapon at the fleeing car.

I fired five of my six rounds at the receding car. The car continued its path southbound in the alley. I saw the police car that had been hit, sitting in the alley, and it was not chasing the suspect. I thought it was my partner who had came around from the front of the liquor store. I did not see anyone sitting in the car, though, so I ran up to it, and, as I looked into it, I saw two officers in the front seat. They were both bent over and it appeared they were trying to get on the floorboard of the front of the car. I hollered at them and asked them if they were alright. They replied that they couldn't get up, someone was shooting at them. I told them that it was me shooting at the car that was driving down the alley. I told them that the suspect had just robbed a liquor store and had just run me over with his car. After I told them what had happened, they sat up in their car and began to chase the suspect's car that was just turning out of the alley. I returned to the alcove and found my badge. At about this time my partner Chuck drove into the alley, and I got into our car.

"What in the hell is going on!" Chuck said to me. "I heard several shots fired. The liquor store was robbed, and the suspect had a gun and left the store with the money in a paper bag."

"Just a little thing like getting run down by a car!" I replied. "That damn suspect hit me with his car when he was escaping. Another patrol car had driven into the alley as I was being hit by the car. As I was shooting at the car that was getting away, they thought he was shooting at them. So they got down in their car to avoid being shot, they said. They then left to chase the car out of the alley. I heard their siren a short time ago. Let's go see if they caught him."

"I just heard a broadcast saying that they needed help. The dispatcher said that this suspect is on foot, and that the other unit needs additional units to set up a perimeter. They are about two blocks away from us. Let's go see if we can give them a hand and catch your bad guy."

After Chuck told me about the broadcast, he drove the car to the location where the other unit was. We entered a residential area about two blocks away from the back alley. When we got to their location, we noticed the suspect's car had spun out and was in the middle of the street. One of the officers was at their police car, which was behind the suspect's car. As we arrived at the location, additional units also arrived, as well as several motorcycle officers. There also was a field sergeant at the location. Upon our arrival, the field sergeant was directing the other units and the motorcycle officers to set up a perimeter around the location. We were informed that the suspect had apparently left the car before the first unit arrived. It was felt that he was still in the general area and a search was going to be conducted for the suspect. As the other officers began to search the general area and set up a perimeter Chuck and I went to examine the suspect's vehicle. The sergeant informed us that the vehicle would be our responsibility, and that, to his knowledge, no one had approached the vehicle.

We went to the location of the suspect's vehicle and began an examination. The vehicle was a 1959 Plymouth Fury, and its rear window had been shattered. We looked into the front seat of the vehicle and located a pistol on the right passenger floorboard. The pistol was a .38-caliber revolver, two inch, with brown grips. On the front seat we located a brown paper bag full of money. We believed this was the money that the suspect had taken from the liquor store. Looking into the back of the car through the rear window, we observed that two of my rounds had struck the rear of the back of the driver's seat and that they were lying on the rear floorboard. We observed that another of my rounds had hit the window molding and was lying on the backseat. The fourth round had hit the front windshield above the radio, which was located in the center of the dash. We found that round in the corner of the windshield and side window. We were able to account for four of the five rounds that I had fired at the vehicle. We did not find the fifth round in the car. Further examination of the vehicle did not reveal anything further. Once I gathered up my spent rounds, the gun, and the bag of money from the car, we returned to our car, I placed these items into the trunk and, we locked the trunk. We then returned to the sergeant's car to get further directions to assist in the search for the suspect.

The search for the suspect had run into its second hour, and the he had not been located. There were approximately a dozen officers conducting the search that consisted of areas between the houses, alleys, and garages. The sergeant was preparing to order some of the officers to start knocking on the doors of the houses to ascertain whether or not the suspect had entered a house. We heard an officer hollering from down the street, approximately a block away from the suspect's car.

"I think I found him! He is down here underneath a parked car. At least someone is down here under this parked car. I pointed my gun at him and told him to get out from under the car, and he is ignoring me. Send Reynolds down here to see if he can identify the guy under this car as being that guy who ran over him."

I ran down the half a block or so to where the officer was and looked under the car. Sure enough, the person under the car was the person I had seen in the car that had hit me. Several other officers joined me, and we surrounded the car. After the sergeant was notified that the suspect had been found, he put out a code four at the location. He further asked all units to join him, and, upon their doing so, he dismissed the officers so that they could resume normal patrol. Once he had accomplished that ,he joined us at the parked car that the suspect was under.

We again ordered the suspect to come out from under the car. The suspect still refused to come out and would not engage in conversation with us. The sergeant told us that if the suspect continued to refuse to come out from under the car, he would get on the air and request a K-9 unit to meet us at the location. We told the suspect that we were going to bring a dog to the location and that the dog would be sent under the car to get him out from under it. The suspect still refused our request.

Within a half hour, the K-9 unit showed up at our location. The dog was brought to the car the suspect was under and was given a command to start barking and growling. The dog did so. The suspect still did not come out. The dog was ordered to go under the car, and did so. While watching underneath the car, I saw the dog hunch over and crawl under the car. When the dog got to the suspect, it began biting the suspect on the suspect's arms and legs. As soon as this happened, the suspect hollered to call off the dog, and that he would come out. The dog was called off and ordered out from under the car. The dog then came out from under the car by way of the front of the car, and the suspect came out from under the car by the way of the rear of the car.

We took the suspect into custody and placed him in the rear seat of our police unit. We took the suspect to the station, where we interviewed him and placed him under arrest for robbery. During the interview, he admitted that he had robbed the liquor store and that he had used the gun that we had found in his car. He stated that the money we had found in his car was the money that he had taken during the robbery. He also stated that after he had hit me with the car, he had driven out of the alley and that his back window had shattered while I was shooting at his car. He had not been hit by any of the bullets that I had fired, but he had been hit by the shattered glass from the rear window. After he had gotten out of the alley he had driven a few blocks, and after making a left turn his car has spun out and became disabled. As he was getting out of his car, and before he could retrieve the gun or money, he saw a police car enter the street. He ran down the street a short way, and it was then that he crawled under the car.

We booked the suspect into our jail at the station and completed our crime, evidence, and arrest report. After doing so, we were approached by the field sergeant. The field sergeant informed us that the suspect's car had been impounded and was being held for further investigation. He stated that our reports would be turned over to detectives for further investigation and filing of charges. He said, "Reynolds, I see from your reports that you had fired five shots out at that location. I also see from your reports that you can account for four of those five shots. I just want to let you know that I have to make a shots fired report and that report will be reviewed by a shooting board. This shooting board will determine whether or not you were justified in firing those five shots. At this time, I see no problem with this shooting, and in my opinion it was a good shooting and you were justified for what you did. I only see one problem. You have to account for all the shots that you fired. You're going to have to go back to that alley and find that fifth shot before I can complete my report, so I suggest that you get busy doing that because I want to go home sometime this morning. It's already 8:00 a.m. and we are on overtime, so don't waste any time in getting that done."

Chuck and I went back to the location, and it took us over an hour to find that fifth round. We finally located it in a telephone pole, about halfway down the alley from where I was firing my revolver from. It was about six feet up on the pole from the ground. From all the evidence obtained, it appeared that four of my shots had struck the rear window of the car on the driver's side. The round that had struck the telephone pole was probably the first shot I fired. Not too bad, considering this was the first shooting that I had been involved in. I just felt fortunate that I had not shot the suspect and that we had been able to take him into custody without his being shot. The injuries he had received from the dog bites were good enough for me.

After we returned to the station, we found out that the other two officers who had been in the patrol car that the suspect had hit were OK. They had not received any injuries from the traffic accident. I had received some bumps and bruises from being hit by the car and knocked down in the alcove, but I was not seriously hurt. This was one time that I was glad that I had on a leather jacket. It probably saved me from a lot of injuries from the impact of the car and the ground.

The next war story I am going to tell you is probably the most memorable morning of my career. This occurrence was the closest that I had ever come to being killed while serving the police department. This occurrence was reported in newspapers across the country. It was even reported in my hometown newspaper in Alliance, Ohio. What happened that morning just tends to show you that anything can happen at any time, and a person has no control over his destiny.

It was during the early morning hours of Saturday, April 28, 1962. Chuck and I had just left roll call and were driving eastbound on Slauson Avenue. We had just come northbound on Broadway and had made a right turn onto Slauson. I was driving the patrol car, and noted that it was approximately one o'clock in the morning. We were in the process of heading out to our patrol area.

All of a sudden, the radio blared out the following transmission: "Shots fired, officer down. Suspects are still at the location. All available units respond to Fifty-seventh and Broadway, code three."

I turned to Chuck and said, "We just passed Broadway; Fifty-seventh street is in University Division, and it's only a couple of blocks north of Slauson. We are going to respond to that call, so hang on; I'm going to get there as fast as I can." That being said, I made a quick U-turn and, after putting on the red lights and siren, I drove to Broadway Street. When I reached Broadway, I made a right-hand turn and headed northbound. As I approached the intersection of fifty-seventh and Broadway, I observed a police car parked at the curb and facing south. There was no one in the police car, and, as I observed the activity on the sidewalk adjacent to the police car, I saw a crowd of unruly people. Among the people I saw a police officer lying on the sidewalk. I further observed another police officer standing a little north of the first officer, and he was waving and pointing to a crowd of about twelve persons who were running northbound on the sidewalk. The officer was hollering, "They just shot my partner!"

I observed the persons running northbound on the west sidewalk and saw them come out into the street. Feeling that there was nothing I could do for the two officers on the sidewalk, I pursued the persons I seen running northbound in the street. They had crossed the street and were running northbound on the east sidewalk. When they reached a building located at 5606 South Broadway, they ran up the steps and entered the building. Just as they entered the building, I had stopped my police car and double-parked at the location. Chuck jumped out of our car and ran up the steps and into the building that the suspects had entered. After turning off the car, I jumped out as well and ran toward the steps and the front door of the building. I had not had time to grab my nightstick, nor my hat from the rear seat. I had been able to grab my three-cell flashlight that had been lying on the front seat. As I ran up the front steps of the location, I noticed that there were two swinging front doors that lead inside. The doors were closed, and I had no idea where Chuck was, other than that he had entered the building.

I opened the right door and entered the building. I found I was in a small hallway with a flight of stairs to my right, leading upstairs. As I looked up this flight of stairs, I saw approximately twenty African American males coming down the stairway toward me. As I raised my flashlight to shine it up on them, they immediately grabbed me as they came off the stairs. The momentum knocked my flashlight out of my hand.

Around seven of the males had surrounded me and grabbed me and picked me up off of my feet. They carried me to my right into what appeared to be a cloakroom. The cloakroom was about the size of a twelve-by-ten-foot room. As they were carrying me into the cloakroom I heard them shouting: "Kill him! Kill the white devil! Get his gun and kill him with it. Take his gun away from him and shoot him!"

I was carried into the corner of the cloakroom and slammed into a five-gallon water bottle. The bottle was sitting on top of a stand. The stand broke, and a five-gallon water bottle rolled across the room. (This large water bottle was used to hit another police officer over the head with outside of the building a short time later.)

After I struck the water bottle, I fell to the floor. The same six or seven males kept striking me on and about my body with their hands and feet. I continued to struggle against their weight and attempted to free myself from their hold. I struggled physically as much as I could and attempted to break free of their grasp, but there were too many of them for me to be able to do that. At the time they had my arms pinned above my head, and I could not get my hands down to my weapon. All the time they were screaming that they were going to kill me. As I was struggling to get my hands to my gun, I felt someone remove my gun from its holster. I felt the gun being placed into my left rib cage. At that moment, knowing that there was nothing physically I could do to keep myself from being shot, my body and my mind seemed to relax completely and await what was going to happen to me. While this was going on, I was hearing shots being fired outside in front of the building. I also heard screams from the same location.

Almost the precise moment that my gun was pushed against my left rib cage, I heard a voice scream, *"All of you! Get up off of him. If you don't get up immediately I'm going to shoot you."*

I then heard a shot fired inside of the room I was in. After the shot was fired, the person holding my gun dropped it to the floor, and I heard the gun strike the floor. I then heard another command shouted by the person who had been screaming.

"All of you get up and place your hands on the wall and turn your backs to me. Anyone that does not do that will be shot."

All of the males who had been fighting with me and lying on top of me began to get off me, and that allowed me to scramble out of the corner and stand up. As I stood up, I noticed that a police officer I knew from Seventy-seventh Division by the name of Jade was standing in the room. He had his gun drawn and was pointing it at the males who had gotten off of me and was further ordering them to get against the wall.

"Are you all right, Reynolds? I saw your uniform pants sticking out from under all those African-Americans who were on top of you. I knew a police officer was underneath them. I fired a shot in the ceiling. My next shot would have been fired into them. Can you help me search these guys?"

"Yes, I'm alright. Let me pick up my gun, and we will search all of them." That being said, I walked into the corner and picked up my gun and put it back in my holster. Jade and I put all the African-Americans in the room up against the wall. It turned out that there were seven of them. All seven of them had been on top of me. I began to search each one of the males. At the time I searched them, I tore their suit coats up the back and opened up the belts on their pants and searched underneath their pants. I was searching for any concealed weapons that they might have on their person at the time. I did not know what to expect, and I did not find any weapons during my search.

Jade and I kept the seven males against the wall. After we had searched them, we waited a short time, until other officers joined us in the cloakroom. After we were joined by other officers, we placed the seven males into handcuffs supplied by the other officers, in addition to our own. Jade then took the suspects out the front door of the building in order to transport them to the police station. (It wasn't until that time that I became aware of what had happened out in front of the building. I would not know the full impact of what had happened until much later.)

After the suspects had been taken out of the cloakroom, I sat down in the corner of the cloakroom and suddenly realized that I was unable to walk out of the building. I had received some serious injuries to my person while I was struggling with the suspects. It turned out these injuries consisted of a brain concussion, broken thumb, and several bruises and abrasions on and about my body. An ambulance crew came inside the building and into the cloakroom and loaded me up and transported me to a central receiving hospital, where I received medical attention for my injuries. When I was taken outside of the building, I was oblivious as to what was occurring outside. It wasn't until later, when I had read the papers and seen the pictures, that I found out what had happened while I was inside of the building and being beaten by the individuals that we had arrested.

I was released from the hospital around four that morning. I was taken to University station so that I could make a report about what had happened to me. When I arrived at University, I was taken to the roll-call room, and, once inside the roll-call room, I observed many police officers and detectives milling about. I was asked to identify the seven males who had assaulted me while I was inside the building. There were approximately forty eight-by-ten photographs, both facial and full-length, laid out on the roll-call tables. I was to walk through the tables, looking at each photograph, and identify the seven males who had assaulted me. I was able to pick out all seven individuals from the more than forty photos that were lying on the tables. I was sure of the identification of the seven males due to the fact that the seven males I picked out were photographed in their clothes, and their clothes were torn. I knew at the time that these were the persons who had assaulted me, because I had been the person who had torn their clothes.

After making my identification of the suspects who had assaulted me, I got together with a detective and completed a crime report. The crime report showed that I had been assaulted at the time of the incident, and the crime report was titled, "Assault against a police officer, with intent to murder." The crime report listed the suspects who assaulted me by name. That was the first time that I learned the names of the suspects who had assaulted me. Six of the suspects were adults, and one was a juvenile. The detective informed me that all seven suspects had been arrested and booked on a charge of assault with intent to commit murder on a police officer.

After I completed the report, I looked around the room and noticed there were between twenty and thirty police officers in and around the roll call room. I started around the room looking for Jade. I found Jade in the coffee room. After getting a cup of coffee I sat down with Jade. As I sat down, I took off my leather jacket. I thanked my leather jacket for taking a lot of the blows and saving me from any life-threatening injuries.

"Thank you so much, Jade, for saving my life. At the time, I thought I was going to be killed. Once I realized physically that I could not prevent myself from being shot, my whole body went limp, and my mind seem to accept the fact that I was going to be killed. It seems when my mind accepted the fact, my body was ready to accept what was going to happen to me. At that time, I seemed to be at peace with myself, and I was not afraid of what was about to happen to me. It was really a weird feeling, but I don't recall being frightened."

"I'm just glad I went inside that building," Jade said. "I don't know why I did. When we got there, and a lot of fighting was going on outside between other officers and the suspects, I just ran up the steps and into the building. That's when I saw your uniform sticking out from among those suspects."

"Well, I can tell you, I wouldn't be sitting here talking to you now if you had not come into that building. I still have not found out what happened to my partner, Chuck; have you heard?"

"I talked to him a couple of hours ago. He was here, but I think he's left already. He told me when he ran into the building the preacher was coming down the staircase by himself. The preacher ran into that cloakroom and out the back of it into the auditorium. Chuck chased after him. Chuck chased him through the auditorium and out the back door and across an alley and into a house on the other side of the alley. He caught him inside the house and brought him back out to Broadway. By the time Chuck got back to Broadway, the incident at the mosque was over. The preacher was brought down here. Chuck also recovered a briefcase full of Black Muslim literature. The briefcase was turned over to intelligence division. By the way, did you know that building we were in is a Black Muslim mosque and all the suspects are Black Muslims?"

"No, I did not know that. I have never heard of the Black Muslims, and do not know anything about them. I guess I'm going to have to learn about them, and I'll owe one of them thanks."

"Why is that?" Jade asked.

"Hey, thanks that he didn't shoot me."

After talking to a lot of the officers who were involved in the incident, and reading the newspaper accounts of what happened the following facts were revealed.

1. The incident became known as the Black Muslim riots of 1962. It was the start of the riots and demonstrations in Los Angeles that would come later.

2. The building I was in was Muhammad's Mosque Number 27.

3. A total of eight officers were injured that night. One officer was shot, one officer was beaten and hit over the head with the five-gallon water bottle, and the rest, including myself, were physically assaulted and treated for their injuries. All of the officers were placed I.O.D. (This stands for Injured on Duty.)

4. Seven Black Muslims were shot outside the mosque. One died from his wounds, and one was paralyzed.

5. The leader of the Black Muslims was Profit Elijah Muhammad, based in Chicago.

6. Malcolm X was a leader in Los Angeles. He founded an inner circle in the Black Muslims called the Fruit of Islam.

7. Fifteen Black Muslims were arrested, out of the more than thirty who were involved in the incident.

I had been placed off duty because of my injuries. I had been off duty for about a week when I went to central receiving hospital and got a release from the doctor, which would enable me to go back to work. I received a return-to-duty slip from the doctor and went by the station to let them know that I was returning to duty. (The following morning I had just had another birthday on May 9. I had just turned twenty-three.) When I got to the station and told the watch commander I was coming back to duty, I was told that the captain was in and that he wished to see me. I went into the captain's office, and the captain asked me to have a seat. I gave the captain my return-to-duty slip and told him that I was feeling fine and that I would be returning to work on the morning watch the following morning. The captain got out from behind his desk and came over to the couch that I was sitting on and sat down beside me.

"I'm glad to see that you're feeling OK. It will be a pleasure to have you back on the morning watch. I just want to inform you that I am going to implement two felony cars. Our division is being plagued by burglaries, and the community is very upset and has been after me to do something about it. In looking at the pin maps, where the burglaries are mapped out by where they are occurring, and at what time, I have come to the conclusion that we have several cat burglars working the area. As you know, a cat burglar is a burglar that enters homes while the people are sleeping and removes whatever property at that time. Our citizens, for good reason, are really upset. There's nothing scarier than an intrusion into people's houses while they are sleeping. It looks like we have more than one cat burglar working our division. We also have another burglar working the division as well. This is a burglar that seems to be operating between the hours of three and six in the morning. I feel if I put the felony cars out to work this problem, I will have better success than what we have been having. As I said in the past, I was going to put the police officers on these cars that had the most felony arrests in the past few months. You and Chuck are the number-one car in felony arrests. When you come in tomorrow morning, be prepared to work the felony car. You know, this means that you will not be subject to any assigned radio calls. By the way, that was a good job that you and Chuck did at the Black Muslim mosque. The original two officers who stopped to investigate the selling of clothes out of the trunk of that car were University officers. One of them was shot with his partner's gun, and his partner was beaten senseless. If you had not arrived when you did, who knows what shape they would've ended up in. In my opinion, your arrival saved their lives. This just goes to show that we are all on the same police department and that one division can help out another. You will be getting a citation and a commendation for your participation in that riot. Now, why don't you go home, get some sleep, and come back and catch my burglars!"

"Thank you, sir, so much, for your faith in Chuck and me. We are a good team, and we will do our best to catch those burglars. I really appreciate the chance you are giving me to work the felony car." After shaking the captain's hand, I left his office and went home to get ready to come back to work the following morning. I was still living in San Pedro, and the drive back and forth to work took an extra hour out of my day.

The following morning when I came back to work, I met with my partner Chuck in the coffee room. We said our hellos to each other and shook each other's hand. Both of us stated that we were glad to be back working together. We discussed how we were going to work the burglary problem that we had been assigned. We were both in uniform and had been given a plain car to work out of. The car had a radio with all of the frequencies necessary to monitor the radio traffic in the division. It also had two plug-in spotlights. The car had a rack for a shotgun and racks on the doors to put our nightsticks into. This was going to be the first time I did not have to place my nightstick in the backseat. We had been told that we no longer had to wear our uniform hats, either in the car, or in the field. We were also allowed to remove our badges from our uniform jacket. This would allow us to be less identifiable in the car as well as out of the car. We decided that we would just do what we normally did. We would drive the alleys and shake, rattle, and roll. We each bought black knit hats to wear.

One of the areas that one of the cat burglars was working was in the Watts area. The other area that a cat burglar was working was in the north end of the division. The straight burglar, who is a person who enters a home that is unoccupied, was working just outside of Watts in the South end. We decided that we would take on the burglar in Watts first.

The area that the cat burglar was working in was approximately one half mile square. The burglar was taking mostly money and jewelry. His MO was to go in an unlocked door or window of a single-family residence between the hours of one o'clock and three in the morning. The burglar would not ransack a house, and it appeared that he was looking for items in plain sight and items that he could carry away in his pockets. In all the reports that we checked, we found no sign of him taking any electronic items, cameras, or weapons. This told us that we would be looking for a person who was not carrying any property other than property that would fit in his pockets. Thus far this burglar had not been seen, nor had a car been heard leaving any of the victim's locations.

We had been working the area for approximately one week, and we had not been successful in coming across our burglar. We had been shaking down every suspicious person who we encountered in the alleys and on the streets. We had come across several persons who had warrants out on them for their arrests and persons in possession of narcotics. We had put approximately six people in jail in that week, but we had not jailed our burglar. We were parked in an alley in an alcove between two garages, and it was approximately one thirty in the morning. We had been parked in this alley before, but had not come across our burglar. As we were sitting in our plain car, with the engine off and the radio turned off, we observed an individual come out into the alley. The person was coming out of the rear backyard of a house. This house did not have a garage at the rear of it, so it was easy to see that the person was coming from the house. The person came out into the alley and turned in our direction. The person walked up to the alcove, where our car was parked. Upon reaching the alcove, the person looked into the alcove and saw our car sitting there. At this time, both Chuck and I were sunk down in the front seat and could not readily be seen. The person started to approach our car, and, as he did so, both Chuck and I opened our doors and jumped out of the car. Upon seeing this, the person ran back through the alley to the yard that he had just come out of and ran into the yard. Both Chuck and I immediately began to chase this person. I was in front, and Chuck was behind me. I was just entering the rear yard of the house that the person had ran into when I saw him climb a six-foot fence that separated the house from the neighbor's house. As I ran into the yard, the person jumped over the fence and went out of sight.

I ran to the fence, with Chuck just behind me, and climbed over it. When I got on top of the fence, I saw the suspect climbing another fence on the other side of this yard. I jumped to the ground and ran across the yard and climbed that fence and dropped on the other side of it. As I did so, I saw the suspect picking himself up off of the ground. He had fallen on the wet grass. As I ran toward the suspect, he got up and ran to the rear of the house that was at our location. As he approached the rear of the house, I noted that there was a back door and a landing with three or four steps. The suspect ran toward the back door and at that time, I had caught up with him. I tackled the suspect as he was attempting to run up the steps. We both fell on the steps at that time. I was on top of the suspect, and I was attempting to handcuff him when I felt Chuck come up behind me. I looked over my shoulder at that time, and saw that Chuck was swinging his sap down toward the suspect's head. At the same time Chuck was swinging his sap, a light came on in the house and someone opened the rear door. I quickly placed my left hand over the suspect's head and took the full blow of Chuck's sap on my left hand. Fortunately, I was wearing a short cast that was protecting my broken left thumb. (It was the thumb I had broken in the Muslim riot.) The blow struck me on the knuckles of my left hand, but was cushioned somewhat by the cast. It still split open a couple of my knuckles. I cried out in pain, and at the same time, I heard a woman cry out in pain. "What are you doing to my son?"

Chuck and I then picked the suspect up and handcuffed him. The woman in the doorway told us that the suspect was her son and that he lived there. She further stated that he was only seventen years old, and she did not think that what we were doing to her son was right. We explained to her that we had caught her son coming out of one of the neighbor's yards, and that we suspected him of burglarizing the neighbor's house. We also told her that we felt he was going to go through the car we had been in. We told the boy's mother that we would be going back to the neighbor's house where we had seen him in the yard and felt that we would find out that their house had been burglarized. We also asked the boy's mother to go through his pockets to see if he had any property in his possession that she found did not belong to him. We told her that if the neighbor's house had not been broken into and her son did not have any stolen property in his possession, we would be letting him go. At this time she looked at her son and asked him if what we said was true. Surprisingly, he told her that it was. He reached into his pockets and pulled out some miscellaneous jewelry and some cash. He told his mother that he had taken the jewelry and the cash from the neighbor's house.

"You officers might want to look in our garage. I have a mind to believe that you will find other stolen jewelry in there. You see, my son told me he was buying and selling jewelry at school. He said that a lot of kids wanted to trade jewelry, so he was setting up a business in the garage. He's been trading and buying jewelry for quite some time now, but I suspect it's not jewelry from the school. You see, my son has a job, and I believed that he was using his money to run this little business out of the garage. Now, I don't believe that is true."

Chuck and I then took the suspect to the garage. We entered the garage and turned on the lights. We saw a display of jewelry set up on a workbench. We asked the suspect if this was jewelry he had taken in other burglaries and he stated it was. We asked him how long he had been breaking into houses. He replied he started breaking into houses only in the past year. At that point, Chuck and I gathered up the jewelry that was located on the workbench. We informed the mother that we were going to take her son down to the station and arrest him for burglary. We told her that she was able to ride to the station with us, and that we would, in all probability, be bringing her and her son back home. Since he was a juvenile, and was cooperating with us, we would not be detaining him. A petition would be filed against him in juvenile court, and he would have to appear at a hearing. She agreed to go to the station with us. After going to the neighbor's house and confirming that it had been burglarized, we drove to the station.

In talking to the juvenile at the station, we were able to clear up a lot of the burglaries that had occurred in this half-mile square radius around the juvenile's home. We used the map of the area and the reports that we had gathered on the prior burglaries, and, between these items and the juvenile, we were able to pinpoint a lot of the burglaries that the juvenile had committed. In all probability, a lot of the other burglaries could be attributed to him as well. The juvenile also informed us that he had never broken into a house. He stated that he only went into houses where doors and windows were unlocked. He admitted that in some houses the people had woke up, but that he had always been able to flee the house before he was discovered. The juvenile stated that he hadn't gotten into trouble before, and that this was the first time that he had been arrested. When we checked for a record on the juvenile, we were unable to locate one. It appeared to us that the juvenile was telling the truth. Because of his cooperation and the recovery of the jewelry, and the cooperation of the mother, we released the juvenile to the mother's custody and took them both home. We were just grateful that we had been able to catch our cat burglar.

Chuck and I were sitting in the coffee room at the station, drinking coffee. We were getting ready to go end-of-watch. We had completed our reports and booked all the jewelry into evidence. The case would be turned over to the detectives that morning, and they would sort it out. The sun had come up, and it was going to be another gorgeous day. We had changed into our street clothes and were relaxing before going home.

"Partner, I want to thank you for taking that blow to your hand. If you had not done that, that mother would have seen me hitting her son alongside his head. I would have been in deep shit, him being a juvenile and everything. I was just pissed off that we had to chase him. I did not even think about him being a juvenile."

"You would have done the same thing for me. I'm just glad I did it too. She would've seen the whole thing. I think she is grateful that her son did not get hurt and that we treated him properly, as we did her. I like it when things turn out this way. You know, it is just like a game of chess. We are playing a game of chess, and it's up to us to win, not our opponent. But during the game, you have no animosity towards your opponents. The bottom line is winning. Besides, I already have a cast on this damn left hand. I'll just enlarge the bandage a little bit to cover my knuckles for a while, and no one has to know about this."

"Okay, Reynolds, I owe you one. Next time I will stop and think about it before I do anything like that again."

"Chuck, in this game, we don't sweat the small stuff, and nothing is big. Now, like when I was close to being killed a week or so ago, that is big. I can take a couple of lacerated knuckles. Let's go home."

(I still have the scar on my knuckle from that sap.)

A couple of days later, I met Chuck in the coffee room of the station. It was around nine o'clock in the morning. We had decided to take a night off and come in and talk to the burglary detectives. We wanted to find out what they were doing on the burglary cases with the cat burglar that we had given them. We also wanted to talk to them about the burglar who was working the south end of the division. We were going to start working on this burglar, so we wanted to find out what we could about the burglar's MO. The burglary detectives worked five days a week, eight hours a day. They worked between Monday and Friday and were off on the weekends. Since they did not work at night, it was necessary for us to meet with them during the day. We knew that the only detectives who worked overtime, weekends, and at night were the homicide detectives. There had been many a homicide on which we, working with them, had done the preliminary investigation at the crime scene.

We went to the detective division, and we located the burglary detectives. The first thing we did was ask them about the cat-burglar case. They explained to us that they were locating several of the burglary victims and were getting identified some of the jewelry that we had booked into evidence. They also told us that the juvenile we had arrested was a gold mine. It seemed that the juvenile was working with them, and he was assisting them in recovering a lot of the property that he had sold to his high school friends. This property consisted of jewelry and watches. The detectives had been going around to the homes of the kids from school and were recovering a lot of property. They told us that they were clearing a bunch of cases, and that they were grateful to us in that we were able to catch the suspect.

After we told the burglary detectives that we were going to start working on the burglar that was working in the South end of the division, they gave us the following information about the suspect's MO:

1. The burglar was taking all sorts of property, including TVs and other electronic items, watches, money, and any items that could be carried.

2. The burglar was entering houses where people were not home. Sometimes people found their doors open and not locked when they returned home to find their house burglarized. They insisted that they had locked their door. Other people had found their door jimmied and broken into. Other people could not say whether or not they had left their door locked. There were no other signs of entries other than the front doors. There were no broken or open windows in any of these cases. The detectives felt that the suspect might be using lock picks.

3. No fingerprints had been found at any of the locations, which suggested that the burglar was wearing gloves.

4. The suspect was burglarizing single-family homes as well as apartment units. The apartment units were either first- or second-story units.

5. All the victims had either been on vacation or away visiting at the time that the burglary occurred. This seemed to indicate that the suspect was staking out the locations and knew when the residents would not be home.

6. It also appeared that the suspect had to be driving a vehicle. A lot of the property that had been taken could not have been carried off and would've had to be placed in a vehicle.

7. There were not any reports of the suspect being seen. Either no one had seen the suspect at any time, or they had seen the suspect and had not recognized the fact that he was a burglar. It was felt that the burglar was working between the hours of midnight and 5:00 a.m. because the neighbors of the victims were in and about their residences from 5:00 a.m. until midnight. The burglar should have been seen at some of the locations. If the burglar was to work freely without detection, these would be the ideal hours to work. Most people are sleeping after midnight, and those who are working are getting up at 5:00 a.m. This was also true with housewives with children. There was no guarantee that this was the case, though, and we would just have to play it by ear.

Chuck and I started to work the south end area, where this burglar was working. We first decided to shake down anyone we saw in the area who would either be going into or coming out of a residence or apartment. We also concentrated on anyone who was coming or going with a vehicle. After a few nights of doing this, we found that we were encountering too many people who were either coming home after partying or leaving to go to work. Most of the people who we stopped and questioned lived in the residences in question or were visiting. We did not seem to be getting anywhere, so we decided to limit the people who we were stopping based on some other priorities. One of the priorities was that they were either carrying something into or out of the residence. They also had to have access to a vehicle.

We continued to shake, rattle, and roll in the area for the next week, with no success. We would patrol the streets and the allies, looking for any suspicious activity and/or persons. We would stake out certain locations by parking on the streets, in the allies, and even in between buildings. We would get out on foot and walk through the neighborhoods. We were making our share of arrests for narcotics, assaults, and stolen vehicles, but we had not caught our burglar. We stopped a lot of people who we felt were potential burglars, but did not have any evidence to show that they were up to anything criminally wrong. We were getting to know a lot of people in the area who would benefit us in the future, but were of no benefit to us in the present. We were getting frustrated in our inability to catch our burglar.

And then our luck changed. We were parked in between two parked cars on 108th Street, just west of Central Boulevard. The area we were in was almost exclusively apartment buildings. The apartment buildings ran side-by-side in a north-to-south direction. The apartment buildings were two-story buildings, and the stairs to the second-story units were in the street side of the buildings. There were twelve of these buildings. There were areas to park between the buildings. Several of our burglaries had occurred in these buildings. We were parked on the street, south of the apartment buildings. The area to our south had been cleared, and construction was going on. New apartment buildings were being built in this area, and it was fenced off. It was around four o'clock in the morning. The area was very quiet, and there were no pedestrians on the street or in and around the apartments. The vehicle traffic was very light, with only an occasional car passing us on the street.

"Well, what do you think, partner?" Chuck said to me. "Let's give it another hour, and then I'm ready to go get something to eat. We've been sitting here for a couple of hours now, and we haven't seen anything move that has been of interest. I think we need to go to another location."

"You're probably right," I said. "We will give it another hour, and then we'll leave. If nothing else, we can shake down some of these cars that are passing us, just for something to do. You never know what you can come across when you stop a car. Who knows, we might even find our burglar in one of the cars."

About a half hour later, as we were getting ready to wrap it up, we saw a car coming in our direction from Central Avenue. This car pulled over and stopped approximately a half a block east of where we were sitting. It parked along the street in front of one of the apartment buildings. We watched as the driver of the car got out and stood in the street, looking around. We noted that the driver of the car was dressed in a post office uniform and was wearing gloves. After a short time, the driver of the car went around the front of his car and to the steps of the apartment building that was adjacent to his car. He went up the stairs and out of our sight.

"Did you see that guy get out of that car down there?" I said. "He was in post office uniform and wearing gloves. I'm sure he's not out here delivering mail from his personal car. He wasn't carrying any mail that I saw. What do you think that he's up to? Do you think he has a girlfriend up there who he's coming to see before he goes to work?"

"Could be, but if that's what he's doing, he better be quick about it, because I'm sure that he probably has to go to work shortly. You know, even our postal employees are entitled to a little on the side. We will just sit here and see what happens."

In less than five minutes, we observed the person in the postal uniform appear at the top of the steps. Now he was carrying something that appeared to be rather large and that had a towel draped over it. As he got to the steps, he checked out the streets and the parking area below him. When he saw that there was no one on the streets or in the parking area, he came down the steps. When he got to the bottom of the steps he looked up and down the street and then started walking toward his car. When he got to his car, he opened the back door and put whatever he was carrying into the car and closed the door. He again looked up and down the streets and then went to the driver's door of his car.

"Let's get him!" I said.

Chuck and I both bailed out of the car and ran down the street toward the suspect's car. We now felt that he was at least a suspect, if not our burglar. I did not start our car and drive down to the suspect's vehicle. We got out and ran down on foot. I did not drive our car down to the suspect's car because I felt by the time I got the car out from between the two cars to the front and rear of my car, it would be too late.

We ran up to the suspect's car and got there just as he was sitting down in the driver's seat. He had seen us running toward him and was attempting to put the keys in the ignition. Chuck ran up on the driver's side of the car, and I ran up on the passenger's side. We drew down on the suspect, and I was pointing my weapon through the passenger window. Chuck was pointing his weapon through the driver's side window. Both of the windows were down.

"Drop the car keys on the floor, and put your hands on the dashboard!" Chuck yelled. "Don't do it, and you're *history*."

I jumped in the front seat with the suspect and slid across the seat up against him. I stuck my weapon in his ribs and told him not to move. The suspect had put his hands on the dashboard as Chuck had requested. He turned and looked at me with a shocked expression.

"I have him covered, Chuck. Put your gun away and pull this sucker out of the car."

"No problem."

At that time, Chuck opened the driver's door and grabbed the suspect behind his back, pulled him out of the vehicle, and spread him out on the street. I left the vehicle by way of the passenger door and came around the rear of the car to the street where Chuck had the suspect spread-eagled. I then opened the driver's side rear door and saw the object that had been covered with the towel was still covered with the towel and lying on the rear seat. I took the towel off of the object and found the object to be a twenty-one-inch TV. I closed the door and told Chuck that we had a TV in the back of the car. We then picked up the suspect and leaned him over the front of his car and began to search him. In his rear pocket we found a screwdriver and a pair of pliers. In his front pants pocket we found a set of lock picks. In his rear pants pocket we found his wallet with his driver's license. We also found a pair of latex gloves in his front pants pocket. The suspect was still wearing the gloves we had seen him wearing.

"What are you doing with this TV?" I said. "We saw you come down the steps from that apartment building with this TV. As you know by now, we are police officers."

"The TV belongs to a friend of mine. I was just helping him out by taking the TV to get it fixed. It's broke, and he did not have time to take it to the repair shop and asked me if I would do it for him."

"You always carry a screwdriver, pliers, latex gloves, and lock picks with you when you do favors for your friends?" I said. "How do you explain that? Chuck, why don't we take him and put him in our car? I'll go up the stairs of that apartment building and see what I can find. You take him and I'll take the TV. I'll pick his keys up off the floor and take them with me."

We took the TV and the suspect up the street to our car. I put the TV in the front of our car, and Chuck got in the back seat with the suspect. I then went up the stairs of the apartment building where we had seen the suspect. An apartment approximately halfway down the walkway had its door standing ajar. I noted that the door lock had been jimmied and that the door and the door frame had damage to it. This damage appeared to be pry marks that could've been made by a screwdriver. I knocked on the door and stated I was a police officer. No one answered me, so I went into the apartment. There was no one inside the apartment. In the front room I saw a stand that had nothing on it. It appeared that a TV had been sitting on the stand.

I came out of the apartment and noticed that the lights had come on in the apartment next door. I knocked on the door, and it was opened by the person who lived there. I told him that I was a police officer, and that I felt his neighbor's apartment had been broken into. I asked him if he knew where their neighbor was. He told me that his neighbor was on vacation, but would be back the following day. I asked him if his neighbor had a TV, and he stated they did. I asked him if he would recognize the neighbor's TV if he was to see it, and he stated he would. He further stated that he had been in his neighbor's apartment many times watching his neighbor's TV. I asked him if he could come down to the street and identify the TV I had in my police car. I also told him that I wanted him to look at a person who I had down in my police car to see if he recognized him.

The neighbor came down to my police car with me. I showed the neighbor the TV sitting on the front seat of my police car, and he stated that it was in fact his neighbor's TV. I had him look at the person sitting in the backseat with Chuck to see if he recognized him. He stated that he had never seen this person before in his life. I asked him if he had ever seen the person in his neighbor's apartment, and he stated he had not. I then walked the neighbor back up to his apartment. He told me that he would secure his neighbor's apartment and watch after it until his neighbor got home the following day. The neighbor stated he would put a padlock on the front door. I thanked the neighbor for his help and went back out to our patrol car. I told Chuck that I thought we were ready to head for the "barn" (station.)

Several days later, I went to the station and talked to the burglary detectives about our suspect. They informed me that he was good for a lot of the burglaries in the south end. They said that they had cut a deal with him and only charged him with a couple of the burglaries in turn for him telling them about all the burglaries he had committed. He had told them that he worked at the main post office in Watts. He said that he was a postal clerk and sorted mail inside the post office building. He told them that he picked the houses and apartments that he burglarized by checking the vacation notices and out-of-town notices that people had filed in order for their mail to remain at the post office, to be picked up later. That way, he knew when he went to a location that the people would not be home. He had told the detectives that if he did not find the front door open, he would pick the lock with his lock picks. If he could not get the door open with the lock picks, he would pry it open. It turned out that he was a mainline dope addict and was supplying his dope habit with the proceeds from the property he pawned.

• • •

One morning about a week later, I was working the felony car with a partner by the name of Dean Smith. Chuck was on a day off, and Dean filled in for either Chuck or me on our days off. I had worked with Dean for a few days before, and he and I got along just fine. He'd been on the job for a little over six years and had been working Seventy-seventh for the last two years. Dean was about six foot two and weighed about 240 pounds. I guess you could say he was a big guy. He was a very jovial guy, and when he gave you a bear hug, you knew he was no one to mess with. Dean was always smoking cigars.

The one thing he did not like to do was drive, and any time we worked together, I would drive the car. This particular morning we were working the north end and were still looking for additional burglars. We had a cat burglar working in the area we were patrolling. Chuck and I had been working in this area for the past week, so I was familiar with the area and where the burglaries were occurring. As usual, we would patrol the alleys, stake out various locations, and shake down anything that moved.

This particular morning I was driving the plain car, with the lights out, down an alley. As I always did, I was driving the car at a speed less than two miles an hour. We had the brake lights fixed on the car so that they did not come on when you hit the brake, so I was basically letting the car idle down the alley and would break occasionally to keep the speed from increasing. This way, the car was not making any noise as it moved down the alley. Dean was slumped back in his seat and was smoking his always-present cigar. He would keep his hand cupped over the cigar so that the light from the cigar was not seen. He also had a habit of knocking his ashes onto the floorboard as opposed to knocking them out the window. Obviously, this was done so that the cigar would not be seen by anyone. The alley we were driving down was only wide enough for one car to drive through. The alley was lined on both sides by garages and fences. The fences were wood or cinderblock and would have gates opening onto the alley. The only way a person could come out into the alley was through these gates. I guess you can say it gave the appearance that the alley was walled in on both sides.

It was about three o'clock in the morning, and we had been patrolling the alleys for around two hours. As I was moving slowly down the alley, approximately six car lengths in front of us we saw a gate open on the right side of the alley. This would be on the passenger side of my car, or on Dean's side of the car. At the time the person opened the gate, he took a step out into the alley and began looking up and down the alley. We noticed that the person was holding something in his right hand. The person was about five foot ten, 140 to 150 pounds, slender build, and in his late twenties. He was wearing dark clothes.

"Look at that guy down there," Dean said. "What do you think he's holding in his hand?"

"It looks to me like he's holding a pair of shoes," I said. "I'm damn sure that's what he's holding. I think we just found our cat burglar. Now the question is, what is he going to do?"

I kept the car creeping down the alley and would hit the brakes occasionally to keep the car's momentum from increasing. As I was doing this with the car, we saw the suspect—of course, now he was a suspect—take another step out into the alley and look up and down the alley. He was still holding the shoes, and we noticed that he was barefooted. All of a sudden the suspect noticed our car. He again looked up and down the alley and then looked back through the gate into the rear yard where he had come out from. We knew at that time that he was considering his options. As we saw it, the suspect had three options. He could either go back into the yard where he came from; or he could run down the alley, away from us; or he could run up the alley and try and run by us. The suspect chose the third option, and began to run toward our police car on Dean's side of the alley.

"Reynolds, put the car lights on and hit the gas. He is not going to get by our car. We've got him blocked in between the car and the fence."

As Dean said this, I did just that. As the car sped up toward the suspect, Dean opened his passenger door and jammed his right foot into the door so that the door would be blocked. As the suspect came running alongside the car, as the car was traveling down the alley, the door hit the suspect and knocked him to the ground. Just prior to the door hitting the suspect, and when I saw the suspect at the front of the car, I hit the brakes. The impact of the door had knocked the suspect to the ground, and when the car stopped, the suspect was lying on the ground between the car and the fence, just under the open door.

"I guess you chose the wrong option. I guess your option was lucky for us, but not so lucky for you," Dean said, as he was leaning out of his door and looking down at the suspect. Dean then held his cigar out the car door and flicked his ashes on the suspect.

I pulled the car forward, and as I did, Dean got out of the car and went over to the suspect. He picked the suspect up and placed the suspect it against the fence. At the same time, I stopped the car and got out of the car. I walked back to where the suspect has been lying and found a pair of shoes that had been scattered in the alley. I picked up the shoes and joined Dean, who was holding the suspect. We searched the suspect and found that he possessed no weapons or burglar's tools. We placed the suspect in the back of the police car and drove down to the gate that we had seen him come out of. Dean stayed in the car with the suspect, and I went into the back-yard through the gate. Just inside the gate and up against the inside of the fence, I saw a TV. I then went to the back door of the house and knocked on the back door. In a short time, the lights came on.

"Police officers," I said. "Would you please come to the back door? There is nothing to worry about. I just would like to talk to you."

"Just a minute, I'm coming. What is it you want?"

An elderly man came to the back door and opened it. He was standing inside the door in his pajamas. I again identified myself and showed him my badge. I explained to him that I believed his house had been broken into. I asked him if he owned a TV, and if he did, could he look to see if it was still in the house.

After going inside the house and coming back to the back door, the elderly man told me that his TV was gone. He could not understand what had happened to it. He had been watching it just before he had gone to bed.

I asked him if he would come out into his backyard with me and look at a TV that was sitting in the backyard up against the fence at the gate. He said he would, and both of us walked out to the fence and looked at the TV. The man told me that the TV sitting on the ground was his TV.

"How did my TV get out here?" he said. "The last time I saw that, it was in the front room. I certainly did not put my TV out here. Why would I put my TV in my backyard? That doesn't make sense. This is crazy. I'm going to take that damn TV and put it back in the house."

"Let me talk to my partner. We're going to have to dust the TV for prints. If my partner can do it, we can do it here. If not, we are going to have to take the TV into the station to do that. I will be right back."

The victim went back into the house, and I went back out into the alley and to our police car. I asked Dean if he could print the TV. I told him that I had found a TV in the backyard and that I got the owner to identify the TV as being his. Dean told me that he could dust the TV for prints. He said that he had a print kit in his duffel bag that he had put in the trunk of our car. At that time Dean got his print kit and went into the yard through the back gate. I remained in the car with the suspect.

"I see you are not wearing any gloves. You know that we are going to get your prints off that TV. So why don't you tell me why you went in that house and took that TV."

"Man, can I put my shoes on? My feet are cold. And they hurt from running up that alley, and I got a headache from hitting that damn door. I almost made it by your car. If I had gotten by the car, you would've never caught me. This is just a bunch of bullshit. I don't know anything about that damn TV. This is a humbug. I'll be out in forty-eight hours. Go on and do what you got it do, but you aren't getting no confession out of me."

"That's cool with me. We got you cold turkey even if your prints aren't on that TV. You are guilty as sin. We have all the probable cause we need to put your ass in jail. So that's just what we are going to do. We'll let the detectives sort it out. You're probably good for a lot of the burglaries that are going down around here. You better think up a good deal to ask for when the detectives talk to you."

In a short time Dean returned and told me that he had gotten several lifts off the TV. He told me that he had left the TV with the victim after the victim signed a receipt stating we'd given the TV to him. Dean further stated that he did not see the necessity of taking the TV in and booking it as evidence. He could testify that the TV was returned to the owner at the scene. Besides, it was almost time for the six o'clock news, and the victim wanted to watch the news. We took the suspect back to the station where we booked him for 459 PC (burglary). After booking the suspect and finishing our reports, we got a cup of coffee and then went home. (The suspect was made on prints and also had his prints matched on other cases.)

• • •

It was now June of 1962. Chuck and I were again working the morning watch, and were out in our plain car. It was beginning to warm up, and the division was experiencing a big problem with the prostitutes. The prostitutes, or streetwalkers, were filling the street. It seemed that Figueroa Street was the street of choice on the part of the prostitutes. They would walk up and down the sidewalk and solicit the cars. There was a hot dog stand at the corner of Figueroa and Florence. The prostitutes would congregate at this hot dog stand. Their presence at this corner was causing a lot of traffic jams and causing the pedestrians to avoid the corner. Our watch commander had asked the two felony cars to work these prostitutes and to eliminate their activity; in other words, he wanted that corner cleaned up.

Chuck and I and the other felony car were going to the corner early in the morning and loading up the prostitutes into our cars. We would bring them to the station and take them into the detective bureau, where we would identify them and run them for wants, or warrants. If they had warrants out on them for their arrests, we would then arrest them on the warrant. Most of these warrants were for failure to appear on other prostitute arrests. We continued to do this until we had brought all the prostitutes into the station for identification. We would inform them that we did not want to see them back on the corner.

On one occasion, when we were in the detective bureau with about a half a dozen of these prostitutes, I noticed a new probation officer there. He was with his training officer, and they were completing a burglary report. I asked the training officer if I could use his probation officer for a while, and he told me that I could.

"I'd like your help in searching these prostitutes who we've just brought in," I said. "I have to interview each one of them, so I'd like you to search them as I take them into an interview room. I want to make sure they don't have any weapons on them. A word of caution: don't search their hair. They are all wearing wigs. They have a habit of putting razor blades in the hair of their wigs. If you search the wigs, you will cut your hand on the razor blades. They do this because some of the other girls like to grab the wigs and pull them off of their heads, and then run off with their wigs. Also, they keep their narcotics stashed under the wigs. This way they know that no one will steal their stash from them."

The probation officer then began to pat-down search three of the prostitutes who I had in custody. After he finished patting them down, he informed me that they had no weapons on their persons.

"That's not going to work," I said, "you need to search them better than that. You need to search inside their bras and to search their crotch area. If you're going to find any weapons, that is where the weapons will be."

"Don't I have to get a police woman to search that way? I was taught at the academy that only a police woman should search the private parts of a female."

"There are no police women working here at this time. So we have to do what we have to do to get the job done. Just consider it a direct order from a senior officer, and I will take any responsibility for them filing a complaint against you."

The probation officer then approached one of the females. He apologized to her, but told her that he was going to have to search the area of her private parts. At that time, he patted her bra down and reached inside the bra. He jumped back with astonishment and with a sheepish look on his face. He began to pat down her crotch.

"This female has got balls! And she does not have any boobs! In fact, this female is not a female. This female is a male! Are the other two you want me to search also transvestites?"

"Yes, they are," I said. "They are all three transvestites. We might as well have a little humor in our night. Thank you for your assistance. You did a good job. Just goes to show you things are not always as they appear to be. Consider this a lesson learned about this job. You never know what to expect."

Now back to our prostitute problem. The girls did not heed our advice about staying off the corner, so we had to go to plan two. I had told my fellow police officers that while I was working the Harbor Division I became aware of an amusement park in Long Beach. This park was called the Pike. It was located on the waterfront in downtown Long Beach. A lot of sailors frequented this park. All we had to do was load up the prostitutes and take them down to this park. By the time they would get back, it would be after we went off duty. So that is just what we did. For the next several nights we loaded up our cars and drove the girls down to the park in Long Beach. We told them that they could make more money down there from the sailors than they could make up in Watts. As none of the girls had ever been out of Watts, they were surprised to be in an amusement park in Long Beach. It turned out that they could make twice the amount of money that they were making up in Watts. After a while, I arranged with some taxi-cab drivers to come by the corner and take the girls down to the park. After a while, the girls would solicit their own rides down to Long Beach. Not all of the girls would go down to the park, but enough of them would go so that it solved our problem. As things worked out, the girls were better off because they could make more money, and we benefited in that they were not on our corner.

• • •

Several nights later, Chuck and I were having coffee in the coffee room at the station. An officer walked into the coffee room and got himself a cup of coffee and walked back out. The officer's name was Bill Swift, and I had worked with him when I first got to Seventy-seventh Division. He had been on probation and had been assigned to a car I was working with another officer named Rada.

"Do you know that officer?" I said to Chuck. "Do you know the story behind him?"

"My answer is no to both of those questions. So what is the story?" Chuck replied.

"I was on a day off, and he was working with Rada that morning. They had just come out of roll call and were in the parking lot getting into their police car. They heard a broadcast of a pursuit on the Harbor Freeway. A highway patrol car was chasing a stolen car southbound on the freeway and was asking for assistance. Rada told Swift to jump in the car, and that they were going to go over to the freeway to attempt to intercept the fleeing car. As you know, there's an on ramp to the freeway just across Broadway Street, out behind the station. As they were heading in that direction, the highway patrolman and the fleeing car had came off the Harbor Freeway at Slauson. They were traveling southbound on the road parallel to the freeway, coming down toward the station. Rada drove to that road just as the fleeing car was speeding by. The highway patrol unit was a short distance behind the fleeing car. The car hit the on ramp to the Harbor Freeway and was going up the on ramp to get back on the freeway. The pursuing highway patrol car passed by Rada's car and followed the fleeing car up the on ramp. Rada immediately started up the on ramp behind the highway patrol car. The fleeing car lost it before he made the freeway and went off the on ramp into the ice plant alongside the on ramp. The highway patrolman bailed out of his car and started to run up to the suspect's car. Rada told Swift to get on the radio and put out a broadcast that the fleeing car had spun out and that they were code four, and to give their location. Rada got out of the car and came around the front of the car, and was running up the on ramp, toward where

the highway patrolman was going. Swift had opened his passenger door and got out and kneeled behind it and placed his
weapon on the open window frame. He was broadcasting on
the radio when he capped off a round, accidentally. The bullet
that he had fired went through Rada's right hand as he was
running up the on ramp. Can you believe that?"

"You have got to be kidding me! And he is still working here?
How did he make his probation? Is Rada still working?"

"Rada turned out just fine. He was off for a month or so, but
he's back to work. I've seen him around and have talked to
him. As you notice, Swift is an African American. As you
know, we do not have many African Americans on the job. I'm
not saying that's good. And I'm not saying that's bad. I'm just
saying that's the way it is. I'm not saying that had anything to
do with his making his probation either. I'm just telling you
the story, and I'm just telling you like it is." (Swift Would end
up a Captain, accidents happen.)

• • •

Now let's go to my next adventure. It was toward the end of
June, 1962, when I was informed that I was being drafted into
the US Army. I had received a notice through the mail, from
my draft board, in the state of Ohio, that I was to enter the US
Army in July. I had registered for the draft on my eighteenth
birthday, while living in the state of Ohio. This was quite a
shock to me, and I attempted to be exempted from the draft. I
notified the department that I was being drafted. The department informed me that they would give me a leave of absence
for the time that I was required to serve, and my job would be

waiting for me when I came back. The department also stated that they would contact my local draft board and request that I receive an exemption because I was a Los Angeles police officer. Deputy District Attorney McKesson also notified my draft board that I was to appear in the Black Muslim trials, coming up later that year. He also requested that I be exempted from going into the service. Neither of these requests was approved. The Ohio's draft board stance was that they did not care what responsibility I had to the city of Los Angeles. The Ohio draft board stated that I was filling their quota and that I was to report to Fort Ord, California, for basic training on July 23 of 1962. This left me no choice other than changing a Los Angeles Police Department uniform for a US Army uniform. I completed my basic training and was assigned to the 291st MP Company at Redstone Arsenal, Alabama. I spent my entire army career at that location.

Muslim Riot 1962. Scene outside of mosque

March 14 1966 article on being run down by robbery suspect

Chapter 3

Seventy-seventh Division Patrol

August 1964–August 1966

It is August of 1964, and I am back with the department, full-time again. In the last two years, major changes have taken place in the country, the department, Seventy-seventh Division, and with me. I am trying to figure out where my place is in all of these changes. The next six years will prove to be the most challenging years in my career. I am going to break away from the war stories to set the stage for what is to come.

First, I will reflect on my life over the last two years. While in basic training, at Fort Ord, I had heard of a police officer being killed in Seventy-seventh Division. The police officer had taken my place on the felony car when I left for the US Army. It was his first night out working the felony car. He was driving it when he began to chase a stolen car. During the chase of the stolen car, he lost control of the police car and hit a telephone pole, which subsequently killed him. The person he was chasing was caught and identified as a Ronald Green.

Ronald Green was convicted of auto theft, but did not have to answer for charges with respect to the death of the police officer. I bring this up because later I would encounter Ronald Green. (The story about my encounter with Ronald Green will come later.)

Police work and the way it was being done had changed quite a bit during my two years' absence. It would continue to change drastically over the next six years. I do believe that the next six years of my career would really impact my life and would influence me greatly. Some of the case law that came down out of the courts during the next six years would change the way police work was done. The following are some of those cases:

1. Map versus Ohio, 1961. The exclusionary rule came out of this case. It dealt with either illegal evidence and/or illegal confessions being obtained from suspects, and it led to the doctrine, "fruits of the poison tree." This basically meant that evidence would be excluded from court, and that any evidence obtained as a result of the illegal evidence and/or illegal confession would also be excluded from court.

2. Miranda versus Arizona, 1966. This decision dealt with the rights suspects have at the time they were to be inter-rogated. It stated that prior to interrogating a suspect, the suspect was to be advised of the following rights: You have the right to remain silent. You have the right to the services of an attorney, and if you cannot afford an attorney, one will be provided for you free of charge. Anything you say can and will be used against you in a court of law. Once advis-ing a suspect of these rights, you were to obtain a waiver prior to talking to the suspect. The waiver would consist of the suspect's acknowledgment of understanding these

rights and giving up these rights and agreeing to talk to the law enforcement officer, without an attorney present.

3. Terry versus Ohio, 1968. This case was known as the stop and frisk case. It stated that a police officer had probable cause to frisk a suspect who they were detaining. The frisk consisted of a pat down to the outer garments of the person, period. This pat-down search could only be the searching for a weapon. It did not allow you to search the person's pockets.

4. Ramey versus California. This case dealt with arresting a person who was inside their residence. It stated that a police officer needed an arrest warrant prior to entering a person's residence in order to arrest them. A police officer could enter without a warrant only under emergency circumstances.

5. Chmiel versus California, 1969. This case stated that you could search an area that was only within reach of the arrested person at the time of arrest.

Prior to these decisions, the police officer's responsibility was to arrest and convict criminals. A police officer wore two hats. The first hat was worn when dealing with the general law-abiding public. You were hired to protect and serve these people. Your job was to protect their rights that they had under the US Constitution that allowed them to live in peace and tranquility. You treated them with courtesy and respect. It did not matter what race, sex, age, religion, or culture they came from. You treated them all equally. The second hat worn was worn when a police officer dealt with a criminal. The criminal did not have any rights. How the evidence was obtained, with respect to physical evidence and/or confessions, was immaterial. The criminal was to be arrested and convicted for the criminal offense. This was done to protect the law-abiding public. It was also done without any animosity toward the criminal. It was done only to rid the streets of the criminal element, and in so doing to allow the law-abiding general public to enjoy their constitutional rights. When the courts start applying constitutional rights to everyone, including criminals, the balance between serving the law-abiding general public, and protecting them from the criminal elements in the country, was lost.

The chief of the Los Angeles police department, Chief Parker, retired in 1966. The only good thing about this was that patrol officers could wear short-sleeve shirts and not have to wear a tie. Chief Parker had insisted on the wearing of long-sleeved shirts and ties, because he did not like to see tattoos on his officers' arms.

Apollo landed on the moon in 1969. I guess the Rockets that were being made at Redstone Arsenal ended up working. My only claim to fame was that I had guarded the base, where the rockets were being made, for two years.

The Los Angeles police department now had seventeen divisions. Two divisions had been added. These divisions were in the valley and were called the Foothill Division and the Van Nuys Division. The population of Los Angeles was now over three million people, and the city was now 498 square miles. Los Angeles was the third-largest police force in the country and was outnumbered only by New York and Chicago.

The then United States president, President Johnson, signs the civil rights act on July 2, 1964.

Malcolm X, of the black Muslims, is shot to death on February 21 of 1965.

The official start of the war in Vietnam was in August of 1964. The United States would not withdraw from Vietnam until 1973.

Demonstrations in the United States, as well as in Los Angeles, were starting to heat up. There were demonstrations for civil rights. Hate and discontent toward the police was occurring in Seventy-seventh Division. The police were being called *pigs*. Protest against the Vietnam War and the burning of draft cards were prevalent. College demonstrations were occurring throughout the country. *Free love, free drug use, sit-ins, love-ins, Woodstock, flower children, hippies, yuppies, PCP, LSD, pills, marijuana, flower children,* and *turn on, turn off*, were all buzzwords.

• • •

When I came back to work at Seventy-seventh Division in 1964, I found my old partner; Chuck was still working there. Chuck and I hooked up and worked together again. For the next several months, we patrolled the Watts area of Seventy-seventh Division, working the night watch. We came to work at 4:00 p.m. and worked until 12:30 a.m. It was like I had never left Seventy-seventh Division. The people and the places were the same people and places I had dealt with two years prior. The criminal activity had increased, and the radio was as busy as ever. I revisited all my old places and redeveloped my informants and knowledge of the activity that was going down. It was becoming harder to get information out of the suspects who we were arresting. It was also harder to search them. The criminals, as well as the citizens, were becoming more anti-police and anti-white.

I had been assigned to the Fortieth MP Company, which was headquartered at Spring and Hope Streets, in downtown Los Angeles. This was where I was to fulfill my active duty, reserve status. We met one weekend a month to drill and train. We were to go to summer camp to Fort Ord, California. I had a two-year obligation to complete my required army duty. While attending these meetings, I found that a lot of the reservists were police officers. They were police officers from all over LA County. We had police officers in the Fortieth MP Company from the cities of Covina, Inglewood, Burbank, El Monte, and various other cities.

I had been working several months when I found out that Sam Cooke had been killed in our division. Sam Cooke! He was one of my favorite singers, at the time. A song, recorded by him, that was released after his death made a big impact on me. "A Change Is Gonna Come, (Yes It Is)", was the song. It spoke to the changes that were occurring in our society.

According to the investigation that had been done by our homicide detectives, Sam Cooke was shot by Bertha Franklin, manager of the Hacienda Motel at 9137 S. Figueroa Street. He had been shot on December 11, 1964, between 2:30 and 3:00 a.m. The investigation showed that he had picked up one of our prostitutes on Figueroa Street and had gone to the motel with her. The hotel was known to be a motel that was used by prostitutes to turn their tricks. While at the motel, Sam Cooke was ripped off by the prostitute. She took his clothing and money and fled the room and disappeared. He went looking for her wearing only a sports jacket and his shoes. He went to the manager's office and got into an altercation with the manager. The manager shot him with her .22-caliber revolver, and he died as a result of one gunshot wound.

CHAPTER 3

Sam Cooke's clothes and money, estimated to be three thousand dollars, were never found. The prostitute was identified and was picked up and questioned. She would not admit to being a prostitute, nor would she admit to having the clothes or money. She did admit to being at the motel with Sam Cooke and claimed that he had kidnapped her. A coroner's inquest was held and it found the shooting to be justified.

About a week after the Sam Cooke homicide, Chuck and I were again patrolling the streets.

"You know, Chuck, that killing of Sam Cooke really bothered me," I said. "I know we've handled many a homicide scene. And I've never felt bothered about any of the deaths before. But this one really bothered me. You know, we've heard that his killing wasn't as the detectives said it was. We've heard it was a hit, either by the Muslims, or behind his record contract. I'm sure it was as the detectives said it was, but wouldn't it be fantastic to be the detectives investigating it?"

"What are you saying?" Chuck replied.

"I am just saying I think I have found out where I want to go on this job. Ever since I got back from the army, I've been wondering where I wanted my career to go. You know, we've done a lot of preliminary investigations at the scenes of homicides, but we've never worked a homicide to solve it. What I want to do is work a homicide from beginning to end. So I'm going to try and get into homicide somewhere and do whatever it takes to do that."

"You know, the only way to get into the detectives, let alone homicide, is that you have to be asked by the detective division. It's kind of like the good-old-boy scenario. You know, I scratch your back, you scratch mine. But, if that's what you want- it's what you want."

"Sooner or later I will get myself into homicide. Hopefully, it will be here at Seventy-seventh Division. We carry the highest rate of homicides of any division in the city. We both know that there's at least a homicide a week down here. There's never a lack of work, working homicide."

"Why do you think Sam Cooke was down here? That rip-off was the oldest trick in the book. The whores are always ripping off their tricks. They know the johns are not going to report it. With his money, he came down here."

"I don't know, but I do know he would have been bigger than Elvis Priestly!"

The year 1965 started off with a lot of hate and dissension in the streets. The black community and south-central Los Angeles was becoming rebellious against white society. The Black Muslims were really pushing their doctrine and were distributing their newspaper throughout the community. Their newspaper was soliciting the blacks in the community to join their movement against the white government. They were saying that any black who did not join in their movement would be ostracized. Their position was that anyone not siding with their movement was considered an "Uncle Tom."

The Caucasians that were living in Seventy-seventh Division were being targeted by the rebellious black youth. Most of the Caucasians were elderly and could not move out of the area because of a lack of income. They owned their houses and could not leave. They became easy prey and were burglarized, robbed, and assaulted. Their cars were stolen and their property was maliciously damaged. Whereas in the past, it did not matter whether you were white or black, anyone was subject to becoming a victim of criminal activity. Now more of an emphasis was put on the whites in the community, as opposed to the blacks. The police were being called racist pigs or white devils. The battle cry on the streets was "Get Whitey."

An example of this was an arrest that Chuck and I made on February 11, 1965. It was around ten fifteen at night, and we were patrolling the alleys and streets in the vicinity of the 111 Street and Slater Avenue. We observed two young black juveniles half carrying and half dragging a drunken Caucasian. Both of the juveniles had clubs in their hands, and the victim had been beaten about the head and shoulders. We jumped out of our car and ran toward the juveniles. When the juveniles saw us, they dropped the Caucasian victim and took off running. I was able to catch one of the juveniles, and Chuck was able to catch the other. The suspects had thrown away their clubs. After taking the juveniles into custody and retrieving the clubs, we went back to where the victim was lying on the sidewalk. We requested an ambulance be dispatched to our location. We then talked to the victim and learned he had been walking down the sidewalk when he was accosted by the two suspects. He stated he lived in the neighborhood and had just been to the liquor store and was returning home when he was accosted by the suspects. He stated that they had beaten him about the head and face area with clubs and had robbed him of his property. His property consisted of his money, wristwatch, and ring. He further stated that the two suspects had told him that they were going to take him to the fields and kill him. We placed the suspects under arrest for assault with intent to commit murder. When we searched them, we found the victim's property in the pockets of one of the suspects.

Another example was a call we received one evening around eleven at night in March of '65. "All units, robbery suspects there now at 128 East 110th Street, units respond code two."

Chuck and I jumped the call and told communications that we would handle it. As we approache the location, we noticed that it was a single-story, single-family residence. The residence had a front yard and was set back off of the sidewalk, approximately twenty to twenty-five feet. As we approached the residence, with our lights out, we noticed two persons come running out the front door of the house into the yard area. We immediately jumped out of our car and ran to the yard area with our guns drawn. We hollered at the two persons to raise their hands and to get face down on the ground. As we said this, we got to within fifteen feet of the two persons. They raised their hands but did not get down on the ground. We ran up to them; Chuck put one of them on the ground, and I put the other on the ground. We handcuffed them, and as Chuck stayed with them, I went into the house.

When I got inside the house, I observed a female Caucasian woman, approximately seventy-five years of age, lying on the living room floor. She had what appeared to be bruises and abrasions to her upper arms, neck, and cheek area. She was crying at the time.

"Please go check on my husband in the back bedroom. They were in there with him and beat him. He's lying in bed. He is an invalid and wheelchair bound. Please go see if he is okay."

I immediately went into the bedroom and, upon entering, observed her husband lying in the bed. He was severely beaten about the head and chest area. At the time he was unconscious and could not respond to my questions. I ran back outside, went to my patrol car, and requested that an ambulance respond to my location.

Another unit had showed up at the location, and Chuck had given them two suspects and asked them if they would transport the suspects to the station for us. I informed the unit that there were two victims inside the house, and that it appeared that the husband was in critical condition. I told them that the wife had been beaten as well, but that she appeared to be OK. I asked them to notify the homicide detectives as to the occurrence, and that I felt the husband was not going to make it. I asked them to tell the watch commander that we will be at the Martin Luther King hospital with the victims.

The ambulance then arrived and, after loading up the woman and her husband, left the location for the hospital. I requested another unit respond to the location, and upon their arrival I had them secure the crime scene. I told them that either I or homicide detectives would be coming to the scene at a later time. Chuck and I then went to the Martin Luther King hospital, and, upon our arrival, were told that the husband had died and that his wife was going to be admitted as a result of her injuries.

I briefly interviewed the wife and was told that the two suspects who had run from her house had come in the house and had stated they were there to rob them. She stated when they went in the bedroom to talk to her husband, they began beating him and hollering at him to show them where our valuables were. He kept telling them that we did not have any valuables, and that any money we had we would be given to them. She further stated that when they got through with him, they came out and began hitting her and asking her for valuables. After ransacking the house and finding no valuables, the suspects had left.

Chuck and I returned to the scene, and, by that time, the detectives had arrived at the residence. I gave the detectives the information I had and turned my statements over to them. I informed the detectives that the two suspects from the location were at the station. I further told them that the two victims were at Martin Luther King hospital, and that the husband had died. I asked them if they wanted me to book the suspects for them, and they stated that they did not want me to arrest the suspects—they would handle the case from there out.

The detectives later informed me that the wife had recovered from her injuries and had identified both suspects in standing lineups. Charges of murder, assault with intent to murder, and burglary had been filed on both suspects.

Over the next four months, Chuck and I received seven accommodations for the arrests that we made during that time. We had made three arrests from spotting stolen cars while they were being driven. In two of these instances we had to chase down the suspects after they had jumped out of the cars. We made one arrest of a burglar who was seen coming out of a house. We caught him as he was running from the scene. The other three arrests were for possession of narcotics for sale. The arrests had resulted from observing dope deals going down at various liquor stores in the Watts area. It was now August of 1965, and Chuck and I were about to get involved in the biggest occurrence of criminal activity in the history of the city of Los Angeles.

LA Race Riot 1965

(aka the LA Watts Riot)

To tell this war story, I am going to put the cart before the horse. I am going to list the statistical information that came out after the riot had occurred. The reason I am doing this is that the story is better told in reverse. I spent the entire six days of the riot, involved in the riot. I did not go home for those six days. After the statistical portion, I will take the riot and separate it out on a daily basis. I feel the story is best told in this fashion.

STASTICS

Area involved: 46.5 sq.miles. The riot started in Seventy-seventh Division, and spread out to the west and north into Newton, University, and Central Divisions. The riot spread to the east of Seventy-seventh Division and into the county, which was the Firestone sheriff's Division.

Response forces: 932 Los Angeles police officers, 719 LA county sheriffs, and 13,900 national guard soldiers from the First Battalion, 160th infantry, the First Battalion, 111th armored Calvary, First Battalion, Eighteenth Armored Calvary, and the Fortieth Armored Division, including military police.

Length of time rioting occurred: six days, from August 11 to August 17, 1965.

Population: Seventy-seventh Division, 100,000 persons, 10 percent non-black. Watts, 29,500 blacks, 66 percent with no income, and 30 percent on welfare. LA County was home to 600,000 blacks.

Property damage: $200 million—1,000 buildings looted and burned.

Type of property: liquor stores, war surplus stores, gun stores, hardware stores, chain stores (White Front, Market Basket), pawnshops, markets, retail stores, and small businesses. There were no houses or churches that were torched. Any business with, Negro Owned signs in its windows was not torched.

Injuries: There were 1,032 persons injured, that were known of. Of these persons, 90 were police officers, 136 firemen, and 10 were national guardsmen. There were 36 deaths, including two police officers and one fireman.

Arrests: 3952 were arrested; 3438 were adults and 514 were juveniles.

What caused the riot: Some say police brutality and harassment. This was disproved, and race relations in Los Angeles had been among the best in the country. The blacks in the community wanted to be policed by black police officers. Yet any time black police officers worked in Seventy-seventh Division, they were called Uncle Toms by the populace. At the time of the riot, there were only a half a dozen black officers working out of Seventy-seventh Division, which had 207 police officers.

White merchants were taking everything out of the community and putting nothing back. The black community felt they were being exploited by the white businessmen. They felt they were being overcharged for goods that they bought.

The McCone commission contributed the rioting to the high jobless rates, poor housing, and bad schools.

Various gangs, within the community, were felt to be the cause of the rioting.

The Black Muslims, although not the original parties involved, were felt to have organized the rioters, after the start of the riot, in order to continue the riot in a rebellious state.

Personally, I felt that the rioters rioted because "AM beats NAM." As a suspect once told me, something is better than nothing. Once it was realized that the police could not prevent looting or burning, the word spread like wildfire. It became a situation in which people would get what they could. Everyone felt that someone was going to get whatever there was to get, so why not let that someone be himself? A lot of the property obtained by the rioters was just thrown any way in the streets. Since only locations that had merchandise of value were looted and burned, this premise holds up.

The First Day: Wednesday, August 11, 1965, 4:00 p.m.–Thursday, August 12, 1965, 5:00 a.m.

It was a hot, sultry August night, and Chuck and I were on patrol, working the night watch. We had come on duty at 4:00 p.m. It was now around six o'clock, and we were patrolling in the Watts vicinity.

"It sure is hot!" Chuck said. "I wish we didn't have to wear these long-sleeved shirts and these damn ties. Even though they are breakaway ties they still cause you to keep your shirt buttoned up."

"I know, life is a bitch," I answered. "I hear there is going to be a full moon tonight. You know what they say about a full moon: someone will get killed tonight. Of course, we both know that a full moon only means that a lot of people will be out on the street. This heat and a full moon will cause the streets to be crowded with people. It will also cause a lot of drinking to be going on. All the moon does is give the people extra light at night and makes them want to be out of their houses. Look at the streets now, they are already crowded with people, and it's only a little after six o'clock."

"Well, we can expect to be busy. I'm glad it's your night to keep the books and my night to drive. You're going to be doing a lot of writing."

"Well, partner, a guy's got to do what the guy's gotta do."

"All units in the vicinity respond to an officer needs help call at 116th Street and Avalon. The California Highway Patrol is requesting help at that location," the radio blared.

"Let's jump that call!" I said. "We are only seven blocks from that location." We were in the Imperial Courts housing project at Imperial Highway. Imperial Highway was the main highway that ran east and west through the Watts area. All of the traffic from the east side of Los Angeles traveled this highway to get to the west side of Los Angeles. There were no east/west freeways to travel on. The airport and the ocean, along with many businesses, was on the west side. A lot of people working in these businesses, or going to the beach and airport, would travel this road. The traffic on Imperial Highway was always heavy. A lot of Caucasians travel this highway.

We traveled the seven blocks with our red light and siren on. 116th Street was one block south of Imperial Highway. As we reached Avalon Boulevard and were making a left turn, we were joined by two other LAPD units. When we made the corner, we saw two California Highway Patrol vehicles and two motorcycle officers in the street a block from the corner. They were surrounded by a group of forty to fifty blacks. The group of blacks was very unruly and was shouting at the highway patrolman. Chuck pulled our police car up next to the highway patrol unit that was facing north. The crowd had the highway patrol officers, who were out of their vehicles, surrounded. There was a lot of pushing and shoving going on between the four Highway Patrol officers and the crowd. I noticed that there was a black male and a black female in one of the highway patrol cars. I grabbed the shotgun out of the rack and bailed out of our car. Chuck also bailed out and brought his nightstick with him. The other two LAPD unit's officers also bailed out with their shotguns and nightsticks. The six of us formed a skirmish line and walked into the crowd around the highway patrolman's vehicle. We pushed the people back away from the highway patrol cars and hollered at the highway patrol officers to get in their cars and on their motorcycles. One of the highway patrol officers took another black male into custody and pushed him into the unit that had the other two sitting in it.

The crowd was saying that they were going to take the three suspects in custody back out of the car and not allow the highway patrol to take them away. The crowd began chanting, "Get Whitey, Get the Pigs!" All of a sudden, rocks and bottles were being thrown at us and our police units. I hollered at my fellow officers to get back in our cars. I told the highway patrol officers that we would form a wedge with our police cars and for them to fall in between our cars, in order to drive away from the location. I then noticed that there was also a tow truck at the location. This tow truck had a car hooked up to it. I told the tow truck driver to bring up the rear, and I ran to my patrol car. Chuck was already in our car and had it running. The other two LAPD units joined us, and we formed a wedge in the street, and the CHP cars and motorcycles got in between our cars. The tow truck got behind the CHP motorcycles.

The crowd at the location had now increased to around a hundred people. As I looked into the crowd, I was able to see several people who were throwing rocks and bottles at our police cars. Several of the missiles hit our car and broke the front and back windows. A lot of the rocks were hitting our car, as well as the other units. Once everyone was in place in our caravan, we drove out of the area by going north on Avalon Boulevard. When we reached Imperial Highway, we took a right-hand turn and headed east. Once we got away from the crowd, the highway patrol units continued on east down Imperial Highway, and we headed for Seventy-seventh Station. Our car was unsafe for us to drive because of the windows being broken out. We wanted to get another car.

At the station we learned that the highway patrol officers had stopped a drunk driver, and that the suspect's family and friends had tried to keep them from taking the suspect into custody. Little did we know at the time, but this was the start of the Watts riot.

Chuck and I were at the station, drinking coffee and deciding what our next move was going to be. The watch commander had told us that the crowd out at Imperial Highway and Avalon was becoming very unruly and increasing in numbers.

"Chuck, I can identify several of those people that rocked our car. What do you say? I say we go back out there and pick them up. We can get a plain car, and that way we can be on top of them before they know who we are. I don't think they should be able to get away with what they did."

"Reynolds, if that's what you want to do, that's what we'll do. But I'll tell you one thing: I'm going to get a shotgun so that we will each have one. If we are going to have to pull some of them out of that crowd, we are going to have to show some firepower."

"Well, let's get it done! It's around eight thirty, and we still have a lot of time left on our shift. If we make those arrests, it will eat up the rest of the time we have left on our shift, and afterward we can go home."

"I wonder why those highway patrol officers were down here in Watts to begin with. They usually stay on the freeways. Maybe that drunk driver was on the freeway, and they followed him down into Watts. I heard he lived right there where they stopped him. His brother was in the car with him, and they let him go. Then I heard he ran and got their mother. Then the mother tried to take her son away from the highway patrol officer. Like you said, a hot night, a full moon, and liquor cause people to do funny things."

"Chuck, while you get a shotgun, I'm going to tell the watch commander that we are going to check out a plain car and go back down there and look for the suspects that stoned our car. I think we also need to pick up some sandwiches to eat on the way. I'm starving!"

Chuck and I got into our plain car, picked up some sandwiches and soft drinks from one of our frequented spots, and headed in the direction of Imperial Highway and Avalon Boulevard. As we got to within a couple of blocks of Avalon, we noticed that the sidewalks were loaded with people. When we got to Avalon Boulevard, there were over two hundred people at the intersection. The intersection had a gas station on the southwest corner. The gas station had been taken over by the crowd of blacks. There were at least a hundred people in the gas station. Some of them were carrying merchandise out of the gas station store. Others were filling up cars, bottles, and any container that would hold a liquid, with gas. There was no way we could stop this activity from occurring, because of the numbers of people involved. There was also no way that we could locate the suspects we were looking for, because of the volume of people gathered at this location.

"Damn, them people have taken over that gas station! I don't have to second-guess what they're going to do with that gas. We better radio this in to the watch commander and let him know what's going on out here. This mob is going to eventually cause some problems, and a lot of trouble. What do you think, Chuck, should we head back to the station?"

"Let's drive on down to Central Avenue and see what's happening there first. I want to see what the people from Imperial Court's housing project are doing. If they've got wind of this, and they probably have, they're going to be up to no good. You know how they hang out at Central and Imperial Highway, where the traffic light is. They wait for a car to stop at the red light, on Imperial Highway, and then run up to the car and rob the person. Sometimes they even take their car. The victims are always white persons driving through Watts, going to the airport or to work over in the beach area. Half the time they don't even report the robbery, they are so scared, and they just want to get out of the Watts area."

So we drove on down to Imperial Highway and Central Avenue, and, as we approached the intersection, we observed a crowd of about twenty juveniles on the northeast corner. The juveniles were throwing rocks and bottles at the cars on Imperial Highway that were heading west , and had stopped for the red light. We saw two juveniles breaking into a car that was waiting on the red light. They had broken out the driver's side window of the car. They were trying to pull the driver out of the car.

"Chuck, you take the one on the passenger side, and I'll take the one on the driver's side, just like we always do. Just like when we take down a stolen car. Just drive the car right up against the front of that victim's car. The minute you hit the front of his car, we will bail out. I think we should get the victim too, and throw him in our car and then get the hell out of there. We don't need to worry about his car, it's history."

Within seconds, Chuck had done just that. He rammed the victim's car with our car. At that moment, we bailed out and grabbed the two suspects before they knew what was happening. I took my suspect down onto the street and turned him over and cuffed him. Chuck did the same with his suspect.

I hollered at the victim, sitting in his car, "Get out of your car and get into our car, and do it right now! We have to get you out of here before it gets any worse. Don't worry about your car, it can be replaced."

The victim jumped out of his car and ran toward our car. I hollered at him, "Get into the front seat, not the backseat! Open our back doors before you get in."

As I saw the victim doing this, I pulled my suspect to his feet and noticed that Chuck had done the same with his suspect. Chuck and I ran to our car with our suspects, and, as we get to the car, we put the suspects in the backseat, and I jumped into the backseat with them. Chuck slammed the back door shut and jumped into the front seat behind the steering wheel. The victim had gotten himself into the front seat of our police car, and then closed the door and lay down on the seat.

The people at the location have now increased to approximately twenty to twenty-five people. They are throwing rocks and bottles at our car as we sped away from the location. We headed back down Imperial Highway westbound, and, as we were driving, we noticed that the street was full of people on both sides. When we reach Broadway Boulevard we hung a right, heading north, and headed back to our station. We took our suspects and the victim to Seventy-seventh Station. While we were driving back to the station, we were hearing radio calls over the radio. These radio calls were for units to respond to disturbances along Imperial Highway. Molotov cocktails were being thrown at passing cars. Traffic was being disrupted by crowds of people coming out into the streets and harassing the cars. There were calls from police units asking for assistance in apprehending suspects.

"Chuck, after we take the victim back to the detective bureau and put the suspects into the holding tank, I'll go talk to the watch commander. While I am doing that, you can take a crime report from the victim. Then we will take on the two suspects."

"OK, I can do that. I'm going to take a robbery, auto theft, crime report. I'm going to make it a crime in progress. I'm going to have a unit go out there and see if we can recover his car. I doubt that we will be able to do that, but anything is worth a try."

I went into the watch commander's office and told him what we had. I also told him that the activity out on Imperial Highway was out of control. I told him that gas was being taken out of the gas station at Imperial Highway and Avalon, and that I was sure it was to be used for Molotov cocktails.

"Have you heard the radio calls that are being assigned to our units out there at that location?" the watch commander said. "We do not have enough radio cars to handle the calls that are coming in. I have informed our captain about what's going on out there, and he has authorized me to go to twelve-hour shifts. The night watch is going to work until five a.m., so you won't be going home. We are going to run two shifts, one from four p.m. until four a.m., and one from four a.m. until four p.m. I want you to talk to our captain, who is in his office. I want you to tell him what you been doing. The highway patrol officers from that earlier occurrence you were at have booked three members of that family. Just for your information, the drunken driver was Marquette Frye, twenty-one years old, and the two persons who tried to take him away from the officers were his brother, Ronald Frye, twenty-two years old, and his mother, Rena Frye, forty-nine years old. The captain wants an update, so go see him."

I went into the captain's office and updated him on the information I had, from what I had seen out on Imperial Highway. I also informed him of the arrests that we were making, and the activity that revolved around it. The captain then asked if Chuck and I would take him out to Imperial Highway, so he could see firsthand what was occurring. I told him that we could do that. We could finish up our arrests, and after we had done so, I would get Chuck and be with him shortly.

I found Chuck in the detective bureau with the victim. Chuck told me that the victim's car had been firebombed and that the responding officers who we requested to check on the car were unable to do anything about it. Chuck also told me that our two suspects were both juveniles. He suggested that we arrest and book them and file detain petitions on them and detain them in juvenile hall.

"That sounds good to me," I said. "The captain wants us to take him out on Imperial Highway. He wants to see what's going on out there. I told him, but he wants to see for himself. Let's run him out there, and we can book and transport these juveniles after we do that. I doubt if we'll be able to get hold of their parents, anyway."

After assuring ourselves that our victim was able to find someone to come and pick him up at our station, Chuck and I went to the captain's office. We took the captain out to our plain car and drove him out to the vicinity of Imperial Highway and Avalon Boulevard. We were unable to drive down Imperial Highway. The traffic had been stopped in both directions. Roadblocks had been set up on Imperial Highway, four blocks east and four blocks west of Avalon Boulevard. The roadblocks were set up by using patrol cars. The officers at the roadblocks told the captain that unruly crowds controlled the streets inside of the roadblocks, and that it was unsafe for the traffic to drive on Imperial Highway. Looking down Imperial Highway, you could see a multitude of cars that had been vandalized and/or set on fire. All the time that we were out there, the radio was reporting locations where looting was taking place. Most of the looting that was occurring, at the time, was north on Avalon Blvd. We took the captain back to the station. At the station we learned that a lot of the businesses in the area were closing up, and that the owners were going home. It was now around midnight, and the only places open at the time were liquor stores and fast-food places. Our police units were making arrests for theft and malicious mischief, but could not control the streets.

Chuck and I finished up our reports on the arrest of the two juveniles and transported the juveniles to juvenile hall, where we detained them on the charges of attempted robbery and attempted auto theft. As I had suspected, we were unable to contact their parents. That was now the responsibility of the Juvenile Hall intake officer.

On the way back to the station, we stopped in to eat at a restaurant in downtown Los Angeles. The radio in our car was still broadcasting calls of disobedience in the streets, down in Seventy-seventh Division.

"What do you think, Chuck? Do you think this will blow over, and when the sun comes up, the streets will get back to normal? Do you think when that full moon goes down and the sun comes up, it's going to be a brighter day?"

"I really don't care what the sun brings. I'm going to be home in bed. This has been some night, and I'm not sure I want to see many more nights like this. We still have around three hours until end of watch. That gives us enough time to make another arrest. I thought hot August nights were to be spent in Reno."

"Well, one thing is certain, I won't be going home. When we get off this morning, I am going to sack out at the station. I have everything I need in my locker at the station. Would you believe I even have my army clothes in my locker? I am supposed to leave this Saturday to go to Camp Roberts for my active reserve, two weeks' summer camp."

"I am glad I am not committed to the army like you are. Funny, my draft board is in Pennsylvania, and they didn't mess with me like Ohio messed with you. I am only a year younger than you are, but I already have an exemption because I'm in the police department. Anyhow, let's get back to work, enough of this bullshit."

We left the restaurant and drove back to Seventy-seventh Division. When we got into our area of responsibility, we got on the radio and cleared ourselves, making us available for radio calls. We immediately received a radio call to go to the liquor store at 103rd Street and Lou Dillon Street, and see the man holding a theft suspect. This was one of our favorite liquor stores. It was owned by a Mexican by the name of Bob Martinez. He was a promoter of boxers and had a stable of boxers and a gym. He had owned the liquor store, which was right in the middle of Watts and across the street from the Jordan Downs housing project, for years.

Chuck and I had known Bob Martinez, since we had worked together. Bob knew everyone in Jordan Downs and did not take any trash from them. All of his clerks in the liquor store were members of his family. Every night we worked we stopped by to check on him and to exchange information. He had a large business office in the back of his store, where we would kick back and enjoy each other's company. We had made a lot of arrests out of his parking lot, and because of us stopping by every night, at different times, the riffraff would stay away from his store.

As we drove down 103rd Street from Central Avenue, we noted that the street was full of people. The activity taking place was not unusual. It definitely wasn't as it was on Imperial Highway. There were no signs of looting or unruly behavior. (This would all change in a couple of days.) It was about one quarter of a mile from Central Avenue to Lou Dillon Street. We parked our car in the parking lot of the liquor store and went into the store. The inside of the store was one big room that measured about twenty-five by twenty-five square feet. The room had a horseshoe-shaped counter that wrapped around the entire room. The clerks could walk around behind this counter from one end of the store to the other end. There was a door behind the counter in the middle of the room. This door led into the back of the store, where storage space and the office were located. All of the merchandise, from the liquor to the potato chips, was kept behind or in the counters. This made shoplifting impossible. Bob was behind the counter.

"What's up, Bob?" I said. "We got a call telling us you had a shoplifter here for us. You don't normally have shoplifters, and if you do, you take care of it yourself. If you need help, that's what we're here for, so what it is?"

"Hey, Reynolds," Bob said, "it's good to see you. Hey, Chuck, it's good to see you too. You guys know I wouldn't call you over nothing. This guy just pissed me off. He's in the back office, and my cousin is sitting on him for you. Gilbert had left the back door unlocked after a delivery this afternoon. When I came down here a little while ago I found the suspect in the back. He was trying to run out the back door with a case of whiskey."

"There's got to be more to it than that, Bob," I said. "We'll take him in and book him for the attempted theft. If that's what you want. Why don't you tell me what's really going down?"

"I'm hearing on the news about what's going on over on Central Avenue and Imperial Highway. That is not far from here. If the people in Jordan Downs get wind of what they're doing over there, they will be doing it over here. That means that none of the businesses on 103rd Street are safe. So I want to set an example early of what I'll do if they try and loot my store. When they see you carting this guy off, they will know I mean business. I'm going to tell you right now that I and my cousins will be armed with shotguns and rifles. No one's going to burn or loot my store. I worked too hard getting where I'm at, and I'm not going to have my store burnt down. If things get that bad over here, I'm closing the store, and we will be inside and on the roof with our firepower. Just so you guys know, if you come by here, what to expect."

"Bob, I guarantee you if you need any help protecting your store, in the future, Chuck and I will be here for you. Let's just see how the wind blows, and we will worry about it if it happens."

Bob took us back to his office, and we found his cousin sitting on the couch with the suspect. Chuck and I hooked up the suspect and walked him out the front door. We lingered in front of the store with the suspect in order to show the people in Jordan Downs what was going down. We then loaded the suspect up in our car and drove to the station. We did not encounter any criminal activity on the way to the station, and that part of the division had not been impacted, as of yet. After completing our reports and booking the suspect, it was now close to five in the morning.

"Well, partner, I'm going end of watch and heading home. Are you sure you're not going home, Reynolds?"

"It makes no sense for me to go home now. Besides, I don't know what tomorrow is gonna bring. I might be needed around here, and I'm single and don't have anybody to worry about me at home. I will just sack out here in the cot room upstairs, and that way, if they need help, I'll be here. You take care, and I'll see you later on today. Today is Thursday, August 12, of the great year of 1965. Just think—we have Friday to look forward to. It's going to be Friday the 13th. I will have to go play with the army on Saturday. I wonder what bad luck we'll find on Friday."

Chuck left and went home, and I went down to the watch commander's office. I told the watch commander that we were end of watch, and that Chuck had gone home, and I was going upstairs to sack out in the cot room. I told him I would be upstairs if he needed anything, and to call on me if he did.

Seventy-seventh Division is a two-story building. The first floor contains the front desk, the watch commander's office, the jail, the record bureau, the detective division, and the captain's office. It has several other offices that are used by administrative personnel. The second floor contains the roll-call room, the coffee and lunch room, the restrooms and showers, the cot room (where officers sleep when they have court in the morning), the vice and narcotics offices, and the stairs to the roof. The property room is in the basement of the building. The station fronts on Seventy-seventh Street, just east of Broadway Street. The rear of the building and the station's parking lot fronts on Seventy-sixth Street. There is a chain-link fence around the rear parking lot of the building with two exits and entrances into the parking area.

Second Day: Thursday, August 12, 1965–Friday, August 13, 1965

I woke up around noon, and, after I showered and shaved, I put on my uniform and went down to the watch commander's office. As I went into his office, I noticed that the police station was loaded with police officers, half of whom I did not know. I got a cup of coffee, sat down with the watch commander, and asked him to brief me on the situation.

"I can tell you this, it's not good. The crowd out there, in the south end of the division, has grown to over fifteen hundred persons. We have got over one hundred officers out there now, fighting that crowd. We have already had nineteen police officers injured. There have been over fifty cars destroyed, including ten of our police cars. By the way, your car was the first car we lost. We are calling in officers from all over the city. We are also bringing in Metropolitan Division tonight. By the time you go to work at four, there'll probably be other officers coming down here."

"Were any of our officers hurt seriously?" I asked.

"We had two serious injuries that caused the officers to be hospitalized. You know Stu—he tried to take a looter out of a crowd, and was stabbed in the back in the process. And then McKnight got a cinder block to his head. They were driving down San Pedro Street and the cinder block was thrown off the top of a building and came through their windshield. The rest of the officers have received minor injuries from rocks and bottles and cinder blocks being thrown at their cars. That's how we lost most of our cars. Most of the officers will probably get return-to-duty slips from central receiving hospital. I expect a lot of them will show up tonight."

"Well, I have four hours before I report to roll call. Is there anything that I can do in the meantime?"

"As a matter of fact, there is something I want you to do. I'll put you on the clock. And you can start your shift at noon. I have four officers up on the roof, guarding the station. I would like you to relieve one of them so I can put that officer back out in the field. They have not tried to do anything to the station yet, and I don't anticipate a problem. But we need to be prepared for anything, and I don't want to get caught with my pants down."

"No problem; I'll go up there right now and relieve one of the officers up there. I will stay up there until four o'clock roll call."

I left the watch commander's office and went upstairs to my locker and got my Sam Brown belt, with my equipment, and put it on. I also got my riot helmet out of my locker and put it on. The helmet reminded me of my football helmet. It was made of hard plastic that came to the ears. It had a strap that ran under the chin, to hold it on. It was white and had a small black bill. Chuck and I had not worn these helmets the previous evening. I then went up on the roof of the station and relieved one of the officers who was up there. He gave me the shotgun that he was using, and left.

For the next four hours, I walked around the roof of the police station. While I was up there, I surveyed the area to the south of the station and the area in the back parking lot. The area to the south of the station was the area that the now-rioting was occurring. Funnels of smoke appeared on the horizon, at several locations. I could hear the sirens of police cars and fire trucks racing to the scenes of the fires. There did not seem to be many fires at that time. The weather was still sunny and hot, and I worked up a sweat up there on that roof. The back parking lot was full of police cars. They were coming and going all of the time. I could see that a lot of the cars were not Seventy-seventh cars. I could also see that a lot of the officers were motorcycle officers who were arriving in cars. A lot of the cars arriving were bringing in prisoners with them. Our division was becoming a very busy place.

At around three forty-five in the afternoon, I left the roof and went down to the watch commander's office and informed him I was going to roll call. I then went upstairs and went to the coffee room to get a cup of coffee. The hallway, roll-call room, and coffee room were full of police officers. I counted over fifty officers milling about the second floor of the station. I met Chuck in the coffee room and asked him if he had his riot helmet, and he stated that he did. Chuck and I then went into the roll-call room. At around four o'clock the watch commander came to the roll-call room and briefed us as follows.

"To start out with, I want to welcome the officers from other divisions. As you know, we have a major disturbance in the south end of the division that has grown in size. Everyone here will be working a twelve-hour shift, so don't expect to get off until tomorrow morning at four o'clock. I also want you to know, as you can see by the watch bill, I am placing all of you visiting officers with Seventy-seventh Division officers. This is because the Seventy-seventh Division officers know the division. You are going to find your radio very busy. First and foremost, answer your calls. Don't hesitate to ask for assistance should you need it. We already have twenty officers injured from this occurrence.

"To continue, I have to advise you that the use of deadly force is for the protection of life, not property. If you encounter looters or fire bombers, you can use deadly force only if they are threatening your person or the life of another person. If you can manage to get the lawbreakers into custody without the use of deadly force, I advise you do that. You are going to hear their battle cries in the streets: BURN BABY BURN and GET WHITEY are their battle cries. Do not let that upset you to the point that you overreact.

"We estimate there are in excess of seven thousand people on the streets and becoming involved in the activity. By the end of the night tonight, we will have around 350 police officers on the streets. The first stores out there to be looted were the gun shops, war surplus stores, and liquor stores. Be aware, there are a lot of guns out there on the streets. And you know what happens when you mix liquor with guns. Just remember, the looters and firebombers are down on the streets, but the snipers are up on the roofs. I'm here to tell you that the liquor is flowing like water out there."

"And finally, a word of caution,—*Get Whitey* means police officers, firemen, businessmen, and any other unfortunate white person who comes into the area. An example of this is all the unfortunate persons who have been caught down on Imperial Highway. Right now there are over fifty cars down there on Imperial Highway that have been abandoned. We are making no effort at this time to remove those cars. We are setting up a perimeter at this time. That perimeter will be Vermont on the west and Alameda on the east. On the north we are using Slauson Avenue, and, to the south, 120th Street. This does not mean that you cannot enter inside the perimeter. It is just defining where the activity is either occurring or expected to occur."

The watch commander then dismissed the roll call and posted the watch bill on the blackboard. All of the officers went to the blackboard to check their assignments and find out who they were working with. The watch commander came back to where Chuck and I were sitting and asked us to meet him in the coffee room. We stayed in the roll-call room until all the officers had left. We then went to the coffee room and met with the watch commander. In a short time, we were the only three persons left. After getting coffee we sat down with the watch commander.

"As you can see by the watch bill, you two are still working together. I want you to go out there in your plain car. I want you to know that I have notified communications that you are not to receive radio calls. What I want you to do is monitor the radio calls and respond to any calls you want to. You will be able to shake, rattle and roll, as you always do. You can switch your plain car with any other plain car at any time you deem it necessary. I want you to do this, both tonight and tomorrow night. Reynolds, I see you are going to the National Guard on Saturday morning. I think the National Guard will be coming down here tomorrow. Anyhow, when you leave Saturday morning, I'll put Dean with Chuck to replace you, if this thing continues. In case you do not know it, Seventy-seventh Division is now the riot field headquarters."

After the watch commander had said this, both Chuck and I thanked him for his faith in our abilities. We told him that we would do what we could to assist the other officers. We all three then left the coffee room, the watch commander went downstairs to the his office, and Chuck and I went out into the parking lot and got into our plain car. It was going to be an interesting evening.

"Did you sleep well last night?" Chuck asked.

"Not really. I guess I got about five hours' sleep. I went up and guarded the station, on the roof, from noon until roll call. I also heard that Stu and McKnight are in the hospital. Stu got knifed and McKnight got hit with a cinder block, through the windshield of his car. I know one thing; I'm not going to wear this damn tie. It's too hot! We also can not wear these helmets; everyone will make us as the police."

"You've got any suggestions as to what we are going to do?" Chuck said.

"We will do just what the watch commander said to do. Let's shake, rattle, and roll and see what we come across. We probably need to reconnoiter the area and see what our best bet is. I'm thinking we probably won't do much until it gets dark. Then we'll just hit the alleys like we always do."

The first thing we did was drive down Broadway until we reached Imperial Highway. We drove east on Imperial Highway, and, as we approached Avalon Boulevard, we noticed that the activity in this area was as it had been the previous evening. We had to weave our way through a lot of abandoned cars, and sometimes we had to avoid bricks and bottles being thrown at our car. We noticed that the gas station at Imperial Highway and Avalon was still being used to obtain gas for Molotov cocktails. A lot of the activity had moved up northbound on Avalon Boulevard. All of the north-south streets that we passed until we reached Central Avenue were full of people. We drove up central Avenue to 103rd Street. There was not a whole lot of activity on Central, and, as we drove down east on 103rd Street, we did not observe any looting. We stopped at Bob's liquor store and found that he was open for business as usual. We went inside and found that Bob and four of his cousins were behind the counters.

"Hey, my friends, what it is," I said. "It looks like the riot is not slowing you guys down. What is the good word?"

"There are no good words," Bob said. "For your information, if you can believe what I'm hearing, 103rd Street is going to burn tonight. All these assholes in Jordan Downs are over there on Avalon and Imperial getting their piece of the rock. The word is that when there's nothing left over there, they're going to come down on 103rd Street. At the first sign of trouble, I'm going to close up, and we are going to go up on the roof and spend the night up there. What are you guys going to do?"

"We are going to do whatever we have to do. We will check on you throughout the night. You are better off than we are. You can shoot people to protect your business, but we can't. But if people end up shooting at you, we can shoot them for that. We will see you later, and good luck." Chuck and I then went back and got into our car and left the area.

We drove over around Avalon Boulevard where it crosses Century Boulevard. We reconnoitered the area and came to the conclusion that there was an eight-square-block area around Imperial Highway and Avalon Boulevard that had been turned into a seething battleground. This seemed to be the hot spot at the time. The damage from Molotov cocktails seem to be confined to automobiles. At the time there were not any buildings on fire in that area. Looting of the liquor stores and markets continued. The radio was very active with radio calls for assistance from the general public. Most of the assistance requests were coming from the businesses in the area and from people who had fled their vehicles. The streets were littered with broken glass, debris, smashed concrete, bus benches, broken street barricades, trash cans, and rocks. There were four burning cars on Imperial Highway. Small packs of wild-eyed youths rampaged through the broken glass and the rubble-strewn riot area around Imperial Highway and Avalon Boulevard. Fire trucks and ambulances were bombarded by bricks and chunks of concrete, and were forced to turn back unless escorted by police patrol cars.

The police in the area were forming wedges and were pushing back the youths gathered at the intersection. They would get several of the youths and bring them back to their patrol cars and put them inside the cars. Then they would drive out of the area, and other police officers would move in. As they drove out of the area, their cars would be bombarded by rocks and bottles. As soon as the police officers would leave, the streets would fill up again with the rampaging rioters. Although their tactics were good, they were outnumbered. Indiscriminate shots were also being fired in the area. It was becoming impossible for the police to contain the area, and we knew that they were fighting a losing battle.

It was around seven o'clock at night when Chuck and I left the area. We drove to Imperial Highway and Vermont, where there was a restaurant that we frequented. We went inside the restaurant and ordered coffee.

"Can you believe what is happening down there?" I said to Chuck. "Here we are, about a half a mile away from that, and there is no problem here. It's like a world away from that uncontrolled anarchy. We need to make a plan about what we are going to do. I think we need to drive in there and get those people whose cars are being firebombed and bring them back here to the restaurant. When we get them to the restaurant, they can either go to the station and make a report, or they can call someone to come and pick them up and take them home. We can do that a couple of times, and when they recognize our car, we can go to the station and get another car and do the same thing. What do you think, Chuck?"

"That sounds like a plan to me. It won't do us any good to join the police officers who are trying to control that down there. And since we can't shoot anybody, we can't control any of the activity that's occurring. I do not see this ending soon. If anything, it's getting worse. There has got to be a a thousand people down there. And from what I'm hearing on our radio, it's escalating and moving north up Avalon and then east on 103rd Street. I'm afraid Bob was right. Since 103rd Street, east of Central, is the main business district in Watts, it has to be next."

For the next three hours we did just that. We would drive down Imperial Highway, and when we saw any Caucasians, either in cars or running in the street, we rushed in with our vehicle and picked them up. We worked Imperial Highway from Avalon east to Central Ave. There were times when we had to use the side streets to get out on Imperial Highway. We did whatever it took in order to get in and out of that area. A lot of our driving tactics were by way of the alleys that we knew so well. We had changed our car three times and were fortunate that we were not recognized during the course of those three hours. I don't remember how many people we got off that street and out of that area, but it was a lot. We took them all to our restaurant, and most of them just wanted to call someone to come and pick them up and not be bothered with making a police report. Most of them indicated that they would report it to their insurance companies to seek restitution for their cars. I think that most of them were just happy to be alive. I know that I was happy that they were alive. We even picked up some police officers and took them back to the station when we changed our car. The officers were injured, and their partners hooked up with other officers and stayed in the action.

The last time that we went to the station, we heard that the news was advising everyone to stay off Imperial Highway. The watch commander also told us that barricades and roadblocks were being set up on Imperial Highway, at Alameda on the east and Vermont on the west, to divert traffic off Imperial Highway. We also learned that sixty-three rioters were arrested and that forty California highway patrolmen and 195 sheriff's deputies were on the line with our police officers now. The law enforcement force was now almost five hundred strong. The sheriff's department had a reserve force of 283 men en route to the fighting zone, including cadets and jail guards pressed into service. This reserve force was going to muster at 120th Street and Broadway. The watch commander also told us that a catering outfit had set up a kitchen at that location, and if we needed something to eat, we should go there. It was now eleven o'clock at night, and we still had half our shift to finish, so we decided to give it a try.

I drove down to 120th Street and Broadway. As we got to the location, we noticed that the kitchen had been set up in a vacant field. They had tents and picnic tables set up and had a full kitchen. I also noted that there were three sheriff's buses parked in the field there. I parked the car, and we joined a lot of officers who were sitting at the tables under the tents. Most of these officers were sheriffs, but there were a few LAPD officers eating at the tables also. Everyone was eating steaks. When we went to the kitchen to get our steaks, we found that they were all out of steaks. The steaks were being replaced by hamburgers, so we ended up eating the hamburgers.

Chuck and I joined the LAPD officers that were eating. Some of these officers we knew, and others we didn't.

"How is your hamburger?" one of the LAPD officers said. "It's too bad you didn't get here earlier; you could have had a steak. You see those buses over there? They are full of deputy sheriffs. They just got here about an hour ago, and they have all had their steaks. They told us they are a reserve force, and they're waiting here until it's decided what's going to be done with them. One thing I know is whatever they do end up doing, they will be doing it on a full stomach."

"I heard about them while I was at our station. They are cadets and jail guards who have been pressed into service," I said. "I don't see why it would be so difficult to decide where they're needed. It's certainly not here, eating up all the steaks. Leave it to the sheriff's to find the food. But on the other hand, they are welcome to join us. We certainly do need their help, there's no doubt about that."

We hung out with the other LAPD officers for a while and then left the kitchen. We decided to head back over to Bob Martinez's liquor store. When we got to 103rd Street, we saw that there was a large crowd at a liquor store on the southeast corner of 103rd Street and Central Avenue. They were looting the liquor store. We detoured around the corner and came up to Will Rogers Park, which was north of the liquor store.

We drove into the park and stopped behind some trees and parked our car. We had hopes that we could pick off some of the looters as they left the liquor store. As we were watching the looters, a car pulled up and parked in front of the liquor store. Three adult male blacks got out of the car and joined the looters inside the liquor store. In a short time, they came back out of the liquor store to their car. They opened the trunk of the car and loaded the trunk with liquor that they had brought out of the store. They then drove their car about a half a block away from the liquor store and parked at the curb. They waited until the crowd had dispersed from the liquor store. When there was no one at the liquor store, they drove back and parked in front of the store. Two of them got out of the car, and the third stayed in the car behind the steering wheel and kept the car running. One of them stood on the corner and watched the traffic that was going by. The other one placed some Molotov cocktails inside the broken-out window of the store. He lit the Molotov cocktails, and the two of them ran back to the car, got into the car, and the car sped off northbound on Central Avenue. As they turned the corner, the store window blew up, and the store was on fire.

As they drove by Will Rogers Park, we came out of the park and began to follow them northbound on Central Avenue. I got on the police radio, told communications that we were following a wanted vehicle, and asked that a unit join us in pursuing this car. I gave our location as northbound on Central Avenue from 103rd Street. I stated I wanted the radio car to approach us from the south. We had driven approximately ten blocks when I saw a police car pull in behind us from a side street. I told communications to inform them of the description of the car that we were pursuing. I also told communications to tell them to stop the car with their red lights and siren, and that we would block the car in from the front. I also informed communications to let them know that the car was wanted for burglary and arson.

We continued to follow the car northbound on Central Avenue for a few more blocks. The radio car behind us flashed their lights after they had gotten our communication over their radio. We caught up with the suspected car, I pulled my car around the left side of that car, and, as we drew up alongside the driver, Chuck pointed his gun out the window at the car and I hollered at them to stop. At the same time, the radio car put on their lights and siren, and pulled up to the rear of the car. We boxed the car in and forced it to the curb and caused it to stop. We all jumped out of our cars and the four of us ran to the car and ordered the suspects out of the car at gun-point. At that point, we pulled the three suspects out of the car and spread them out on the sidewalk and searched and handcuffed them. We then searched the inside of the car and found about a half a dozen Molotov cocktails on the backseat. I placed the Molotov cocktails into one of the liquor boxes and put the box in our trunk. I got the car keys out of the ignition of the suspect's car and opened that trunk. There were three cases of liquor in the trunk of the car. We loaded the liquor and one of the suspects into our car. The other two suspects were placed in the rear seat of the radio car. The suspects were all taken to Seventy-seventh Division, where they were arrested and booked for burglary and arson. We booked the liquor that we removed from the car as evidence. We took the Molotov cocktails to the police garage and poured out the gas into a gas container and threw the bottles and rags in the trash. When we got done booking the suspects and completing our reports, it was after four on Friday morning. Seventy-seventh station was a madhouse.

Rows of uniformed officers were writing complaints from scores of persons standing in two rows, some with bloodied skulls and cut faces and hands. A police radio blared out incoming reports: "Yellow cab overturned, shots at Avalon and Imperial, man pulled from car on Imperial Highway, car overturned, officer in trouble." Deputy Chief Roger E. Murdoch was in command, operating from the first floor, watch commander's office. A sergeant was taking dispatches next door. He came in every minute or so with written or verbal messages. Grim-faced officers were in constant movement through the corridors. More than a score of newsmen and photographers jammed the main lobby. They are waiting on the only phone to call in their reports. Outside a full moon bathed the grim streets.

"I think it's time to wrap it up." I said. "I have been working since noon yesterday, and it's now almost five o'clock on Friday morning. We are going to have to do this again in a few hours. I'm going to go upstairs and hit the sack. I think you should go home too, Chuck; you've been working for over twelve hours."

"I will have to agree with you, Reynolds. We have had a busy night, and I have a feeling Friday night is going to be even busier. I don't think this station can hold any more people than what it has inside it already. I haven't ever seen so much brass around here as I have seen tonight. I've just seen Inspector Gates and Inspector Powers go in the captain's office. I'm sure it's not good news they are bringing to the captain."

"Friday the 13th has just started. I heard that Farley is at the hospital. He got hit by flying rocks and injured his hand. Gordon Weeks is also at the hospital, after being struck in the left leg with a cinder block. I am sure that some of those officers that we brought to this station have gone off duty. Today has not been lucky for them. I'm also going to have to take a shower before I sack out. I smell like gas from those Molotov cocktails. I wonder how many other stores those guys have fire bombed. What do you think Chuck?"

"My guess is that this was not the first one. They sure looked like they knew what they were doing. One guy keeps the car running, one guy acts as a lookout, and the other guy does the firebombing. All of this after they looted the store. They must just like to see fires. They could have driven off after they got their liquor and not set the place ablaze. Makes you wonder sometimes about human behavior. Some people just do some things because they can do it. They don't have any conscience to bother them about their behavior."

"Well, that's for their shrinks to figure out," I said. "Enough of this! As I said, I'm going upstairs and get a shower and go to bed. I will probably be back on the roof this morning when I get up."

I went down to the watch commander's office and told him that we were end of watch. I also told him that I was going to be up in the cot room and would be catching up on my sleep, and if he needed me to send someone up to get me. And that is just what I did.

Friday, August 13, 1965, noon–Saturday, August 14, 1965, 6:00 a.m.

I was sitting in the watch commander's office, drinking a cup of coffee and waiting on him. The station was very busy, as you can understand, and he had a hundred and one things to do. It was around noon, and I had just come down from upstairs after changing into my uniform. After briefing his sergeant, the watch commander came over and sat down with me.

"Good to see you again, Reynolds. What I want you to do is get yourself a shotgun. Then I want you to patrol the outside area of the station. You will find several officers out there who you can help out. I don't have a lot of time to brief you on what is going on, but your watch commander will brief you at roll call tonight at 4:00 p.m.. I can tell you that the riot has jumped our perimeter and now has increased to a twenty-one-square-mile area. Reports are coming in from the command center, and it appears there is some organization to the riot. The Black Muslims are still circulating their newspaper and urging the black community to resist the white devils. Our station is in the middle of the riot now, and we have rioting going on, on all sides of us. The area around Imperial Highway and Avalon Boulevard is now a mop-up area. There is nothing left down there to loot or burn. Oh, by the way, you will be on the clock. So go out there and see what you can do until your roll call. Thanks for sticking around. We can use you."

I left the watch commander's office and went to the room where they issue police officer's equipment. I am told that they do not have any shotguns left to issue. I then go up onto the roof of the Police Station. Up on the roof, I look around the surrounding area. Everywhere I look I see smoke. The heaviest smoke is to the southeast, where Watts is located. There are fires burning all around the Seventy-seventh Division. I then go over and look down into the police parking lot behind the station. It is a beehive of activity. I see that all the police officers' private vehicles are parked on the adjacent streets. The whole parking lot is now being used for police purposes. There are two large LAPD buses in the parking lot, and police officers are loading prisoners into these buses. The maintenance garage is full of black-and-white police cars, and there are several additional cars surrounding it. It looks like a car salvage yard down there. All of the cars are dented and smashed up from cinder blocks. The maintenance people are just replacing windshields and other windows as fast as they can, in order to get the cars back into service. I see officers down in the parking lot in all kinds of different uniforms. There are LAPD officers, sheriffs, highway patrolmen, US marshals, and representatives of numerous other law enforcement agencies. I can also see LAPD officers patrolling the perimeter of the station and walking up and down the streets in front of and behind the station.

While I'm up on the roof, I reflected on what had happened as well as what was happening right now. What started out to be, in my opinion, fun, recreation, or hoodlumism has now turned into anarchy. What started out to be *Am beats Nam* (something is better than nothing) has now turned into "Burn, baby, burn." I thought about the definition of anarchy: the complete absence of government and law, political disorder and violence, lawlessness, disorder in any sphere of activity. Anarchy is activity that leads to disorder, rebellion, riot, and insubordination. Was this what was taking place? I thought about the arrest that we had made earlier that morning. It did seem that there was an organized purpose, with respect to what the suspects had done. First, the windows of the liquor store were broken, then the store was looted, and then the store was set on fire. From what I had learned, this was a routine pattern that was now occurring throughout the riot area. It was also being said that the word in the streets was that if you were in the streets, and you were black, you were expected to join in the activity. If you did not join in the "movement," you were considered the enemy. That being the case, you were subject to the same treatment that whites would receive. In other words, anyone not joining in the riot was considered an Uncle Tom.

I then thought about police brutality being a cause for the riot. Was there police brutality in Watts? I had worked in Watts for over two years, and I had not seen one instance of police brutality. The law-abiding citizens were treated as fairly as anyone else would be treated. If there was police harassment, it was aimed at the criminal and ridding the black community of the non-law-abiding persons. I am sure there were times when the criminal was harassed, and, in some cases, physical force was used in order to arrest them. I myself personally did not consider that police brutality.

I then went down on the street and talked to several of the officers who were patrolling the parking lot and adjacent streets on foot. All of the officers had received minor injuries over the past two days. I knew some of the officers, and others I did not know. They were all assigned to light duty and had come back to work rather than stay home. All of them felt that they needed to be doing something to assist their fellow officers. Most of them had been hit by cinder blocks, rocks, or other thrown objects. A couple of the officers were the same officers that Chuck and I had picked up on Imperial Highway. These officers again thanked me for what I had done for them. They told me that their mission was to protect their fellow officers' private cars, and to assure that no damage came to the cars.

I then got to thinking about some of the arrests we were making, prior to the riot occurring. We were arresting people for what was known as victimless crimes. We made arrests for being drunk, using or possessing narcotics or dangerous drugs, gambling, and prostitution. These crimes were against the law, but were these laws really necessary? What if there were no laws against drinking, gambling, prostitution, and drugs? It would surely save us, the police, a lot of time and trouble. It would also take a lot of money out of the hands of criminals. If the black community, as a whole, wanted to participate in these illegal activities, so be it. I would be all for the legalization of these particular crimes. I knew that I could never work vice. I hated narcotics and drugs and what they did to a community, but if they were all legalized and addicted persons were treated, like for alcohol, I think the community would be better off.

It is now four in the afternoon, and Chuck and I are sitting together in the roll-call room. It is so full of police officers, the rear doors were open and officers were standing in the hall. I'm sure that the sheriff's roll calls are as crowded as ours are. The watch commander is preparing to brief us prior to us going out into the field.

"I am sure you all are anxious to hear what I have to say about what is happening out there in the streets. First of all I'd like to tell you that all of Watts is burning. Whole blocks are on fire. Not only the original places that were being burnt, such as liquor stores, gun stores, war surplus stores, and markets, all businesses are being looted and burned. We are fighting on two fronts now, so you need to be alert. The rioters own the streets and the snipers own the rooftops. We have reports of sniper activity all over the riot area. Not only are we being shot at, the firefighters are being shot at. There are over one hundred fire companies being deployed to the riot area. A lot of the fires they can't put out because of the sniper fire.

"The National Guard, Fortieth Armored Division, is coming in to assist us. I have been told that there will be between five thousand and ten thousand national guardsmen here on the streets by ten o'clock tonight. They will be arriving on your watch, so you are to assist them in any way you can. Remember, they are coming here to assist us. I know that national guardsmen are going to be put on the fire trucks in order to protect them while they are fighting the fires. I'm sure that their mission will be to sweep the streets and set up road-blocks.

"We are getting radio calls on the average of one every two minutes. You will continue to answer your radio calls and take whatever action is necessary to conclude the call. Right now, as I speak, all of Seventy-seventh Division is within the perimeter of the riot. The riot now has encompassed University and Newton Divisions. The cities of Inglewood and Gardena, to the west of us, are not engulfed in the riot. In fact, when we ran out of shotguns, we went to Sears, in Inglewood, and got all they had. We have also gotten shotguns from the various gun stores that have not been affected by the riot. So, after roll call, I assure you, each and every one of you will be given a shotgun.

"That brings me to my next comment. Only department-issued sidearms and shotguns will be used during the course of this riot. No personal weapons and/or additional firepower will be taken out on the streets with you. I know that you all feel that we are restricting your use of deadly force. But thus far, no police officers have been killed, nor have any of the rioters, that I am aware of. I do not know what the National Guard's policy is going to be, nor do I know what type of weapons they are coming here with, but our department still only authorizes shotguns and .38-caliber revolvers.

"The original location of the riot, at Imperial Highway and Avalon, is now an area that we can get into. The day watch has been down there in a mop-up action. All of the derelict cars are being towed out of the area. The day watch has stayed on the fringe of the riot and is picking off any violators that they have an opportunity to catch. We are not committing ourselves to the main riot area and are awaiting the National Guard. There is no way we can keep the rioters from rioting. So I suggest, on your watch, you only answer your radio calls, and you work the fringes of the riot until the National Guard gets here. At that time, we will reevaluate our position.

"OK, if there are no questions, let's go to work. I will post the watch bill up here on the blackboard, so you can see what unit you are working and who you are working with. I know a lot of you from other divisions don't have our frequency on your radio. I have tried to pair you up with our officers, so you have communications. A lot of our communication will be on the tack frequency. Anyone who has communication problems please see me after roll call. Remember that a lot of different law-enforcement officers are going to be on the streets, and communication between you and them will be nonexistent.

"I have one more thing to tell you that I failed to mention earlier. All arrest and bookings related to the riot, such as looters and arsonists, will be done on the short-form drunk arrest report. You do not have to name a victim, and you do not have to make crime-and-arrest reports. There are buses in the back parking lot to load your prisoners onto. The buses will be taking the prisoners down to the main jail. We have set booking cages up in the jail to facilitate the booking procedure. This way you can avoid spending a lot of time booking the prisoner. Only serious felonies—such as robbery, murder, or burglary—need crime-and-arrest reports."

After the roll call, Chuck and I went downstairs, and after we were given a couple of shotguns, we went out and got into our car. We sat there awhile and watched the activity around the police parking lot. We see all the cars leave the parking lot, full of the officers who had been at the roll call. We turned on our car radio and heard calls coming out constantly. There was no delay between one call and another. The calls were everything from shots being fired to buildings being looted. A lot of the calls were from police officers asking for assistance. Other calls reported new fires being set. A lot of the calls were now for incidents occurring in Newton and University Divisions. We were both overwhelmed by what we were hearing. We looked at each other and were speechless for a few minutes.

Chuck turned to me and said, "What now, coach?"

"I really don't know, Chuck. Why don't we go down on Imperial Highway and see if there's anything there to be done? We can then work our way up Central and see what's going on in Watts. From the radio broadcast, it appears the heavy activity is in the north end of our division and in Newton and University. I am really wondering if Bob's liquor store is still standing. We might try and get by there later and see how he is doing. Then, I guess we will just shake, rattle, and roll until the army gets here. By the way, remember I have to join the army tomorrow morning, so we can only work until 6:00 a.m. That is when I will have to leave."

"Since you are driving tonight, I will just go along for the ride. Wherever you take me is OK by me. We might want to jump some of the calls and help out. We can always shake down some cars for stolen merchandise. Those would be easy arrests."

I then drove our car out of the parking lot got on the Harbor Freeway and started driving south toward the Imperial Highway off-ramp. Looking toward the east, while driving down the freeway, I saw that the sky was still full of smoke. This heavy smoke was coming from the area of Watts, and I was sure it was on 103rd Street. The traffic on the freeway was lighter than usual. I attributed this to a lot of white people not using the freeway because of it running through south-central Los Angeles. Several fire trucks passed us, on the other side of the freeway, northbound.

I got off the freeway at Imperial Highway and went east toward Avalon Blvd. When I got to Avalon, I noticed that there was a lot of activity. The activity was not as it had been the past two nights; it was police activity, as opposed to rioters. Police officers were walking and standing on the street, and a lot of tow trucks are in the street hooking up the abandoned cars. The police officers were holding their shotguns at port arms and were protecting the tow truck operators. As we got to the gas station on the corner, I noticed that there were police personnel in the gas station, and they appeared to be preventing anyone from coming into the gas station. There were a few people meandering down the street, but they didn't appear to be causing the officers any trouble. What a difference this was from what had been happening here last night! Since it appeared that our help was not needed, I continued to drive west on Imperial Highway and reached Central. I started to go north on Central Boulevard and ran into a lot of traffic. Central Boulevard was congested with cars and pedestrians. When I reached 103rd Street, the crowd was really dense and the area was still active with looters. We could see down 103rd Street and see that the fires were still burning. The crowd then began throwing rocks and bottles at our car. After some of these rocks and bottles hit our car, I made a U-turn and drove out of that area as fast as I could.

"I'm sure glad we got out of there," I said. "I guess we will have to try to get to the liquor store after it's dark."

"I do not know if they knew we were the cops, or if it was just because we are white," Chuck said. "But they sure were hell-bent on getting us. Last night we couldn't drive on Imperial Highway. Tonight we can not drive down 103rd Street. Just like Bob said, when Jordan Downs gets the word, 103rd Street is going to burn."

"Let's go to plan B and look for a car we can stop. We need to get off the streets and wait till it gets dark. You and I don't work too well when it's light out."

For the next several hours, we stopped several cars and came up with several arrests of looters. It was easy to book them because of the short-form arrest reports. The only hassle was booking the evidence we took out of the cars, and impounding the cars. We did this until around midnight that night. At midnight we went over to our restaurant on Vermont and got us something to eat. While we were in the restaurant, a lot of people came up to us and asked about the conditions of the riot. The waitresses in the restaurant wanted to know if the riot was going to reach them, and we told them that we did not know. Everyone in the restaurant was very concerned about their safety. We simply told them that the best safety for them would be to go home and to not remain in the area. We advised the manager of the restaurant to close. After dealing with this situation inside the restaurant, we went back outside and got into our car and headed for Bob's liquor store.

The National Guard had been coming into the area since around ten o'clock that night. They transgressed various streets in the three divisions. The use of vehicles and national guardsmen on foot was effective in moving crowds off the streets. They set up roadblocks around the perimeter, which was now a forty-square-mile area. The inner area was twenty-one square miles. The outer perimeter was to keep vehicles from entering the inner perimeter, and the area between the two perimeters was patrolled by police officers and squads of national guardsmen. This concept seemed to work in containing the riot area and giving it definition. The inner area was not entered initially by the National Guard, and it was given to the rioters. Eventually, by pushing the rioters away from the outer perimeter and into the inner perimeter, the riot was confined to the inner perimeter.

We came into Watts from the west side. As we were approaching Bob's liquor store, we noted that 103rd Street looked like a war zone. Bob's liquor store was the only business not burned or looted on all of 103rd Street. A lot of people were still out and on the streets, but it appeared that most of the looting had already been done. We pulled into the liquor store parking lot and drove around to the alley behind the building. As we got out of our car, Bob and his cousins hollered at us from the roof of the liquor store.

"We are up here on the roof. Wait just a minute, and I'll come down and let you in the back door."

Bob opened the back door of the liquor store, and we went inside. Bob look like he hadn't slept in a week. For that matter, he had not shaved either. He took us into his office and offered us some coffee. We all sat down and relaxed for a few minutes and just enjoyed our coffee.

"What have you guys been up to?" Bob said. "I guess my store is the only store left that can open for business in the morning. You would think it was Vietnam out there today. There were a lot of times where they tried to get my store, but we put some fire down on them and they backed off. I don't know if we shot anybody or not, but tell you one thing—they know we are up here."

"The National Guard has come in and they will clear the streets." Chuck said. "We have already seen them, to the north, and they're working their way down to this area. I'm sure they will be coming down 103rd Street by tomorrow. It's a good thing you guys were up there on the roof. But you better watch yourself: snipers are on the roofs, and if the police or National Guard takes you for snipers, you're liable to get wasted."

"Well, hopefully we won't have to be up there much longer. If we see the National Guard pushing through here, we will get the hell off that roof. I think all of Jordan Downs was out here on the street today, and all of them have their houses full of looted goods. I did see the cops out here a few hours ago, and they did shoot one of the looters coming out of the hardware store."

"I will be joining the National Guard in a few hours, Bob," I said. "Maybe the next time I see you, I will be in a different uniform. You and your cousins take care, and we will see you later. We got to get back to work."

"You guys take care too. When this is all over, we will go out and get ourselves a nice dinner, as long as it's Mexican food."

Chuck and I then left the liquor store and drove down 103rd Street to Central. At the time we were driving down the street, there were very few people left on the street. The sky was still lit up by the fires that were occurring to the north of us, but it appeared that the fires on 103rd Street had either burned themselves out or had been put out by the fire engines. It was now getting close to our end of watch time, so we headed back to the station. At the station we went up to the locker room and changed our clothes. I put on my Army fatigues and packed my duffel bag. Chuck and I said our good-byes. Chuck said he would tell the watch commander we were end of watch and that I was heading out for the army. That being said, I went downstairs and left the building and headed for the Fortieth MP Company's armory.

Saturday, August 14, 1965–Tuesday, August 17, 1965

I would spend the next three days with the Fortieth MP Company, and I would be assigned various assignments in the riot area. It was a long three days, and I did not get much sleep, nor did I shower or shave. I wore the same set of army fatigues for the entire three days. I worked with a multitude of other MPs, so I am not going to address who I was with and when I was with them. During the course of these three days, there were many incidents in which we were shot at by snipers, and we returned fire. We did not make any arrests, but we did turn looters and rioters over to law-enforcement personnel. There were occasions when I joined up with law-enforcement officers and assisted them in chasing down and catching violators. I am going to pick out some of these instances and address them as war stories. I will address them on the days that they occurred, but not list each day separately.

I had reported to the armory Saturday morning at eight. The commanding officer told our Fortieth MP Company that we were still going to go to summer camp. The company was going to leave twenty MPs back in Los Angeles to set up traffic-control points for the Fortieth Armored Division, which was to come in with their tanks. He asked for volunteers to stay back and do this. I was one of the volunteers, and, out of the twemty volunteers, eighteen were police officers. I was the only volunteer that had seen action, thus far, in the riot. Our lieutenant, in the guard, was also going to remain with us and would be our commanding officer. He was not a police officer, and ran an ice-cream parlor in real life. We would be issued fully loaded M-1 rifles, .45-caliber pistols, and steel helmets. Six jeeps would be furnished to us for transportation. The jeeps would be equipped with radios and communications, and would be set up through a radio operator at the command post. The command post would be located in a school at 108th Street and Figueroa. After being issued our weapons and our jeeps, we proceeded to the school.

I am now sitting in a classroom at the school, with the nineteen other MPs, waiting for our lieutenant to come in. Our caravan of jeeps had gotten to the school at around noon. Upon our arrival at the school, we found out that the Fortieth Armored Division was also using the school for their command center. The school parking lot was loaded with half tracks, jeeps, personnel carriers, and LA County Sheriff's buses. The gymnasium in this school was being used has a property room for weapons and or stolen merchandise that had been recovered from the riot zone. Prisoners were being brought to the school by both army personnel and police officers. These prisoners were being placed on the sheriff's buses and were transported to the LA County Jail. The school was as crowded as Seventy-seventh Division police station had been. Ninety percent of the people at the school were National Guard troops as opposed to police officers.

"I see you all made it down here to the school," our lieutenant said. "This classroom is going to be our headquarters. I am going to set our radio operator and the radios up in this classroom. Our assignment has changed, though, and I'm going to brief you on what you can expect to be doing. The Fortieth Armored Division tanks are not going to arrive until either late tonight or tomorrow morning. An inner and outer perimeter has been established in the riot zone. These perimeters are going to be manned by personnel from the Fortieth Armored Division. Your job is going to be to check the roadblocks and traffic control points on the perimeters. A curfew is going to be implemented at 8:00 this evening. This curfew will last until dawn and will be in effect until further notice. What this curfew means is anyone on the street after 8:00 p.m. is violating the law, and can be arrested for curfew violation. Anyone you find on the streets tonight, after 8:00 p.m., you have the right to pick them up and hold them for this violation. You can either bring them here or load them on the buses in the parking lot, or you can take them to any police station, and that station will accept them. All you need to tell the booking officer or the transportation officer is your name, rate, and rank, and where you picked the person up, and the rest will be done by them."

The lieutenant continued, "You will be working twelve-hour shifts. I am going to put four men in each jeep and we will put two jeeps out on each shift. The other four I will keep here and rotate them as needed. While you are out there checking on the TCPs,(traffic control points) I expect you to call in every two hours for a status report. Other than that, you will be on your own, and can go anywhere inside the outer perimeter. Just keep in mind that there are a lot of snipers out there shooting at the police and the fire trucks. I have been told that the Fortieth Armored Division personnel were very successful last night in sweeping the streets. Tonight should be a different matter, with a curfew in effect. At least the people who are not involved in the riot will be in their houses and not on the streets. Anybody on the streets, either walking or driving, is fair game, and you should not have any trouble identifying the looters and arsonists from the law-abiding citizens. Now you figure out who is going to work with whom and who is going to work, which shift, and let me know. Whoever is going to work the first shift can start as soon as they're ready to go out."

I let the other MPs know that I was going to work the second shift from midnight until noon. I told them that I had not been to bed the previous evening, and I needed to get some rest. I had seen that there were some cots set up in one end of the school gym. This end of the gym was divided from the rest of the gym by a partition that ran across the gym floor. After telling them that I did not care who I worked with, I left the classroom and found a cot to catch some shut-eye on.

My squad woke me up around eleven o'clock that evening. My squad consisted of three other MPs. One of the MPs was a LAPD officer who I did not know. Another was a police officer from West Covina. The third MP was a nineteen-year-old kid. It was decided that I would drive, since I knew the area. They told me that they had received information that the outer perimeter had been lifted, and that the riot zone was now limited to that area inside the inner perimeter. The inner perimeter consisted of a twenty-one-square-mile area. There was still activity occurring outside of the inner perimeter, but squads of the Fortieth Armored Division and the police were being sent to the sporadic activity. Our orders were still to check the roadblocks in and around the inner perimeter. We got our weapons, steel helmets, clips of ammunition, and rounds for our .45s, and went out to our jeep. I got in the driver's seat, and the other LAPD officer got in the other front seat. The West Covina police officer and the nineteen-year-old got in the backseat of the jeep. The lieutenant had given a map containing the marked roadblocks to one of my squad. I examined the map and was sure that I knew all of the locations of the roadblocks. We checked our radio to make sure it was working, and it was. We notified communications that we were on the road!

I was driving down Forty-Eight Street, at San Pedro, and was heading for a roadblock to check out when we received our first sniper fire. I heard what I believed to be rifle shots being fired. I heard the pinging of the bullets off our jeep. The nineteen-year-old, who was sitting in the backseat, asked me what I was running over in the road. He said whatever it was, it was hitting the back of the jeep. I told him that I was not running over anything, someone was shooting at us and that was their bullets bouncing off the back of the jeep. He immediately got down on the floor of the jeep and stated, "Let's get out of here." I drove out of the area, and we continued to head for the roadblock. This was the first time that we had been shot at, but it would not be the last.

We had been checking roadblocks, for around two hours when we came to a roadblock at Broadway in Manchester. This roadblock was being manned by four Fortieth Division national guardsmen. They had the entire street blocked off with barricades, and to one side of the barricade they had a .30-caliber machine gun mounted on a tripod. Three of the four had M1 rifles, and the fourth was manning the machine gun. The four of us got out of the jeep with our M1 rifles. We went up to the national guardsmen and asked them how they were doing. Before they could reply, we all heard and saw a car coming southbound on Broadway toward the barricade. The car was about a block north of the barricade, and was picking up speed. The car was a 1959–60 Buick.

"That car is not going to stop!" someone said.

"Get on that .30-caliber gun!" someone else said.

"He is going to run the road block!" I said. "We need to shoot at the car."

About this time the car is within a hundred feet of the road block, and coming faster. The four of us MPs began to shoot at the car with our M1 rifles. The national guardsmen on the .30-caliber machine gun began to shoot at the car with his machine gun. The other national guardsmen ran out of the street and sought cover. The car crashed through the j°barricade, and we continued to shoot at the car as it came through. The car went out of control about two car lengths' south of the barricade and spun out and hit the curb, where it stopped. All of us ran to the car and found a driver slumped over the steering wheel. A couple of the MPs pulled the driver out of the car and laid him in the street. The driver had been shot several times, and the windows of the car were blown out. I went over to the car and looked inside. There were no other persons inside the car, but the backseat was full of Molotov cocktails. I got the keys out of the car ignition and opened the trunk. The trunk was full of cases of liquor.

One of the MPs got on our radio and notified communications of the incident, and requested an ambulance and police be sent to our location. After doing this, the national guardsmen at the roadblock again secured the roadblock with the barricades. In a short time, an ambulance showed up at our location and examined the person who had been shot. They told us that they would remove him from the location, but that he was not going to survive. They asked us if we had reported it to the police, and we told them that we had. They then gave us a medical treatment receipt and asked us to give it to the police when the police arrived. At that time they left the location with the suspect. I looked at the MT,(medical treatment slip) and written on it were the initials DOA.

When the ambulance was going down the street, I saw several police cars approaching our location with their red lights and sirens on. I recognize the cars as being LAPD radio cars. All of the cars got to our location and pulled up and stopped. The officers got out of their cars, and I noticed one of them to be a sergeant. He came over to me and nodded.

"Do you want to explain to me what happened here?" he said. He looked me in the eye, and I saw signs of recognition in his eyes. "Is that you, Reynolds? What are you doing in that uniform?"

I then recognized him as being a sergeant I had worked for when I worked at the Harbor Division. "Yes, it is me, Sergeant Steele. I am now working out of Seventy-seventh Division. I've changed my uniform today because the Army has better firepower than LAPD has, as you can see by what happened here. Where are you working now days? I know it is not at Seventy-seventh."

"I am working at Metropolitan Division. I have been working there for the past year. So tell me, what is this all about?"

"It seems that the driver of that car did not want to stop at the roadblock. When he got too close for comfort, we had to stop the car from hitting us, so we shot at the car with our M1 rifles and that .30-caliber machine gun you see over there. It seems that he got hit by some of our gunfire. If you look in his car over there, you will find Molotov cocktails and cases of liquor. Besides, he should not have been on the street. There is a curfew, as I understand it, that started at 8:00 PM."

Another police car had driven up at that time, and a lieutenant had gotten out and had approached us. He walked up to Sergeant Steele and asked him for a briefing on what was taking place. He looked at me and nodded. Sergeant Steele told the lieutenant what I had told him. It was obvious to me that the lieutenant was Sergeant Steele's commanding officer. The lieutenant talked to Sergeant Steele and then came over to me and nodded again and left.

"Reynolds, you guys are going to have to stay here for a while. That was my lieutenant. He is going to Seventy-seventh to notify the homicide detectives and have them respond. As you know, Seventy-seventh Division is not far from here. The detectives will want to talk to you."

"I am afraid I can't do that. I have my orders from my lieutenant, and those orders mean that I'm out of here. Those national guardsmen you see over there at the roadblock can tell the detectives anything they want to know. You take care, and who knows, I might see you down at Metro someday. Tell the detectives that we will come to the station and see them later on this morning, around eight. Oh, by the way, here is the MT slip from the ambulance."

My squad and I then got into our jeep and drove off down Broadway and headed for another roadblock. We did not talk to each other about what had just happened, and we were just relieved to be out of there. We put new clips into our M1 rifles as we drove down the street. I found out later, when we talked to the detectives, that the nineteen-year-old kid with us had not fired his weapon.

We had heard from the police officers who we were running into, that there was a lot of activity over on Central Boulevard, north of Slauson Avenue. So, around four in the morning, we headed in that direction. I drove northbound on Central Boulevard, and, as I passed Slauson, I noticed that we were in a dense business area and most of the businesses had been burned and looted. All of a sudden, we were being shot at. We could see the snipers shooting from the rooftop of a building on the west side of the street. I could see the persons firing their weapons. I stopped the jeep and hollered at everyone to get out and get behind the jeep on the passenger side.

We all took up positions of concealment behind the jeep and returned fire. We could see three persons on the roof of the building who were firing at us. They were firing rifles, and, from the sound of the firing, we determined that they were firing .22 rifles. They would jump up and fire at us and then go out of sight. The bullets from the shots they were firing were hitting the street on the other side of the jeep, and a couple of the bullets did in fact hit the jeep. As I was kneeling in the street and firing my M1 over the passenger seat of the jeep, I felt something strike me in my left calf. It was a sharp, piercing pain, but it lasted for only a moment. After the initial pain, the pain became a dull, nagging pain. We continued to fire at the suspects on the roof, and in about five minutes they stopped firing. (It seemed like we had been firing back and forth for an hour.)

"Do you think we shot them?" the nineteen-year-old kid said.

"I don't know," I said. "They either ran out of ammunition, or have been hit, or they have left. One thing I do know, though, is we are getting out of here. You guys get back in the jeep. I have to check my leg." I drove the jeep over to Seventy-seventh station and drove into the parking lot. The parking lot was full of police cars and police officers coming and going. My squad went into the station to use the restroom, and I stayed at the jeep. I looked at my leg and found that the skin had been broken, in my calf. I could see the raw meat of my calf, but it was not bleeding. I did not know what had struck me in the calf, whether it was a bullet or a chipped piece of the street. I got a first-aid kit we had in the jeep and put some salve and a bandage over the wound.

After doing this, I went into the station and found my squad. We went back to the detective bureau and located the detectives that were investigating the crash of the roadblock earlier. I knew both of the detectives who were handling the case. We all gave them statements as to our involvement in the incident. The detectives told us that they could see no problem with the incident, and that we were justified in doing what we had done. They confirmed the fact that the suspect, who had ran the roadblock, had died. They gave us their business cards to give to our lieutenant, in case he had any questions.

When we left the station, we noticed that the sun had come up. We got in our jeep and decided to go get something to eat. We drove over to the city of Inglewood, found a restaurant, and went inside and ate. Everyone in the restaurant came up to us and asked us about the riot. They all wondered if the riot was going to escalate and come over into Inglewood. We assured them that it was our opinion that the riot was being controlled, and with a curfew, the streets were safer than they had been. We left the restaurant, checked some more roadblocks, and went back to the school at 108th Street and Figueroa.

Only one incident occurred on Sunday morning, while we were on patrol, that is worth mentioning. I was driving the jeep southbound on San Pedro Street around Eighty-ninth Street. At this location, there was a commercial bakery called the Golden Crust Bakery. The bakery had been looted, but it had not been burned. There were big glass plate windows in the front of the building that faced the street. The windows were broken out of the building. As I was driving by the building, out the corner of my eye I noticed some furtive movement. The movement was coming from inside the bakery. I immediately thought that the movement could be looters who were inside the building. I had driven a short distance by the bakery, so I made a U-turn and headed back toward where the bakery was. I told my squad about seeing the movement in the window of the bakery, and that I was driving back to the bakery to see what the movement was. As I came out of my U-turn, three black males jumped out of the bakery window and ran north up the sidewalk. The suspects disappeared into the houses and apartment buildings. When I got to the bakery, I stopped the jeep and looked into the broken-out windows. Inside the broken-out windows, and on the floor behind them, sat a .30-caliber machine gun on a tripod. The weapon was pointed out toward the street, and it had an ammunition belt in the receiver and the breech was closed. We all jumped out of the jeep and ran up to the bakery and went inside through the broken window. When we examined the weapon, we found that the ammunition belt had been put into the breech upside-down. This would jam the weapon and not allow it to be fired. We figured that the male suspects we had seen run from the location were attempting to fire the weapon at us, as we passed by the bakery. We loaded the weapon up in our jeep and later, when we went back to the school, we turned it over to the property officer.

On Monday morning, we had the honor to play bodyguard to the governor of the state of California, Governor Brown. Governor Brown was provided a tour of some of the Seventy-seventh Division area, including Watts. Governor Brown, along with some other dignitaries, and the press were in a motorcade that we escorted with our jeeps. The governor got out of his vehicle, at several locations, and talked to the crowds at these locations. The motorcade, and Governor Brown, ended up at the Jacob Riis high school. The governor had lunch with high-ranking National Guard officers at this location.

The following article appeared in the *LA Times* newspaper on Monday morning. This article was titled:

Now We Understand—Black Muslims Here Figure in Riot Start

Marquette Frye, 21, whose arrest for drunk driving Wednesday night set off Los Angeles' bloody Negro rioting, was a surprise guest speaker Sunday before a meeting of black Muslims. Frye told the meeting that Muslim leader Elijah Muhammad "has been teaching the doom of the white man for a long time and now we understand. These troops do not mean a thing. They haven't seen anything yet."

John Shabazz, minister of Muhammad's Mosque No. 27, said, "All of this is part of a general awakening. Some are responding in one way and some in another. Some are trying to destroy the white image before them and others are following the only man they know (Elijah Muhammad) who can free them."

The Black Muslims had been passing out handbills since the violence first erupted, advertising the meeting and bearing the headline, Stop Police Brutality.

I talked to a young black woman who I knew at Bob's store later on Monday afternoon. I asked her why they had rioted. I told her I thought that the blacks were not discriminated against in Los Angeles. I felt they could live where they wanted to live, they could get a job anywhere, and I did not see any segregation. I told her I felt that the blacks were justified in feeling they were mistreated in the South, but that I did not feel they were mistreated in Los Angeles.

"You are right," she answered me. "We are not segregated against in Los Angeles. My father and grandfather fought that in the South. What my generation wants, here in Los Angeles, as well as anywhere, is to live in our own society. We want to live by our rules, not your rules. We do not want to be judged by the white man's court, nor policed by the white police. We want our culture to be the predominant culture. We want to live, how we want to live, not how you want us to live. We want our hairstyles, our clothes, our music, our language, and our food to be where it's at. I am nineteen years old, and all my friends and people my age are after this."

On Tuesday morning, August 16, 1965, I was told by my lieutenant that we were going home. He told us that the curfew had been lifted, and that we were no longer needed. He stated that our Fortieth MP Company was going to stay at Camp Roberts until the coming weekend. Since it was too late for us to go to Camp Roberts, we were going home. Our two-week commitment was over, and we could go back to our regular jobs.

We loaded up our gear and drove our jeeps back to our armory. After I turned in my gear, I went out to my car and drove home. My time spent in the Los Angeles riots was over.

• • •

It was June 8, 1966, at about one thirty in the morning,. Chuck and I were on patrol, and we were in the vicinity of the Imperial Courts project. I was thinking back on the last ten months. It had been ten months since the LA Watts riot had been put down. I had been patrolling the streets in Seventy-seventh Division and Watts and reminiscing on what has happened since the riots. The main streets of the division, and of Watts, had looked like a war zone. A lot of the streets did not have any businesses left open on them outside of a few mom-and-pop stores. Most of the businesses that were open were black-owned businesses. In Watts, 103rd Street was completely void of any businesses, with the exception of Bob's liquor store. There was rubble everywhere, and burned-out hulks of nonexistent businesses stood like naked skeletons. The streets had an eerie feeling to them, and it was like ghosts hid in every burned-out building. All of the liquor stores were gone, with the exception of Bob's. All of the furniture stores, hardware stores, and any store that sold anything of value were no longer standing.

Everyone was wondering why the blacks, living in the area, had burned down their own community. The blacks in the area felt that it was not their community; it was the white business-owners' community that got burned down. I felt that it was my community. The streets were my streets. All of the liquor stores, and the people around them, whether they were black or white, were my people and my stores. There were a lot of good people in Watts, and now these good people were suffering. I looked at the people in Watts as two separate groups of people, and it had nothing to do with the color of their skin. There were the law-abiding citizens, and there were the criminals. The ones that had gained from the riots were the criminals in the street. They had lost nothing, and their days went by as they had prior to the riot. It was business as usual for them.

Federal and state funds were being promised to be spent in the area, in order to rebuild the buildings and bring in new programs. There already was an attempt in progress to clean up the rubble. The state was mandating that the contractors who were being hired to do this hire their labor from the labor pool in Watts. The state was promising the people of Watts jobs, education, transportation, and additional welfare. But the contractors, working in Watts at the time, were unable to hire the majority of their labor from the available labor pool in Watts. I guess some of the reasons for this were (1) you could make more money, being on welfare, than you could picking up bricks; (2) you could make more money, dealing dope, robbing, and stealing, than you could using a pick and shovel; (3) it took a desire and ambition to overcome laziness, and that was too hard to do; (4) all of the good, hard-working persons in Watts already had a job; (5) it was "Whitey's" job to clean up the mess; (6) this meant that you had to work a five-day, forty-hour week. You would have to get up in the morning, five days a week. Every day would not be a Saturday or Sunday.

I thought about Sam Cooke's song, "A Change Is Gonna Come." Would I be able to cause a change to occur within the community of Watts? Every day I hoped that an arrest I made would cause a change. I never felt that it would be impossible to cause change, and every day I talked to friends of mine in Watts, I knew that I was doing it for myself and them.

There had been changes made within the last ten months in Watts. The Black Muslims were becoming more aggressive in the community. They were becoming more demanding on the citizens of Watts. They were distributing their newspaper and insisting that the black community join in their movement. They were using aggressive tactics and intimidation. A lot of the blacks in the community feared them.

The Black Panthers were gaining in strength as well. Their aggressiveness was directed toward the police department, as opposed to the community. They displayed openly defiance for authority. They carried weapons openly, and would gather at the courthouses and other places that the public had access to. There had been several attempts by them to shoot at and kill police officers.

A black organization with the initials *US* (United Slaves, led by Ron Karenga) received a federal grant to form an organization called CAP (Community Alert Patrol). The federal grant supplied them with vehicles, radios keyed to the police frequencies, and video cameras. They would listen to the police radio calls on their radios. Then they would respond to the locations that the police were going to. Once they arrived, they would videotape whatever action the police took. This was supposedly to show the police brutality that was occurring in the community.

The gangs in Seventy-seventh were gaining momentum. They had learned from the riots that there was safety in numbers and more profit to be made by combining their resources. Each of the project areas had their individual gangs. There were gangs on the Eastside and the Westside. There were gangs to the north and gangs to the south. There were gangs in the high schools, and there were gangs in the junior highs. Gangs were ever present in the streets as well.

Several changes had occurred within the police department as well, as a result of the riots. The biggest change was that of communications. Our radios had tactical frequencies now, and we could correspond between the individual radio cars. We could also go to frequencies that enabled us to hear the activity in other divisions. Bulletproof vests had been issued to those officers who wished to wear them. When Chief Parker retired, we were able to do away with our ties and long-sleeved shirts. A short-sleeve shirt was part of our standard uniform.

We were allowed to purchase and carry our own revolver, and not have to carry the city-issued weapon. We could wear our riot helmet at any time we felt that our safety was in peril.

Demonstrations in the streets of Los Angeles were heating up. I do not know if the LA Watts riot had any influence on this or not. There were street demonstrations occurring in support of civil rights. There were demonstrations occurring in protest of the war in Vietnam. There was draft card burning and US flag burning. There were sit-ins and love-ins in public places and parks. All kinds of subversive groups were becoming very vocal and very active. There were hippies and yuppies, beatniks, and flower children participating in the demonstrations. All of these groups were predominantly made up of Caucasians.

On a personal note, I was dating a girl who I would marry before the end of the year. I had taken up waterskiing at the Colorado River with several of my police-officer buddies. I had bought a ski boat and was spending a lot of time waterskiing. I had met my wife to be at the Colorado River while skiing. I planned on staying in San Pedro, and managing the apartment building I was living in, after I got married. Any change in these plans would have to come after I had children.

I was brought back to reality and my thoughts were interrupted by the following radio call: "Unit twelve Z fifty-five needs assistance code two, at one-three-one-five East 114th Street. Rocks and bottles are being thrown at them. The rocks and bottles are being thrown by a group of thirty to forty persons."

"Chuck, jump on that call! We are only a short distance from that location. I am going to go into the area from Central

Avenue. That address is in the Imperial Courts projects. Tell communications that we will be at the location within five minutes."

I drove us to the location and entered the Imperial Courts projects from Central Avenue. As I made my left-hand turn, heading west, I saw the requesting unit parked in the street at the location. Both officers were sitting in the car, and there was a group of thirty to forty persons to their west, approximately thirty yards in front of their car. The group of persons was screaming out obscenities and was still throwing missiles at the police car. The back window of their police car had been broken out. I drove past their police car, at the people, and when they dispersed, I made a U-turn and came back alongside the other police car. The people regrouped and began throwing bottles and broken cinderblocks at our police vehicle. At this time I yelled at Chuck and the other two officers in the other police car: "All of you make notes of their clothing so we can identify them later. I can identify four of them by their clothing. See how many you can identify and write it down, and we're getting the hell out of here."

The four of us left the location in our two police cars and drove out to Central Avenue. We parked in a parking lot across the street from where the rock-throwing had occurred. The other two police officers got out of their police car and got into the backseat of our car. We compared notes and found we were able to identify six of the individuals who had been throwing rocks and bottles, and three that were also in the group. We all agreed that the thirty to forty people in the group were all juveniles and/or young adults. We continued to sit in the parking lot and watched the group that had now grown to approximately fifty persons. I got on the radio and asked for assistance and for any units to meet us in the parking lot. I told communications that we were engaged with a group of approximately forty juveniles and male adults that had been throwing rocks and bottles at our police cars. Communications informed me that four metropolitan units would be responding to our location, and would meet us in the parking lot. In a short time the four metropolitan units rolled up and joined us in the parking lot. The officers were in uniform, but were all in plain cars. We all got out of our cars and joined each other in the parking lot. I recognized two of the metropolitan officers as classmates of mine, from the police academy. Their names were Maki and Potts.

"Hello, Maki and Potts, it's good to see you." I said. "I did not know you guys were working metro. Thanks for showing up. I'll tell you all what we got here, and then you can see what you think. Look over there across the street, and you will see that group of fifty people in the Imperial Courts projects. They threw rocks and bottles at both of our police cars, and we have identified nine of the parties involved. Here is the description of the nine who we were able to identify. As you can see, some of them are still over there in front of the crowd. What I suggest we do is to put our patrol cars out here, and you four metro cars go get behind the group in the projects. You can do that by going up to 112th Street and go around and come in the back door of the project. We will talk to each other on the TAC (tactical)frequency, and when you get in place, you let us know. Once you are in place, we will sweep in the front door on 114th and come in with our lights and sirens. We will jump out and wade into them with our nightsticks. There is a walkway through the projects behind where they are gathered. I am sure most of them will run from us, down that walkway. What do you think?"

"Sounds like a plan to me," answered Potts. "Give us the list you have on the descriptions of the suspects. We will get around behind them, and when we radio you we are there, we will start walking toward Central, through the project. Anything else we need to know?"

"Only thing I can think of is that I'm sure the suspects are members of the Bounty Hunters. The Bounty Hunters are the primary gang in the Imperial Courts projects. During the riots they were out on Imperial Highway and Central Avenue, pulling people out of their cars and robbing them. Chuck and I have dealt with them before. They do have access to guns, but I did not see any weapons on them tonight. That's not to say that they don't have guns on them, so treat them as if they did. OK, if we are ready, let's get the show on the road, and we will meet you at the pass."

The metro officers got in their cars and left the parking lot. We stayed in the parking lot and awaited their communications. In a short time, we received intel from the metro officers that indicated that they were in position and would be moving through the projects in one minute. Our two units put on the red lights and sirens and sped across Central Avenue and down 114th Street toward the crowd, which now numbered in the fifties. When we got to within thirty yards of the crowd, we jumped out of our cars, with our nightsticks, and began to run toward the crowd. The crowd immediately dispersed and began to run away from us, westbound through the project. I began chasing one of the persons that I had identified, throwing rocks at my car. After a short foot pursuit I was able to catch up with him. I tried out my best football tackle on him, and it worked. I took him to the ground and handcuffed his hands behind his back, and picked him up. (He turned out to be an adult.) Our plan worked too, and we forced a good portion of the crowd into where the metro officers were waiting. After all was said and done, we had nine suspects in custody. Six of the suspects were juveniles: two fifteen-year-olds and four seventeen-year-olds. Three of the suspects were adults. We arrested them all for 405 PC, Riot and 23110b V.C., Throwing Substance at Vehicle. We loaded all the suspects into our cars and took them to Seventy-seventh Division station, where we booked them on the aforementioned charges. On our way out of the projects, we stopped and picked up some bottles and rocks out of the street to book as evidence.

After booking all of the suspects, we went up to the coffee room with the metro officers, to talk about the reports. It was decided that we would make all the reports and put the metro officers in the reports as witnesses and/or arresting officers. The metro officers would transport the juveniles to juvenile hall for detention. (One of the fifteen-year-olds was released to his parents because he did not have any prior arrests.)

"Tell me a bit about Metropolitan Division, Potts." I said. "How long have you worked there, and what do you actually do at Metro?"

"We do a lot of things, and I've been there a little over a year," Potts replied. "First of all, we have citywide jurisdiction. As you can see, we use plain cars. We work stakeouts, surveillances, protect VIPs, participate in SWAT operations, break up demonstrations, and fill in for detectives, on loans. Oh yeah, and we also shake, rattle, and roll. You know—shake the doors, rattle the bushes, and roll over the rocks. That's what we were doing down here in Seventy-seventh Division tonight. The Los Angeles Police Department formed Metropolitan Division in 1960. Right now we have sixty officers and work in two

WAR STORIES LIVED BY A L.A. COP

platoons. Because of the increase in street demonstrations, our captain is going to enlarge our division."

"Tell me more about these loans to detective divisions."

"A lot of times when detectives go on vacation, they need fill-ins to work for them while they are gone. So we will go work that division, for that detective, for one month. It gives us a break from metro, and it gives the detective division extra strength. We are chosen on a volunteer basis. We don't have to work the loans if we do not want to."

"I think I would like to work metro. I eventually want to get into a detective bureau, somewhere. My ultimate goal is to work homicide, here at Seventy-seventh Division."

"From what I've seen you do tonight, I think they would accept you down at metro. That plan of yours worked out exceptionally well. If you put in for metro, I will give you a good recommendation."

"So will I," said Maki.

The metro officers then left the station with the suspects to be placed in juvenile detention. We went down into the detective division, and completed our reports on the crimes and arrests of the suspects. After everyone had left the station, I went into the watch commander's office and filled out a transfer request to metro. The next transfer, I transferred to Metropolitan Division.

103rd. Street after the 1965 Riot.

Photo from 1965 Riot. I am on the right just behind the girl
looking at the camera.

Chapter 4

Metropolitan Division

August 1966–November 1967

Metropolitan Division was located in the basement of the central police station in downtown Los Angeles. The division had a roll-call room, a locker room, and offices for the staff. I now had a one-hour drive up the Harbor Freeway to get to work. I had used a couple of days off to get settled in at my new assignment. I was assigned a locker and had brought all my equipment and uniforms and placed them in it. I was preparing myself to report in to the lieutenant in charge of the Metropolitan Division. I knew at the time that this was the lieutenant that I had briefly met during the riots. I also knew that I had disobeyed his orders to stay at the scene of the shooting and await the arrival of the detectives. Would he remember me? As I walked into his office, I figured that I'd just play it by ear.

"Good morning, Officer Reynolds, have a seat." Lieutenant Bright was in fact the same lieutenant who I had met previously. "You got here just in time; we are having a briefing in the roll-call room this morning. We are going to brief all our personnel on our tactical alert status. As you know, we have two platoons. Our A platoon is assigned to days and our B platoon is assigned to nights. You will be assigned to the B platoon. We have thirty officers assigned to each platoon. At this time one of our main duties is to disperse demonstrations. This is what the roll call training is going to be about this morning. Do you have any questions?"

"No sir," I answered.

"I think I have met you somewhere before. I never forget a face. I just can't place you. Where have you worked at before coming here?"

"I have worked at the Harbor Division, and at seventy-seventh division."

"Have you ever worked out in the Valley?"

"No, I have never worked in the Valley. If we have met before, it would have been at the Harbor Division, or at Seventy-seventh."

"Well, I can't place you now, but I will sooner or later. It's not that important right now, so you get ready for roll-call training, and we will talk again."

I left the lieutenant's office and went to the roll-call room, where Sgt. Gomez was ready to brief us on tactical alert status.

Sgt. Gomez briefed us as follows: "You are aware that under the First Amendment, people have the right to assemble and to freedom of speech. As you know, we are having demonstrations in the streets and in public places by a lot of different groups. At times these groups become unruly and go beyond their rights to assemble and speak. These groups we are dealing with have the right to peaceful protest, but this does not mean that everyone with opinions or beliefs to express may do so at any time and at any place. The law also does not sanction riotous conduct in any form or any demonstrations, however peaceful their conduct or commendable their motives, that conflict with properly drawn statutes and ordinances designed to promote law and order, protect the community against this disorder, regulate traffic, safeguard legitimate interest in the private and public property, or protect the administration of justice and other essential governmental functions.

"The law also allows for assembling a legal force. Assume that city police have confidential information that a mob action is being planned for a time, some hours from now, and that they wish to assemble a police force in order to deal with this. That force that the city chooses to assemble will be us. Both of our platoons are going to have tactical alert status. This means, depending on the size of the crowd and who the participants are, we will activate either one of or both of the platoons. The platoon, or platoons, will be responding to the location of the demonstration and will take immediate action. The decision to respond will be based on information available at the time. This information will confirm that the demonstration is no longer peaceful and is in violation of a law. The demonstration is now an unlawful assembly. Criminal acts, such as impeding traffic, destroying property, assaults, vandalism, malicious mischief, or theft might have already occurred. We also have the ability to disperse a group prior to criminal acts occurring. If it is anticipated that the assembly is leading to the inciting of a riot or any of the aforementioned criminal acts, we have the legal authority to disperse the group. We have the power to use auxiliary weapons of any kind, such as nightsticks, tear gas, and physical force.

"The bottom line is that the chief does not want any of these demonstrations to lead into another Watts riot. If the demonstration is peaceful and no laws are violated, we will not become involved. Based on where the demonstration is taking place, the police of that division will handle it. There will be no tactical alert status. Just remember that the primary duty of our division is to keep the peace, and that duty rests with state and local officials. And to do this, they must necessarily have power to command obedience, preserve order, and keep the peace, and no person or power in this land has the right to resist or question its authority, so long as it keeps within the bounds of its jurisdiction.

"There are a lot of groups out there that are demonstrating against the war in Vietnam and for their civil rights. Some of these groups feel that their intent is good. Unfortunately we are not in a position to take sides; we're only in position to uphold the law. On the other hand, some of the groups out there are only looking for personal gain, and have nothing better to do. There is a lot of drinking, use of drugs, and malicious mischief attached to their activity. Irregardless of what group we run into, our duty is to disperse the group, and that's what we will do. Does anyone have any questions about what our responsibility in a tactical alert will be?"

There were no questions, and we all left the roll-call room and went to get coffee and sodas. I circulated among all the other officers and introduced myself and got acquainted with as many as I could. They all seemed like good officers, and I felt I had made the right decision in coming to Metro.

• • •

It turned out that I was at many demonstrations over the time I spent in Metro. I will pick out three of these demonstrations, and speak to them here as war stories.

The first demonstration I participated in as a member of the tactical alert squad was at the Beverly Wilshire Hotel in Century City. It was around seven at night. President Johnson was at the hotel. A group of approximately five thousand persons had gathered in front of the hotel to protest the Vietnam War. A picket line had been set up in front of the hotel, and barricade tape had been stretched across in front of the group. There were 150 police officers deployed on the picket line. The crowd was becoming unruly, and our chief felt that the crowd was a threat to the president. A tactical alert had been implemented at the hotel. Both of our platoons had been put on alert, and we were in the basement of the hotel—our status was on standby. We were a force of sixty officers. The LAPD Motorcycle Traffic Division had also been placed on alert, and was with us in the basement of the hotel. They were a force of fifty motorcycle officers.

Our chief, Chief Parker, was on the roof of the hotel with the head of the Secret Service, Mr. Potters. Mr. Potters had told our chief that the crowd was not to come into the hotel. He also stated that he did not think the chief could keep the crowd from doing this with just his police officers, and that he should activate the National Guard. This was the president of the United States, and the crowd was placing his life in jeopardy.

Chief Parker turned to Mr. Potters and told him that he would handle the demonstration. He then turned to his captain and instructed him to contact the lieutenant in the basement of the hotel and tell him to get the reserves on the picket line. Once the reserves were on the picket line, the lieutenant was to give a dispersal order. If the crowd did not disperse in the allotted time given them, the lieutenant was to order the picket line to disperse the crowd. There was to be no one left standing in front of the hotel after the dispersal of the crowd was accomplished.

In the basement of the hotel, our lieutenant told us we were to go out and deploy on the picket line. He stated that a dispersal order was going to be given, and if the crowd did not disperse, we were to disperse the crowd. He further stated that we would not be making arrests at the time we dispersed the crowd. The arrests were to be made by the police officers who were presently deployed on the picket line. Our duty was to move the crowd, and their duty was to arrest those that were remaining. The motorcycle officers were given the same instructions by their lieutenant. We all then went outside and deployed on the picket line.

When we got outside, we joined the officers that were already on the picket line. We filtered in with them and alternately had one of them, one of us, and one of the motorcycle officers. This sequence ran throughout the picket line. This gave us about 260 police officers on the picket line. At the time, I noticed that the crowd was made up of mostly male Caucasians. There were a lot of females in the crowd as well, and there were children. Some of the children were in strollers. A lot of the members of the crowd were holding picket signs. The signs were stapled to one one-by by-one pieces of wood. The crowd was being very boisterous and loud. They were chanting, "Get out of Vietnam," "End the war," and "Bring our troops home." The crowd was pushing against the barricade tape and was threatening to come through the barrier. Once we were in place on the picket line, our lieutenant gave a dispersal order.

"I am declaring this assembly an unlawful assembly. I am ordering you to disperse and retire peacefully to your abodes within five minutes. Failure to do so will cause you to be arrested for failing to abide by this dispersal order."

We waited out the five minutes given to the demonstrators on the picket line. We held our nightsticks at port arms, and the motorcycle officers revved up their motorcycles. At the end of the five minutes, the demonstrators had not disbursed, so we were given the order to disperse them. Two hundred of us, including Metro, the motorcycle officers, and ninety of the original police officers, waded into the crowd to disperse the demonstrators. The other forty-plus officers held back to arrest anyone who was left in the area. Our initial impact caused the crowd to turn and start to run away from the area. We were swinging our nightsticks at anyone and anybody, and the motorcycle officers were running into anyone and anybody. People in the crowd were swinging their picket signs and sticks at us as they ran. They were throwing wine bottles at us as well. People were falling to the ground as a result of these actions. The police officers behind us were taking the people on the ground and the people standing around into custody. Buses for transportation, and medical units, had been brought to the front of the hotel. The people that were taken into custody were taken to the buses and medical units for treatment and/or arrest. After around twenty minutes of this action, there was not a person standing in front of the hotel.

I had confronted a lot of people that night, and my arms were so sore from swinging my nightstick that I could not pick them up. I had been hit by a lot of sticks, but the sticks did not impact my mission. (After this demonstration, the demonstrators started to use two-by-fours on their picket signs, and used them as weapons against us.) We all assembled back in the basement of the hotel after the disbursement of the crowd was completed. A few of the officers had been hit by bottles that demonstrators had thrown at them, and they had received minor injuries. Some of the officers had minor bruises and abrasions from fighting the demonstrators. We heard later that it was the same for the injured demonstrators. No one received any serious injuries. The *Los Angeles Times* newspaper had been at the scene and taken a lot of photos that were in the morning paper. Not one of the demonstrators had gotten into the hotel. Our tactical alert had been successful.

• • •

The next demonstration I'll address occurred at Pandora's Box on November 12, 1966.

Pandora's Box was a teen club located on Sunset Boulevard. It was the center of the Sunset strip youth scene. By the summer of 1966, the young scene-makers were clogging the sidewalks and snarling traffic along the 1.8 mile stretch. The strip was a main thoroughfare between Hollywood and Beverly Hills. The politicians were under pressure from the local property owners and other nearby businesses to clean it up. Since Pandora's Box was in the county, the LA county sheriffs were arresting the juveniles in the area for curfew violations. As weekend arrests mounted, the teens and young adults eventually protested with weekend street demonstrations, at times numbering as many as two thousand demonstrators. A demonstration was planned for Saturday, 12 November 1966, and this demonstration turned into something of a riot. Some rowdies in the crowd smashed store windows, disabled, an LA city bus, and threw rocks and bottles at passing motorists. This activity, on the part of the juveniles and young adults, flowed over into the city of Los Angeles. A tactical alert was called for, on the part of the city of Los Angeles, and we responded to the location. (The demonstration had been called, but scarcely organized, by RAMCON—the Right of Assembly and Movement Committee, headquartered in the Fifth Estate coffee house at 8226 Sunset.)

We were called in to assist the sheriffs with handling a crowd of an estimated two thousand juveniles and young adults. The street disturbance was now occurring in both the county and the city along Sunset Boulevard. A plan was put into place wherein that we would approach the rioters from the city side, and the sheriffs would approach them from the county side. Both the sheriffs and a Los Angeles police department would provide buses at the location to load the violators into—the sheriffs would transport their violators to the county jail, and LAPD would transport their violators to the city jail at Parker Center. At the time the tactical alert took place, it was approaching midnight, and therefore a curfew violation was enforceable. We used both of our platoons to quell this disturbance, and, as a result, we ended up arresting over two hundred violators.

The Los Angeles County Board of Supervisors decided to get tough, and unanimously rescinded the "youth permits" of twelve of the strip's clubs, thus stamping them off-limits to anybody under twenty-one. There continued to be demonstrations against this move on the part of the LA county board of supervisors, but no criminal violations occurred as a result. Notables who were behind this movement were

Sonny Bono, who wrote the song "We Have as Much Right to Be Here as Anyone," and Buffalo Springfield, who wrote the song "There's Something Happening Here." Roger Corman, who was a Hollywood legend at the time, cranked out a low-budget exploitation flick entitled *Riot on Sunset Strip*.

• • •

The next demonstration I'll address occurred at Griffin Park on July 2, 1967. This demonstration was called a love-in by the local media. Griffith Park is a city park with a lot of wooded areas, adjacent to the LA city zoo. The park had a merry-go-round, and it was a local gathering place for the hippies and yuppies. The "love-in" had attracted more than four thousand persons on this day. It was the largest such gathering since an Easter Sunday, when more than six thousand persons massed at Elysian Park without incident. Earlier in the day, fourteen adults and twelve juveniles were arrested for possession of marijuana. A man wearing only a loin cloth was arrested for lewd conduct. Another was arrested on arson charges after setting a grass fire in the area. A man found carrying a billy club was arrested for violating the state's deadly weapons act. A traffic alert had been broadcast about five in the afternoon, when traffic became congested in the area. The Los Feliz Boulevard and Golden State Freeway entrances to the park were closed. About ten-thirty at night, two city fire companies extinguished a blaze in an automobile parked near the park's merry-go-round.

A tactical alert was called, and we responded to Griffith Park as a result. We deployed in the form of a skirmish line and surrounded the Griffith Park area, around the merry-go-round. A dispersal order was given, with no results. The crowd of males and females, appearing to be young adults, did not disperse. The crowd, as a whole, appeared to be high on alcohol and/or drugs. Rocks and bottles were thrown at us at this time, and absurdities were being voiced by the crowd. We attacked the crowd with our nightsticks in an attempt to move them out of the park. As we continued our sweep of the area, an unknown individual came up behind me and stabbed me in the back with a broken wine bottle. The bottle hit my uniform belt and slid up into the skin of my back. Two other individuals had attempted to grab me from the back. I had turned toward the individuals and was struggling with two of them when Sergeant Gomez came up. Sergeant Gomez started to struggle with the person who had stabbed me when he noticed that I was profusely bleeding from the back.

"You have been cut in your back. Go seek medical treatment from one of the medical units. I will take care of these guys for you," he said.

At this time, the three suspects turned and began to run into the woods. Sergeant Gomez ran after them, and I ran after Sergeant Gomez. We chased the suspects into the woods and entered a very dense bushy area of the woods. At this time we were running up a hill, through the underbrush. There appeared to be a path through the bushes, but we were unfamiliar with where the path led to. I heard Sergeant Gomez scream out in pain and disappear through the bushes ahead of me. I went to the location where I last saw him, and found that there was a hillside behind the bushes that dropped off about twenty feet. He had run over this hillside and fell to the bottom of it. The suspects, apparently being aware of where the path went, had taken a left-hand turn on the path and had disappeared on up the hill, out of sight. Sergeant Gomez had hurt his back and was unable to walk out of the area. I went back to the paramedics and got them to come up with a stretcher and get Sergeant Gomez out of the hillside area. He eventually would go off duty as a result of his injuries. I went back to the merry-go-round area and assisted my fellow officers in clearing the park. By the time we had cleared the park of the hippies and yuppies, we had made twenty-nine arrests and had impounded seventeen illegally parked cars. I never did find the three persons who had assaulted me. After clearing the park, I went to central receiving hospital, where I was treated for my injuries. I did not allow them to place me in an off-duty status, and returned to work.

• • •

Another big part of our job at metro was staking out locations where a multitude of crimes were occurring. For instance, if liquor stores were being robbed repeatedly in a particular division, we would stake out the liquor stores in hopes of catching the suspects. Different places that we staked out were banks, liquor stores, food stands, markets, and delivery trucks. We would always stake out the location inside, even the delivery trucks. We would carry shotguns with bird shot instead of double O buckshot. The reason for this was that we were to injure the suspect if we had to shoot them, as opposed to killing them. I caught several suspects during the stakeouts. I never had to fire my shotgun, and just the sight of it caused the suspects to give up and allow me to arrest them. The only time my shotgun discharged on a stakeout was as the result of an accident. Let me tell you that story. Don't you tell anyone this story, because the only persons who know the story are myself and my partner.

My partner and I were staking out a liquor store out in the valley. Metro was staking out ten liquor stores in the valley that evening. We were working in Van Nuys Division, and they had had a rash of robberies. Our purpose was to catch the suspect, who was working alone, while he was robbing the liquor stores. They had called us in to eliminate the problem. Thus, it led to the liquor stores being staked out. At this particular liquor store, the only place to stake it out was in the beer cooler.

The time we were in the liquor store ran between 6:00 p.m. and 2:00 a.m. The suspect's MO showed that he would rob the liquor stores during this time span. His preferable time was just as the store was about to close, which would be 2:00 a.m. We had been in the beer cooler from 6:00 p.m. until around midnight. We had to move around a lot to keep warm, even though we had our coats on.

"Partner, I think I have an idea." I said. "I saw a row of trees across the street from this liquor store when we came in here. Those trees border a field across the street, and there are no houses or buildings directly across from this liquor store. I say we get out of this damn cooler and get warm. We can go across the street and conduct our stakeout from inside those trees. I have some binoculars, and we could watch the store from over there. If anything goes down, we can be on top of it from out there."

"Sounds good to me," my partner answered. "We can tell the liquor store clerk that we will be outside of the store and watching from outside. We will tell him to give us a high sign when he is closing the store. Let's do it."

We left the store and went to our plain car that was parked half a block away, on the street. I got my binoculars from the car, and we walked back to the liquor store and went across the street to the trees. At the trees we sat down in among them and concealed ourselves at that location. I laid my shotgun down on the ground in front of me and began watching the liquor store with my binoculars. My partner sat down and laid his shotgun across his knees. We sat there for the next two hours, and we traded off watching with the binoculars every twenty minutes. At around two o'clock, I was watching the store with the binoculars and had my shotgun lying on the ground between my legs. The clerk came out of the store and gave us the high sign, which indicated he was closing the store. He was standing on the sidewalk and was setting a silent alarm on the front door of the liquor store.

I was telling my partner that it was time for us to wrap it up, and at the same time I started to stand up. As I started to stand up, I began to pick up my shotgun off the ground. As I was picking up the shotgun, a fallen branch from the tree, which was caught in the trigger guard of the shotgun, caused the shotgun to go off. The bird shot from the shotgun traveled across the street and hit the windows of the liquor store. I could hear the bird shot hit the windows and heard the *tat, tat, tat*. The bird shot did not hit the clerk, but it scared the hell out of him. I could see him activate the silent alarm, and then run back into the store and close the door. He got behind the counter and went out of sight.

"We better get the hell out of here. I think he set off the silent alarm. Patrol units are going to respond to this location, and I don't want to be here when they arrive. I don't know how that branch got caught in that trigger guard, but it did. I'm damn happy that bird shot did not hit that clerk."

After I said that, we ran to our car, and after we got into it with our shotguns and the binoculars, we took off. As we were driving off, we heard the siren of an approaching radio car. The radio car passed us after we were about six blocks away from the liquor store. It was obvious that the radio car was going to the liquor store. We went end of watch that night, and we did not hear anything about what had happened at the liquor store. We had not gone back to the liquor store to ask the clerk what he had told the police, either.

The next night while going end of watch, after working another liquor store in the valley, we were approached by a couple of other officers.

"Did you guys hear about the drive-by shooting that occurred at the liquor store you worked last night? Too bad you weren't there when it went down." The officer stating this continued. "Tonight we worked the liquor store that you were in last night. The clerk told us that just after you left, he was closing the store and setting the alarm when a shot rang out. He turned and looked and saw a car driving by on the street. He then ran into the store and hid behind the counter. He said that the front windows were hit by the shot. We could see where the shotgun pellets hit the window."

"No, I did not hear about it." I replied. "Did he get a description of the car?"

"No, you know how that goes, a big, black four-door sedan. That is what they all say. He made a report, but I'm sure that case will never be solved. You guys have a good night, and I'll talk at you later."

• • •

Every month listings of the loans that were available were posted on the bulletin board. These loans were to various detective divisions, and lasted for a month. If anyone was interested in working the loan, he would place his name in the space provided. I watched this posting every month in hopes that a loan would show up to a homicide division. My ultimate goal was still to work as a homicide detective, and that was the main reason I came down here to metro. I got lucky when a loan was offered to Seventy-seventh homicide detectives, starting the September 1, 1967. I applied for the loan, and my request was approved. I reported to Seventy-seventh homicide on that date and worked at that location for the next month.

While I was working there, I made it a point to volunteer for everything there was to be done. I was on call every weekend, with another homicide detective. I went to every autopsy that there was a need to go to. I took evidence down to the crime lab to be analyzed. I sat in on interviews with various suspects and witnesses and assisted in the interviewing and interrogating. I canvassed neighborhoods looking for witnesses at the crime scenes. I was inquisitive and asked many questions of the homicide detectives. I let it be known that I was interested in obtaining a full-time position within their homicide squad.

When my loan was up at the end of September, the lieutenant of the section asked me to come back for another month.
My lieutenant at metro agreed to allow me to spend another
month with homicide at Seventy-seventh Division. At the end
of the second month, I was asked to transfer into Seventy-
seventh homicide. I put in my transfer request, and it was
approved. I then transferred into Seventy-seventh homicide
in November of 1967. The use of the Metropolitan Division
as a stepping-stone had worked out well for me. I was now,
officially, a homicide detective.

Chapter 5

Seventy-seventh Homicide Detectives

November 1967–January 1976

I would spend the next eight years working Seventy-seventh homicide. I would become a seasoned homicide detective during this period and become known throughout the Los Angeles County as an expert in the field. Many things happened during these eight years. I am going to redress some of these events here prior to going into my war stories. This will allow some insight into the cases I will address later. It will also allow me to not have to stick to a timeline over these eight years. I also will not have to stop in the middle of telling a story and relate to what I am about to tell you now. Bear with me, and I'm sure that the pieces will fall in place.

Education:

I knew that if I was going to become proficient at my job as a homicide investigator, I would have to couple my field experience with education. I attended Harbor Junior College, in Harbor City, from January of 1968 until January of 1972. I earned an Associate in Arts Degree in Police Science. I attended the California State University, Los Angeles, and on June 15, 1974, I earned a Bachelor of Science Degree in Police Science and Administration. In 1975, I received a basic certificate, intermediate certificate, and advanced certificate from the Commission on Police Officers Standards and Training. These certificates were awarded by the state of California Department of Justice. I joined the California Homicide Investigators Association and received annual training through this organization.

I felt if I was going to work homicide, I would have to be able to define homicide. I would need to know the definitions of the crime, the elements of a crime, and the types of evidence that was necessary in order to make an arrest. Not only did I need to know how to make a lawful arrest, I would need to know what was needed to file a case, try a case in court, and convict a person of the crime. The following is what I learned.

Homicide: the death of a person, caused by the hands of another person, is a homicide. A homicide can be justifiable, excusable, or criminal.

Justifiable: an intentional homicide committed under circumstances necessity for duty without any evil intent and without fault or blame, no guilt. (Self-defense, police in the line of duty, and state executions are examples.)

Excusable: a homicide committed by accident or misfortune and doing any lawful act by lawful means, without criminal negligence or without any intent.

Criminal: a person who unlawfully, and knowingly, recklessly, or negligently caused the death of another human being. Criminal homicide is broken down into three classifications.

The classifications are murder, manslaughter, and negligent homicide.

Murder First Degree: Death is a result of committing or attempting to commit certain felonies. (Rape, robbery, burglary, arson, kidnapping, or flights from a crime are examples.) Unlawful homicide with malice, forethought, premeditation or other intent to kill the person must exist at the time of the act. Premeditation precedes the killing, for even a moment.

Murder Second Degree: Unlawful homicide where malice was not aforethought, and there was no premeditation. Felony, other than those listed in first-degree, is committed and the defendant causes the death of another. Transferred intent is a third-person homicide. Extreme indifference to a human life and the intent is to do serious bodily harm is also a third-degree murder.

Voluntary Manslaughter: to recklessly cause the death of another person. It is done in a heat of passion, or anger, or rage. There is no chance to cool off. Must be adequate provocation that naturally and instantly causes a normal person to experience rage, or anger, and act uncontrollably. Mere words or gestures alone are not enough to reduce murder to manslaughter. Examples would be adultery observed, batteries, along with words or gestures, or trespass, along with words or gestures.

Involuntary Manslaughter: when, with criminal negligence, a person causes another's death, or commits an unlawful act, not amounting to a felony.

Negligent Homicide: Examples would be vehicular homicide, failure to act—such as a pit bull dog kills a person, or a person does not seek medical aid for an injured person—and, in any case, not covered in the murder/manslaughter statutes.

I also learned that there were three facts that had to be proven in order to convict a person.

1. The homicide was a crime, and was not justifiable or excusable.

2. The crime was committed. There was a guilty mind, evil intent, or criminal purpose behind the act. The state of mind could be based on knowingly, recklessly, negligently, or intentionally committed the crime.

3. The person committing the crime did in fact commit the crime. This could be proven by direct evidence, physical evidence, or circumstantial evidence.

Now let me give you a few cases I handled, and see if you can determine what is the most serious crime that you can charge each person with. All the evidence needed to get a conviction is there. The district attorney will always have the ultimate choice as to what charges are being filed on the person. Every person I arrest I charge with murder and let the lesser charges be determined by the district attorney. See if you can figure out what charges would be filed on suspects from the facts I have given you.

1. A suspect is in the backseat of a cab and is attempting to rob the cab driver with a revolver. The suspect has placed the revolver against the back of the cabbie's head as the cabbie is driving down the street. The suspect tells the cabbie, "This is a robbery" and orders the cabbie to pull over to the side of the street. The cabbie starts to pull the cab over to the side of the street, when the cab hits a bump in the road. The suspect's gun goes off, as a result of the cab

hitting the bump, and the bullet enters the cabbie's head and kills him instantly. (1st Degree Murder).

2. The suspect is at the city dump, firing his .22-caliber rifle at rocks. It is a misdemeanor crime to fire a firearm within the city limits. The bullet ricochets off a rock and hit a four-teen-year-old child riding by on a bicycle. They bullet fired from the .22-caliber rifle kills the fourteen-year old child. (Involuntary Manslaughter).

3. Two guys are having a verbal argument in a bar. Both of them are threatening to kill each other. The suspect draws a revolver from his waistband and points it at the victim, who he had been arguing with, and pulls the trigger. At that precise moment, the person he had been arguing with moves to the side. The bullet strikes the bartender behind the bar and kills him. (2nd. Degree Murder).

4. The suspect comes home after a night of drinking, goes upstairs to his bedroom, and finds his wife in bed with another person. The suspect pulls out his gun and is going to shoot the two of them, but has second thoughts. He goes back downstairs and gets a beer and sits on the couch and drinks it. He then goes back upstairs and shoots his wife, and the person with her. Both of them die from the gun-shot wounds. (1st. degree murder). –

5. Now that you've figured that out, what would you charge him with if he had shot them the first time he was up there? (Involuntary Manslaughter).

6. What makes a successful homicide detective? Remaining objective and working your case through a process of elim-ination, as opposed to tunnel vision.

Rank: When I first went into homicide, I went as a police officer in rank. I had not taken the sergeant's test because of the
fact that if I made sergeant, I would have to leave the detective
bureau. A lot of detectives were in the same position. Once
you made sergeant, you had to go back to patrol. In 1970, the
Los Angeles police department came up with a study of the
detective bureau, called the Jacob study. This study proved
that a lot of detectives would not make rank because of the
above-mentioned situation. As a result of the study, the city
created detective positions that would allow detectives who
passed the sergeant's test to stay in detectives at a higher pay
grade. The positions they created were an Investigator One,
Investigator Two, and Investigator Three. An Investigator
One position was equal to a police officer, an Investigator Two
position was equal to a sergeant, and an Investigator Three
position was a working investigator position or a coordinator position. I was appointed to the Investigator One position
in 1971, to the Investigator Two positions in 1972, and to the
Investigator Three position in 1974. I had to take written and
oral tests in order to be make the Investigator Two and Three
positions.

Family. My wife Patricia and I had two sons while I was working Seventy-seventh homicide. Robbie was born on October 8,
1969. Troy was born on December 26, 1972.

Watts. Many changes had occurred in Watts since I was gone.
Federal and State money had flowed in like water running
downstream. A multipurpose center was built in Watts, just
north of 103rd Street and east of Wilmington Boulevard. This
multipurpose center had a medical treatment facility, including an emergency room. It had classrooms to teach persons
what to eat for better nutrition and how to raise a family. It

468

4725

had a narcotic rehabilitation classroom. It also had a welfare office. The state would pay a person sixteen dollars a day for attending these classes. The classes consisted of four hours of instruction per day. Attendance rosters were kept, and students needed to sign in when they attended the class; a lot of people just signed in and left and collected their money each week.

A new hospital, called the Martin Luther King General Hospital, was built in Watts. This hospital was built even though a measure on the ballot for its building was voted down by the voters. This hospital was to become my third home, after work, and my residence.

Most all of the liquor stores that had been looted and burned during the riot were now back in operation. Keep in mind that these were not state-owned liquor stores; they were privately owned and were mini markets. Everyone in the neighborhood shopped at the liquor stores. That is why I developed informants at all of these liquor stores. Everyone at a liquor store knew everyone else, and their business. It was also where there was always a dope dealer. A new central market was built on Central Boulevard, between 103rd Street and Imperial Highway. All of the businesses along 103rd Street in Watts were either rebuilt or replaced. There remained a handful of buildings that were yet to be torn down. A new fine arts and culture center had been built and was open on 103rd Street as well. New bus lines had been established, in order to increase transportation needs. Will Rogers Park had been restructured, and a swimming pool was put in, as well as basketball courts and a recreational center.

Seventy-seventh Homicide. The Seventy-seventh homicide unit consisted of four two-man teams and a coordinator, who acted as the lieutenant in charge. This coordinator position was an Investigator Three position. (I would become the homicide coordinator in 1974.) The homicide detectives worked a five days a week, Monday through Friday, from 8:00 a.m. until 4:00 p.m. A team of homicide detectives was on call from Friday at 4:00 p.m. until Monday at 8:00 a.m. This team was to handle any homicides that occurred during that period of time. The four homicide teams rotated that duty. If more than one homicide occurred, the on-call team would handle as many as possible. Homicides were classified into two types. The first type was called a solved homicide. This was a homicide that was solved in a very short period of time.The case could be wrapped up during the preliminary investigation. Everything was present at the time of the homicide. The victim, suspect, and witnesses were present at the time, and the physical evidence and/or confessions were gained within a short time of the homicide occurring. The suspect was known at the time, and was either in custody, or could be placed into custody. The second type of homicide was called an unsolved homicide. This was a homicide in which you did not have any direction. The suspect was unknown, and there were no witnesses to the occurrence at the time of the preliminary investigation. This type of homicide required a continuous seventy-two-hour investigation, in an attempt to get direction and/or information on the homicide that would lead to it being solved. This was called a follow-up investigation. It had been proven that if no direction and/or information were obtained within seventy-two hours, the unsolved homicide would be difficult to solve.

The Seventy-seventh homicide unit handled between 92 and 134 homicides a year, in the eight years I worked there. The average year was 120 homicides. Each team handled a minimum of thirty homicides a year. The homicide unit carried an average 86 percent clearance rate. Year in and year out, Seventy-seventh homicide led the city in the number of homicides they handled and the number they solved. Each team had a minimum of five unsolved homicides going on at any given time. Contrary to what TV, books, and movies will show, a homicide detective is never working only one case.

The Homicide Investigation. First of all, you have to remember that a homicide investigation, in those days, was not done with the help of DNA, computers, video recorders, cell phones, the Internet, and the analysis of physical evidence such as what is seen on TV today. A homicide investigator, in those days, was only as good as the information he could obtain. The majority of that information came from people the detective talked to. This information was gathered by footwork and not through the computer.

The first thing done at a crime scene was to sketch the crime scene. The sketch of the crime scene would include the location of the body, of any physical evidence, and of anything attached to the crime scene. Next, photographs would be taken of the the body and any other physical evidence present. The location would then be dusted for fingerprints. In Los Angeles, we had specialists who we called to photograph the crime scene and dust for fingerprints, at our direction. The body was always examined in the presence of a coroner, who had responded to the scene to remove the body. The suspect would always be transported to the station for interview purposes, and not talked to at the crime scene. The same held true for any witnesses who were present at the location. The homicide investigator would be the person to gather the physical evidence and transport it to the crime lab for further analysis. Identifying fingerprints lifted at the crime scene was the responsibility of the person who had lifted the prints. The case was to be proven based on the direct evidence, testimony, and the physical evidence obtained at the scene. A confession was always to be the frosting on the cake. This means you do not need a confession to make your case. Therefore, if you do not obtain a confession, the case is still solid.

Now that I've made a good detective out of you, I'm going to take you to a weekend that I was on call and handled five cases. Two of these cases were solved cases, and three of them were unsolved cases. The two solved cases were pretty much wrapped up that weekend, but the other three took a period of time to solve. I will conclude all of the cases for you. I am going to refer to the victims by the use of colors. This will make it easier for you to follow each case. The colors are red, white, blue, gray, yellow, black, and brown. My partner on these cases was Rex Simpson.

Rex and I were notified by the watch commander, on Friday night at 7:00 p.m., that there was a homicide in the division. The watch commander stated that the scene was being protected by the patrol officers, and that a witness and/or suspect had been transported to the station. The watch commander requested us to come in and investigate the homicide, and he stated that the photo lab had been notified and they were responding to the crime scene. The watch commander was told that we will be at the crime scene within the hour.

We responded to the crime scene, and arrived at 7:45 p.m. The crime scene was a residential house that was mid block between other houses. It was a single-story house that sat back off the street. The patrol officer at the scene informed us that they had received a radio call of shots fired at the location. They had received the call at 6:45 p.m. They had arrived at the location at 6:50 p.m. and had entered the location. The ambulance crew had also arrived and had entered the location with them. Inside the location they had found the victim lying on the living room floor. A woman was sitting at the kitchen table inside of the location. The ambulance crew had pronounced the victim DOA. A radio car had been notified, and when they arrived, they transported the woman who had been inside the location to the station to await the arrival of the investigators. The patrol officer stated that it appeared that the victim had been shot, and that no one had contaminated the crime scene. He further stated that the victim had not been moved by the ambulance crew, nor had any evidence been removed from the crime scene. The female that had been taken from the crime scene to the station, and they, as well as the ambulance crew, had all left through the rear door of the residence. This was done so that the crime scene would not be walked through and contaminated. The patrol officer then gave investigators the crime-scene log, which listed everyone who had arrived at the crime scene and left, by time sequence. I then asked the patrol officer to remain outside and continue to keep the crime-scene log and log in people who I would be contacting, as they arrived. I asked him to notify the watch commander and have the watch commander notify the coroner, who would respond to the crime scene. Rex and I then entered the crime scene.

When we entered, I observed the victim lying on the floor face-down just inside the front door. There was a blood pool on the floor around the victim's head, and there were blood splatters on the inside of the front door and the wall surrounding it. To the left of the door was a table against the wall that contained some carryout food and a bottle of wine. There was also a potted plant on the table. Upon checking the plant, I found a .38-caliber revolver with a two-inch barrel. The revolver was lying in plain sight and was on top of the dirt in the plant holder. I left the revolver in the location that I had discovered it. Rex started to do a crime-scene sketch, which consisted of the front room, and I continued to inspect the rest of the house, which appeared to be unremarkable in nature. After doing this I concluded that our crime scene consisted of just the front room of the house. The photographer from the photo lab arrived at that time, and we directed him to take photos at the location. We had photos taken of the victim, the gun, the front room of the house, the blood and blood splatters, and the items on the table. Once the photos were taken, I retrieved the revolver from the plant, and Rex took the blood samples from the wall and door. I examined the cylinder of the revolver and found one spent shell casing and five live rounds in the cylinder of the weapon. (Later I had the revolver dusted for prints and would find the suspects prints on it.)

The coroner arrived at the location, and we made an examination of the body with him. It was found that the victim had been shot once in the right temple. The victim's body was warm to the touch, and no rigor mortis was present. The coroner took a liver temperature by inserting a meat thermometer in the victim's liver. The liver temperature was 96°. This indicated that the victim had died approximately three hours ago.

It was now 9:30 p.m. The contents of the victim's pockets were removed by the coroner, and the victim was tentatively identified from his driver's license as being Mr. Gray. There were no other injuries noted to the deceased person. From the victim's driver's license, I found that he was a male negro, thirty-four years old, six feet tall, and 210 pounds black hair and brown eyes. The coroner removed the body of Mr. Gray and transported him to the LA County coroner's office. Rex and I asked the patrol officer to check the neighborhood for witnesses, and we returned to the station.

We located the woman who had been brought in from our crime scene at the station. Rex preformed a GSR, gun shot residue, test on the woman's hands. This is a test used to discover traces of gases and smoke from the explosion occurring at the time a shot is fired. It will show whether or not a person has recently fired a firearm. We then allowed the woman to use the restroom, in the company of a police woman. (You do not want a person to use the rest room before you administer the test and have them wash their hands and destroy your evidence.) I then took the woman back to the detective bureau and placed her inside and interview room. Rex went to the tape room and inserted a tape so that the interview with the woman could be tape-recorded. After assuring himself that the tape was recording, he joined me in the interview room.

I asked the woman, who still had her purse, if she could identify herself to me. From her purse she produced a driver's license and handed it to me. The driver's license identified her as Mary Smith, F/N, thirty-two years old, five feet five inches, 120 pounds, and had black hair and brown eyes. I asked her if she needed anything to eat or drink, and she responded by saying she would like some coffee and a cigarette. I went and got some coffee, and when I came back, I gave her a cup and pulled out my Pall Mall cigarettes and gave them to her. I then told her that we were investigating the death of the person at her house, and that we wanted to talk to her about that occurrence. I asked her if she was willing to talk to us about the occurrence without an attorney present, and she answered she was, and did not need an attorney. She stated that she was about to have a nervous breakdown, and could she drink the coffee and smoke a cigarette before I questioned her. I told her that would be fine, and that I would leave the pack of cigarettes on the table and she could smoke as many as she wished. I left the room and turned off the tape. Rex phoned communications and asked them to pull the tickets on any calls made to the police with the crime scene address. We wanted to determine who had notified the police that shots had been fired at the crime scene location. We started the tape and went back into the interview room and entered into a conversation with Mary Smith.

"We identified the person lying on the floor of your front room. His name is Mr. Gray. Do you know him?" I said.

"Yes, I know him; he is my ex-boyfriend. I broke up with him over six months ago. He became very abusive and would hit me and holler at me all the time. I called the police on him a couple times, but they would not do anything to him. I finally told him to leave my house, and he did. I haven't seen him in over six months."

"How did he happen to be there tonight?" I asked.

"I came home from work around four o'clock and found him sitting in my kitchen. I forgot all about him having a key to my house, so he must've let himself in. I asked him what he was doing in my house, and he told me he just came by to renew an old acquaintance. He said that he would have dinner with me and a few drinks. I told him I did not have anything in the house for dinner or to drink. I also told him that I was tired and did not want to entertain anybody that evening. He told me that we did not need to either eat or drink; all we needed to do was go to bed and have sex. I became very afraid of him at that time and was afraid that he would rape me. I told him that if he would go out and get something to eat and drink, and allow me to take a shower and clean up, I would reconsider allowing him to stay. He told me he could do that, and he laughed, and stated that he would be back in about a half hour. He then left to get something to eat and drink."

"Had he physically or verbally threatened you in any way during that time he was in your house?" I said.

"He did not have to. The inference was there. I know him, and I know what he was thinking. He was thinking he could just take me at any time, and that's why he came back to my house."

"What did you do after he left your house? Did you lock the door? Did you call the police? Did you do anything to protect yourself?" I said.

"No, I did not lock my door. It would not have done any good, because he had a key. No, I did not call the police. I felt I might be able to handle the situation myself. I thought that when he came back, I would eat and drink with him. Then I would tell him that he had to leave, and that I was tired and was going to bed. I thought I would go to the door and open the door and show him the way out. I got my gun, and I put it in the flower planter beside the door. I thought if he would not leave, I would show him my gun and order him out of my house. I was not going to let him hurt me. I knew that if I did not do something this time, he would only come back and rape me again."

"Rex, could you go get us some more coffee? Thanks, partner. I think she needs a cup, and I know I do. We'll wait until you get back before we continue." I had done this for two reasons. The first reason was that Rex had to check our tape, and the second reason was I wanted her to relax a little before we got into the shooting. Mary continued to smoke my cigarettes. Rex came back in a few minutes, and Mary and I started to drink our coffee.

"So tell me, Mary, what happened when he came back to your house. Did you two get into it, or what?" I said.

"I waited until I heard his key turning the lock on the front door. I was standing behind the front door. I opened the door and took the takeout food and a bottle of wine from him. I placed them on the table next to the planter where my gun was. I told him at that time that we could eat the food and drink the wine, but that he was going to have to leave once we were done. He was not going to spend the night at my house. I guess that made him mad, because he told me he wasn't going to spend money on me and not have sex with me. He grabbed me around my shoulders, and started to try and kiss me and force me back into the front room. I tried to fight him off, but he was too strong. He started to molest me, and was trying to take off my clothes when I reached over into the planter and got my gun. I pointed my gun at his head and pulled the trigger. The gun went off, and he fell to the floor, and I ran into the kitchen and called the police. Then I just waited until the police arrived. Then they brought me down here. That's the whole story, as I remember it. Did you find my gun? I don't remember what I did with it."

"Yes, I found your gun back in the flower planter. Is the gun registered to you? We are going to have to book you on this. You know we are going to arrest you for murder, but we will tell your story to the district attorney, and we will see what comes out of it. You can keep the rest of my cigarettes and take them with you. They will allow you to keep them in jail. I'm sorry it came to this, but it appears to us that you did not have any other choice. We will explain that to the district attorney on your behalf. Try to pull yourself together, and you will be able to get through this."

"Yes, the gun is mine, and it is registered to me. Thanks again for the coffee and cigarettes. I am really sorry that I shot him, and I wish he hadn't come over to the house."

Rex and I left Mary Smith sitting in the room, and we went out to talk about the case.

"The GSR test showed that she had fired a weapon with her left hand." Rex said. "What do you think about her story? I think the tricky part is going to be her planting that gun. That shows premeditation, on her part, to shoot him. Do you think she planned to shoot him from the start?"

"I think the district attorney will have to decide that. She says that she was just going to use the gun to force him to leave the house. The rest of her story fits the physical evidence that we found. The gun and the flower planter were on the left side of the door. She would have used her left hand to get the gun, and to shoot him. The gunshot wound was to his right temple, and the blood splattering on the wall and door were from a left-to-right angle; she was standing in front of him, facing the door, and he was facing the interior of the room. I don't think she was justified in shooting him, but I don't think she planned on doing it. Let's take her down to the women's jail and book her, and then come back and do our paperwork."

We took Mary Smith and the evidence that we had gathered out to our car. We placed the gun and blood samples into our homicide kit, in the trunk of the car, and placed Mary Smith in the backseat. I got a time and mileage check from communications, and we took Mary Smith to the woman's jail and booked her. We then returned to the station and took our evidence inside and booked it into the property room. (A homicide kit is a wooden box, kept in the trunk of the car. It contains everything from coveralls to coin envelopes. A time and mileage check is used when a female is transported, so you are covered if she later claims you raped her at the time.)

It was now one o'clock on Saturday morning, the following day. Rex and I were in the detective bureau working on our reports. The watch commander came in to the detective bureau and told us that we had another homicide. He informed us that we had a female victim at the location, and that there were no suspects in custody. The radio car officers were standing by, awaiting our arrival. Photos and prints had been notified and were responding to the location. The coroner had not been notified.

I told Rex that I would go to the location and cover the scene of the homicide. He could remain at the station and finish working on our reports. That way we would save time, and, if I needed anything, I would call him from the scene. I then left the station and went to the scene of the second homicide. (Time is the most important asset a homicide investigator has. Time is not to be wasted.)

I arrived at the scene and met the radio car officer who was standing by at the location. The location was a single-family home, located mid block in a residential area. There were houses on either side of the home and houses across the street. All of the houses had driveways running down between them, and garages to the rear. The street was full of cars parked along the curb on both sides. The radio car officer told me that upon their arrival, the woman from across the street was at the location. She was the reporting party and was the person who had found the victim. She had gone back to her house across the street and was waiting for me at that location. The radio car officer's partner was in the house with her. They had not canvassed the neighborhood, thus far, and were waiting for us to arrive. They had secured the scene, and the ambulance had been there and pronounced the victim DOA. He handed me the MT slip that the ambulance crew had left with him. He had gone inside the house with the ambulance crew and found the victim in the bedroom. After finding the victim, both he and the ambulance crew had left the house and had not been back inside. He was filling out the crime-scene log, and would have it for me upon my request. I thanked him and asked him to stay and wait for the photo lab and fingerprints to arrive at the scene and log them in upon their arrival. I then walked into the house where the homicide had occurred. The room I walked into, upon entering the house, was the front room of the residence. Directly behind the front room was the kitchen. A hallway between the front room and kitchen led to the bathroom and bedrooms on either side of the bathroom. The victim was in the front bedroom, which would be the bedroom located on the street side of the house.

The victim was lying on the floor between the bed and the wall that was the outside wall to the bedroom, on the street side. She was wearing a nightgown and had what appeared to be a jagged cut to her throat. There was blood all over the bed, floor, victim, and the adjacent walls of the bedroom. The amount of blood indicated that the victim had bled out. This was the probable cause of death, in my opinion at the time. There was a six-inch steak knife lying on the floor between the victim and the bed. The bed had two pillows and two sheets on it that were in disarray. There were woman's clothes lying on a chair that was to the other side of the bed. Blood had been tracked across the floor of the bedroom, in the direction of the bathroom. Bloody footprints were on the bathroom floor, and blood was on the bathroom sink. The bloody footprints on the bathroom floor led into the bathroom and out of the bathroom. I then checked the second bedroom, the front room, and the kitchen. In a kitchen drawer, I found identical steak knives to the one that was in the bedroom. In the front room I found a half a dozen beer cans sitting on a coffee table in front of the couch. There were also munchies on the coffee table. There was a pair of women's shoes on the floor under the coffee table. Other than the items mentioned, the rest of the house was unremarkable.

I drew a crime-scene diagram of the location and placed all the items mentioned above in this drawing. The photographer from the photo lab showed up at the scene, and I had him photograph the entire scene, including all of the rooms, the victim, beer cans, steak knives, blood, and footprints. The fingerprint technician arrived, and I had him fingerprint the entire bedroom, bathroom, front room, and kitchen. While he was doing this, I went across the street to talk to the neighbor who had found the victim.

The neighbor told me that she was close friends with the victim. She stated that they were both single women, and that they got together from time to time. She had come home Friday night at around eleven o'clock and had seen that the lights were on in the victim's house. She called the victim on the phone, but there was no answer. She was still seeing the victim's lights on around twelve thirty on Saturday morning. This was unusual, because the victim was always in bed after eleven thirty. She called the victim again, on the phone, and there was still no answer. She decided to go over to the victim's house and check on her. At that time she went across the street and up on the porch of the victim's house. The front door to the victim's house was standing open. She called out to the victim, but got no answer. She then went into the victim's house and found the victim lying on the floor of the victim's bedroom. Upon seeing all the blood, she felt that the victim was deceased. She used the victim's phone to call the police. She waited in the front room until the police arrived. After the police arrived, she told them what she saw and asked if she could go back to her house. She had been in her house since that time.

I used the neighbor's phone and called the station and talked to my partner. I told him that I could handle the crime scene and asked him to call the coroner, and have the coroner respond to the scene. I also asked him to send a criminologist to the scene. I wanted the criminologist to gather the blood samples for typing. I then entered into a conversation with the neighbor.

"Did you see anyone in or around the victim's house when you came home?" I asked the neighbor.

"No, I did not see anyone over there."

"When you were over at the victim's house, did you see anything unusual about the inside of the house?" I asked.

"When I was sitting on the couch, waiting for the police to get there, I noticed that her TV was gone. She had a nineteen-inch color TV that was in an ivory case with black trim. The TV had rabbit ears sitting on top of it, and they were gone too."

"Does the victim have a boyfriend?" I asked.

"I guess you could call him a boyfriend. He comes over about every other week, and stays with her from about six until about ten at night. She never knows when he's coming; he just kind of stops by. She told me that he keeps telling her he's going to leave his wife, but I guess he never did. She doesn't tell me much about him, and I just see him over there occasionally. I've never been over there when he's there. He looks to be about thirty-five to forty years old. He's a real big guy; I would say over six feet tall and weighing over 230 pounds. I don't know his name; we have never met."

"What kind of car does he drive, and did you see it over there tonight?" I asked.

"He drives a pickup truck with one of those cabover campers on the back of it. I don't know what kind of truck it is, but the truck and camper are white. I don't know the license number, 'cause I never looked at the truck. I just see it parked over there in front of the house sometimes."

"What is the victim's name, and does she carry a purse? I looked through the house, but I did not see a purse," I said.

"Her name is Cecilia Yellow. She does carry a purse, and she keeps it in her top dresser drawer in her bedroom. She never takes it out of there unless she is going to leave the house. She was married before, but that was a long time ago, and her ex-husband does not live in California. I have never seen him, and he has never been to her house, that I know of. She doesn't have any children, either. I don't know about any relatives, I've never seen anyone at her house."

I gave the neighbor my business card, and told her if she thought of anything else, or saw the boyfriend come around, to please call me. I then went back across the street to the victim's house, and met with the photo lab technician and the fingerprint technician. The criminologist had showed up at the scene. I had to keep the photo technician at the scene in case there was something under the body that needed photographed when we removed it. The fingerprint technician informed me that he had been able to get several fingerprint lifts. He had gotten lifts from the beer cans, the bathroom sink, the coffee table, the TV stand, and a dresser in the victim's bedroom. He did not get any fingerprints from the steak knife that was in the victim's bedroom.

I had the criminologist take blood samples from various locations, including the bathroom sink, the floor of the bathroom, the blood around the victim, and in various places on the bed. I also had him take samples from the wall in the victim's bedroom. I looked in the dresser drawer in the victim's bedroom and found her purse. The purse had a wallet in it that contained money and the victim's driver's license. The victim was Cecilia Yellow, ,female negro, thirty-six years old, five feet four inches, 115 pounds, with brown hair and brown eyes.

It was interesting that the suspect had not taken the victim's money.

The coroner arrived at the location, and we conducted an examination of the body. The victim did in fact have a jagged cut across her neck that severed her carotid artery and cut through her windpipe. The coroner stated that the wound was consistent with the steak knife being the weapon. He also found several bruises and abrasions to the victim's arms and chest. It was his opinion that they were recent injuries, and that there had not had been time for blood to coagulate beneath the skin. The coroner felt that the cause of death was the knife wound that led to the victim bleeding out. A liver temperature was taken, and the reading was 93°. The coroner felt that the victim had died sometime between nine and ten o'clock the previous evening. He removed the victim and transported her to the LA county coroner's office. The three technicians at the crime scene left with their evidence to be analyzed. As I was leaving, I noticed that the next-door neighbor's lights were on, and I decided to go talk to the next-door neighbor.

The neighbor told me that he had seen the victim's boyfriend's truck parked out in front of her house earlier on Friday evening. Sometime after ten o'clock the previous evening, he noticed that the truck was gone. The neighbor told me that the victim's boyfriend was always parking his truck across his driveway. He called the police a couple of times about the truck blocking his driveway. One time, the police came out and wrote a ticket and put it on the truck. He did not know the license number of the truck, but gave me the same description of the truck that the neighbor across the street had given me. He had not heard or seen anything at the victim's house that previous evening. He had not seen the victim's boyfriend at her house that night. He had just seen his truck.

I then left the location and returned to the station. I had the beer cans, steak knife, and other steak knives from the kitchen, the victim's wallet and money, and sheets from the bed with me to book as evidence and for safekeeping. (I had the three technicians sign as witnesses to the money.) The coroner had placed a seal on the front door of the victim's house. This was pending notification of the next of kin. Anyone breaking that seal was committing a crime and would be arrested for it. Not to say that it wasn't done, on occasion.

I met Rex at the station and briefed him on what the crime scene investigation consisted of. I told him that we needed to identify the boyfriend, and that I thought he was our prime suspect. Our suspect could also be someone who broke into the house and killed her and took the TV. The purpose would've been robbery, even though the money wasn't taken.

Rex showed me what he had done on the first case in my absence. He had started the murder book on that case. (A murder book is a book where you file all the information you gather on a case from the beginning to the end. The book is indexed into sections and starts with a chronological log, where everything is listed in a date and time sequence. There are sections in the book for your reports, photographs, analyzed evidence, witnesses' statements, crime–scene diagram, and other miscellaneous reports.)

It was now around five o'clock on Saturday morning, and we decided to go get something to eat. After we ate, we canvassed both neighborhoods around the two crime scenes in search of additional witnesses. We did find a witness at the second crime scene who had seen the boyfriend's truck at the victim's house but did not see it leave, nor did they see the boyfriend leave. We found a witness at the first crime scene.The witness lived next door to the suspect's house. This witness told us that she had seen the victim go into the suspect's house at around three in the afternoon that Friday. She stated that she knew the victim because he had lived at the suspect's house some time ago, and she had met him. She saw him come back out around four thirty that afternoon and then come back to the house at about five thirty, carrying a package. She saw him go into the house, but did not see anything or hear anything after that.

We returned to the station, and I booked the evidence from the second crime scene into the property room. While I was working on the reports from the second homicide, Rex called the coroner's office and found out that our two autopsies were going to be performed on Monday morning at eight o'clock. Rex also called communications and asked that the time slips on any calls with respect to our second crime scene would be pulled. He also requested that any calls coming from the witness's house (who had called in on the pickup truck blocking his driveway) at the second crime scene also be pulled. Rex called the traffic division and requested a search for a parking ticket that was issued at the witness's address, in hopes of finding the ticket that had been placed on the boyfriend's truck. I made up a murder book on our second homicide and filled out the chronological log. I made out a list of things to do on the second homicide. Rex had done this on the first homicide, while I was at the second homicide scene.

List of things to do on the Green homicide:

1. Attend autopsy at 8:00 a.m. on Monday. Recover bullet and take to ballistics. Determine cause of death. Determine if the corner has notified the next of kin.

2. Take gun to SID [scientific investigation division] and have gun printed and ballistics checked against bullet, if we get one.

3. Take blood samples to SID.

4. File case by Tuesday morning.

5. File all information and reports in the murder book upon their being returned to us after approval.

6. Check on photos.

List of things to do on the Yellow homicide:

1. Identify the victim's boyfriend.

2. Attend the autopsy on Monday morning at 8:00. Determine the cause of death. Determine if the coroner has notified the next of kin.

3. Check communication tickets for sources of calls.

4. Check traffic division for traffic ticket put on boyfriend's truck.

5. Check on fingerprints lifted at crime scene as to identification of prints.

6. Check on photos.

7. Check for any other crimes with same MO, method of operation.

8. File all information and reports in the murder book upon their being returned to us after approval.

Rex and I made sure that all of our reports had been completed and submitted to the watch commander for approval. We had given the record clerks two death reports, two crime reports, two evidence reports, and one arrest report to be typed up and given to the watch commander. The record clerks had completed the reports, and they were in the watch commander's office. It was now after five o'clock on Saturday afternoon, and. we had solved one homicide and had some promising leads on the other. We decided to sleep at the station and save the two hours that it would take to drive home and come back in, in case we needed to. The likelihood of a homicide occurring on a Saturday night was great, and not to disappoint us, we got woke up at eight o'clock that Saturday night. The watch commander told us that there had been a homicide, inside a house, on 108th Street. There were three victims that had been shot inside the house, and they were children. The photo lab had been notified and had quoted a delay. The scene was secured by the patrol officers, and they were awaiting our arrival.

The both of us got dressed and were out at the scene in a half hour. The scene turned out to be a single-family home in a residential area. The home had steps leading up to the front door, and there was a front porch to the home. We got out of our car and approached the front of the home. We noticed that the ambulance crew was still at the scene, and that the patrol officers were at the scene as well. I also saw a woman sitting on the front steps of the house. I went up and talked to the officers and the ambulance crew and was told that there were three children inside the home that had been killed by gunshot wounds. They had each been shot in the back of the head. The ambulance crew handed me the MT slips on each of the victims and asked if they could leave. I told them that they could. I asked the patrol officer who the woman was who was sitting on the steps. The patrol officer told me that it was the children's mother. She had not been there when they arrived at the location, but had driven up while they were examining the scene. The patrol officer had been outside on the sidewalk at the time, and she had gotten out of the car and came up to him and told him that this was her house and the children inside were her children. The patrol officer had asked her if she knew that the children had been shot, and she stated that she did. The patrol officer had told her that she would need to talk to the detectives, and that the detectives were on their way out to the location. He then attempted to put her in his car, and she resisted, and stated she would sit on the steps until the detectives arrived. At that point, the ambulance crew had come out of the house with his partner, and he allowed her to wait on the steps.

I went up to the woman sitting on the steps and asked her name.

"Sissy Sanders, don't you remember me? I talked to you briefly about a month ago. Remember, I killed my neighbor, and I was arrested for it. You're not the detective that handled the case, but I talked to you at the station before they booked me."

After looking at her for a moment, I realized that I did know her. She was a good-looking woman, thirty-two years old, five feet two inches, 110 pounds. She had the kind of body you wanted to see in a bikini at the beach. She had been in a physical altercation with her female neighbor. They were fighting on the sidewalk between their two houses. She had stabbed her female neighbor with a knife, which ultimately led to her neighbor's death. She had been charged with the murder, but at her arraignment, a female judge by the name of Betty Best had allowed her to be released on her own recognizance, pending her trial. The judge felt that the case could be proven to be self-defense. I had been at the station when Sanders was brought in by the patrol officers on that case. Another team of homicide detectives from our division were handling the case and had sent her into the station from the scene. I had put her in an interview room, and had gotten her a cup of coffee and given her some cigarettes.

"I do remember you. Now, can you tell me what this is all about?"

"First of all, you're going to want the gun, and it's here in my purse. Then you're going to want to know who shot my three kids, and I can answer that too. The answer to that is, I shot them." After saying that, she handed me her purse and told me I had her permission to get the gun out of the purse, and that she was ready to now go to the police station.

I opened the purse and found an RG .38-caliber revolver inside the purse. I checked the weapon and found six spent shell casings inside the gun. I asked her if the revolver was hers, and she replied that it was. She also stated that it was the gun that she had used to shoot her children with. I advised her that I was placing her under arrest for the killing of her children and advised her of her rights, and got a waiver of her rights from her.

"When did you shoot your children, and where have you been?"

"I guess it's been about two hours now, since I shot my children. After I shot them, I went over into Watts and I shot my ex-boyfriend. I tried to shoot his new girlfriend, but I guess I missed. I only had three shots in the gun, but I know I hit him with one of them. I did blow out the window of his business."

"What are the names of your children, and what are their ages?" Her reply was Red, twelve years old;White, six years old; and Blue, four years old.

I asked the patrol officer to call a radio car to the scene and have them transport her to the station for me. I also asked him to check and see if there been a shooting in Watts, within the last two hours, and if there had been, to let me know. I asked Sissy if she would consent to a GSR (gunshot residue) test, and she said she would. I got the test from our homicide kit and tested her hands. I found gunshot residue on her right hand. I looked around and found that while I had been talking to her, the photographer had showed up at the scene. The photographer, Rex, and I then walked into the house.

When we entered the house, we were in the front room. To the left of the front room was the kitchen. Behind the kitchen was a hallway that led to three bedrooms and a bathroom. The first victim was found in the kitchen. The victim was a twelve-year-old girl, and she was standing up between a refrigerator and clothes dryer. Her back was toward us. She was facing the wall, and she had been shot in the back of her head. She appeared to have squeezed into the small space. The victim was fully clothed and did not appear to have any other wounds to her person. The victim's body was cool to the touch, but rigor mortis had not set in.

The other two victims were on the floor of the master bedroom at the back of the house. They were both on their stomachs and were facing each other. There was an area of approximately two feet between their heads. Their faces were buried in the carpet, and they both had gunshot wounds to the back of their heads. One of the victims was a four-year-old male and the other was a six-year-old female. Both of the victims were cool to the touch, but rigor mortis had not set in. Both of the victims were fully clothed and did not have any other wounds, with the exception of the gunshot wounds.

I had the photographer take all the necessary photos of the crime scene and the victims. I had made a diagram of the crime scene, showing the locations of the victims. There was not any physical evidence to gather at the crime scene. Rex had notified the coroner, and upon the arrival of the coroner, all three bodies were taken from the crime scene and transported to the LA county coroner's office. We all left the crime scene, and Rex and I returned to the station.

When we arrived at the station, we were met by a couple of police officers who informed us that they had just taken a crime report at Martin Luther King General Hospital. They told us that our suspect, Sissy Sanders, was a suspect on their crime reports. The victims on their crime reports were the ex-boyfriend of Sanders and his new girlfriend. The ex-boyfriend owned a business on 103rd Street in Watts. It was a house decorating business. The two victims were working in the business, earlier in the evening, when Sanders appeared outside the business and shot at them through the business window. Three shots had been fired, breaking out the window, and one of the shots struck the ex-boyfriend in the shoulder. The other victim, his girlfriend, was not injured. The police officers also stated that they had driven by the business on their way to the station and verified that the window had been blown out. They had recovered two spent rounds from the interior of the business. At the emergency room of the hospital, they had also been given a bullet that was taken out of the boyfriend's shoulder. I told the police officers to go ahead and finish their crime reports, and to leave the bullets with me, and I would book the bullets for them. I told them that I would get their reports later and file charges against Sanders for the shooting. I then thanked them for their good work and allowed them to leave.

Rex and I then went back to the detective bureau and found Sissy Sanders in an interview room. The two officers that had brought her in were waiting for us in the detective bureau. They told us that they had not talked to her at all and had just placed her in the interview room. They asked us to take their handcuffs off of her and give them to them so they could leave. While I was doing this, Rex went in to set up the tape recorder for our interview with Sissy Sanders. I was noting the date and time (Sunday, 12:10 a.m.) on my notebook, when the watch commander walked in.

"Glad to see you are in here; you got a dead body out there in a liquor store parking lot. Your crime scene is secure, but there are no suspects in custody. It appears he is the victim of a shooting. The liquor store is at 106th Street and Compton, in Watts. Don't you guys ever go to bed? I'll tell the radio car that you're on your way. This has to be patrol's lucky night: that's two homicides you will be going to from the station. We did not have to call you in from home."

"Could you hold that radio car that was just in here talking to me?" I answered. "I will get Rex to go out to the scene, and I want them to go with him. If he has plenty of help out there, he can cut them loose. I have to stay here at the station and conduct an interview."

"You got it. I can do that," the watch commander answered.

"What's going on?" Rex said as he walked up. "Did I hear the watch commander say that we had another homicide? I got your tape set up. All you have to do is turn it on. I agree with you, and I will go handle the scene. You handled one last night without me, and I can do the same for you. You need to talk to her while she's hot, anyhow. I'll take that radio car and have them follow me to the scene. I'll let you know when I know what we got out there. Good luck on your interview. Catch you on the flipside. I seem to recall that you have an informant who hangs out at that liquor store. Hope it's not him, and time has caught up with him."

"Yeah, so do I hope it's not him. I know his family well. He scores dope at that liquor store now and then. He is a mainliner and shoots up. It's a wonder the dope hasn't got to him."

Rex left and I went and got Sissy and I a cup of coffee. I knew she liked it black, like I did. I had gotten her black coffee before.

I always talk to persons I have brought to the station with coffee and cigarettes. Sometimes the person I'm talking to wants soda, so I will get soda instead of coffee. I talk to the person I am interviewing or interrogating, as anyone would carry on a conversation. I converse with them in their comfort zone as opposed to mine.. I never take paper and pencil into the initial conversation, just me, coffee, and cigarettes. Paper and pencils scare some people. The minute you write something down, they don't want to talk. Like the reporter that tells you it is off of the record, and you read about what you said that next day in the paper. My first conversation is just the beginning. Once I get the story I want, and it's on the tape, I then go back over it with the person. It's easier for a person to tell the story again, once it's out in the open. The second time I go over the story, I write the story and have the person read and sign the written copy.

I also include a statement that says they gave their story to me, free and voluntary, and I did not promise them anything for telling me their story. If I have gotten a waiver to Miranda rights, I can use the story in court. I can use a story without a waiver, if a suspect takes the stand and his or her story changes. This way my taped statement is always good, no matter what. Miranda allows you to talk to a suspect, as long as you don't ask them questions about their involvement in the crime you are investigating. If you do ask them questions about the crime you are investigating, and they admit to participation, you cannot use that admission against them. But, under California law, if they take the stand to testify to an alibi, you can use an inadmissible statement to challenge what they are now saying. Your inadmissible statement goes to the truth of the matter. This then allows a court or jury to decide which they're going to believe: what the suspect is saying on the stand, or what the suspect told you at the time. I always felt that I could talk to any suspect, at any time, and for as long as I wished. As long as I was careful, I could get the results that I was after. If the statement was not useful, I then just put the tape in a file and did not use it unless the suspect took the stand. Of course, the trick was to have your case be a solid case and not need a confession. In addition, Miranda rights do not apply to conversations with victims or witnesses. Miranda rights apply only at the time that you suspect the person you're talking to participated in the crime.

I started the tape, then went into the room where Sissy was and gave her the coffee. I offered her a cigarette, and she took one. We both settled in and sized each other up. I couldn't believe how calm she was. You would think she was going to watch TV or something.

"Sissy, do you use any other names?"

"No."

"I'm going to have to advise you of your Miranda rights. You have a right to remain silent. You have the right to the services of an attorney, and if you cannot afford an attorney, one will be provided for you, free of charge. Anything you tell me, can and will be used against you in a court of law. Do you understand your rights?"

"Yes."

"Do you wish to give up your rights, and talk to me at this time, without an attorney present?"

"If you'd let me tell it my way. I don't mind telling you. I got it all planned out. I don't need an attorney, yet. Besides, I already got an attorney from the last case. He would only tell me not to talk to you."

"So you're saying you don't want your attorney here, and you will talk to me without him."

"That's what I'm saying."

"You have been a busy girl tonight. Why don't you start from the beginning, and tell me about your night."

"You mean, when my kids were alive?"

"That would be a good place to start."

"We were all in the house, and around six o'clock at night I sent Red to the store to get some milk. Then I took White and Blue into my bedroom. I told White and Blue we were going to play cowboys and Indians, and I showed them my gun. I got them to lie down on the floor, with their heads together. I then told them to hide their eyes in the carpet. When they had done what I told them to do, I took my gun and shot them both in the back of their heads. It was over fast for them, and they didn't suffer."

"Which one did you shoot first?"

"I shot White first, and then Blue. It was like right away. You know, no time between the shots. Just Bang! Bang! I checked them, and they were both dead."

"This was with the gun I took out of your purse?"

"Yes, that's the only gun I used all night. I only had six shots to fire from it, and I fired three at home and three later. If I had more bullets, I could have done a better job at my ex-boyfriend's shop. Is he still alive? I know I did not hit his girl-friend with a bullet."

"Yes, he is still alive, and he will be OK. He has made a report against you, but I think that's a minor problem for you. The real problem is going to be your kids. Let's get back to that."

"OK. Can I have another cigarette and some more coffee?"

"I will go get us the coffee, and here are some smokes. Help yourself."

I left the room and checked the tape. I then went and got us each some coffee—so far, so good. I had gotten a waiver that would hold up in court. I had what appeared to be the gun that was used. I could show malice, forethought, and premeditation. I could tie in my evidence with each piece supporting the other. I went back over it in my head. Bodies, gun, and premeditation, two victims covered and one to go. I would have to cover the boyfriend and his girlfriend too.

I went back in the interview room and gave Sissy her coffee. She thanked me, and we got started again. I asked her to explain what had happened to Red.

"A little while after I had shot White and Blue, Red came back from the store. I met her in the kitchen. I had put my gun away in my pocket. She gave me the milk and change. Then I told her I had dropped my purse behind the dryer and I needed it to put the change in. I asked her to squeeze in between the dryer and refrigerator, and see if she could get my purse. She did that, and when she was squeezed in there, I shot her in the back of her head."

"Did that kill her?"

"Yes, it did. Just like White and Blue, real quick and fast. That's how I planned it to go, over quick, no pain, no suffering, and no regrets on my part. I put the gun in my purse—my purse did not fall behind the dryer, and I had just said that to get Red to crawl in there. After I put the gun in my purse, I left the house. I got in my car and drove over to Watts. I forgot to tell you, I called you guys and told you that there had been a shooting at my house. I didn't give them my name, though."

"How long have you been planning on this?"

"About a month, I guess. That's when I got into that fight with my neighbor. It all started when my boyfriend left me. It always happens. I get a boyfriend, and he gets tired of the kids. He always wants me and everything is OK, and then the kids get in the way. Then he looks for a better relationship, and he flies the coop. This isn't the first one that's done it. I get a good one, and he always leaves me. That's why the neighbor lady and I fought. She was saying that he was good to go, in leaving me."

"Tell me about after the kids."

"After I called the police, I drove over to my ex-boyfriends shop, in Watts. When I got there I saw the two of them through the window. They were at the counter and were talking to each other. That should have been me with him. I got so mad, I didn't even go in, and I just took my gun and shot at them through the window. I fired the gun until it wouldn't shoot anymore. I must have fired three shots, because I had used three shots on the kids. I saw him grab at his chest, or arm, and they both went down behind the counter. I got back in my car and drove back home. When I got there I saw the police were there, so I got out of the car and told them who I was. You know the rest."

"How long were you together with your ex-boyfriend?"

"About a year. We came out here from Texas. I met him in Greenville, Texas. That's where I was living before we came to California. He had his business there, and moved the business here."

"Were any of the kids his?"

"No, they all had their own fathers, but none were his. I had two other kids when I was in Texas. They were in between Red and White. I need to tell you about them too."

"Where are they now?"

"Oh, they are dead. The first one I smothered in his crib, shortly after he was born. I think it was around six months after he was born."

"Were the police involved in his death?"

"No, it was ruled a SIDS death. I called 911, and the ambulance came. Then the police and the coroner came. They had an autopsy and ruled it accidental. Then I had to get a mortuary to cremate him. The second one was two years later. That one I just called the mortuary, and they came and got her and cremated her. There was not any investigation or autopsy involved in her death. You can check with Texas and find out about them. It was in Greenville, Texas, and I want you to check it out." (Later on, I did just that, and confirmed what she told me. Both deaths were listed as accidental; cause of death on both of them was listed as SIDS.)

"So why are you telling me about the two kids in Texas? I would not have known about them if you hadn't told me. You know, I am going to run your record, but I wouldn't have found out about them. There wasn't a crime attached to the deaths, and you weren't arrested."

"If you look at it, I've killed five of my kids, I've killed my neighbor, and I tried to kill my ex-boyfriend and his new girlfriend. I am going to get a jury trial and plead not guilty by reason of insanity. What's a jury going to think? I have to be crazy. The court will give me two years in Atascadero, and then I'll be found sane again. Then they will let me go, and I won't have to worry about having kids again. I'm going to get my tubes tied, and I'll find a new boyfriend, before I get too old. I started having kids when I was eighteen. None of them were planned on or wanted to begin with. I was just unlucky.

Once this is over, I will make sure I won't let kids get in my way again."

"I am going to get us some more coffee and check on my partner. I'll be back in a few minutes." With that, I left the interview room and checked my tape. It showed over an hour's worth of conversation, most of it hers. And letting her tell her story, I had gotten all I needed for a case against her, and more. I did not have to solicit any information. When I went back into the interview room to write up her statement; I would fill in some gaps about the gun, other family members, and any other pre-plans she had made, with respect to her killing her kids.

Rex was not back yet from the scene of our new homicide, nor had he called in. I got some more coffee and took her a cup. When I gave it to her, she asked how long it would be until she went to jail. I told her we had to go back over her story, and we would be booking her after that. I left the room and went outside for some air, and to gather my thoughts.

Outside, I pondered the case. I could normally deal with people killing people, but I did not handle children's deaths very well. They were innocent children and look to adults for guidance. They had no real control over their life, at an early age. Adults could take advantage of them and manipulate them. I blamed a lot of the misguided youth in Watts on their parents. On the other hand, some teenaged youths did set their own futures, despite their parent's style of upbringing. When a juvenile sets their course, the parent no longer has any influence or control. I called that maturity on the part of the child. This could happen as early as twelve to thirteen years of age. Once this mind-set occurs, the parent no longer has any influence on the child. The child has set his or her path to follow, and the parent cannot change the direction of that path, no matter how hard they try. At this point the parents have to give up responsibility for that child and realize that they are no longer having an impact on their child's life.

A prime example of this was the increased gang activity in Watts. Time and time again, I had to deal with the parents of a gang member who had been killed, or the parents of the gang member who had killed. The parents always wanted to know where they had gone wrong, in bringing up the child. I had to explain to them that if they raised their child properly, they had no control over what the child had done, with respect to joining or being in a gang. That being the case, the child had to take responsibility for his actions, not the parents. On the other hand, if they had allowed the child to fend for themselves, in the streets, then they had to accept part of the accountability for the child's actions.

The Cripps and Bloods were becoming the two main gangs in Seventy-seventh Division during this time. There was a lot of competition for control of turf. They were absorbing other gangs into their sets. As a result, there were a lot of killings, which brought publicity, which brought notoriety and respect. The more they read about themselves in the paper, the stronger they felt their gang got. Reputation in the streets was where it was at, and identification in the paper helped build their image. The two gangs developed a color identification: red being attached to the Bloods, and blue being attached to the Cripps. Gangs, such as the Bounty Hunters, integrated themselves into these two gangs. The selling of dope on the streets became their most profitable crime. Other crimes involved robbery, auto theft, and murder. Control of territory led to turf wars, which led to the "shoot them before they shoot you" mentality. The bigger and badder the gang was, the better reputation it earned. By the 1970s, there was no place in Seventy-seventh Division that was void of gangs.

With respect to Sissy's children, they were still at the age that they were solely dependent on her, and look what it had gotten them. I wondered if I had done everything that I could do to avenge their deaths. Could Sissy get away with it, as she had planned? Would a jury buy her story? The only way I could defeat an insanity plea would be through the premeditation on her part. This would probably beat a temporary insanity plea, but what about insanity, period? I guess that determination would have to be left to the professionals. My only hope was that the state would come up with a better shrink than the defense did.

Rex came back to the station just after I finished writing Sissy's statement. I told him what I had learned from her, including the killing of the two kids in Texas. We decided to transport Sissy to the women's jail and book her, and then go eat at the Pantry restaurant in downtown Los Angeles. We ate there often, when we were working a case we called an all-nighter.

After booking Sissy, we got to the Pantry around five in the morning. The pantry was a well-known restaurant, famous for its breakfast. The restaurant stayed open twenty-four hours a day, seven days a week. Its trademark was fresh celery and carrot sticks at every table. The waiters were all males, and the clientele were of all stages in life, from millionaires to bums. There was only one purpose in mind when you went to the Pantry, and that was to eat a good meal, at a good price.

Rex and I each ordered the ham and eggs, over medium, and with home fries. The coffee was hot and black, and I could smoke—what more could you ask for on an early Sunday morning? Reminded me of when I was a kid and my mother sent me to church on Sunday morning, and I skipped church and hung out at the local restaurant. Some people called these types of restaurants greasy spoons. Take my word for it: the food was good and the coffee was hot and black.

"I can't believe how cold and calculated that Sissy is. She would have had everything going for her if she chose a different path to take, instead of developing such a black heart. She sure has good looks going for her. It's no wonder she was able to get so many boyfriends. What do you think, Rex?"

Rex sat back and took a deep breath and let it out slowly. He was a thinker and never said much, but when he did speak, it was never without thinking first. I guess that's why we work well together. We both respected each other and each other's opinions. We had complete trust in each other, and this led to our solving our cases more than any other team in our section. We spent more time together than we did with our wives. Both of us were dedicated to our job, the department, and the cases we handled. Our families were important to us, but the job took a priority over the family, at times. Rex did not have any kids, and I had two at the time. Both of my kids were infants, ages one and three. I felt that I had a few years yet before I needed to spend any quality time with them. For now, I would let my wife raise them, and I would make the money and solve my cases. There would be time later for teaching them how to play sports.

After some thought on the matter, Rex answered me. "Well, I think she thinks she got it all figured out. You know how juries are. They always go away from the facts of the case and evaluate the suspect. We will have a strong case against her. But with her looks and appeal to the jury, she will have a strong case too. Like she said, she has to be crazy to do what she did. And we don't know what she has planned to show caused her to get crazy. The juries love to hear about abuse as a child and sympathize with the victim of physical, emotional, and sexual abuse. Knowing her, as we do, she will have some trump cards to play. And with the law today, if she wins, she will be right about what she has said. Once she is found to be sane again, and the shrinks have rid her of all her misgivings, she will walk. Just like this moratorium against the death penalty. Society does not sign on with executions anymore. I bet we don't go back to executions, and if we do, I bet we will not see California use it again."

"You are probably right about that," I said. "We have gotten some death sentences on our cases, but none have been carried out. It certainly is not a deterrent, at least not here in California. I wonder if it is still used in Ohio, where I'm from. The only place I know it's being used now is in the streets. Funny how we see it used all the time with the gangs. Do you think it is a deterent in the streets?"

"It's used for intimidation, and the threat of death, but I think the gangs don't pay much attention to it. Some of the gang-bangers do run and hide from the threat, but others believe they can overcome the threat by striking first. You know: have gun, will use gun. Speaking of guns, let me tell you about our new case. It's going to be a whodunit case. Not a self-solver, mama and papa homicide."

"OK; it's your dime."

"First of all, the victim is not your informant. The victim is Coal Black, M/N, thirty-two years of age, five foot ten, and 160 pounds. He lives in the Imperial Courts. It's a good thing

California has a law making it a crime not to carry identification. He had his driver's license on him."

(California changed this law later and did not require a person to carry identification. A jogger was stopped in San Diego at 4:00 A.M, jogging, and was arrested for not carrying identification. He was found guilty. The case was appealed and was won on the appeal.)

"I'm sure his prints will verify this is him. The liquor store clerk said it was him, and he got his name because he was so black. It's his real name to. He had old tracks on the inside of both arms. I'm sure he is hype, a mainliner." A mainliner, for those readers who may not know, is a person who introduces dope into their body by using a hypodermic kit. They insert the dope, into their veins, with a needle.

Rex continued, "He was shot three times at close range. All of the shots were to his chest. There was smudging to his shirt and tattooing to his chest. There were no exit wounds. He was shot with a .38 or nine-milimeter automatic. I recovered three shell casings, probably from a Browning or Colt. He had been shot within the hour, prior to my arrival. His liver temperature was 98 degrees. There were no other wounds on his person. I found him lying faceup in the back of the parking lot. From the victim's position, I would assume the shooter was behind the liquor store, in the alley. The victim was just outside of the alley. The shooter could have been in a car when he shot the victim. If he was, he was riding shotgun, or in the right rear of the car. The shell casings were all in the alley to the right of the victim. If the weapon was a right-handed weapon, it would throw the shell casings to the right. Not many left-handed guns out there. Anyhow, the victim was dead before he hit the ground."

"Did you come up with any witnesses?"

"No, the parking lot was empty when I got there. You could have thrown a bowling ball all over that lot and not hit anyone or anything. Kind of unusual, not to find any Lookey Lous at the store when I got there. Tends to make me think no one wants any part of this killing. It strikes me strongly of a killing over dope. More like an assassination, know what I mean?"

"Yes, I do. We have seen it before. The victim must have pissed someone off. How about after you got there, anything turn up?"

"I talked to the liquor store clerk. You know, that store is a small store. They only have one clerk working in the store at night. Of course, he did not see anything. He said he heard the shots, and called the police. He said it had been a slow night, and the parking lot did not have a lot of people around, that he could tell. Most of the regulars had already left. No one came into the store and told him anything after the shots. He identified the victim after I got there, when I took him out to see the victim. I talked to everyone that came to the store when I was there, and no one admitted to seeing anything. It's funny, because they always want to see if they know the victim. I also think they want to see the blood and guts too. Like at a traffic accident, when people slow down and even stop to look. We wouldn't have any traffic jams, if people weren't Looky Lous. The only ones at this scene were those who wanted to be as far away from there as they could get. It's kind of like they already knew who was killed, and how. It's going to be hard to find someone to talk about this killing. Sure hope your informant can come up with something on this one. We are going to need it, I'm afraid."

"Any chance of tire tracks in the alley? I know that alley is paved, and used for dope deals all the time."

"No, I had the photo lab take pictures of what was back there, but don't hold out any hope for something. About all we got are the shell casings and the body."

"A lot of cases we have just had the body and have to work the case backward. We have to identify the body, and trace the victim's steps from being killed, in reverse, as opposed to up to the time they were killed. Either way, we have to take the place of the victim. All other crimes have a victim to work with, but not ours. We have to put their shoes on and become them to get the job done. Only the family gets satisfaction out of our work. If you believe in reincarnation, there are a lot of people walking around in other bodies that are thanking us, I guess. The shell casings are a plus, though, if we find the gun."

"The coroner said the autopsy will be on Tuesday, he thinks. Depends on what they get through with Monday. We got four of their Mondays' work. You do know that tomorrow is Monday, and we have the four autopsies scheduled. We better get back to the station and put our reports together on these two cases. We could get another case before Monday morning. At least when Monday morning gets here, the lieutenant won't dump on us for awhile. The good news is we got two solved, out of the four."

"I guess all good things must come to an end, and this break-fast was a good thing. I only eat breakfast after an all-nighter. I never eat breakfast when I get up and come to work. I just have coffee and cigarettes. At least I give my wife a break, and she doesn't have to get up when I do, and cook me break-fast. Sometimes the kids wake up, and she has to get up with them. You're lucky you don't have kids, but I wouldn't trade them in for anything. I will enjoy our lives together later. OK, let's go do it. I'll do all the reports on the Sissy case, and you can handle the Coal Black case. Then we can go home and sleep sound, I hope. You know, they say we have seventy-two hours to get direction on a case." (Today a TV show is called *48 Hours,* as if the best chance to solve a case is gone after only two days, not three.)

Rex and I went back to the station and finished the reports and turned them in to the watch commander. We then went home to catch some shut-eye. We could not go to Coal Black's residence; yet, we did not know if it was truly him. The coroner was going to run his prints as quickly as possible, but we knew it wouldn't be for eight to ten hours. We had that time to sleep. We both knew we would be back to work that night, whether we got another case or not. We were now living inside a seventy-two hour window on two cases.

I was drinking coffee and smoking out on my deck, at home, in San Pedro. I had just bought the house a month ago. It was the second home I had owned, me and the bank. This house was the house of my dreams. Ever since I moved to San Pedro, I wanted to own the house that sat on a hill and looked out over the San Pedro waterfront. This house did just that. I had an unobstructed view all the way to Long Beach. The whole inner and outer harbor was at my doorstep. I could see the entire San Pedro waterfront and all that came with it. All of the watercraft, from tankers to sailboats, that came and went, did not escape my view. The house was a four-bedroom, two-bath, and custom-built house, of over three thousand square feet. There was plenty of room for the four of us. It was my pride and joy, when I was home to enjoy it. That was the problem I was having currently— being home.

I had gotten a few hours' sleep, after getting home and going straight to bed. But the family was up and active, and my two boys were good to go. My wife tried to keep them quiet, but you don't keep two boys quiet in the afternoon. I had finally given up trying to sleep and had decided to join them. The wife had gotten on my case again, about the hours I kept. You know—why I didn't at least transfer to another job within the police department that was more like an eight-hour day job with weekends off. Better yet, quit the police department and get a job with a little sanity attached to it. I had heard this before, but it was becoming a normal routine on her part. She complained more often now, and said she felt like a trophy on a shelf, as opposed to being a wife. I knew there were good points to what she said, but I could not give up my job. It was part of me and who I was. Our troubles were probably my fault, but I didn't listen too well, and just kept hoping she would change; I knew I wouldn't. The arguments always led to me walking away and coming out on the deck. That's how I had gotten to where I was at: I was watching the fishing boats coming back into the inner harbor. I had given up fishing in the ocean when I got married. Fishing had been my second passion, my first passion being the police department. Wasn't giving up my second passion enough?

I had called Rex and talked to his wife. She had told me he was still in bed. After some small talk, I told her to tell him I would meet him at the station around seven o'clock,—it was now 5:00 p.m. She said he had told her to get a time from me for him to meet me, and that he would make it. I thanked her and told her to take care. I had about an hour and a half before I had to leave, so I analyzed the four cases again.

I first examined what evidence we had. There are several types of evidence, the first one being direct evidence. Direct evidence is testimony on the stand by either victims or witnesses. Witnesses are either laypersons or expert witnesses. Laypersons can testify only to what they know. Expert witnesses can testify to opinions or conclusions on their part. Another type of evidence is physical evidence. This evidence is based on a person's senses: their touch, smell, hearing, and sight. Real physical evidence is things such as a body, fingerprints, blood, firearms, and other solid objects. Trace evidence is things such as hair, fibers, and anything uncovered by the use of a microscope. Another type of evidence is circumstantial evidence. Circumstantial evidence is a set of facts that would lead a reasonable person to believe in a conclusion. A case cannot be proven with just one form of evidence; you must corroborate it with one or more of the other forms of evidence. In other words, you cannot convict on a confession alone, or on just having the murder weapon.

I used what I call the four *I*s to gather evidence. The first *I* is *information*. Information is gathered through people. It is also gathered through records and paper trails such as police files, utilities's bills and records, bank statements, and employer records. The second *I* is *identification*. This is identifying the body, witnesses, and any other persons of interest that would help you solve the case. The third *I* is *interviews*. Some examples are any statements or admissions made by anyone other than a suspect. The fourth *I* is "I confess." Anyone who participates before, during, or after, the crime, and gives a statement about their involvement in the crime, is confessing.

The short version of what I was attempting to do, when work-ing a case, was use the four *I*s to uncover the three types of evidence (direct, physical, and circumstancial). Then I must tie the evidence together to make my case, and identify the suspect. Next I filed charges that will lead to the conviction and sentencing of the suspect. Only then did I feel I had been successful. Sometimes the district attorney did not let the case go to court, and plea-bargained with the defense attorney. The defense attorney was after a lesser sentence, thus leading to less time served on the case. After a conviction of the defen-dant, the judge could give a lesser sentence as well, including probation. I could not worry about those things happening; I had no control over what they did.

In the Gray and Red, White, and Blue cases, we had the evi-dence necessary to file our cases. We had direct evidence and physical evidence in both cases. A few loose ends had to be tied up, but the loose ends would be tied up sooner rather than later. We would be able to file charges within the forty-eight hours we had, to keep the arrestees in jail. We needed to file charges and have the suspects arraigned on charges in the fort-eight hours, or we had to let them go. We would be ready to file charges on Tuesday, and we had until Wednesday at 10:00 a.m. Weekends and holidays were considered dead time, and they did not count as part of the forty-eight hours.

In the Yellow case we had physical evidence, but no direct evi-dence or circumstantial evidence. We were looking for a park-ing ticket to identify the boyfriend's truck and the boyfriend. We had prints from the scene that we hoped would identify a suspect. We also had a missing TV to locate. The one thing we didn't have was the use of an informant. Informants were good for street crimes, but usually not good when it came to domestic-violence cases. Most of the time, domestic-violence cases were a family matter. This was true especially if there were no witnesses to talk about the crime. In our society, we love to talk. If only the suspect knows about the crime, and they don't talk about it, only they know. If they talk, then we have to find the person who they have talked to. So far, I did not know what the situation would be in the Yellow case. If it was a rip-off, the word might be on the street. It would be worth a try to put out my feelers, but I wanted a better direction before I did that. I would have to give this case a little time to develop.

The Black case looked to be the most difficult one to solve. This case would really need an informant. So far we had only the shell casings, but not the gun. Tracing the shell casings would be almost impossible, but we had to give it a try. If we recovered the bullets during the autopsy, we could determine what type of ammunition we were looking for. Then we would check all the local gun shops for sales of that type of ammunition. We really had to find a reason for the killing. Was the killing over narcotics, a robbery, personal, or a random killing? We needed to get right on it tonight. Random killings were the hardest to solve. Usually the victim was just at the wrong place at the wrong time. The gangs were good at committing random killings. They were called drive-by shootings, or "don't tread on my turf" shootings. Some of the gang killings were committed for initiation into the gang, or for status. I hoped this killing was not a random killing.

I left the house around six thirty that night. I picked up the boys and hugged them and told them I loved them. My wife asked me if I would be home that night, or was it going to be another all-nighter? I told her I did not know. I did not bring my work home with me, and I never discussed my cases with her. What do you say, "I just saw three kids with their brains blown out"? The good thing was that by working overtime, the money paid the bills. Homicide and narcotics were the only two jobs on the Los Angeles Police Department that I knew of, that you could work unlimited overtime. We did not have to get approval, most of the time, to work overtime. We got paid time and a half for it too. Sometimes I made more money in overtime than I got paid for in regular time. But I knew that no matter how much I worked, I would never get rich working for the Los Angeles Police Department. I did like money, but not well enough to give up my job, even though it would have probably made my marriage better if I did.

I met Rex at the station around seven o'clock. He had been at the station for about an hour before I got there. Rex had contacted the coroner's office, and found out that Coal Black was positively identified through his fingerprints. We decided to go to his house first and make the notification of his death. We would then go back to the scene and look for witnesses. I also wanted to look for Johnny, my informant. If anyone in Watts knew anything, it would be him.

Before we left the station, we checked on the status of our prints on the Yellow case. We found that the fingerprint division had not run the prints for a match yet. They had to do a hand search,(to go through the finger print cards ,on file, one by one, by hand. and at the earliest, it would be done tomorrow. We found out the same thing on our traffic ticket. Were we the only ones to work on the weekend? Our autopsies were still on for the coming morning at nine o'clock. The other two autopsies, Yellow and Black, looked like they would be on Tuesday. No one was in firearms, so we had to just hang onto the shell casings from the Black case. We notified the watch commander that we would be on the air if we were needed, and left the station.

Rex and I got into our car, and, as we did, Rex turned to me and made the following comment. "Do you think you will be able to get Johnny on this Black case? He does hang out at the liquor store, sometimes, doesn't he?"

"Tell you what—you drive, and I will think about it. Let's go make the notification first, and see what we can find out there. Maybe his family has heard something. I will bet they already know about his being killed. It has already been over nineteen hours since it happened. News travels faster than that around here. The grapevine is full of grapes out here, and I am sure they have been squeezed for information. We just have to find the right grape. Johnny will probably be one of those grapes to squeeze, but let's see if we can find another one to squeeze first."

I got to thinking about Johnny. I called him Johnny-come-lately, because he was everywhere in Watts, but nowhere, if you know what I mean. Sometimes he was hard to find, and sometimes I had to just wait until he got a hold of me. I had known him almost ten years now. He was in his late thirties, and was a little guy, about five feet five inches and 140 pounds. I met him in 1962, when I was working the felony car. Remember the plain car? I picked him up in an alley, and thought he was a burglar. It turned out he was a hype, and just hurting at the time. I took a liking to him and fed him and gave him some money to fix his problem. After that we hit it off. I met his wife and kids later. Through the years I helped him out as best I could. Some of the money I gave him was mine, and some of it I got back by "chitting" it to cases I made with the information he gave me. When I had a case I solved with his information, the city would pay me back for what I spent in order to solve the case. If I did not have a case at the time, I ate it. I figured, over the years, I came out ahead. Johnny was one of the best sources I had. He just could not give up the dope. I could relate to that in that I could not give up cigarettes. I had been smoking since I was thirteen years old, and started smoking with a corncob pipe and corn silk.

The thing about informants was that they were like wives; you didn't share them with anyone, even your partner. You also did not burn them. If you could make your case on their information, without using or revealing them, OK. But if you couldn't make your case without them, you did not force them into court and lay them out. You just had to dig harder on the case, and if you couldn't make the case, you let it go. This did not happen to me often, but it did happen. I had informants of all types. Remember, anyone who gives you information is an informant. I had informants all over Watts, and I would get information for other investigators, even sheriffs, but I never gave up my sources. Does that remind you of the news media? Rex knew Johnny, but just by seeing me with him. He was along with me when we went by Johnny's house, sometimes, and was with me when I took Johnny to lunch. But Rex had never talked to Johnny directly, and I respected Rex for that.

Rex was driving us toward the Imperial Courts housing projects, but he was driving pretty slowly. He always drove slowly when there was something on his mind. I guess he could think better that way. Knowing Rex like I did, I knew he was waiting on me to ask him what was on his mind. I gave him a few more blocks to put it together, and then I asked him, "What's on your mind, Rex?"

"I hate to make these notifications; you never know how a person is going to take it. I like it better when the coroner has to make the notification. Sometimes I think about what my wife would do if some cop came to my house to notify her I wasn't coming home. You know, we have made more notifications than our share, but it never is easy. Here it is Sunday night, approaching eight o'clock, and we could be going to the ball game at the Dodger Stadium."

"If it helps you, I think this is going to be an easy notification. My gut feeling tells me she already knows that Coal Black has passed on. If we were going someplace other than Nickerson Gardens, I would leave you in the car while I made the notification. But there is no way I'm going to leave you in the car; you're going to come with me. You'd be about as safe in the car as if you were tied to some railroad tracks, with a train coming."

"Like I would stay in the car! If I did, you would not have anyone to protect your backside. And if anybody needs their backside protected, it is you. You can get into the god-damnedest situations I have ever seen. You don't know when you're well off. Having a partner like me probably keeps you around longer then you were meant to be around. You walk around in these projects like you own them. About half of the time I have to run to keep up with you. You know, it makes no difference if everybody knows you out here in Watts; someday the wrong person is gonna step in your path. I keep telling you that, but I know it don't do any good."

"Well, here we are again in the beautiful Imperial Courts, the home of the rich and famous, due to profits from dope, welfare, and prostitution. If we could get rid of that stuff, the good people that live here could call this home. Now it is called the ghetto. The way I go through these projects, they think I'm either big and bad or crazy. One thing they don't like, and are afraid of, is a crazy person. I got them fooled because I am not big and bad so I have to be crazy, and a crazy person might shoot them. Anyway, we are here, and that's the unit we are looking for. Not too much going on down here tonight, quiet as a graveyard. There is a little humor for you, to cheer you up, partner."

"I do not know who is crazier, you or me. I am working with you, so I have to be."

"Come on, partner, let's get it done." After saying that, I got out of the car and waited for Rex to get out. Rex got out, and we walked up to the front door of Coal Black's unit. The units in the housing project always reminded me of long apartment buildings, similar to the apartments I used to manage in San Pedro. I knocked on the door, and in a few minutes the door was opened by a heavyset woman. We identified ourselves as police officers. I told her I was Detective Reynolds, and I introduced Rex. I asked if we could come in. She motioned us into the house and walked away from the door. She walked into the kitchen, where there were three children sitting at the kitchen table. She then told the children to go upstairs, that she had business to take care of. The children gave us the once-over and ran out of the kitchen. She then pointed to the table, and we all three sat down at the table. From what I could see of the house, it was very neat and clean. The kitchen smelled of ham hocks and beans, and reminded me I was hungry. This was a comfortable home. She was a good woman.

"If this is about Coal, I know he's dead. I always told him that the streets were going to catch up with him, and damn if I wasn't right. The only good he ever did for me was to father the three kids."

I waited a few minutes, and then I said, "When did you find out, and who notified you?"

"It was about five o'clock this morning when I found out. Everyone in the projects knew. They were beating down my door, to tell me. They woke me up, and the kids too. When I opened the door, they were all out there, trying to be the first to tell me. They were all those kids that run loose in the projects. I don't know them; I stayed in the house. I don't want my kids to be out there, running with them. They all just said that Coal was dead, and that he'd been shot. I don't know what happened, and I don't know who did it. You need to talk to those dope friends of his. I kept telling Coal that we should have stayed in Arkansas. If we had just went back home, this would not have happened. If he had not got hooked on dope, out here, we could have had a good life. It is just not fair! Me and the kids try to do it right, and see where that got us. What do I tell them now?"

"I am really sorry for your loss. I am going to give you a card with my name and phone number on it. On the back of the card is the coroner's phone number. You will need to call the coroner to make arrangements for Coal. You can call me anytime, and I will do whatever I can to help you. My home phone number is on the card too, so you can call me there as well. Now I have to ask you—was Coal dealing drugs?"

"Lord have mercy! Yes, he was, up there at the liquor store. He dealt what he couldn't use. He kept saying he was going to get out of it, but he never did. He was a good man, in that he never took my welfare money. He took care of his habit himself. He just could not get that monkey off of his back. I don't know who he works for, but someone gave him the drugs to sell. He told me about what he did, sometimes, but never who he was working for, or with. He always told me I was better off not to know."

I felt bad for her, but did not know what I could say to help her. She was going to have a hard time raising those three kids. Maybe later, I could get the welfare social worker to move her out of Imperial Courts. Imperial Courts would soon eat those children up, and they would become part of the landscape, sooner or later. Rex and I then left the unit and walked out to our car. There was an eerie silence in the projects as we got to our car. The word was out, that the heat was in the projects. I wondered how many sets of eyes were watching us at that moment. At least we did not have high-rise buildings like they did in New York or Chicago. I had been in them, on extraditions and investigations, in the past, and I wanted no part of them. I would take the projects in LA over high-rises anytime. The only thing good about high-rises is the workout you get climbing the steps.

After Rex and I got into our car and were driving out of the projects, my stomach started talking to me. "Let's go over to Stops Bar-B-Q and get some ribs. It's only a couple blocks away," I said to Rex.

"Did the smell of those ham hocks and beans make you want some soul food?" Rex said.

"You know, we can't do good work on empty stomachs. I want to talk to Irving and Simon for a minute. Besides having the best food in town, sometimes they have the best information.

I don't know if they will be on top of this case, but it is worth a try."

Stops Bar-B-Q was a take-out, eat-inside restaurant, located at Imperial Highway and Central Avenue. It was circular and had a horseshoe parking lot around it. The rear of the restaurant was fenced off and faced away from the streets. Everyone in the Imperial Courts ate at this restaurant, sooner or later. The restaurant was especially busy when the welfare checks came out. The cost of the food was reasonable, and the portions served were large. When you are on welfare, Mother's Day comes twice a month.

The restaurant was owned by two Jewish brothers, Irving and Simon. I had known them forever, and knew that they had both been in the concentration camps during World War II. They both had their concentration camp numbers tattooed on their forearms. They never mentioned it to me, though, and I never asked them about the camps. I had been to Irving's home on several occasions and had had dinner with him and his wife. He would always give me a quart jar of his barbecue sauce to take home. I had tried many times to get his recipe, but he would not give it up. Most of the time I went to the restaurant; I would park inside the rear fence and go in by way of the back door. I would then eat in their office and out of sight of anyone in the restaurant. While I would eat, we would share information. We always looked out for each other, and knew that we were fast friends.

Rex and I were eating our barbecue and talking to Irving at the Stops Bar-B-Q. Irving had heard about the death of Coal Black, but he had heard nothing with respect to how he was killed, or who killed him. After talking about it, we all three came to the conclusion that he had been killed as a result of a robbery, or out of disrespect. Either way, it appeared that no one had the answer. Everyone was talking about the shooting, but no one was talking about who had done the shooting. We finished our meal, and thanked Irving for his hospitality. Irving assured us that if he heard anything, he would let us know.

We went back to the liquor store at 106th and Compton and found that the parking lot was empty. There were a few winos sitting in front of the store, drinking their short dogs of Thunderbird and Gallo wine. They did not even remember what day it was, let alone anything about the homicide. It was obvious that the heat was on. As far as the parking lot was concerned, no one was willing to hang out there. It would be quite some time before the parking lot became active again. The liquor-store clerk told us that he had heard nothing about the homicide, and he did not expect to. We checked all the houses in and around the neighborhood with the same results: nothing.

We spent the next hour or so looking for Johnny-come-lately. We checked all his spots, and could not find him. He had numerous spots, where he crashed, after he took a fix. The spots we checked were burned-out buildings, which were left over after the riots. There were also vacant houses that he crashed in, but he was not around.

At around eleven that night, our radio came to life: "Unit one-two-W-one-two, handle a homicide at six-one-three East Eighty-ninth Street, code two. There is a patrol unit and an ambulance at the scene."

It was our call, so I answered the call, and Rex drove us to the location. The location was a two-story duplex, and the scene was in the unit upstairs. We entered the unit and found the two patrol officers and the ambulance attendants inside. There were also a dozen teenagers in the unit. The unit was a two-bedroom unit, with a kitchen, front room, and bathroom. The teenagers were all sitting around in the front room and kitchen, with the officers watching over them. The ambulance crew directed us to the bathroom, where we found the deceased in the bathtub. The deceased was fully clothed and was a teenage female. She was lying on her back, and only her head was exposed. The rest of her body was underneath the water, which was a milky white in color. There were several empty milk cartons lying around on the floor of the bathroom. The ambulance crew informed us that they had pronounced her DOA upon their arrival, which was less than ten minutes ago. In their opinion, the girl had died of an overdose. One of the patrol officers entered the bathroom, and told us that one of the teenagers told them that the milk had been poured into the bathtub water.

There were six teenage girls and six teenage boys in the apartment. Rex and I interviewed them all separately, and put together the following story: The deceased was Denise Brown, fifteen years of age. They had all been partying, at the location, when Denise had fainted. They had put her in the bathtub and filled it with cold water, to revive her. They knew that she had taken some pills, and were afraid that she had overdosed. She had been arguing with her boyfriend and was upset. Her boyfriend had been showing an interest in one of the other girls. When the cold water did not revive her, they decided to try the milk. One of them had been told that milk would revive you, if you took too many pills. So they had went to the store and bought a bunch of milk and poured it into the bathtub. When she still did not come around, they called 911. After some pressure, they all admitted to dropping pills and smoking some marijuana. Several of the girls had pills in their possession: yellow jackets, bluebirds, and red birds. The pills consisted of amphetamines and barbiturates.

The coroner arrived, and after further examination of the body we observed no injuries to the deceased. We had drained the water out of the bathtub and removed the deceased. Several traces of the pill capsules were found in her mouth. There also was mucus coming out of her nose. It was the coroner's opinion that she had overdosed on the pills. That being the case, the question to be answered was whether it was an accidental overdose or a suicide. The coroner then removed the deceased to the his office. We had been told the deceased's residence address, and the coroner asked us to make notification, and have someone come to their office to identify the body.

Rex and I had photographed the scene, both prior to the deceased being removed from the bathtub, and after she was removed. Outside of the photos, there was no physical evidence and / or fingerprints to obtain at the scene. We had taken all the pills from the teenage girls and informed them that we would need to talk to them later. We also reminded them that it was a crime to be in possession of the pills. The mother of the girl who lived at the location had come home while the coroner was at the scene. We turned over custody of the young girls to the mother and asked her to make sure that they got home safely. We then told all the boys to leave the location and go home. All the boys were over the age of seventeen. Rex and I then left the location to go make the notification of the deceased death.

"The good news is this is not a homicide," Rex said as he was driving down the street. "It's going to be up to the coroner to decide if it is a suicide or an accident. If the cause of death turns out to be from the pills, it will be his problem to resolve, not ours."

"I have been thinking about that, and I have a suggestion. I can remember two teenaged girls that overdosed and were dumped in the streets. One happened when I was on loan to homicide from metro. We found her in the street, and the detectives that handled it just wrote it off to an overdose. The second one was found in an alley, and it was handled by one of our teams a little while ago. It was also written off as an overdose. As you know, they dump these bodies in the streets so that it will not bring heat back to the location the deceased overdosed at. So in the case of an overdose, there is no investigation, no arrests, and no justice. We found this girl in an apartment, and I am sure those other girls will be able to tell us who she bought the pills from. They probably bought their pills from the same person. If we can find that person, we can charge them with second-degree murder, for furnishing the pills that ultimately led to the girl's death. Who knows, we might be saving another teenaged girl's life by getting whoever it is off of the streets. What do you think, Rex; you think it is worth a try?"

"Why not, partner, it only means we will be working five cases out of this weekend, instead of four. What's another case mean at this point anyhow? I will make a deal with you; I will stay in the car this time while you make the notification. If you agree with me, I will work this overdose with you; refuse, and you are on your own."

We arrived at the deceased's home, and noted that it was in a residential area on the east side of the division. Her house was one of several that were located in a horseshoe-type court. The address indicated it would be one of the back houses. I got out of the car and headed toward the sidewalk that ran down between the houses. Rex also got out of the car and joined me. I knew he wasn't going to stay in the car. He had just been pulling my chain. I also knew that he was as interested in working this case as I was. As we were walking down the sidewalk, toward the back of the horseshoe, we heard loud music and loud voices coming from one of the back houses. It was now after three o'clock in the morning, but it was not unusual for a party to be going down. We soon noticed that the party was at the deceased's house. The front door was open, but a screen door was closed. As we approached the front screen door, it opened suddenly, and a middle-aged woman stepped out onto the porch and greeted us.

"This is about Denise. Isn't it? I am her aunt, and I just called to report her missing. They said I should come down to the station, but I guess they sent you instead. She should have been here hours ago."

"We work for the police department, as you have already guessed, and yes, this is about Denise. Is Denise's mother inside the house?" I spoke as casually as I could.

"Is Denise dead?"

"We think she is. We have a fifteen-year-old girl down at the coroner's office to be identified. We have come here to notify her mother that she needs to go to the coroner's office and see if the girl the coroner has is, in fact, Denise." Again I tried to be as casual as I could.

"I will notify Denise's mother for you. If you notify her, she will have a heart attack. She has high blood pressure and a bad heart, and this news would kill her. I will know how to approach her and tell her, so you give me your card and the coroner's phone number, and I will see that someone goes down there to identify Denise. If you tell her, you will damn sure have to bring an ambulance out here, and you are going to have two dead bodies."

After getting the aunt's identification and recording it, I gave her my card with the coroner's phone number on it. She assured me that the notification would be made, and that she would call me for information on Denise's death later in the morning. She would also let me know when the identification had been made, and when the mother was told about Denise's death. I had told the aunt that we expected the cause of death to be from an overdose of pills. I had also told the aunt that Denise had been found inside a house, where a party was going on. Rex and I walked away from the house, and were walking down the sidewalk toward our car when we heard the screen door slam, and then heard the following, hollered in a loud voice.

"Denise is dead! She is in the morgue, and we have to go down there and identify her!"

Rex and I looked at each other and looked back toward the house. All of a sudden, we heard screams coming from inside of the house. We ran to our car, got in, drove a block away, and parked on the opposite side of the street. We decided to wait to see if an ambulance was dispatched to the location. I used the time to think about the case. The scene that we had just been at was only going to give us a body and a cause of death. If the cause of death was due to an overdose of pills, the coroner's protocol would give us the pills as physical evidence. If we were to identify a suspect, we were going to need direct evidence, in the form of testimony, to convict. That meant that the teenaged girls had to testify, or a suspect had to confess. I was betting my nickel on the girls. Oh yeah, and an ambulance did arrive and take Denise's mother away from the home. We found out later that her mother was OK.

That morning I left my office around seven o'clock and went to attend the two autopsies we had scheduled at the coroner's office. The two autopsies were going to be on the Yellow case and the Gray case. I took the gun from the Gray case with me, in case I recovered a bullet to match to the gun, and in case I did, I would drop them off at firearms for ballistics. I took the steak knife along as well, to show the coroner on the Yellow case. Rex stayed at the station to put the five cases' murder books together, and to brief the captain on the five cases. A murder book is a three ring binder that contains every thing on a case. The binder is used to either file a case or work a case. It is given to the district attorney to use at the time he files a case. He will tell the investigator what he wants out of the murder book, to file a case, and the investigator will give him copies of what it is he wants. The murder books on the Gray and the Red, White, and Blue cases had to be taken to the district attorney to file the cases with. The other three murder books were going to be left to work on.

I returned to the station around noon and briefed Rex on the two autopsies. On the Gray case, the cause of death was ruled as a result of a gunshot wound to the head. A bullet had been recovered, and I had taken it, along with the gun, to firearms. They stated that, in all probability, they would get a match. I also took a blood sample of the victim's blood to the Scientific Investigation Division (SID) to be compared to the blood samples we removed from the scene. At that time Rex told me that he had completed the murder book on the Gray case, and that the case was ready to file. Rex filed the case later on that day. One count of murder was filed against the suspect, Mary Smith. Later on, the case was plea-bargained, and Mary Smith pleaded guilty to manslaughter and was sentenced to two years in a women's prison. Two years to the day, after Mary Smith was sentenced, she walked into the station and asked to see me. She looked very tired and drawn, and told me that she had just gotten out of prison that day. She laid a pack of Pall Mall cigarettes on the counter and told me they were mine. She stated that she had promised herself for two years that the first thing she would do upon her release was give me a pack of cigarettes. She said that the night that I had interviewed her, she had smoked all my cigarettes, and would not have gotten through the interview without them. Without the cigarettes, she would have had a nervous breakdown. That being said, she turned and walked out of the office, and I never saw her again.

On the Yellow case, the cause of death was ruled as a knife wound, administered to the neck, which cut the carotid artery. The coroner had stated that the steak knife I showed him, in all probability, caused the wound, or at least one like it. He had further stated that there were fresh abrasions on the victim's arms and hips. These abrasions were consistent with a physical struggle with the assailant. The victim had not been raped, nor were there any other cuts and/or lacerations on the victim's person. Rex told me that he had checked with fingerprints while I was gone, and that presently there was no make on any of our prints from the scene. Rex said that SID had typed the blood, and the blood on the bed and floor and walls was our victim's. The blood on the sink, the bloody fingerprints, blood on the victim, bloody footprints, and some blood on the bed was of a different type, and we could assume that it was the suspect's blood. The information on the parking ticket had not come back yet.

Rex told me that we were ready to file on the Red, White, and Blue case, pending the autopsies. He had completed one murder book for the three victims and had compiled all the reports and information into that one book. He had also included the ex-boyfriends and his new girlfriend's reports as well. Rex suggested that when we filed the cases, we tell the district attorney about the pending case, with respect to Sissy's neighbor, and ask him to consolidate all of the cases into one trial.

Rex had also made an undetermined death report on the Denise Brown case and had started the murder book on that case as well. The coroner had notified him that the autopsy would be scheduled for Wednesday. Denise's aunt had called and told him that she had made the identification of Denise, and that the mother was home recovering from her purported heart attack. The aunt had been told that we would be getting back with her later.

It was Tuesday afternoon, and Rex and I were back at the station. Rex had been to the coroner's office, and had attended the two autopsies that we had had scheduled that morning. In the Red, White, and Blue autopsies, three bullets were recovered, one from each victim. They appeared to be consistent with the gun that we had. The cause of death in all three of the autopsies was ruled as a gunshot wound to the head. Three bullets were also recovered in the Black case. The cause of death in the Black case was gunshot wounds to the chest, one penetrating the heart. Rex had taken all the bullets; the gun from the Red,

White, and Blue case; and the shell casings from the Black case to firearms. Firearms had compared the bullets while Rex was there and stated that the bullets in the Red, White, and Blue case had been fired by the gun that Rex had provided, and the bullets in the Black case were consistent with being fired from the shell casings that had been submitted. The bullets and the shell casings in the Black case were .38 calibers.

I had gone to the district attorney's office and had filed charges on the Sissy Sanders case. The district attorney agreed to consolidate all cases she was being charged with into one trial. Later on that year, Sissy Sanders had her trial. She had asked for a jury trial, and was found guilty of the murders she had committed, by reason of insanity. She was sent to a mental hospital, and was to remain there until she was proven to be sane. Two years later, I read an article in the paper where she had tried to hang herself at the mental hospital. She had been transferred to a women's prison because she was a security risk at the mental hospital. I went to the mental hospital to find out what had happened, and was told that she had been told that she was not going to be released. It was felt by the staff that she was still mentally incompetent. She then attempted to hang herself with her belt. It was felt that the attempt was not a serious attempt, but she was transferred for security reasons. The staff felt that she felt she should have been released in two years, and it had been two years, to the day, when they told her she would never be released. Three years later I had a visitor from UCLA. who was working on her thesis, who wanted to know if I could get her a visit with Sissy Sanders. The student's thesis was on the criminal mind of a woman who kills her kids. I contacted a captain I knew at the prison to set up the interview, and he told me that it could not be done. When I asked him why, he said because Sissy was not there, that she had escaped. I asked him how she had escaped, and he told me. She had convinced the warden she had the civil right to attend the Watts festival, which is held every year, at Will Rogers Park. The warden let her go to the park with a female officer and a state car. The female officer came back, but Sissy and the state car didn't come back. The captain felt that there was a lesbian relationship between Sissy and the female officer, maybe even the warden. The bottom line was that Sissy was gone. When I asked him how long she had been gone, he said over a year. I asked him why they had not contacted me, I had all the background on Sissy, and all the addresses of her past residences. My captain friend answered only, "Why do you think?" Why do I think? I think the escape was covered up…"

We were in the station, and it was Tuesday afternoon. We had put the murder books up on the Gray and the Red, White, and Blue cases. We told the captain the two cases were cleared cases, and we were pondering what to do when I got a call from the traffic citation records unit. They informed me that they had found our parking ticket on the Yellow case. The license plate of the truck had been run for wants and warrants, and it was found that the registered owner of the truck was a Buddy Lilly. Neither the truck nor Buddy Lilly had any warrants out on them. Buddy Lilly was also the legal owner of the truck. I asked them to mail me a copy of the parking ticket, and I thanked them very much for their work. Rex and I then went to downtown records and pulled the jacket (criminal record file) on a Buddy Lilly. We were able to determine, through the contents of the jacket, that this was the right Buddy Lilly. He had a record for gambling and several simple assaults against his wife. He did not have any felony arrests. We took a copy of his prints, a booking photograph, and his personal information, including his residence address, out of the jacket. He was thirty-six years old, six foot two, and 230 pounds. We took his prints over to the fingerprint section, which was in the same building we were in. We asked them to compare his prints with the prints lifted at the scene of the Yellow homicide. They made Buddy Lilly's prints on the coffee table, bathroom sink, and beer cans. We had just placed him inside our homicide scene. Better yet, we had placed him there when the homicide had occurred. His prints were on the bathroom sink, in the victim's blood.

We went back to the station and made up a photo lineup, which is a card with five photographs and the suspect's photograph on it. All of the photographs are similar in appearance. We drove by the suspect's residence and saw that his truck was there. I took a picture of the truck, and we left. We were sure that we were not seen at the suspect's house. We then went back to the station and located similar photos of trucks, and made up a photo lineup card on the truck. We took the cards out to the witnesses at the Yellow homicide scene. We showed the cards to all the witnesses, and they picked the suspect out as the one who was the victim's boyfriend. They picked his truck out as the one that they had seen parked at the victim's house on many occasions, including the night of the homicide. We now had the suspect, and his truck, at the homicide scene at the time of the homicide. We knew, from the suspect's jacket, that he worked for the garbage company. The address of where he worked was in his jacket. We wanted to search his truck at the time we arrested him, so we did not want to go to his house to arrest him. Without a warrant, it is a lot easier to search a vehicle than it is to search a house. Because of the mobility of a vehicle, the courts are more flexible with a search of a vehicle. We were looking for the victim's TV, and felt it would be in his truck, as opposed to in his house. We decided that we would go by his house tomorrow, in the afternoon, while he was working. That way we could talk to his wife, without him there, and maybe she would tell us something useful. We would then go stake out his truck, at his work site, and try and pick him up, rolling in the truck after work. Besides, we had an autopsy to attend in the morning on the Brown case. We would take a night off tonight; we had no idea when the next night off would be.

It was around ten o'clock in the morning, and Rex and I had just gotten back to the station after attending Denise Brown's autopsy. The cause of death had been ruled an overdose of amphetamines and barbiturates. The coroner asked us to interview the persons at the party again, in an attempt to show whether the victim intended to kill herself, or had just taken too many pills accidentally. The classification of death was going to be left open. A coroner's inquest might become necessary in order to classify the death as either a suicide or accident. We had informed the coroner that we were going to make an attempt to show the death as a homicide. If we could show the death was caused by the hands of another person, we could show the death was a homicide—the rationale being that the person who furnished the pills did in fact cause the victim's death.

Rex and I had been analyzing our three cases to decide how we were going to proceed. On the way back to the station, we had driven by Buddy Lilly's place of employment, and noted that his truck was in the parking lot. "Rex, I need to go by

Johnny's house and talk to his wife. It is unusual that he has not surfaced by now."

"We need to get those girls into the station as well. We need to find out who that pill pusher is who sold them the pills, and what's with Denise. Did she commit suicide, or was it an accident? The girls should be able to shed some light on that question. I can do that while you are looking for Johnny."

"After I check Johnny out, I can go by Buddy Lilly's house and talk to his wife. When I get through talking to her, I'll come back and help you with the girls. Once we get the girls' story down, we can go stake out Buddy Lilly's truck and go from there."

I left the station to drive to Johnny's house, and Rex started to work on getting the girls into the station. As I was driving, I was thinking of what would be the best approach to use with Mrs. Lily. I would probably tell her that I was following up on a complaint by the neighbors. The complaint was that her husband was abusing her again. Then I could lead into asking if her husband was seeing anyone else. I could ask her if she knows of another woman. That way I could find out if there was another woman in the picture, thus leading me back to the victim, Ms. Yellow.

I got to Johnny's house and I talked to his wife about where he was. She told me that she had not seen Johnny since early Saturday morning. She was not overly worried about him because he had stayed away longer than four days before. I told her that I really needed to talk to Johnny, and for her to have him give me a call, day or night. I then asked her if she needed anything, and she told me she was OK. After talking to the kids a while, I left Johnny's house and went looking for him. I spent the next three hours trying to find Johnny. I revisited all the spots I knew where he could be. I looked high and low for him, in the places he hid, out of sight, and the places he hung out, out in the open. I had one more place to go in my search for Johnny, but I was getting worried. Had Johnny overdosed? Had he left Watts, for some reason? Was he avoiding me, or avoiding someone else? These were all unanswered questions, and I intended to answer them, for the sake of his family as well as for my own sake.

The last place I had to look for Johnny was at Bob's liquor store. I had an informant there who knew Johnny as well as I did. The informant's street name was Popsicle, and he got around Watts almost as much as Johnny did. He did not use hard narcotics, but he was addicted to dangerous drugs. He always had a handful of pills in his pocket. It was a shame, because he was a suburb athlete. When he was not at the liquor store, he was at Will Rogers Park, playing basketball. His mother, Mrs. Williams, was always after me to talk him into giving up those damn pills. I found Popsicle at the liquor store, and while we were talking, he pulled a handful of pills out of his pocket. Every time I got together with him he did this. He even did it once in the presence of uniform officers who were with us at the time. I think he liked to show that he could commit a crime in front of me and get away with it. He knew I would not bust him for possession of dangerous drugs. We owe each other too much to make it be a big deal. I always ignored what it was that he did and gave him the benefit of the doubt. Popsicle told me that he had not seen Johnny since the past Saturday, when he had seen him at the liquor store. I asked Popsicle if he knew any pill pushers up around Fremont High School, and he told me he did not, only at Jordan High School. I then told Popsicle to take care, and get in touch with me if he saw Johnny. I then left Bob's liquor store and headed for Buddy Lilly's house.

As I got out of my car at Buddy Lilly's house, I noted that it was a well-kept piece of property. It was in a residential area, and had houses on both sides. I felt that my game plan of telling her I was answering a complaint by the neighbors would work. I knocked on the door, and a rather good-looking woman answered. I identified myself and asked her if she was Mrs. Lilly, and she stated that she was not, she was Ms. Rose. I then asked her if she was the common-law wife of Buddy Lilly and she answered that she was. (A lot of couples did not get married and lived in a common-law relationship. If they split up, the man would just walk out, and the woman would keep the kids and go on welfare. It was easier that way, and did not take an attorney and a bunch of money to split the sheets.) I asked her if I could come in the house, and she stepped back from the door and waved me inside. I entered the front room and observed three young children watching a TV in the front room. The TV was sitting on top of a dresser, and the TV was the victim's, Ms. Yellow's, TV. My game plan had just changed, and I was going to have to set a new course of action.

"I am here about that TV you have sitting there. Could you tell me when it was that you got the TV?"

"Buddy brought that TV home a few days ago. He told me that someone had thrown it out in the trash, and that he had picked it up and brought it home. He told me he wanted to give it to the kids to watch. As far as I know, the TV came from his work. He picks up stuff all the time, from other people's trash, and brings it home. Is he in trouble, or something?"

"No, but I will have to take the TV with me. You see, some woman and her husband were arguing over this TV. She wanted to keep the TV, and he threw it in the trash. When she found out the TV was gone, she called the trash company to try and recover it. They told her that they did not have it, and the driver might have kept it. That's how I learned Buddy had the TV. All you will have to do is give Buddy my card when he gets home, and tell him I have the TV, and that he is not in any kind of trouble. Can you call him at work and tell him?"

"No, they don't allow him to receive calls at work. I will have to wait until he gets home, to tell him. He gets off work at four this afternoon."

I then picked up the TV and left the house. It was good news to know that she could not call him. We would be able to pick him up after work, and he would not know that we were coming. He would also not know that we had the TV. I put the TV in the trunk of my car, and I drove by Buddy's work site again. I went to see where would be the best place to take Buddy into custody. His truck was still parked in the parking lot, and I felt that we could take him into custody as he left work and started to get into his truck. We did not have to worry about searching his truck now; I had the TV. We would not even need to impound his truck. We could leave it where it was. Sometimes the Lord does good things.

I met Rex back at the station, and we compared notes. He had finished interviewing all the girls, and had even interviewed several of the boys who had been at the party, including the victim's boyfriend. He had found out that two of the girls who had had pills at the party had been with the victim when they all bought pills from the suspect. They had bought the pills on the Saturday before the party. They were sure that the pills the victim had taken were the same pills that she had gotten from the suspect on Saturday. None of them had any pills, and that's why they bought the pills on Saturday. The girls, and the victim's boyfriend, said that the fight between the victim and her boyfriend was not serious. The victim had taken the pills to feel good, not to commit suicide. Rex had written up all their statements, and had contacted the coroner and informed him of the results. The coroner was going to classify the victim's death as an accidental overdose. This was good for us, in that the victim had not caused her own death by committing suicide.

Rex also told me that he had identified our suspect. The two girls who had bought the pills from the suspect, with the victim, had told Rex that they knew the suspect by his street name of Big Daddy. Rex had found several Big Daddies in the mug books, and had shown the mug books to the girls. They had identified the Big Daddy they knew and picked him out of the mug books. The suspect's name is Clarence Colder, and he was thirty-two years old. Rex had run the suspect's record and found out that he had several arrests for possession of dangerous drugs and possession with intent to sell. He was currently on the street, and Rex had an address for him. In conclusion, Rex told me that we had a case on Clarence Colder. We had two girls to testify to the victim's buying her pills from the suspect, and their statements would connect the suspect, through the pills, to the victim. We also had several witnesses who would testify to seeing the victim ingest the pills.

We left the station and headed out to take care of Buddy Lilly. On the way, I briefed Rex about what I had done. I told him that the TV was in the trunk of our car. We drove to the parking lot that Buddy Lilly's truck was in, and we staked out the truck. We had to wait about a half hour until Buddy came out from work.When he came out into the parking lot, we recognized him from the photographs that we had obtained from his jacket. When he got to his truck and was about to get in the driver's door, Rex and I came up behind him and placed him under arrest. He did not offer any resistance. I informed him that we were placing Δhim under arrest for the murder of Ms. Yellow. We placed him into our police vehicle and drove him to the station. When we got to the station, we placed Buddy in a holding tank. I went out to our car and got the TV out of the trunk. I brought the TV into the station and placed it on a desk in the detective division. I placed it in such a way that Buddy would see it when I brought him back to an interview room. I then got Buddy out of the holding tank and brought him back to the detective room, past the TV, and to an interview room.

Rex set up our tape and then joined Buddy and me in the interview room. I had gotten us all coffee, and we were taking a minute to size each other up. Rex gave me the nod, which I knew meant that he wanted me to take over the interview. Buddy was drinking his coffee and looking at the table. He would not make eye contact with either me or Rex. He looked like a scared, defeated man, but not a man that was going to give in easily. I knew that seeing the TV had an effect on him. I decided that taking an aggressive approach would be the best tactic to use on him, so I started the conversation.

"Before I give you your rights, Buddy, I want to tell you a few things. I do not need you to make a statement to make my case. Anything you tell me will only be frosting on my cake. As you saw, I have the TV that you took out of Ms. Yellow's house. You know I have been to your house, or I would not have the TV. I want you to know that I have told your wife nothing about this case. But you know how women are; they always jump to conclusions. They always get in our faces and do us wrong. That is probably what happened at Ms. Yellow's house; she got in your face. Now, just to let you know, we got your prints, in blood, in the bathroom at her house. We also have your blood on the bed, in the bedroom, at her house. We also will have your bloody footprints, after we print your feet, in the bathroom, at her house. We can put you in her house at the time she was killed. We also have people who saw your truck at her house at the time she was killed."

"So, as you can see, I have an uptight and out-of-sight case. But everyone has a reason for doing what they do. Now you can save that, and tell it to a defense attorney instead of me. But, you will have to wait until you go to trial for him to use it in your favor. If you tell me now, I can tell the district attorney what your story is, and if it is self-defense, we might not even go to trial. You might go home in a couple of days, and not have to bear the expense and embarrassment of a trial. Right now, I am calling the shots. I am the one who will be meeting with the DA to discuss what charges are to be filed. I can either take him a story from you, right now, or I can just go with what I got. Also, I want you to know that I can either go to a female district attorney or a male district attorney. I can get your case heard in front of a female judge or a male judge. If I choose a female DA and a female judge, you know what they will do. They are going to bury you in this case. Females stick together, and always try to put us males down."

"Those rights you have, say that anything you say can and will be used against you in a court of law. They also say that anything you say can and will be used 'for you' in a court of law. Now, if you want to tell me your side of the story, here and now, I will tell the DA what it is you have to say about this case. Otherwise, I'm going to hook-can-book you, and I'll see you in court."

Buddy looked up from the table, and looked me straight in the eye and said, "I want to tell you my side of the story."

"Are you going to give up your rights, and talk to me, without an attorney here?"

"Yes, I am, I don't need an attorney now, and I want to tell you what really happened."

That being said, I advised Buddy of his constitutional rights, under Miranda, and got a waiver from him. I told him that it was his dime, and to just run the story by me, from top to bottom. Buddy stood up and rolled up the right sleeve of his shirt to show me a laceration on his bicep. The laceration was a little larger than a scratch, and it ran horizontal across his arm.

"It was self-defense, and this is where she cut me. I went over there to her house, that night, to tell her I was not going to see her anymore, and that I was not going to leave my wife. We were sitting on the couch, drinking beer, when I told her. She wouldn't believe me, and told me to come in her bedroom with her, and see what I would be missing. I told her no, but she insisted, and I gave in and went into the bedroom with her. We undressed and got into the bed and had sex. Afterwards she asked me if I still was going to leave her, and I told her yes, that this was the last time we were to have sex together. She became enraged and began calling me all kinds of names, and then out of nowhere, she came up with that knife. The one, I guess, you found on the floor in the bedroom. We began fighting over the knife, and I got cut on the arm, where I showed you. We then fell out of the bed, and somehow she got cut on the throat. The next thing I knew, I was laying on top of her and she was bleeding real good! In a few minutes she showed no signs of life, and I knew she was dead."

"Did she get out of bed and go to the kitchen and get the knife?"

"No, she did not get out of the bed. It must've been in the bed somewhere, I guess between the mattress, or somewhere."

"When you'd got the knife from her, did you cut her while you were on the bed with her, or after you fell to the floor?"

"I remember getting the knife from her, but I don't know when she got cut. It could have been on the bed, but I don't remember. I remember us falling to the floor, and that's when she might have got cut. All I know is that afterwards, I dropped the knife on the floor."

"What did you do after you cut her?"

"I went into the bathroom and cleaned up, and then I went back into the bedroom and dressed, and then I left the house."

"What about the TV?"

"Oh, yeah, I took the TV on the way out of the house. I don't know why I took the TV; I guess I was just thinking of giving it to my kids. Our other TV had broken down, so I just thought the kids would have a TV to watch. I knew I could tell them that I got it from my trash route."

The next day I filed a murder complaint on Buddy, and later that year he had a court trial. He was found guilty of second-degree murder. The judge sentenced him to ten years. I guess the court didn't believe his story, entirely. The judge felt that after he had been cut, and having gotten the knife, he could've left the house with no harm, no foul. Sometimes justice prevails, and the guilty are found guilty. Oh yeah, the district attorney was a male, and the judge was a male.

That afternoon Rex and I decided to take a drive by Big Daddy's house. When we drove by the location, we noted that his house was behind another house. His house was actually the garage of the house to the front. There was a driveway leading past the front house back to the rear garage. A fence came off the corner of the garage and wrapped a side yard to the house. The double garage door faced towards the street, and appeared to be framed off so that it would not open. The only entrance into the garage was a regular-sized door on the driveway side of the garage. We could not see any windows in the garage. We parked down the street, a couple houses away, and sat and watched the location. We watched the location for approximately a half hour, and no one came or went while we were watching.

"It looks like the only way into that garage this up the driveway. He could be in there, and then again he could not. I could go back there, and you could go to the front house. That way we will have both places covered. We can keep an eye on each other from the driveway. If he is there, we'll take him down; if he is not, we can stick it out for awhile longer. What do you think, Rex?"

"Sounds like a plan to me. If he is not here, we could cruise by Fremont High School and see if we could spot him. Let's just see if he is here, and if he is not, we will decide then what we want to do. The girls gave me several locations that he hangs out at, when he deals his pills. School has been out for about an hour, and I imagine if he is not here he is over there. The girls also told me that they had never seen him in a car, when

314

I asked about a car. They told me he is always walking on foot, and this place where he lives is only a few blocks from the school. He probably just walks back and forth between his house and the school. One thing for sure, there's not a car in that garage. As big as he is, I don't see how he gets through that door in the garage. I'm ready if you are."

Rex and I got out of our car and walked up to the driveway. As we walked into the driveway, Rex walked up to the door of the front house, and I walked back toward the door of the garage. As I approached the garage door, I saw that a woman had answered the door where Rex was. I noticed that the garage door was ajar. I approached the door and hollered, "Is anyone in here?" I did not get an answer, so I pushed the door open and entered the garage. The only light inside the garage was coming from the open door I walked through.

As my eyes adjusted to the darkness of the inside of the garage, I was able to see that there was no one inside. The inside of the garage was just one large room. There was a large bed, and a sitting area with a chair and couch and a TV. There was a small kitchenette with a small kitchen table and chairs. In one corner there was a toilet, shower, and sink, which were surrounded by a curtain that was pulled open. In the far corner there were two dressers against the wall. There were also several dressers against the near wall, around the area where the bed was. After my eyes took all this in, I walked over to the far corner where the two dressers were. There was a multitude of pill prescription bottles on top of the two dressers. Several of the dresser drawers were open a few inches, and I could see that the drawers were full of pill prescription bottles. Each dresser had five drawers, which would total ten drawers full of pill prescription bottles. All of the pill bottles on top of the dresser showed that the same doctor had issued the prescriptions for the pills. I was able to determine that there were at least ten to twelve different women named on the prescription labels. I started to read some of the dates on the prescription labels when, all of a sudden, the lights went out. The inside of the garage had suddenly gone dark. I looked towards the door of the garage and saw that a person had filled the doorway—and I mean *filled* the doorway. Big Daddy was in the doorway, and I had nowhere to go. As I was drawing my weapon, I heard Rex holler, from outside the garage: "Get your hands where I can see them and back out of the doorway. This is the police, and we're here to talk to you; now, back up!"

Big Daddy backed out of the doorway, and I ran out of the garage. When I got outside I told Big Daddy to get up against the fence, and to face the fence. Both Rex and I had our weapons drawn and were making sure that we would be in no danger. This was a big man. He could have played football for the L. Rams. He faced the fence, and I came up behind him and spread his feet and his hands out on the fence, while Rex covered him. I patted him down and asked him to give me an arm, behind him. He gave me his arm, and I tried to put a cuff on his wrist. The cuff just fit, and I could click it shut one click. I took his other arm and tried to get it behind his back. I could not bring his wrists together, behind his back. (The proper way to cuff people, for safety, is behind their backs.) I gave up and told him to turn around, and I cuffed him in the front of his body. We walked him down the street to our car. We had to slide the front seat forward, all the way, to get him into the back seat.

After we put him in the car, Rex and I looked at each other and shook our heads and sighed. We both knew we would have had a hard time taking him into custody if he had resisted us.

"Where did he come from?" I asked Rex.

"I was coming back there, and I saw him come out of a gate in the fence. He went right to the door of the garage before I could get there. That damn woman tied me up with her fifty questions. That's when I hollered at him. I knew you had to be in the garage. You know they say, the bigger they are, the harder they fall. I wouldn't want to try it with him. I am sure glad we didn't piss him off; we would have had to shoot him fifty times to drop him."

We then pulled our police car up into the driveway that we had just come out of. Rex then went up to tell the woman what we were doing. I pulled out a cigarette, lit it, and sat on the hood of our car. The woman had come out of her house, and was talking to Rex, when I asked her if she had any coffee. She told me she did, and that she would get us some. After she brought us our coffee, she went back into her house. Big Daddy was slumped over in the back of the car and appeared to be nodding off. Rex and I finished our coffee, and I finished my smoke.

"Rex, I have thought up a game plan as to what I think we should do now. Let me run it by you, and you decide what you think about it. When I was inside of the garage, I found hundreds of pill prescription bottles in there. Some of them were in plain sight, and the rest were inside of dresser drawers. They all were written by the same doctor. I saw at least twelve different named women on the bottles. I think Big Daddy is getting his pills from women who are getting the pills from that doctor.

We could work it and maybe get the doctor and the women on distribution of illegal pills. We could really nail the doctor and take a big distributor off the streets. Who knows how far we could go with this case? If we could get Big Daddy to work with us, we probably could make a lot of cases out of it. Or we could notify the district attorney and let him have the case and work it with the attorney general's office. Either way, I don't think we should talk to Big Daddy. We got our case on him for the death of Denise, I am sure of that. I think we should go to the DA and get a search warrant for the garage and bring a DA down here and give the case to them. I have gotten all the mileage out of this case I set out to get, so what do you think, bag it here or go for the doctor?"

"It's really your call, Reynolds, you started this, and I just came along for the ride. We work murders though, not dirty doctors. We got another case to work, and we got our old cases. We only got so many hours in a day. You know what they say: time is our worst enemy, and we never have enough of it. You know we are going to get other cases, and what you're talking about is going to take some time to finish. It's your call."

"Let's let it go here. I suggest we get a patrol unit out here to sit on this garage until we get back with a warrant. We have probable cause to get the warrant, and I can write the affidavit to support it. I think we ought to contact administrative narcotics too. They can put together a task force to handle it."

We got a patrol unit to sit on the garage and told the woman in the front house what we were doing. I asked the woman not to let anyone know what we were doing, and thanked her for the coffee. We took Big Daddy to the station and booked him into the jail on a murder charge. I told him the charge was only for furnishing pills to a girl who overdosed on them. We did not ask him any questions, nor did we read him his rights. This would leave someone else the ability to talk to him and not be effected by him refusing to give up his rights to us.

I went to the district attorney to get the warrant and run our case by them, and Rex went to administrative narcotics to brief them. Later on we all met at the station and we all went out to the garage. We served the warrant on the woman, because she was the landlord of the garage, and the only occupant was Big Daddy. I wanted to be sure of the search and not cause an illegal search to go down. We had left a copy of the warrant with Big Daddy, at the jail. We took over two hundred pill bottles out of the garage, and they dated back two years. There were twenty women's names on them. The district attorney stated he would contact the attorney general's office and coordinate the investigation with them, because of the possibility of welfare fraud and other malpractice on the part of the doctor. He also told Rex and I to bring our case against Big Daddy to him in the morning, and he would file a murder complaint against him. They would arraign him on the murder, and then they could work a deal for his cooperation on the pill distribution ring. With that said, we all left, and Rex and I went back to the station and finished our paperwork so we could file our case in the morning. This left us one case to solve from the past weekend's cases.

It took the task force almost a year to build their case, but when they took it to a grand jury for indictments, they indicted two doctors, six pill pushers, and fifty women on various felony charges. The case made all the papers, and the district attorney, as well as the attorney general, took all the credit. Big Daddy had rolled over for a lesser sentence. Plea bargaining is always about the sentence, not the charge. Hell, I would plead guilty to murder if my sentence was probation. I just hoped that the other two girls that I knew about, who had overdosed, had bought their pills from one of the pill pushers that had went down.

Rex and I were back on the Black case. We still did not know if his death was related to a robbery or a drug deal gone badly. It was Friday night, and we were out, shaking the bushes, rattling doors, and turning over stones. We had pulled the victim's package, in order to identify his running mates. In a case like this, when you have nowhere to go, other than the victim, you worked the case backward. You started with the victim and his associates and tried and come up with some kind of direction. We were back at the liquor store, where the crime had occurred. We knew that our victim did not have his narcotics stash on his person when he was examined by the coroner. We also knew that most dope dealers did not keep their stash on them. That way, if they were shaken down by the police, they would not have their narcotics on them. They usually kept their stash hidden close by, to where they were dealing from. We were attempting to find out if the victim's stash had been taken at the time he was killed. We had found two of the victim's close friends in the parking lot, and they copped out to us that the victim's stash was kept in the Dumpster behind the liquor store. They also informed us that they had checked for the victim's stash, after the victim had been killed, and it was not in the Dumpster. They did not have any information for us on the victim's death, and would not give up who he was dealing dope for. They did not want to go there, and they appeared to be very afraid of whoever it was. It was obvious to us that the friends had taken over the action for the victim. Now they were working for whoever it was that the victim had been working for.

We had just gotten back into our car and were pulling out of the parking lot when we heard a call come out over the radio. A patrol unit was asking for a sergeant to respond to a 187 PC, murder, at their location. They were asking that the sergeant respond to the location code two, which meant to get there as fast as possible, without red light or siren. I jumped the call and told communications that we were responding to the location, and would meet the sergeant at that location. We then drove to the location of the call.

When we arrived, we noted that the location was the upper unit of a duplex. A set of stairs ran up the side of the building, to the upper unit. There was a police car, parked in front of the building, and a female was sitting in the backseat. A police officer was standing alongside the police car, and another police officer was sitting on the staircase. Just as we parked our police car, the sergeant drove up and parked behind us. I walked over to talk to the police officer sitting on the staircase, and Rex walked back to talk to the sergeant. The police officer seemed to be very shaken up and was holding his head in his hands. I was told, by the police officer on the staircase, that the female sitting in the back of their car had just killed her common-law husband, upstairs. She had stabbed him in the chest with a butcher knife, and the butcher knife was still in his chest. I asked the police officer if the female had told him this, and he answered no, that they had seen it happen. He further stated that he and his partner had been upstairs in the living room when it had happened.

Rex and the sergeant came over to where I was standing with the police officer. I told them what the police officer had told me, and suggested to Rex that we go upstairs and check out the scene. I told the sergeant to stand by with his officers, and we would give him a status report as soon as we observed the scene. Rex and I went up the stairs and went in the front door of the unit. The front door opened up into the living room of the unit. Straight ahead was a hallway that went to the back of the unit, where the bathroom and bedrooms were located. Off to our left was the kitchen of the unit. The victim was lying on the floor, in front of the couch, in the living room. He was lying on his back and had a butcher knife protruding from his chest. His hands were wrapped around the butcher knife, and he was dead. In the kitchen, one of the kitchen drawers was standing open. The drawer contained miscellaneous knives as well as other kitchen utensils. The rest of the unit was unremarkable.

I went back downstairs, and Rex used the phone in the unit to call the coroner and photo lab. I asked the sergeant to stand by with the female suspect, and asked the two officers to come back upstairs with me and walk through what they had seen. The officers told me that they had received a radio call to handle a family dispute at the location. When they arrived, they talked to the reporting party, who was the woman in the downstairs unit. The woman had told them that the couple upstairs were fighting and hollering at each other and threatening to kill each other. The officers went up the steps and found the front door open and heard loud voices coming from within the apartment. They went into the apartment and observed the female and the male fighting in the front room. They were physically assaulting each other and screaming at each other. They ran into the unit and grabbed the two persons, one grabbing the female and the other grabbing the male. The officer with the male stayed in the front room with him, and they sat down on the couch. The officer with the female took her into the kitchen. They stated that they had been taught in the police academy to always separate the persons involved in a family dispute, and to talk to them separately, so that is what they had done. The officer was in the kitchen with the female, who was leaning against the counter. The female was telling the officer that her man had done her wrong. She had stated that he was cheating on her and was seeing another woman. Suddenly she pulled open a kitchen drawer and grabbed a butcher knife out of the drawer. Before the officer could stop her, she ran into the front room and toward her husband. Her husband saw her coming and stood up off of the couch. She ran up to him and planted the butcher knife in his chest, before either of the officers could stop her. Her husband fell to the floor and died from the wound. One of the officers tried CPR, but to no avail. They walked through the whole thing for me and felt that it had been their fault. I told them that the lesson learned was that separation means out of harm's way.

Rex stayed at the location to complete the crime scene with the coroner and photo lab. I went back to the station, with the sergeant, and the patrol officers transported the female suspect to the station. I interviewed the female suspect, at the station, after advising her of her rights and obtaining a waiver. She admitted to the stabbing of her husband, and felt that he had got his just deserts. He had been abusing her for years, and she had taken it. She felt he had no right to cheat on her after she had stuck it out with him. He was threatening to leave her for another woman. She had a black eye and some bruises and abrasions on her upper body from the physical altercation she had had, prior to the stabbing. I had the patrol officers take her to central receiving hospital for medical treatment, and then on to the women's jail to book her on the charge of murder. Rex came back to the station, and we finished all the reports and booked the butcher knife as evidence. It was after midnight when we got through with the reports, so we decided to call it a night. I felt sorry for the patrol officers, in that they had learned a lesson the hard way. One never knows what a woman's wrath and scorn will lead to.

It was Saturday morning, and I had just got up and was on my deck drinking coffee and smoking a cigarette. My wife brought me the phone and told me one of my girlfriends wanted to talk to me. She gave me that look that all women have, and then walked away. No matter how many times I told my wife that I had nothing going on, and that all the time I spent away from the house was work-related, she still felt that I was doing something on the side. I answered the phone, and it was Johnny's wife.

"Johnny is in a hospital, in Long Beach. He called me and told me to call you. He wants you to bring me to see him at the hospital. He said he needs to talk to you, real bad. You know I wouldn't call you at your house, if it wasn't important. Please come and get me. I need to see Johnny."

"Did he say which hospital?"

"He said it was the Long Beach Memorial Hospital, and he said he had been shot."

"I will pick you up in a half hour. If he calls back, tell him we are on the way. Don't tell anyone that you have heard from Johnny."

I hung up the phone, told my wife I had to go to work, and left the house. As I was driving to Johnny's house, I was thinking about what could have happened to Johnny. I knew a couple of homicide detectives who worked for the Long Beach Police Department, and I wondered if I should go there first. Come to think of it, it was Saturday, and they probably weren't at the station. I had their phone numbers in my business-card holder, I would call them later. I had better find out what was going on before I called them.

I got to Johnny's house, picked up his wife, and we headed for the hospital. I asked her if Johnny had called back, and she said he had not. I told her not to worry about Johnny; I would take care of them. Whatever it took, I was willing to do it. I had known them for quite some time, and I felt responsible for them. Had I caused Johnny to be shot?

We arrived at the hospital and went to Johnny's room. We went into his room and saw Johnny lying in a bed, and his head was wrapped in bandages. He was looking at us when we came into the room, and gave us a nod. Johnny's wife went over and took his hand. The two of them started to talk to each other, and I left the room to give them some time together. I went to the nurse's station to find out how serious Johnny's injuries were. I showed the nurse my identification and asked her about Johnny's injuries. She told me that he had been shot in the head and had just woken up yesterday. She told me that he had been brought into the hospital on Thursday night. His condition was serious, but he would recover from his injuries. I asked her if the police had talked to him, and she said that they had talked to him on Friday. I asked her when he would be released, and she said it would probably be a couple of days. I thanked her and went back into Johnny's room.

When I walked into Johnny's room, his wife was walking out. She told me she was going to the cafeteria. She asked me to come and get her when I was ready to leave. I told her I would not be very long, and I walked over to Johnny's bed. He motioned for me to sit down in the chair pulled up to his bed. His wife must have used the chair. I noticed that Johnny had an IV inserted into his arm. I sat down in the chair and looked at Johnny for a minute. His head was completely bandaged, and his mouth had wires inside it. I asked Johnny if he could talk, and he nodded his head in the affirmative.

"I will have to talk kind of slow. It does not hurt to talk; the morphine they're giving me for pain kind of works. It is not as good as the stuff I get on the streets, but it will do in a pinch. The good thing is, it don't cost me anything."

"Let's start with the obvious questions: who shot you, and where have you been? I have been looking for you for over a week. Did one of our old cases catch up with you?"

"No, it had nothing to do with any cases you and I worked. It had to do with me seeing something that I was not supposed to see. I saw Tyrone Green shoot and kill Mr. Black down at the liquor store. I score some of my dope from Mr. Black, and I was in there that night when Mr. Black got shot. Tyrone saw me see him do it, and he's been after me, to take me out. He almost got the job done, but here I am."

"Are we talking about the same Tyrone Green who, a couple years back, was driving a stolen car, and a police officer got killed chasing him?"

"We are talking about the same guy. You knew that police officer who was killed, didn't you? You had told me that he took your place on that felony car you used to ride around in, when we first met. That sure seems like a long time ago—better times, better places."

"I am working on the Black case, and I have been looking for you all week. I do not have anything going on the case: no leads, no suspects, and no motive. Why don't you start at the top and run it down for me?"

"You really want Tyrone Green, don't you? You know, there was no one other than me in that parking lot when Mr. Black was offed. And between me and you, you won't find anyone to testify against Tyrone Black. He is a heavy dude, and no one is going to give him up."

"That police officer had two little girls when he died, and they lost their father. I know it's not like Tyrone shot him, but he did not have to run in that car. Besides, even though Mr. Black dealt drugs, he deserves to see his killer go down. You know I will not lay you out if I can't make a case without you. Just tell me what you saw, and I will take it from there."

"This time I want to go with you, all the way. I told my wife I'm going to kick my habit and clean up. I've been in here thinking about me and the streets. The streets are going to get me one way or another. I almost bought it this time. I owe it to her, and you, to do this up right."

"Let me be the judge of where we stand. Just tell me what went down, and I'll decide what I will do with the case. We also have the case of you being shot. If push comes to shove, I will take care of you first; you know that."

"I was at the liquor store parking lot that night, and I had just scored some dope from Mr. Black. I was walking away, down the alley, when this car came into the alley. The car came into the alley real slow, and with its lights out. I recognized the car and knew it was Tyrone's. Tyrone distributes drugs for Tookie, who is the main drug lord in Watts. You know Tookie, I know. Mr. Black is Tyrone's mule, and sells his drugs. Tyrone had his two heavies in the car with him. That would be Humpty and Dumpty. Tyrone was riding shotgun, and when they got to the parking lot, he called Mr. Black over to the car. When Mr. Black came up to the car, on the front passenger side, Tyrone came up with a gun and shot Mr. Black three times. I heard Tyrone say it was for messing up his drugs. Then I saw Humpty get out of the backseat and go to the Dumpster and get Mr. Black's stash. He got back into the car, and they started down the alley, and that's when they saw me. I took off running, between the houses, and got under a car in a garage. They looked for me but didn't find me that night. A lot of people in Watts know that Tyrone, or one of his heavies, killed Mr. Black, but I am the only one who saw it go down. I'm the only one who knows it was Tyrone who shot him."

"What do you think Tyrone meant when he said Mr. Black messed up his drugs?"

"I think Mr. Black was cutting the drugs down. I know a couple of times I scored from him, the drugs weren't what they should have been—you know, not as potent. I didn't get as high as I should have. Mr. Black was probably cutting the drugs and keeping some off the top for himself. If he was, the word would get back to Tyrone, and he made a statement by offing Mr. Black. You don't get away with cutting down drugs; too many addicts will find their drugs elsewhere, or they will knock on Tyrone's door, and he will have to answer to Tookie."

"So that explains why I couldn't find you. You have been hiding from Tyrone. I have been to all of your spots and couldn't find you. Why didn't you find me and let me hide you?"

"I saw you looking for me. I didn't want anyone to see me with you and the word get back to Tyrone. Not that it makes a difference now; he found me and thinks he has killed me. If he finds out I'm still alive, he will find me and do the job up right."

"I will take care of you and your wife, starting right now. Where are your kids?"

"My wife took them to our church and left them at the day care. No one will know they are there."

"When I leave here, with your wife, I will pick them up, and I have a motel I can take them to for the time being—and when you get out of here, you can join them. It will be for the short end of it. The long end of it is that I can find you another place to live. Since you are going to clean up, I will help you do that. I can get you a job as well. Now, tell me how you got shot."

"I was doing pretty good hiding out, but I got to hurting and had to score some drugs. I came out on 103rd Street, and got seen by someone who ratted me out. The next thing I know is that Tyrone and Humpty and Dumpy came down on me and jammed me at Bob's liquor store. It was early in the morning, and the store was closed. They put me in the car and drove off. I was up front, and Dumpy was driving. Tyrone was in the back, behind me, and Humpty was behind Dumpy. Tyrone put a gun to my head and told Dumpy to take the freeway south to Long Beach. No one said anything, and when we got down in Long Beach, they drove around some. The next thing I knew, we pulled into this school, and Dumpy stops. Tyrone puts the gun against my head and pulls the trigger. I kind of jerked my head as he shot me, and I felt the bullet come down into my mouth. It broke my teeth, and I felt the bullet in my mouth. I fell onto the floorboard and played like I was dead. I didn't spit out the bullet and was afraid to move. Dumpy got out and pulled me out of the car. They left me lying there, in the parking lot, and drove off. I remember spitting out my teeth and the bullet, but I must have blacked out, because the next thing I knew was that I woke up here."

"How serious is your injury?"

"The doctor told me the bullet didn't hit anything major. It kind of bounced off my skull and went through my jaw and hit my teeth. He is going to let me out of here in the morning. I won't need a place to stay. No one knows where I live. When I moved to Compton, I made sure that no one knows where I am. I drive up to Watts to score, and keep all my business up there and away from the family. I keep my car in a garage I rented and only use it to get back and forth. That is where I hid out, in my garage. I got all my stuff in the garage and can stay in there a week if I have to. Just check on my family and help me out there. I want to go to court on this, know what I mean?"

"So do I, but I'm not going to put you out front. What I will do is get the district attorney to take this case to a grand jury. That way I won't have to have you go into open court. A grand jury hearing takes the place of a preliminary hearing, and only the district attorney puts on a case, to show probable cause. The defense is not in there and will not know who you are. I still want you to stay at the motel, at least until I get Tyrone and his two bodyguards in custody and indicted by the grand jury. I will take your family to the motel and come and get you tomorrow and take you there. We will see how it goes after that. Like you say, I know Tookie, and if I have to, I will talk to him. I'm sure he doesn't want any heat behind this. What did you tell Long Beach PD?"

"I didn't tell them anything. I didn't even give them my right name. I told them I didn't remember anything, and that I just remembered waking up here."

"I am going to call a guy I know down here, and have him come here, and I will square it away. You were shot in Long Beach, and that will be their case. I also want to get them to put an officer in here to watch you until I can get you out of here. I'll go get your wife and clue her in."

I went out of the room and called my guy in Long Beach and had him come to the hospital. I then went to the cafeteria and talked to Johnny's wife and told her what I was doing. I told her it would take a little while yet, and I would be taking her to get the kids as soon as I could get things squared away. She seemed OK with it, so I went back to Johnny's room to wait on my guy from Long Beach.

When my guy arrived, Johnny and I ran everything by him, and he completed his reports on Johnny's shooting. He agreed with me that he would hold off on his case until we saw how my case went. He told me that they had recovered the bullet, and some of Johnny's teeth, at the school parking lot. The bullet was good for comparison, and looked to be a .38. He had brought a uniform officer with him to watch Johnny. While he was there, Johnny's doctor came in, and, after looking Johnny over, said he would release him the next morning. I thanked my guy and told him I owed him one, and we left Johnny with the uniform officer. I told the officer to leave word with his relief that I would be by in the morning to pick up Johnny.

I went by and picked up Johnny's wife, and we went and got her kids. We went by their house and picked up some things and I took them to the motel where I kept persons I was hiding out. I told Johnny's wife that I would be bringing him by in the morning. I then left the motel and went to the station. I called Rex and told him what had gone down. He said he would meet me at the station in an hour. After I hung up the phone, I went out to Irving's and got some barbecue and brought it back to the station and waited on Rex. Rex got to the station around six that evening, and I told him all that I had learned.

"That Johnny is one lucky son of a bitch! You or I would have been dead, that's for sure. What do you have in mind for us to do now, Reynolds?"

"Well, Rex, I think we should go by records and pull the three suspects' jackets and see what we have on them. I know Tyrone will have a record, and, if I don't miss my bet, Humpty and Dumpty will have records too. I didn't go into it with Johnny because I wanted him to get some rest. We need addresses, cars, descriptions, and photos on all three of them. Once we have done that, we can go by and see Johnny and have him verify the information on them. Then, if you want, we can do drive-bys on them and see what our plan of attack will be. Sound like a plan?"

"Sounds good to me. I would like to see Johnny, anyhow. I knew you would find him, but I never thought it would be in a hospital. How are we going to handle Long Beach?"

"I thought we would ask them along when we take the bad guys down, if they want a part of the action. We will just play it by ear and see what washes out. My guy down there is a good guy, and I have helped him get some arrests up here, so it's not like we are stepping on their toes. We already helped them out by clearing up their case; they had a mystery until I told them who their victim was."

We went by records and found jackets on all three of our bad guys. They all three had records of street crimes and were all from Watts. All of them had done hard time and had been inside together. We got photos, addresses, and car descriptions for each of them. We checked the field-interview cards and found that the three men ran together in the past. Tyrone was a few years older than the other two and had a larger jacket. I felt confident that we had the right guys, but I wanted Johnny to confirm it.

Rex and I then drove to Long Beach to see Johnny. We went to his room and found him sleeping. The uniform officer said he had been sleeping since I had left. I woke him up, and we showed him what we had. Johnny said that our pictures were the three suspects, and that the cars we had were still their cars. Johnny also told us that all three were living together now. They lived on Compton Boulevard, above a secondhand furniture store. The furniture store was next to a liquor store at 109th Street. Their place took up the whole second floor and was where they packaged their drugs. Johnny said that every hype in Watts knew where they lived. The only way to get in was up a flight of stairs that ran off the alley. The stairs ran up the liquor-store side of the building and to a side door at the top. The front windows looked out over the street, and there was no front door. They kept their cars parked in car ports behind the building.

It was now around eight at night. and Rex and I went to the cafeteria to get some coffee and figure out what we were going to do next. We got our coffee, and Rex started the conversation. "I think we have enough to get a search warrant and go for the gun. I don't think we should take the place down without a warrant. For the case we just have Johnny's testimony.

Everything he said fits what I saw at the scene, but it will just be his word against their word. If we get the gun, we can probably tie the gun and Tyrone to both shootings. The good news is that he probably still has the gun. He kept it after he shot Mr. Black and used it to shoot Johnny, if it's the same gun. I'm putting my money on it that it is. They were both shot with a .38."

"I agree with that. We need to support Johnny's story with something. I'm thinking if we wait, what more can we get? Nothing that I know of. If Johnny's right, and no one was there besides him, we won't come up with another witness. If and when we get all three of them, we can try and play one against the other, and see what comes out in the wash. Worst case, we can fall back on Long Beach's case. I say we go for it and take them tonight. We can get a telephonic warrant, and I have a judge who will sign it. I will feel safer for all of us with them in jail. They probably think they are home free, with Johnny dead, and won't be expecting us now. It's only been two days since they shot Johnny. If we wait, there is more of a chance that word gets out."

"I didn't come in here to drink coffee and go home. Let's go drive by the place and check it out and make a roll of the dice then. If we do take it tonight, what are you going to do about your guy in Long Beach?"

"I will give him a call now and ask him if he still wants in with us. I'll tell him it might be a dry run, but once we roll the dice, we will not be stopping in midstream. While I am getting hold of him, you call and get the warrant. My judge is in San Pedro, so we can run by there and get it signed off. We have the paperwork in the car, so we can do it all from here."

I went and found a phone and called my guy, and he said he would be right down to the hospital. I saw that Rex was on another phone, so I went back to Johnny's room to tell him what we were going to do. After I told Johnny, I went out to the car and got the paperwork we needed for the warrant, and met up with Rex. We completed the warrant just as my guy from Long Beach got to the hospital. He came with us, and we went to San Pedro and got the warrant signed. We then did a drive-by on Tyrone's pad.

We saw the pad was just like Johnny had described it. They had fortified themselves against a rip-off, but they had boxed themselves in as well. There was only one way in and one way out. All of their cars were in the alley, and the lights were on up there. The store below their pad was closed. The liquor store was open, but traffic was light. We talked it over and decided to go for it. We did not want to leave and come back and find things had changed, so we got on the radio and asked a sergeant to meet us, with two units and a church key. (A church key is a battering ram to open doors with.)

When they arrived we briefed them on what we were doing. I told them we wanted them to cover the alley at each end, and gave them the location and description of the suspects' three cars and the names and descriptions of the three suspects. The sergeant was a big guy who I knew, and said he would handle the church key for us. I told the officers to hide at the ends of the alley, and if any of the cars moved, to stop them, and if anyone came into the alley, to stop them. That being said, we all went to the alley behind the pad.

The three of us and the sergeant went to the back stairs. There was no one in the alley. We gave the patrol cars a few minutes to get in place, and we started up the stairs. The sergeant was first, and I was next, and then Rex and my guy from Long Beach. As we were almost to the door, several shots rang out, and the handrail next to me was hit with a round. The shots had come from the roof of the liquor store. We all ran to the door, and the sergeant took it down with the church key, and we all piled into the pad. As soon as we got inside, we saw Tyrone and Humpty running at the door. They were coming out with their guns, and we all jumped them before they could get their guns out. We were able to get them down on the floor and get their guns away from them. The sergeant and I were on Tyrone and Rex, and my Long Beach guy was on Humpty. What had happened was they had heard the shots and were running to the door to go out just as we were coming through the door. The timing could not have been any better.

We cuffed the two suspects and were still on top of them when we heard someone running up the stairs and yelling that they were the police. One of the patrol officers came into the room and told us that they had Dumpy in custody, down in the alley. The patrol officer said that after the shots were fired, they saw Dumpy come down off of the roof of the liquor store. He had come down on a ladder that was leaning against the back of the liquor store. Dumpy had run to his car and was trying to drive out of the alley when the two patrol cars boxed him in and confronted him with their shotguns. They had gotten him out of his car and had found his gun on the front seat of his car.

The sergeant called another patrol car to our location, and we had the three patrol cars, each taking one of the suspects to the station and putting them in separate holding cells. We did not want them talking to each other. I showed Rex and my guy the gun I had taken from Tyrone; it was a .38. We then searched the pad and found their narcotics on the kitchen table. They had been packaging the narcotics for sale. The sergeant called another patrol car, and they impounded Tyrone's car for us. We wanted his car because it had been used in two crimes, and we wanted to have the lab go over it for evidence of Johnny being shot in the car. Before we secured the scene and left, we found where the bullet was that had gone into the handrail. Rex dug it out with his pocket knife. We didn't find the other rounds, but we didn't need them. I went up on the liquor store roof, by way of the ladder, and found a sleeping bag and a bottle of wine along with some food. It appeared that Dumpy had been up there when we came up the back stairs. He probably was acting as a lookout while they were packaging their drugs, and saw us coming up the stairs. I had to hand it to them—they had their pad well protected from being ripped off. I still could not believe how lucky we had been. I came down and pulled the ladder down and put it behind the Dumpster. The liquor-store owner had to know they used the roof, but it was not worth our time to jack him up over it, so we let it go.

We put our heads together to see if we had covered all the bases before we left. We had probable cause and a warrant to get into the pad, and an emergency to justify our breaking down the door. (We had also hollered that we were police officers as we went through the door—didn't you hear us?) We had three guns in custody: two from the pad, and one from Dumpy's car. We had two cars in custody: Tyrone's and Dumpy's. We didn't need Humpty's car. We had the narcotics from their pad. We had the bullet that had been shot at us, and we had the three suspects in custody. We could bring the photo lab out in the morning, when it was light, and take photos of the scene. The door to the pad was history, and we could not secure the pad properly, but we had done the best we could. I knew that the pad would be ripped off before the sun came up, but if we had our way, the three residents would not be coming back for their possessions, anyhow. We all left the location and went back to the station.

At the station Rex, my Long Beach guy, and I sat around and talked about how we were going to proceed with the case. We knew we needed to get one of the three suspects to roll over to strengthen our case.

"Let's look at what we got on each suspect,: I spoke up. "We got Tyrone for shooting both Mr. Black and Johnny. We have his gun, which we assume was the gun he used. We will compare the rounds we have from both cases and hope for a match. Remind me to get the round from you on Johnny's case, Guy." We got Johnny's identification of Tyrone as the shooter of Mr. Black and himself."

"Let's look at Dumpy, and see what we got. We got him along on both shootings, and we got him shooting at us. We got his gun also, and a round to compare to it. In the morning, when we go back out there with the photo lab, we can look again for the other rounds.

"I think Humpty is the one we want to turn on the others. We got him along on both shootings, and if we show him he was just along for the rides, he might roll over. I don't want to give either Tyrone or Dumpy a free pass out of any of our cases. I want to convict them of first-degree murder. We won't get a death sentence because of the moratorium against it that's now in effect, but we can get life in prison. We can get the DA to offer Humpty twenty-five years for his testimony against

Tyrone and Dumpy and if he will support Johnny's testimony. What do you think?"

"I think it will work," Rex answered me. "We can talk to all three of them, but we will only offer up a deal to Humpty. After we get that done, I want to eat. This has been a long night, and it is going to get longer. The way I got it figured, is that I will go back out there with the photo lab and get the pictures taken and try to find the other bullets that were fired at us. You can take your guy back to the hospital, and he can get his car and have his bullet sent down to our crime lab. Then you can do what you got to do with Johnny. I will come back here and put our reports together and take the guns and bullets to firearms. I will also get the cars looked at by the lab, either today or tomorrow."

My guy agreed with us and said he could eat something too. He said that we had given him an interesting night, and that he would support us any way he could. He would transfer his bullet, and he did not need anything for his case. If we could get Humpty to roll over on the Johnny shooting, it would strengthen his case, but if we got the convictions we wanted, he would not file his case and just show it cleared. That way Johnny would not have to testify again in Long Beach.

Rex and I talked to all three of our suspects, and, after telling them that Johnny was still alive, it went just as we planed it to go. Tyrone and Dumpy would not talk to us, and Humpty bought our story about just being along for the ride and rolled over on his two crime partners. There is no honor among crooks. There comes a time in everyone's life when they have to look out for number one, and that is just what Humpty did. Humpty told us everything, even about using the roof. He said that Dumpy had been on the roof to protect their back side while they were packaging their drugs. Mr. Black had been killed for cutting their drugs, and Johnny had been shot because he had seen Tyrone shoot Mr. Black.

After going to breakfast, Rex met with the photo lab and went back to the scene. He did get the two bullets out of the wall behind the stairs of the pad, and the pad had been ripped off.

I took my guy back to the hospital, and he got his car and left. He told me I always made life interesting for him, and that we would do it again, but we were going to leave out the part about the shooting at us. I went up and got Johnny, and we went to the motel and got his family. Johnny and I decided that they could return to his house, now that we had all three of the suspects in jail. I was still going to take the case to the grand jury, and talk to Tookie about not looking for Johnny. When I dropped them off, I told Johnny I would still get him that job, and that he needed to stay clean. He agreed with me and said he was going to.

The next day I got the word to Tookie and met him at his mother's house in Watts. I had known where his mother lived for years, and I had met him there before. It was a neutral ground for us, and we both showed each other respect there. As I walked up to the porch, Tookie came out to meet me. He had on a bathrobe and all his jewelry. He looked like Mr. T., except he did not have the same.goatee

"I won't take up too much of your time, Tookie; I just want to run something by you, if it's OK with you."

"It's always a pleasure talking to LA's finest. What it is?"

"I'm sure you have heard about Tyrone and his running mates, and I have a request of you. You know I always tell you what it is, and no bullshit. I got an uptight and out-of-sight case against them, and they are going to go down hard. I don't even need Johnny to testify against them. Besides, Johnny just happened to be in the wrong place at the wrong time. I would hate to see something happen to Johnny. You never know when a favor done will come back to you."

"I think you are going to have a nice day, Reynolds. For me, it's business as usual."

"Thanks for your consideration, and see you on the flip side. Tell your mother good morning for me."

"Tell Johnny to stay off the 103rd Street."

With that said, I got in my car and left. I felt from what had been said that Tookie was washing his hands of it, and Johnny was to stay out of Watts. This would work if Johnny was to clean up. He did not need to come back up here to Watts if he didn't need to score some drugs.

The case all fell into place, just as I wanted it to. We went to the grand jury and indicted all three of the suspects. Humpty got his deal and testified against Tyrone and Dumpy. We convicted all three of them, and Tyrone and Dumpy got life, and Humpty got his twenty-five. My Long Beach guy let his case go, and Johnny got his job, as I promised him. He was working out in El Segundo, at the plant I used to work at. He was staying clean and staying out of Watts.

I had not seen or heard from Johnny for six months when I got a call from his wife. She told me that Johnny had just been found on the steps of their church in Compton, and he was dead. He had gone out the night before and had not come home. She said the Compton police had found him early that morning. He had died of an overdose. She also told me he had been staying off drugs since I had gotten him the job.

She thinks the lord had just called him because they had been going to church every Sunday. She had called me because she thought I would want to know.

I did not know what to say to her. It hit me like a ton of bricks, and it took me a while to find my voice. I asked her if she was alright, and told her that I would come out and help her with Johnny. Johnny must have scored some dope and got a "Hot Shot" of dope—or did someone get to him with the Hot Shot? I never found out which it was.

She told me that would not be necessary, the church was helping her. She told me that when she buried Johnny, she would be taking the children and would be going back to Alabama. She said she had family there. She wanted me to know that Johnny really liked me, and so did she. She then said good-bye, and I never saw her again.

• • •

I know you have heard of murder for hire; how about arson for hire? Sometimes arson for hire can be just as deadly. Let me tell you a war story about arson for hire that turned deadly for the unexpected. In L.A, arson is handled by the fire dep-tartment, but if a death occurred as a result of the fire, the death is handled by the police department.

I was at home when, around ten o'clock at night, I got a call from the station telling me that I had a homicide to come in on, that was the result of a suspected arson. I was also told that the arson might well be the cause of another near-death as well. A second victim was being transported to the hospital, and might not make it. The fire department, their arson investigator, and a patrol unit was at the scene, and a witness was being transported to the station. My partner, Art Sage, was on his way to the station as well. I told the station to tell Art I was on my way and would meet him at the station. I figured if a witness was at the station, we could start with the witness before going to the scene. The body at the scene wasn't going anywhere, and the fire deptartment was probably going to take awhile to complete their job, anyhow.

When I arrived at the station, I found out that Art was there awaiting my arrival. As we had been told, a witness was at the station and was being looked after by a patrol sergeant. We found them in the detective squad room. The witness was a middle-aged male, who was very shaken up, and was trying to regain his composure by drinking a cup of coffee and smoking a cigarette. He was holding his head in his hands and was muttering to himself as we walked into the room. I decided right then that he was a person we were going to have to handle with kid gloves. The witness had several small cuts to his face and neck. The cuts had been treated by the ambulance at the scene, as the sergeant had told us.

Art and I took the witness into an interview room and introduced ourselves. We told him we were investigating what he had seen earlier that evening, and for him to tell us, as best he could, what he had seen. We told him to pretend he was watching it go down on the television, and to take it slowly as he told it to us.

"Am I in some kind of trouble here? I had just went out to get my wife some food, and was driving back home when I hit that guy. I swear I didn't see him; he just came out of nowhere."

After making this statement, our witness started to sweat and wiped his brow with his handkerchief.

"No, you are not in any trouble that I am aware of; just tell it like it is," I replied.

"I was driving down the street, and I was not speeding. I know that 'cause the food was on the seat. It was dark, and it was around eight thirty. All of a sudden, I saw a huge explosion of fire off to my right, and I slammed on my brakes, and the next thing I saw was this guy hits my windshield. He cracked the windshield, and it shattered in on me. I didn't hit the guy; I would have felt that if I did. He was just there, on the hood of my car. I got the car stopped, and he just laid there on the hood of the car. I was starring at him when I saw that house was on fire. That's when I realized that the explosion I had heard was the house blowing up. I swear to you, I did not have anything to do with any of this."

"What happened after you got your car stopped and saw the guy and the fire?" I asked.

"I'll be honest with you; I think I went into some kind of shock. I just sat in my car and stared at that guy. He looked like he didn't have any clothes on, and he was all burnt and all. I don't know how long I sat there, but I heard sirens, ands then the fire department got there. Then the police and an ambulance came, and a cop came and took me out of the car. They said I had to get away from the fire. I didn't even think of the fire. I could feel the heat when I got out of the car. That's when I saw them take that guy off of my car. Then they treated me and brought me here. What about my car?"

"If your car can be driven, we will let you take it home in a little while. Are you hurt at all?' I asked.

"No, I'm not hurt, but I could drink some more coffee. I did call my wife when I first got here, and I told her where I was. She asked me if I was going to jail; am I?"

"No, you're not going to jail; I just have a couple of questions, and then we will be going out to the scene of the fire. We will have a patrol car bring you out to get your car in a little while. Did you see anyone or any cars out there when the explosion happened? You know, like a person leaving in a hurry, or someone who could have been involved in setting the fire?" I asked.

"The only person I saw was the guy on my car. Is he alright, or is he dead? I keep seeing him against my windshield, and not moving."

"We do not know at this time, what kind of shape he is in. We are going to have to get out there and see what is happening now, and start our investigation. We will catch up with you later and let you know."

After notifying the coroner and photo lab, Art and I went out to the crime scene and met up with the arson investigator, out in front of the house. The house was a single-story house that had a front porch facing the street. The fire was out, and the house had been completely engulfed in the fire. The fire deptartment was mopping up and putting their hoses away. There was an ambulance crew standing by at the location as well.

The arson investigator started the conversation. "My name is Ronnie Mobley, and I am in charge of this fire scene. It has been proven, by me, to be an arson fire. In case you don't know it, I'm the one who had you guys respond. There is a dead body inside the house, and I don't do dead people, just arson. And by the way, you got two dead people now. That's why I had the ambulance crew come back here; the guy they took to the hospital was DOA."

"My name is Bob Reynolds, and this is my partner, Art Sage. We work Seventy-seventh homicide and we will help you out any way we can. I'm sure we can work this together and make it work. I play racquetball with the fire crew across the street from our station, and we got a good relationship. If you want to know where I'm coming from, just ask them."

"Answer me this, then: how come it took you so long to get out here? It's almost midnight, and I have been here for almost two hours."

"Let me see how I am going to answer that," I said. "First, we were notified at ten o'clock; second, it took an hour to come in; third, we had to talk to our witness; and fourth, we had to come out here, and here we are."

"Let's get on with it. I want you to talk to the ambulance crew first so they can get out of here, and then we will go inside, and I'll show you your crispy critter."

On our way over to see the ambulance crew, Art and I saw the witness's car sitting in the street. The street had been blocked off by the fire department and the car was facing west and was directly in front of the burned house. The house was to the north of the car and was about thirty yards from the car. The windshield of the car was shattered and broken out. I looked inside of the car and observed some wrapped food on the front seat and broken glass all over the front-seat area. Our witness would not be getting his car back tonight. The car would have to be impounded. Later on I would notify the station to tell the witness and have a patrol car take him home.

Art and I then talked to the ambulance crew. They told us that the guy they had taken to the hospital had died en route. He was able to tell them that he had been waiting for a friend, and he was on the porch of the burned house. He had lit a cigarette, and there was an explosion. The crew had asked him if he was torching the house, and he had nodded his head yes. He would not say who his friend was, and a short time later he had died. Most of his clothes had been blown off in the explosion, but his upper pants had remained on him, and his wallet was still in his pants. The crew had gone through his wallet and found his driver's license and identified him as Willie Williams. They left his wallet with him at the hospital. The crew then gave us their report and MT slip, and we noted that they had listed his death due to blunt-force trauma to the head. The crew then left, and we again met up with Ronnie Mobley.

Before we went into the house, Mobley again took over the conversation. "Ever since the Watts riots, I have been getting a lot of arsons. I bet I got more arsons than you guys got murders. It seems like they learned how to make money by 'burn, baby, burn' during the riot. For my money, some of those fires during the riot were set to cash in on the insurance money. Now everyone wants to cash out and leave Dodge, or get a new business from the insurance money. This is the first house fire I have had, and the first death."

Art spoke up. "Do you have any suspects in mind as a result of your previous investigations?"

"You have got to be kidding me. Don't you know that arson is the hardest crime to solve and the easiest to commit? The person who owns the business hires the arsonist and either leaves town or is somewhere else when the fire goes down. If I can find them, when the insurance company gets involved, they always deny knowing anything. That leaves me with trying to find the arsonist. I usually leave that part up to the insurance company, and do you want to know how many arsonists they have come up with? The answer to that question is zero! Eventually they just pay off the claim, and either the 'victim' doesn't come back to town, or he started a brand new business. My job is to determine the cause of the fire, and that's what I will do here. Now that I have given you your lesson in arson 101, let's go in and I will show you your crispy critter."

We followed Mobley into the burned-out house and worked our way into a back bedroom. When we got into the bedroom, we saw what was left of a person lying on the floor. The person was in a fetal position, but the person's arms and legs were just stumps. The bones were all that was left of the person's limbs. The hands and feet were gone, and the head was just a skull. The rest of the body looked like black charcoal. The clothes were completely burned away. I had seen a lot of dead bodies, but I had never seen one like this before. My first thought was of the suffering he must have gone through. Had the fire killed him or had the smoke? I really hoped it was the smoke. I remember thinking this was probably the worst way to leave this world. It was likely that the only way we were going to identify the person was going to be by dental identification.

A further examination of the room revealed a two-gallon gas can that was a few feet away from the person. The only way out of the room was the door we had come in. Mobley pointed out the path of the fire, which showed that the fire had started at the front door of the house and traveled through the house, and back to this rear bedroom, where the burned person had been trapped. Mobley further explained the chain of events. The two persons had poured gas throughout the house, and the one who was found outside of the house had gone out onto the porch. The person in the back bedroom was still in the back bedroom when the person on the porch lit his match to smoke. The match ignited the gas fumes and gas, and the ignited gas raced through the house and trapped the person in the back bedroom, causing his death. The person on the front porch was blown out into the street, by the explosion, and onto the car. Another gas can was found out in the street, which in all probability had been on the porch with the person on the porch.

We all then went back outside, and Mobley stated he had wrapped up his investigation and was going to leave the scene. He took the two gas cans with him and said he would be in touch. He wished us well on our investigation, and if and when we came up with a suspect, other than the two we had, he would testify to the fact that the fire was arson. We assumed by *suspect* that he meant the owner of the house.

When the coroner and photo lab arrived, Art left to go to the hospital to check on our second person, and I remained at the crime scene to continue the crime-scene investigation. The coroner removed the body, and I had the photo lab take photos of the house, the person inside the house, and the car. Mobley had told me that he had taken photos for his purpose, but I wanted my own photos. While I was having the car photographed, I got to thinking of the crime. I remembered a looting and burning I had witnessed during the riot and recalled there had been three persons involved in that one. There was also a car involved and a lookout person. What about this one—had there been a car and a lookout? How had the two guys gotten here? I was sure they had not just walked down the street with two gas cans. I also knew there wasn't a gas station within miles of the crime scene. I looked up and down the street for a car the persons involved in the fire might have had, and did not find one. The only cars in the vicinity were all cars belonging to neighbors, and the neighbors could not furnish any information about the fire. The strong possibility was that there had been a third person at the scene, who had driven off after the fire, but was not seen leaving the fire. I then called for a tow truck, and had the witness's car impounded and returned to the station to meet Art. The only way I knew to go on this case was going to be through the person who had been identified and was at the hospital. Hopefully Art would come up with something good to work on. I had told the coroner that he had another pickup at the hospital, and he had told me that the autopsies would be in the morning. It seemed that death had taken a holiday the last week, and there were no autopsies lined up.

When I got to the station, Art was already there, and he had stopped by Irving's and had gotten us some barbecue. Art told me that Irving told him to tell me to enjoy the food and to stop by more often. Come to think of it, I had not been to Stops B.B.Q. in a while.

While we ate our barbecue, Art told me what he had found out at the hospital. The person of interest was in fact a Willie Williams, if you were to believe his driver's license. He was a male black, born November 2, 1939, six feet tall, 175 pounds, with black hair and brown eyes. He lived at an address in University Division. The thing that interested Art more was that he had tattoos that included one with the initials *BGF*. We both knew *BGF* stood for The Black Gorilla Family, which was a prison gang that was now active in the streets. This meant that the person inside the house was probably also BGF, and that meant that BGF was into arson, somehow. At least it would be a start and some sort of direction to take. Little did the gangs know that their showing their gang affiliations through tattoos really helped us out at times. A lot of the tattoos were put on their bodies in prison, so we would need to visit the prisons on this one. First we would pull Willie's jacket and see where he had done his hard time and who he ran with inside prison. I felt a lot better after eating my barbecue and talking to Art.

"Art, what did you think of that Mobley?"

"He ought to be a teacher, not an investigator. He can tell us the fire was arson? Like that qualifies him as an investigator! He will get up in court and say that, but not say *who*? I say we don't need him on this one or any other one I might catch in the future. This is my first arson, and I know it is yours too. I hope it is my last, if he is what we get from the fire department."

"The reason I asked you was because I suggest we don't include him in where we are going with this."

"Nothing would please me more than to back-door him."

We left the station and went to records to pull Willie's jacket. We did find out that he was an inmate at Folsom prison and just got out in the last year, after doing a stretch for robbery. We took a set of his prints from his jacket and took them to the coroner's office There we had them print the person we thought to be Willie, and the pathologist confirmed he was in fact Willie Williams. We were informed that our other person would have to be identified by dental records. I told the pathologist that we would be going to Folsom prison in the morning, and that this other person could be an ex-inmate. If they had dental records on file there, we would let them know, and they could try to identify him through their records. I also told him that we would not be attending the autopsies that morning. Other than the direct cause of death, we would not learn anything to aid our investigation. We called Folsom prison and got an appointment to speak with the warden at ten o'clock that morning. We then left the coroner's office and went to the Pantry restraunt for coffee. It was around six o'clock in the morning, and we wanted to talk to OCID (Organized Crime Intelligence Division) about the BGF and to see what they could tell us about them, if anything. We had a few hours to kill before they would be in.

We were having our coffee when I decided to analyze our case with Art. I always found it useful to go over what I thought with my partner. Sometimes I changed my cart in the middle of the stream that way, and headed in another direction.

"I've been thinking about what way we should go on this case," I started out. "As I see it, we have two ways to go. We can go after the owner of the property and show that he hired the two guys to torch the house. If we can prove that, we can show the deaths were the end results of a felony crime, and that construes a first-degree murder. We are usually looking to charge the bad guy who had killed someone over money, dope, or love/sex with murder, but this time it's the bad guys that were killed. I guess the law still applies the same. Or we can go after a third arsonist, if there was one. We can also charge that person with murder. The other crime is the arson. As I understand it, that crime is the responsibility of Mr. Mobley. Am I right so far?"

"So far I agree with you," Art replied. "Mobley did not seem to be interested in our dead bodies. If we are going to work our case from the information we gather from the bodies, why work the case from the owner of the house angle?"

"I was just thinking—if there was no third person, then the only guilty party would be the owner of the house. That would mean we wouldn't be involved after we identify the guy in the morgue. We would clear our case by showing the two deaths were accidental deaths, end of case! Maybe Mobley comes up with a case, and maybe he doesn't. Either way it lets us off the hook. What do you think, Art?"

"I say we keep going in the direction we are going and see what shakes out. If there is a third guy, we find him. If we can't, or if there is no third guy, we see where Mobley is, at that time, and either punt or throw in with him."

"Guess that's why we are working this case together: great minds think alike."

As we were drinking our coffee, I started to reflect on my career in homicide. It was November of 1971, and I had been working homicide at Seventy-seventh Division for about four years, and I had handled over 125 homicides, and I had never had a case like this one. All of my rating reports stated that I was one of the more "seasoned" investigators, and that I had the investigative and interrogative skills, along with outstanding street rapport, to solve any homicide that was assigned to me to handle. My rating reports also stated that my memory was excellent and my tenacity was comparable to that of a bulldog. My conduct at a crime scene was described as professional and thorough. I thought to myself, it would take all of that and more to work through this case. I thought a bit about Art.

I had known Art since I came on the job. In fact, Art was one of the two detectives who I saw talking to that army captain when I was on probation in the Harbor. Art had come up to Seventy-seventh homicide from the Harbor that year, and we had worked several cases together. Art was, in fact, our homicide unit supervisor. (I would have his job in another couple of years.) The one thing Art and I had in common was that we both loved to shoot pool. We would spend our lunchtime in a pool hall a lot of times. Sometimes we would take along a bunch of guys and play nine-ball. Art was a WW II veteran, and he had twenty-five years on the job. He always said he was going to retire at thirty years. I only hoped I could last as long as he had, so far. He was so laid back that thirty was a good bet. Art was a short guy by comparison to most guys on the department. He was probably five feet eight inches and weighed two hundred pounds. He kept his gray hair short and laughed a lot. He would probably go either way on this case, but I wanted it to be his call, not mine.

All of a sudden another thought came to me. I realized why I was feeling so bad about this way to die. I had come close to going out the same way when I was in high school. I had been parked, with my girlfriend, out on a country road. We were in my car, which was an old Nash Statesman. The back of the front seat laid down and made a bed inside of the car, and we had it laid down. It was winter, and the roads were covered with ice and snow. After taking care of business, I left our parking place, which was behind an abandoned building, and was taking her home when I drove into a curve in the road, and a car was coming the opposite way, into the curve. The car crossed over onto my side of the road and was sliding right at me. I drove off of the road, to avoid the car, and my car rolled over onto its top, when I hit the ditch. The other car did not stop but another car, which had seen the accident, did. I crawled out of my car, and the driver of the other car helped me stand up and asked me if I was alright. I told him I was alright, and then I got out my cigarettes and lighter and started to light up. He slapped my hand, knocking my lighter to the ground, and yelled at me, "Do you want to burn yourself up? You are soaked in gas!" I had my football jacket on, and it was soaked in gas from my car. My car was on its roof, and the gas tank had ruptured. The guy then told me he was a preacher, and he asked if there was anyone else in the car. I told him my girlfriend was, and we ran to the car and got her out. She was a bit scared but not hurt. An ambulance showed up, and I had them take her to the hospital to make sure she was OK. I couldn't help but think how lucky we were that we had left the seat down and we both had laid down when the car rolled over. Also how lucky I was to have not lighted my lighter. The image of what might have been has always been with me, and I had nightmares about it and could see us burning up in a fire that could have been.

"Hey you! Wake up! We got work to do," Art said.

"I am awake! I was just thinking about this and that. Are we ready to go? Did you pay the bill?"

"I think it would be nice to give the city some of your time, my friend. I paid the bill only because I lost the last pool game to you. Let's get out of here and go bug those holier than us."

With that said, Art and I went to OCID to find out what we could about BGF. We met with Dan Spots, who was a classmate of mine at the police academy. I asked Spots to give us any information they had on the BGF and explained what we were working on. Spots explained to us that they mainly worked on organized crime families, not street gangs, but he would look into the BGF and get back to us. He told us he would check with Administrative Narcotics and see if they had anything. (In 1973 our department found that street gangs were becoming a real threat to the city and formed the city's first street gang unit called CRASH—Community Resources Against Street Hoodlums.)

We returned to the station, and I called the warden at Folsom. I told him what I was working on and gave him Willie Williams's name and asked for any information he had on him and the BGF. I asked him if they kept dental records on inmates. I also asked for any names of Willie Williams's associates in the BGF.

The warden informed me that they did in fact have dental records of the inmates treated at the prison. He told me that since prisoner rights and rehabilitation became the buzzwords of prison reform, they had to furnish dental care, along with medical care, to all inmates. He informed me that the BGF was an active prison gang at his prison, and they had a complete file on them as to who the members were, who had been discharged, and when and where they had been discharged to. Since they had been under pressure about overcrowding, they had been releasing a lot of inmates early, through halfway houses.

I told him I would be having the coroner contacting him about trying to identify our crispy critter, through their dental charts. I also asked him to see if he could find out who in the BGF had been released into the LA area over the last several years. He said he would get the information to me within a couple of days, and, if I needed anything else, to contact him again.

I could not come up with anything more to do on the case at that time, so I went back to work on my other cases and put this case on the back burner. When some information came in on the case, and it heated up, I would jump back into it. Little did I know at the time how much it was going to heat up.

Several days later I heard from both Spots and the warden on the crispy critter case. Spots called me and told me that the BGF did not have an active gang on the streets. It appeared that they freelanced when they got out of prison and went where the money was. A lot of them worked in the narcotic business, mainly with a black gang run by Raymond Long, also known as Shug. He had found two bars that they hung out at, one being in University Division and the other in Seventy-seventh Division. He wished me luck and said good-bye.

The warden sent me a file on the BGF. The file contained a list of twenty BGF members released into the LA area over the last several years. Of the twenty, two were on parole, and the rest were released through halfway houses. The file also contained complete workups on each member. Willie Williams was one of the twenty. I listed all the names and the two bars in my notebook, and went hunting with Art. We had photos of the twenty BGF members. (I knew Shug and had worked several homicides that he was involved in but couldn't prove his involvement. I also knew that they worked out of University Division, as well, and three of the names on the list worked for Shug.) We would concentrate on the bar in Seventy-seventh first and do some shaking, rattling, and rolling.

The bar in Seventy-seventh Division was on the west side and was in the north end of the division on Vermont. It was a typical neighborhood bar, and, when we entered that night, we noted that it had two pool tables. There were around twenty males and ten females in the bar at the time we entered. Needless to say, we were the center of attention. We sat at an empty table and ordered a drink from the cocktail hostess. Art ordered a beer and I ordered a gin and tonic. We had studied our photos of the BGF members and recognized several of them in the bar. Two of them were the two on parole, so we had them on a parole violation right off the bat. They were associating with known gang members and were in violation of their parole. Several of the males in the crowd left the bar as we were paying for our drinks.

"Looks like they don't like our company Art. Not a bad start for us, though we know we were in the right place. I would have bet some of these guys were from other prisons and the rest were trying to get into prison. I didn't see any of Shug's people in here. Either they were at the other bar, or they don't come into the bars. Now that they had made the big time with him, they were probably in Hollywood at the nightclubs.

"My money goes with the nightclubs. I don't think it's his people we will be looking for, anyhow. I don't see a connection between narcotics and arson. If you are thinking of shooting pool, I will protect your backside. I just shoot pool for recreation, not money, in here. I have a hard enough time keeping my money out of your pocket."

"I had better get my money on one of those tables, if I'm going to do it. I have been watching, and the first table has the best shooter on it, so I guess I'll start there. I'm not going to ask too many questions this time around; we will be back. I am not bringing my *A* game to the table, either. That's for later, when we come back."

I got up and laid a quarter on the table and asked the shooters if I could take on the winner. The two shooters looked at me and then each other, and told me it was a free country. When their game was over, I took my turn and held the table for three games, and then lost on purpose. I did not talk to any of the guys I shot pool, with and none of them were who I had pictures of. I won fifteen dollars and took it to the bartender and laid it down on the bar. I took out a picture I had, of Willie Williams, and laid it on top of the money. I then took out one of my business cards and laid it on top of the picture. Art had got up and was standing by the door.

"This guy got himself killed at an arson fire, and his partner got himself burned up. No one should die that way. I know a third guy was with them, and I need to talk to him. Just in case someone wants to talk to me about it, I will be back in a couple of days. The money is to buy drinks for those three guys I was shooting pool with. I enjoyed the pool games and will be back for another game."

Art and I then left the bar and went to the second bar and played out the same scene. We did not see anyone in that bar that fit our pictures. It proved to be a BGF bar, though, and we knew we would have to come back there. We felt our time had been well spent, and if nothing else, I had some future pool games to shoot.

Later in the week, we were contacted by the coroner and informed that they had identified our crispy critter. They had identified him through dental records, and he was one of the guys we had a file on from the warden. Out of the twenty we had files on, we ended up identifying twelve of them through the bars, but did not get any information on our third guy. I had shown the other ten guys their photos, in the bars, and let them know we knew of them. Two of them were the two on parole, and I let them know I was not there to turn them over to their parole officer, but was just trying to get information on my arson. I worked the bars, on and off, for a month, and did not come up with any good information, but I did make some money shooting pool. I kept seeing the same persons, but they would not budge when it came to talking to me on the arson. I knew the answer to our case was in one of the bars, but I was dealing with ex cons, and they were the hardest to get information out of. Unless I had something to offer them that was profitable to them, they would not talk. Even my putting the word out that I could return a favor was not catching any fish.

Mobley turned out to be a dead end, as well, and pretty much shot down our other way of working the case. It turned out that the "victim" of the fire was an elderly widow lady who was presently in Georgia and would not be coming back to California. She had left to visit her daughter, before the fire, and decided to stay on after the fire. Mobley said the insurance company was handling her, and she was adamant that she was not involved in the fire in any way. Mobley told us that unless the insurance company came up with a witness to the fire who could identify the arsonist, and the arsonist admitted to a conspiracy with the owner, there was no case. In this case the elderly lady was a "victim" and would receive a settlement from the insurance company. He suggested that we write our deaths off as accidental, and move on.

Our case went cold and remained that way until a cold night in December, when it heated up again. I was notified around midnight that I had another arson victim! Another house fire had gone down, and there was another crispy critter inside. The house was in Watts, and Arson was awaiting my arrival.

There wasn't a witness to this fire, and Art was on his way to the scene.

I arrived at the scene within a half hour of being notified and was met by Ronnie Mobley. I asked him if my arrival was quick enough for him, and he ignored me. I then stood back and took in the scene. The fire department had put out the fire, and I saw that the damage was not as great as the other house had been. This house was a two-story house, and the front of the house did not appear to be damaged by the fire. I walked around to the back of the house and found that the back of the house had been completely engulfed in the fire. Mobley came up to me and got in my face. I was really beginning to dislike this guy!

"If you had asked me, I would have told you the fire traveled in this direction," Mobley stated. "I would also tell you that your victim is inside on the couch, in the front room. You are probably going to find that he died of smoke inhalation, not the fire."

"I'll tell you what—why don't we wait on my partner to get here, and then you can educate us both on the fire and our 'victim.' That way you won't have to repeat yourself. I always let my partner do my thinking for me, and that way I don't get second-guessed. Besides, I don't want to keep you any longer than necessary. I know you have better things to do and all you are interested in doing is proving this fire is arson."

At that time Art walked up and joined us. He asked if we were waiting on him, and we told him we were just getting ready to go into the house. Art told us that the coroner and photos were on their way. The three of us then went to the back door of the house and entered. As we entered, Mobley explained the path of the fire to us.

"The fire started at the back door, we just entered, and went from the back door to the stairs. It then went in two directions, one being up the stairs to the upstairs, and the other being into the kitchen and the rest of the back of the house. The fire did not go into the front of the house, and was put out before it could advance. That is why you will find that this victim is not burnt like the other victim was. I am sure that this victim died from the smoke, not the fire."

Mobley then took us into the front room, and we observed our victim lying on the couch. He was laying face down and was fully clothed. His face was buried in a pillow, and his arms were wrapped around his head. It appeared that he had been hiding from the fire at the time he had died. Mobley explained that this was a common behavior of persons caught in fires as they inhaled smoke and became disorientated. The fire had not burned this part of the house. We learned the fire had been fought from the front of the house to the back, and was put out within an hour. We had got lucky on this one. We were going to have a good chance of identifying the victim when the coroner arrived. I felt at the time, the big question to answer was, did the victim live there, or was he setting the fire?

A short time later the coroner arrived. We had already photographed the scene and completed our investigation. The coroner began his examination of the victim, and, as he turned the victim over, I immediately recognized the victim. The victim was one of our photographs of the BGF members by the name of Donnie Davis. This was confirmed when the coroner removed the victim's wallet from his rear pants pocket. I had talked to the victim at the club in Seventy-seventh on several occasions, while shooting pool. At first I was shocked, but then I got to thinking about it. The three victims we had identified from the two fires were all BGF, they all did time at Folsom, at the same time, and they all hung out at the bar in Seventy-seventh. I was more than sure now that our answers were inside that bar. This victim did not live here, I was sure. He had been here setting this fire, but there had to have been someone with him that started the fire that killed him. Could the person with him be the same person, with the two victims on the first fire?

"Tell you what I'm going to do for you guys," Mobley said, bringing me out of my thoughts. "I will identify the owner of this property and notify the insurance company. I will work with them, while you guys work your homicide. We all know this fire is going to turn out to be the same as the last one, arson for hire. I'll keep in touch, later, I'm out of here." That being said, Mobley walked out of the house and drove off.

"He isn't doing us any big favors," Art said, "what he is doing is his job. That's OK. We didn't need him last time, and we don't need him this time. All we will ever need from him, if we ever make these cases, is him testifying to the fires being arsons, and the arsons being for hire."

Art and I had been working the arson cases, on and off, for a couple weeks, and were getting nowhere on them. The victim from the second fire had died of smoke inhalation and was who I thought he was. I had been back to the bar several times and was unable to get anyone to talk about the fires. The BGF had circled their wagons and were on the defense. We were at a standoff, and neither side was giving any ground, until I received a call from the station, at home, late one Saturday night. It was the watch commander.

The watch commander gave me a phone number to call and told me the caller wanted me to call him right away. The caller had called the station, asking for me and stating he knew that I would want to talk to him. The caller would not give his name or where he was calling from. I thanked the watch commander and called the number. When the phone was answered, I gave my name, and the person who answered the phone asked me to meet him at a restaurant in Compton, in an hour, to talk about the fires. I told the person that I knew where the restaurant was, and asked him how I would identify him. He just replied that he would find me, and hung up.

When I got to the restaurant it was three o'clock in the morning. My wife had not been happy about me waking her up with the phone call, but what's new—she had been woken up before, and she would be woken up again. The restaurant was a twenty-four-hour restaurant and was crowded with the people from the bars that had closed at two o'clock that morning. Whoever had called me had picked a good location to meet; we would go unnoticed in this crowd. I had worn my Levis and a baseball jacket, as I always did when I met someone like this. I was able to get a booth in the back, facing the entrance, so I could watch the front door. It cost me only ten dollars. I had gotten my coffee and had checked out the crowd when a person came up from behind me and slid into my booth, across from me. I immediately saw why he had said he would find me; he was one of the BGF members I had a picture of, and I had seen in the bar in Seventy-seventh. He was one of the two members who were on parole and had done time for armed robbery. I had talked to him in the bar, but had not shot pool with him. His name was Tommy Hanson, and he was my height and weight, and was two years older, at thirty-five. I let him speak first.

"I didn't want to talk to you at the bar, for obvious reasons. I can give you the guy you are looking for on those fires, but I also have something that's bigger that I want to give you. But I need a way out. I want to go to Florida with no strings attached to me. My parole is up in two weeks, and I don't want violated. I don't want to go back in."

"Let me ask you this; are you the guy I am looking for, Tommy?"

"No, man, I ain't had no part of those fires. I know the dude that set them up and got the brothers killed. Now tell me what you can get me. Can you get me a free ride if I lay a name on you?"

"Look here, I don't know where you are coming from. If you weren't involved in the fires, why would you need a free ride?"

Tommy sat there for a while, thinking about what he was going to say next. I motioned the waitress over and got some more coffee for us and offered Tommy one of my cigarettes. We both lit up and kicked back and studied each other.

Tommy then broke the silence. "I got another fire I want to talk about, and that one I am involved in, and it's a lot heavier than the two you want. I will give you all of it, but I got to walk. I'm in pretty deep and need a way out, and I figure you are my way out. We can help each other here, but I need proof you got the power to give me what I need."

"Looks like we got us a Mexican standoff here. Without knowing what you got, I can't promise you anything, and you don't want to tell me what you got until I do. As I see it we both need each other, so who is going to lay it out first?" I had a feeling he needed me as badly as I needed him, but I didn't want to play my cards first.

"I can give you the guy on your fires this way. I wasn't with him, but he told me about both of them. He was at both of them, and he set them up. I can give you his old lady too. She was with him when they went down. On the first fire, they were sitting in their car when the fire went down. They had brought the other dudes to the fire, and they were supposed to torch the house and come back to the car. Only that dumb Willie probably lit his cigarette and got them killed. The guy and his old lady just drove off."

"What was the connection between that guy and the two guys that set the fire?"

"He gets his leg men at the bar. He just started freelancing with houses, with these two houses. He has been doing arsons as his regular gig. With the arsons he is the middle man, but the houses are his thing out front. More money that way, you know, cut out the middle man."

"What about the female with him? Is she his wife?"

"No, man, like she is just a hang-on from the bar. As I get it, he uses her to sweet-talk the ladies that own the houses. He gets the houses from the For Sales in the papers. He finds a single old lady who can't sell her house and wants out of here. He and his old lady go there like they are looking for a house to buy. Then he uses his old lady to soft-talk her into giving him a percent of the insurance money, when she collects, for torching the house. Same way payday comes for torching the businesses."

I now had a principal to the fires who I could go after, besides the guy I was after, and she was not his wife. No husband-

and-wife privilege here. I could use them against each other and maybe only have to use Tommy for my probable cause.

"Tell me about the second fire."

"My guy got Donnie to help him on that fire. He had asked me, but I turned him down. The three of them went on that one. He told me that they had parked their car in the alley behind the house. His old lady was driving the car, and he and Donnie were going to set the fire. He told his old lady to turn off the car, and don't start it until they came back. They left and went into the house, and he went upstairs to spread his gas. Donny was supposed to spread gas downstairs. He came downstairs and did not see Donnie. He heard the car running and figured that Donnie had gone out to the car. He went out the back door and lit the fire. When he got to the car, he saw that Donnie wasn't in the car. He asked his old lady why she had started the car, when he had told her not to, and she said that she had gotten cold. They realized that Donnie was still inside the house, and they got out of there. As a matter of fact, they got out of town. I know where they are, though, 'cause he is using me to keep tabs on you. Remember that first night you came into the bar? He was one of the guys that left as soon as you came in."

"What kind of money are we talking here?"

"The front man usually gets 10 percent of the insurance money, and the middle man can get up to 5 percent of that; depends on the payout, or who you are working for. Sometimes the job is for personal reasons, and there is no insurance money. Then it depends on what is offered and what you can get the customer to pay. That's the type of job that has got me into the jam I'm in right now."

"Are you going to give that up now, or are you still going to hold it back? I can tell you this; I will pay you for the two names and their location, upon delivery. I can give you a deposit, as we sit here, and we can go from there. If your other story has you as a player, I would have to go through the district attorney to get you a free pass. From what you have told me so far, I have to suspect that you are ass-deep into this arson-for-hire stuff. I will be up front with you, and if what you have done has not killed anyone, a free pass is an option. I will go to bat for you, and I know I can get the DA to let you slide for the cases. You lay out your case now, and I will take the whole package to the DA and get back to you on where we stand. I will still give you a deposit, if it will help you out. For starters, let's get something to eat; I'm hungry."

We got some breakfast and engaged in some small talk about sports and life on the streets in Watts. We found that we had some things, and people, in common, and we became comfortable with each other. All the time we talked, I felt he was rolling his dice to try and decide if he was going to be safe with me, and I was trying to keep him from seeing how badly I wanted those names. After our eats, and more coffee, and several smokes, he decided to roll his dice.

"You know the Villains, the ones who have the trash collection and disposal company called SAC? They are the biggest in the county, and they are probably the biggest crooks in the county, if the truth were known."

I did know of them; they also sponsored a race car at the Ascot race track in Gardena. I had watched the races at the track and liked their driver a lot. I had also heard that they had pig farms out around Corona. Tookie also had a pig farm out there, and I often wandered if there was a connection there. I answered Tommy, and told him I had heard of them, but did not know the family.

"Check this out: there is a trash company in Gardena called Anderson Disposal. The owner was cutting into SAC's business. A couple of weeks ago they had a couple of their trucks burned. I was hired by the Villains to torch the trucks. Problem was, he had three trucks, and he is still in business. I was supposed to put him out of business. When I went to get paid, they wouldn't pay me and said I had to finish the job. They also told me his house was going to be next, and it would make them happy if he was in it when it burned. Now the trucks are one thing, but the house is another. I don't want no death on my hands like the guy you want has on his. Now I got myself in a vise, and don't know what my chances are with those Villains. They could take me out in a minute and think nothing of it. I mean, are they like the mafia or something?"

"I will have to check it out. I don't know anything about Anderson Disposal or any fires. Let me do my homework and see what I can come up with. What kind of time schedule are you on? How do you contact these people? What have you told them you will do, and what do you want from me?"

"First off, let me say this. When the word came down, through the bar, that they wanted the best out there to torch the trucks, that meant I was the one they were looking for. The trucks take a special talent and a special substance. You just can't pour gasoline on trucks and expect them to burn. Guys like the guy on your fires can't do the job. I had to use Centex to get the job done. It burns hotter and is harder to detect. It can even melt metal, and that's what was needed with the trucks. Now, they wanted to see what they were getting, so I met them in their office and had to show them what they were getting. We agreed on the price, and the rest was history, until I went back to get paid. That's when they let me know there was no payday until I did the other truck and the house. That was a couple days ago. I told them I would have to check out the house and how secure the truck was, now that the other two were burnt. I told them I would get back with them by this coming weekend. What I want from you is a way out. No way would I torch the guy's house, with him in it or not. On the other side of the coin, there is no payday, and maybe getting dead. That's why I decided to hook up with you. What it is that you can do for me?"

I thought about that for a while. All I could see was his word that the Villains had hired him to torch the trucks and wanted him to finish the job, including the house. Then, if his story was true, I would have the burned trucks. Pretty weak case! I wanted those names, though, and I would have to give him something. I knew what I would need from him, but how was I going to sell it to him?

"If we were to help each other, I see it this way. First, I am going to talk to this Anderson and find out what he can tell me. I will have to find out who is handling his case and decide if I am going to cut them in or not. Then I will see the DA and run it all by him and see if he will back me with you and give us the immunity you are after. The DA in Torrance will handle the prosecution. I will go there and ask for an assistant DA to work the case with us, to make sure I cross all the t's and dot all the i's. I will ask them for a grand jury hearing instead of a preliminary hearing. That way I can keep you hidden from the defense when you testify."

"I don't know about all of that, but I do know I want out of here, with no tail on me. I am giving up my meal ticket out of here, but I do admit the cost of the meal is too much. If you can get me expenses, I could live with that. At least I would have my good health and be in Florida."

"Here is the bottom line: I would have to wire you for sound and get admissions on tape from the Villains. They are expecting you back and we would have to have you cook a deal with them on tape. Before we leave here, I want the names of the 'guy' and his old lady. You can keep back their location until I check them out. I will give you the deposit, out front, and do what I got to do. When I got my ducks in order, I will meet up with you and let you know what I got for you from the DA. I would tell you right now that you will get what you want, but I want to show it to you on paper, from the DA. I'm sure I can put it together, but I want it done when we start to play."

"You want me to wear a wire and meet with them and talk about burning the house and truck? Man, I think that's too much. Can't you just use me and what I told you? I would testify for you and then skip town. That's how I got it figured."

"I don't think I can get a case filed with just you and the burned trucks. I got to support that with something else to make a strong case. Does anyone else know about this who can back you up?"

"No, when I took the job I didn't talk to anyone, and I did the job alone."

"Using the wire is the only way, then. Remember, we want to nail them and get them in custody and convict them, not have the case fall apart. That way it will be safer for you, and I will protect your backside through the trial and then get you to Florida."

We both thought about what the odds were of this deal working out for the two of us. Tommy took his time and asked me some more questions, but nothing new came up. Finally he gave in and took the deal. Tommy gave me the two names I was after and their physical descriptions. The names were Bill Henry and Doreen Kitty. Tommy said they both had records, so I should find their rap sheets easily. I gave Tommy my home phone number and told him to call me Monday night and I would set up a meet for Tuesday. I wanted to have him meet with the Villains as soon as possible. That would give me time to meet with Anderson and the DA on Monday. We said our good-byes in the parking lot and I gave Tommy a hundred dollars. Tommy waited for me to leave before he went to his car, but I anticipated this move on his part and doubled back and caught him leaving, so I got the description of his car and the plates. Not that I felt I would need it, but you never know.

Art and I were sitting in Anderson's office at Anderson Disposal, and we were waiting for him to show up at work. It was Monday morning, and I had brought Art up to speed on what I had learned from Tommy. Anderson's business was just outside of the city of Gardena. (The city of Gardena was to the south of Seventy-seventh and was just off of the Harbor Freeway. The city of Los Angeles had annexed a strip of land that ran down the Harbor Freeway and connected with San Pedro. I guess it was done to connect the city with the harbor.) The business was within the city limits of Los Angeles and the arson was under the jurisdiction of LA. I had found out that LAFD Arson was handling the case. I had also gotten the rap sheets on Bill Henry and Doreen Kitty, and the sheets showed that they both had lengthy records. I had contacted the assistant DA in Torrance and set up an appointment for that afternoon. I had briefed him on what I had, and the minute I mentioned the Villains, he agreed to assign a special trial DA to the case and agreed to have him at the meeting.

As we awaited the arrival of Anderson, I was thinking of what I was missing. Something was bothering me, but I couldn't put my finger on it. Had I said enough for Tommy to come through for us? Would he call me tonight, or would he be in the wind? Would the DA give me what I wanted for Tommy? There were a lot of *ifs* to pull this case together. The DA had certainly known the name *Villain* and jumped on my case with both barrels. What had I gotten into here? What would I have without Tommy? It was not time to second-guess myself, and I just needed to go with the flow and see what washed out!

I was brought out of my thoughts by the arrival of Anderson, and we all got coffee and settled into his office. For background, Anderson told us he was a retired navy commander. He had retired out of Terminal Island, and had opened his disposal company about a year ago. He had bought a home in Palos Verdes, and his business grew. He had gotten his incinerator trucks after outbidding SAC for some large contracts with McDonald Douglas and North American. Anderson explained that the trucks could go onto the customer's property, load the classified trash, and it would be incinerated inside the truck. Shortly after he got the contracts, he started to receive threatening phone calls and some threatening letters. The message was always the same: to get out of the incinerator business. He hadn't taken them seriously and had picked up a couple of other contracts. Then his trucks were torched. Luckily, he had had one truck in the shop for repairs, and he had been able to keep the contracts by using the one truck to do the work of two. He thought he could hang on until he got another truck from his insurance, but didn't know how long it would take.

Yes, he was sure it had been SAC that had torched his trucks. They were really upset when he got the contracts away from them. The contracts were worth a lot of money and would turn his business into a profitable one, and he was not going to give them up. He hadn't been in the Navy twenty years for nothing, and he wasn't going to go down without a fight.

"Where does your case stand now?" I asked.

"Ron Mobley is handling it, and he tells me they are working on trying to tie in SAC to the arson. I gave him all the letters and records I have that relate to the case, but you and I both know that he has to come up with a witness, or the arsonist, to make a case. Then he would have to tie the arsonist into SAC. How do you fit into this picture? Mobley told me the police department would not be involved, just Arson."

"Arson was still a crime, the last time I looked, and we handle crimes," I answered. "We might be able to go places Arson can't go and come up with something they can't. It can't hurt having us both looking at this. I suggest you just sit tight, and if we can do something for you, we will. Right now we are working on some arsons that have caused a couple of deaths. We are looking at all the arsons in the area to see if any tie in to ours. It don't appear that yours will, but we have to look at it and eliminate it if it doesn't." I was thinking about what else I should tell him. What if someone else was hired to torch his house before I made my case and got the Villains indicted? Could I work fast enough to do that before Anderson was more than an arson victim? I would wait and see where I was by tomorrow morning and go from there. "Thank you for your time, and we will not bother you again. I'm sure Mobley will do the job for you he should, and if we come up with something, we will pass it on to him."

Art and I left and went to a local restaurant we knew and got something to eat, and put our case together for the meeting with the DA. While we were finishing our coffee, Art looked at me with a puzzled look and began to question me.

"I'm a little confused; are we setting priorities here? You have lost me on where we are going. How are we going to pull this all together? I'm thinking we got two directions to go, and we can't go both ways at the same time. You told me Tommy said our suspects on our arsons were out of town, and we don't know where yet. We need to chase them down, and we need to get right on this Anderson case too. Tell me, what do you have in mind?"

"Well, the way I see it, we meet the DA and get his blessing for Tommy, and I get my phone call from him and hook him up for tomorrow. We meet him and give him his deal and get the location of our arson suspects. Then you can go after them, and I will stay with Tommy ,and we will go after the Villains. How does that sound to you?"

"What about Mobley?"

"What if we tell the DA to call Mobley's case, with respect to Anderson, into his office? That way the case will be coordinated with ours and will be at the request of the DA, and not us. That will get us off the hook with him."

"I'm glad I asked for direction from you. I knew you would be thinking of number one somewhere in there. Not that I care what Mobley thinks of us, anyhow. I think the way you got it figured will fly; let's do it."

We met with the assistant DA and a trial deputy by the name of Troy Dunn at the Torrance DA's office. We laid out our cases for them and showed them where we wanted to go with the case on the Villains. After a lengthy discussion, they agreed with us and stated they would grant Tommy immunity from prosecution if he wore the wire. He would have to testify in all three cases as well. I had also asked them to foot the bill for the cost of getting him to Florida; I explained that after he testified at the preliminary hearings, he would be known to the bad guys and would need to be protected until the trials. Since we would have to pay to protect him anyhow, why not send him to Florida. Dunn agreed to classify him as a protected witness and would place him into a protected witness program, only if he testified and the bad guys were bound over for trial. I agreed and figured Tommy would be satisfied with the deal he was getting.

I had also asked for arrest warrants on Bill Henry and Doreen Kitty. I had explained that they already had left town and they were a flight risk and were already fleeing to avoid prosecution. Dunn had agreed to get the warrants and have them ready for us to pick up in the morning. He also insisted that we coordinate everything through him, and that he would keep all the files in his office. We were to work the cases out of his office, so that he could control the investigation. I didn't like the idea of not having control, but the trade-off was worth giving it up. Dunn took another hour writing up the paperwork and gave me the immunity agreement to have Tommy sign. At least he had not insisted to be present when I talked to Tommy. That was a plus.

It was late in the afternoon when we left the DA's office, so we decided to go shoot some pool. We went to our regular pool hall, which was out in Inglewood. We needed to relax and get away from the stress of our cases. Our meeting with the DA had taken its toll on our brains. We had to think and plan our movements in order to get what we wanted, and come out on top. The DA's always thought they were superior to law enforcement and had to be in control, kind of like the FBI. While we shot pool, Art and I talked about our cases and came to the conclusion that we were still on track. After a while I decided to go to Irving's and get some barbecue, and Art decided to go home.

The next morning I was sitting at a picnic table in a public park in the city of Gardena. I was talking to the groundskeeper and waiting on Tommy to show up. Tommy had called me, as we had planned, and I had told him to meet me at the park. The park was always almost deserted in the mornings, and I liked to use it for my meetings with informants. I had made friends with the groundskeeper some time ago, and, for a bottle now and then, he protected my backside while I talked to my informants. If someone came into the park, he would tell them the park was closed in the area I was in, and he would come over and work around me. That way I knew to check out whoever it was who had come into the park. Art had decided to not come with me, saying "Tommy is your man, not mine." Besides, as we planned, he was going to go get the warrants from the DA and work on getting Bill Henry and Doreen Kitty into custody. When I had talked to Tommy on the phone last night, I had got the phone number he called them at, in San Francisco. Art was going to call their fugitive division and try to get them to find an address, through the phone number, and get them picked up.

It was peaceful in the park, early in the morning, and I liked the solitude it provided, just me and the birds and the sounds of the groundskeeper's mower. I had played a lot of baseball when I was a kid, and I just liked the sight of a baseball field, and there was one here to look at. Funny how some off-the-wall things give a person the peace he is looking for. I thought about the first brain concussion I had gotten. It was at a baseball game, when I was fourteen years old, and I was batting. The sun was setting behind the pitcher, and he threw a high inside pitch that I lost in the sun. The ball hit me in the left temple, and I went down. The next memory I had was waking up in the hospital. There was a man sitting next to my bed, who I thought was my coach, and I asked him if we had won the game. The man answered me and said the game had been ten days ago, and he was my uncle, not my coach. He told me various family members had been sitting with me, 24-7, waiting for me to either wake up or to start playing baseball in heaven.

It wasn't too long before I saw Tommy pull up in his car and park in the ball field's parking lot. I knew it was him because I recognized his car. I watched him get out, look around for me, see me, take something out of his car, and walk over to where I was at. As he sat down at the table, he set a six-pack of beer down, took a church key out of his pocket, opened two of the beers, and gave one to me.

Tommy then said, "Do you think one six-pack will be enough to get us through this? If not, you will need to get the next one, because I only got one."

"Depends on you; it will be enough for me. I got the papers for you to sign, and if you sign them, all we have to do is figure out how we are going to do this. Like I told you on the phone, you got immunity on the fires you set at the Anderson Disposal, for your testimony and the wearing of the wire. We will pay for your relocation to Florida. If it is necessary for you to come back for a trial, we will pay for the round-trip expenses. What I need to know is what is coming out of my pocket for the information you gave me on my other two fires. If it proves to be true, and I don't doubt that it is, and we get them, I owe you."

"I'm thinking five hundred dollars. As long as I can get back with my family in Jacksonville and get away from this hassle out here, I'll be cool—know what I mean?"

"No problem, I can handle that. What I think we have to do is have you set up the meeting for sometime on Thursday. I would like to make the arrest on Friday afternoon. Now, I found out there are two brothers who are in SAC. Which one is it who you are dealing with?"

"All I know is they call him Dom. When I went there for our meeting, his receptionist called him Dom. I don't know about no brother; I only dealt with Dom."

"Let's hope you get Dom to talk to you the second time around. If it's his brother, we will have a small problem, but I think we will be able to take them both, that being the case. Either way, make sure you get what we want on the tape."

We popped another beer and thought some more about how we were going to do it. Both of us knew it wasn't going to be smooth sailing, but we both had a lot riding on the meeting, so we decided to go for it and see where it took us. We finished our second beers and left the park together, in my car. We went to a phone booth, and Tommy made the call. When he hung up, he told me the meeting was a go. He had set it for Thursday at four in the afternoon. We went back to the park and finished the beer and set a meet for the next afternoon to wire Tommy up for the meeting.

I met Art back at the station and found out that he had contacted San Francisco Fugitive, and they had came up with an address for the phone number he had given them. Art had given the two suspects' identification numbers to Fugitive, and they had pulled their jackets up there and had photos on them. They were going to hit the pad tonight. The next couple of days was either going to make our cases or break them.

Art and I ended up winning both directions we had gone. Art won in San Francisco. Both suspects were found and arrested up there, and we went and got them and brought them back to LA. I got Doreen to testify, and we convicted Bill and the two property owners of murder and Doreen of arson.

I had won with Tommy. I had gotten the tape and got Dom and held him to answer for arson at a preliminary hearing. Tommy got his trip to Florida and had made his parole and was a free man.

But as things go, you can never count on the future. It was almost a year later when Art and I were shooting pool and we thought about this case again. We had both been busy with other cases and had forgotten all about this case. We realized that we had never been notified to appear at the trial. We decided to look into why, and when we went to the DA's office we found that the case had been dismissed at a pretrial hearing. We also found that DA Dunn had left the DA's office and was set up in private practice. The judge who handled it had retired and was in the Cayman Islands. The paperwork and my tape were nowhere to be found. And Anderson? He had had his house firebombed and his daughter almost killed, and had closed his business and left the state.

• • •

In October of 1972 the commanding officer of Seventy-seventh Division decided to implement the first unsolved homicide team in the city of Los Angeles. Our division led the city in unsolved homicides, and he wanted to reduce those numbers. (Today television calls this team's work the *Cold Case Files*.) Our homicide coordinator picked Tom McGuine and me to be assigned to this team. We worked this detail for over a year and cleared over twenty-five homicides. The cases were classified one of three ways. One was a case that led to a conviction in court. Another was a case in which the suspect was known, but there wasn't enough evidence to file a case. The third way was a case in which a suspect had not been identified. The most frustrating cases were those in which the suspect was known, but we couldn't get him to court to answer for his crime. Sometimes the streets had their own way of taking care of justice, as we will see later.

In 1973 a crime reporter came to our division after hearing of our unsolved homicide team. He was from England and wanted to do a story on our team for publication in his magazine. He had hopes of influencing Scotland Yard to also develop an unsolved homicide team. The article was published and drew worldwide attention in the law enforcement community. (On Sept. 9, 2009, the article was placed on display in the Los Angeles Police Historical Museum.)

The "Whoduniteam" article was written as follows:

Whoduniteam

They don't wear deerstalker caps and there's not a magnifying glass in sight. But, as far as 27 suspected and convicted Los Angeles murderers are concerned, the legendary 19th century Baker Street team of Sherlock Holmes and Dr. Watson would be no match for 20th century sleuths Tom McGuine and Robert Reynolds. For these two intrepid investigators are the current members of 77th Street Area's Unsolved Homicide Team.

In no way related to Team Policing or any other team concept of law enforcement or investigation, an Unsolved Homicide Team on an area level is a fairly new approach to investigating unclear murders, and an incredibly efficient approach at that.

Still in its infancy as police techniques go, the UHT has compiled an enviable success record. Beginning in October 1972 with an investigation into the fatal stabbing of a son of a retired LAPD officer, the Team has been responsible, as of this writing, for 27 arrests, 18 convictions and 15 cases cleared from the books. Four additional trials are pending.

The Team's entry into a case and its subsequent MO general take the following form:

A homicide is reported to 77th Street investigators. As 77th Street Area is sectored into four geographical areas with one 2-man investigative team assigned to each quadrant, the appropriate pair of investigators begins questioning, searching for leads and witnesses. Evidence is collected and the process of piecing together a life and death puzzle begins. But with more than 100 homicides yearly reported to the area, investigators are frequently not given the privilege of seeing a case through to conclusion. There just aren't enough hours in a working day, nor days in a week, to continue one investigation while beginning on another. The unsolved murder becomes simply another addition to the list of unclear cases in an investigator's log book.

Enter Tom McGuine and Bob Reynolds and the collective experience of the Unsolved Homicide Team.

"We can take on a case for any number of reasons," explains Inv. Reynolds, looking back through a log book of successfully worked homicide investigations. "The case might be particularly violent, with the murderer posing a continuing threat to many citizens. Or we might feel that solving one murder will lead us to a number of other commissions.

"But generally we pick out a case that, quite honestly, has leads which might result in a successful conclusion. One that could have been solved by the original investigators if they just had enough time."

Reynolds, joined by partner McGuine, relates a recent case that illustrates the effectiveness of the Unsolved Homicide Team concept.

A husband and wife team of narcotics peddlers were approached at their residence by some potential customers, ostensibly to make a big sale. In reality, they were to be robbed and killed by the alleged buyers. The husband was fatally stabbed and robbed of both money and narcotics: his wife, although stabbed in the throat and strangled with a telephone cord, survived when the deep throat wound acted as a tracheotomy, allowing her to breathe. She then managed to escape the fire set by the murderers in an effort to hide the killing.

After three weeks in the hospital, the widow fled to New Orleans "in terror that the killers might return for her since she could identify them."

The murder-robbery case was initially tackled by a Seventy-seventh Robbery team that, working on-call weekends, was assigned to investigate homicides.

"Four months later, with the case still unsolved, we received a call from Robbery-Homicide downtown. A witness to a homicide they were investigating said he had information regarding our case. Only he was in jail in Riverside on a narco charge," Reynolds says.

"I went to Riverside, interviewed the man and came back with a pretty good idea who our murderer was. According to the wit, he and a friend had arrived in Hollywood from up north to consummate a narcotics deal. The three supposed sellers had other ideas, however. They shotgunned the wit's buddy and pistol-whipped the wit, leaving him for dead.

"The wit survived the beating and retreated east, later returning to the West Coast to get the guys who had tried to kill him. Instead he was picked up in Riverside and jailed. Hopeful of some sort of deal for his release, and to get even for the beating and murder, he called Robbery-Homicide to ID the three murderers. Robbery-Homicide relayed the information to us. We checked with our snitches and contacts and came up with a verification of the names plus their locations. All three were arrested and the evidence we were able to produce convicted all of them", adds McGuine.

While McGuine and Reynolds were working the second homicide, Art Sage, the Seventy-seventh investigative Homicide Coordinator who had the distinction of being the first Unsolved Homicide "Team," continued with the husband and wife assault and murder.

"I met with the wife of the murdered man," Sage recalls, "and showed her a series of mug shots, including those of the three suspects in the second murder. She immediately spotted one of the three who, by that time, had already received a 187 conviction. That individual is now due to come to trial on the second murder charge."

Two murders: two nearly fatal assaults: two seemingly unrelated cases. Yet both solved and cleared as a result of one month of intensive investigation by 77th Street Area's Unsolved Homicide Team.

Also solving more than its share of homicides is the fairly new Unsolved Homicide Team of Southwest Area. Although barely six months in operation, the Team of Earl Nishirnura and Al Ferrand has cleared one of seven "old and cold" murders along with 13 of 15 more recent southwest homicides.

Many factors have contributed to the UHTs phenomenal success: investigative experience, valuable contacts, even lucky breaks. But one element more than any other in the success story sets UHT investigators apart and above virtually all others: Time! Time to run down leads. Time to contact witnesses and principals. Time to devote to the long, tedious, frequently monotonous sifting of clues and statements. And time is the one commodity most investigators are lacking. Time, it seems, makes all the difference.

Lt. Ron Lewis points out, in addition to time; an essential ingredient to the success of the program is the expertise, dedication, persistence and conscientiousness of the assigned Investigators. These qualities were found in Tom McGuine and Bob Reynolds.

"Bob Reynolds has seven years in homicide and 14 years on the Department. His partner Tom MGuine has spent four years investigating murders and has 11 years with the LAPD. As a matter of fact, Tom McGuine is one of three law enforcement members (along with one each from the LASO and the FBI) listed in the District Attorney's forensic expert directory which is used as a source of reference for Deputy District Attorneys desiring expertise in a wide spectrum of fields.

"Their experience, and what seems to be a knack for the kind of specialized work, has enabled them to clear up some pretty difficult cases."

They've cleared up so many cases, in fact, that it may be a case of misleading advertising to call them the Unsolved Homicide Team.

• • •

Now let me tell you some war stories about three cases that fall into that category of "knowing who the suspects were, but couldn't prove it" category.

I investigated the cases while working the unsolved homicide team. All three cases will come out of the three major drug rings in south central Los Angeles. The first drug ring was controlled and run by Tookie and was based in Watts. The second drug ring was controlled and run by "The Professor," and the third drug ring was controlled and run by "Sugar." (Both of these drug rings controlled the drug traffic to the north and west of Watts.) The first case will come out of Tookie's drug ring and will be taken care of by street justice. The investigation will actually clear two homicides.

In 1970 there was a drug rehabilitation center, located on 103rd Street, called The House of Uri. It was just outside the Jordan Downs Housing Project, and across the street and a little to the west of Bob's liquor store. After a Tuesday night meeting in March of 1971, the director, Marcus Anderson, and a counselor, Cle Adair, were standing in the front doorway shaking hands with the guests as they were leaving the meeting. Two shots rang out from across the street, and both Marcus and Cle were struck by the bullets. Marcus was shot through the shoulder, and Cle was shot in the head. Cle was killed immediately, and Marcus was taken to the hospital in serious condition.

The initial investigation revealed that the House of Uri was an offshoot of the Multi Purpose Center and was being funded by the federal government for drug rehabilitation. Marcus was hired as the director of the program and was receiving federal funds, based on the attendance. Meetings were scheduled three times a week, on Tuesday, Wednesday, and Friday. Every

Tuesday night a dinner was held for the attendees. It turned out that Marcus was a newcomer from New York and was an ex convict with a narcotics record. He was interviewed at the hospital by the original investigators, but disappeared shortly after the interview. At the time he was interviewed, he would not furnish any information about the shooting. (Remember Marcus Anderson.) He revealed only that he and Adair were in the doorway shaking hands with the attendees when he bent over to shake a hand and a shot was fired. The shot hit Adair, and, as he straightened up to run, he was hit by a second shot. He had not seen the person who had fired the shots or where the shots had come from. He had also stated that he had no idea as to who might want to shoot them.

The only information the original investigators got on Cle Adair was that he was an ex convict and had done time for strong-armed robbery. He was also a drug addict and was attending meetings at The House of Uri, where he acted as a councilor. He had been hired by Marcus to attend the meetings and keep the peace during the meetings. He was also getting federal money to attend the meetings.

The case investigation did not turn up any leads or suspects, and the case became an unsolved case. The House of Uri closed down after the homicide, and the attendees were in the wind, as was Marcus Anderson. The only physical evidence recovered were two .30-caliber spent rounds, from a wall inside the House of Uri, and two spent casings from a .30-caliber rifle. The casings were found inside a burned-out building across the street from the House of Uri. The building had been burned down during the '65 Watts riots, and was abandoned and boarded up.

I ran across the case while reviewing unsolved cases in early 1973. Because of the location of the homicide, I decided to look into it. I had not heard of the case, and was curious about why it had gone down. I had been on vacation when it had happened, and that explained why I did not know about it. I knew I had a couple of people I could talk to who might know something about it. It might cost me a few dollars but it would be money well spent if it produced the results I wanted. I had not known the victim, nor had I known anything about the House of Uri.

The first place I went for information was Bob's liquor store. I talked to Bob about the case in his back room at the liquor store. Bob told me he had heard that Marcus was using the House of Uri as a front and was actually selling drugs out of the place. All of the hypes that hung out in and around Jordan Downs went there to get their drugs. They were also getting paid to attend meetings. There had been a lot of talk at the time that Tookie was not happy with the action on Marcus part. He had heard that Tookie had been behind what had gone down, but not who had actually done the killing. Bob further explained that knowing that information was dangerous in itself and could get you dead if you talked about it. Marcus had not reappeared and he had not seen him since he had been shot. No one he knew of had actually seen the shooting go down, nor had anyone seen the shooter. Presently the shooting was history and forgotten about, as far as talk in the streets was concerned.

The second place I went for information was to "Popsicle." I ran into him in Will Rogers Park, shooting hoops. He was by himself, so I got him to take a ride with me. As you might guess, we went to the park in Gardena, and yes, I bought the beer. We were drinking beer and sitting at our favorite picnic table when I popped my first question: "I need to know about a shooting back in 1971 at the House of Uri. A couple of guys by the names of Marcus Anderson and Cle Adair were shot. What can you tell me about it?"

"What is it worth to me to tell you?"

"Let's start out with a hundred dollars and go from there. First I got to see what you got."

"Well, out of the gate I can get you started, but it won't get me into court. That shooting is too heavy! I'll take fifty now and fifty later, if I get to hurting."

"I got the first fifty dollars with me and the second fifty will be there if your information is good."

"First thing you should know is Cle Adair was Tookie's cousin, and he wasn't supposed to be killed. I was tight with Cle, and we did drugs together. He told me Tookie suspected Marcus of dealing drugs out of the House of Uri. He had got the word to him several times to get off 103rd Street. Marcus wouldn't budge, so Tookie got Cle to get next to Marcus and find out what he could. Cle told me Marcus did not know him, and, after he had attended a few meetings, he started buying his drugs from Marcus. Marcus was cutting the cost on the drugs, and a lot of Tookie's trade was going to Marcus. Plus, Marcus was paying them to come to meetings. Cle told me he got Marcus to make him a councilor and put him on the payroll. At the same time, Cle was reporting back to Tookie. Marcus had come out of New York and was getting his drugs from there somehow."

"How long was Marcus operating before Tookie got wind of it?"

"For about a year. It took awhile before the word got up to Tookie. I even went there to score. The price was right, and you even got paid to go there. But then Tookie's dealers noticed they were losing their customers and complained to Tookie. That's when he found out we were going to Marcus."

"So how did Cle end up dead, and Marcus shot?"

"I'm getting there, so don't rush me. After the first of the year, in '71, Cle told me that he was going to set up Marcus to be taken out."

"Was he going to do that at the request of Tookie?"

"No, Tookie did not know Cle was going to do it. It was a cousin thing. Cle told me he was going to do it himself. You know, kind of like helping his cousin out and getting rid of his problem for him. So Cle told me he got Billy Cunningham to be the trigger man."

I had heard that name before, but where? Then it came to me. Billy Cunningham was a named suspect on one of the unsolved homicides I had reviewed. In 1972 a Billy Cunningham was suspected of killing his common-law wife. He had beaten her to death with a hammer in the house they shared in the Jordan Downs. He had been arrested for the killing, but was let go when he denied doing it and it could not be proven. There were no witnesses to the killing, and no physical evidence to connect him to the crime. The hammer was found in the house, but there were no prints on it, nor was there any blood. The victim died as a result of blunt-force trauma to her head. She was beaten so bad that she was not recognizable. The victim was eighteen years old and Billy was twenty-one."

"Tell me about Billy Cunningham!"

"He's a bad dude. He is a psychopath and will beat anyone who disrespects him. The rumors in Jordan Downs, where he lives, are that he has killed two dudes in the projects who disrespected him. Then everyone knows he killed his old lady, but you will never get anyone to talk about it. They are too scared of him; like I say, he's crazy and would put you in an early grave if he knew you were talking about him. Everyone goes the other way when he's around. I couldn't believe it when Cle told me he had got him to help him kill Marcus."

"Okay, let's get back to the killing of Cle and the shooting of Marcus. So far you say that Cle is going to do Marcus on his own. He is going to use Billy to do the shooting. So what went wrong that caused Cle to be shot?"

"I don't know that. All I know is Cle told me he was going to get Marcus into the doorway, after a meeting on Tuesday, and position him so Billy could shoot him from across the street, from an abandoned building. Cle had told me not to go to the meeting that night, and I didn't. I was hanging out at the liquor store to see what was going to go down when I heard the shots. The next thing I see is Billy running down the alley carrying a rifle. He was in the alley behind the liquor store and ran across the street into the Jordan Downs projects. Then, after the shooting and after I saw Billy, I went over there and saw Cle was shot, as well as Marcus. Then I got the hell out of there and I have not told anyone what I saw. Even Tookie had asked me if I saw anything that night, and I told him I wasn't out that night. I don't need that monkey on my back, and I trust you to not lay me out. I'm only telling you now because you asked me what I know. We have been tight, and you know my mother and all, and I know you won't burn me. But like I say, I'm not going to court over any of this. You are going to have to take it from here, without me!"

"Now let's go back to Billy Cunningham. You say that it is rumored he has killed two other dudes; tell me about those killings."

"As I remember it, one was when he was a juvenile, back in 1966. I know it was 1966, because it was the year after the Watts riots. It was a gang thing that went down in the Jordan Downs projects. The Bounty Hunters had come up to Jordan Downs from the Imperial Courts, and were looking to revenge a drive-by shooting down there. There was a shootout, and Billy killed one of them. He was caught on it and did three years in the California Youth Authority. They let him out when he made eighteen years old. That was in 1969. The other killing I heard of him being good for was in 1970. It was in Jordan Downs too. You know, like born and bred in the projects. Billy don't have no car, and don't leave the neighborhood. Anyhow, he got into it with a dude named Joey Rankin one night in Jordan Downs, at the back end of the project, near Ninety-second Street. It was in a cul-de-sac, and Billy was supposed to have shot him dead right there in the street. Again, I'm not saying this is for sure, it's just like I heard it. Maybe he did, and maybe he didn't, but there is a whole lot of people who, if there was a bet on it, they would be on the 'did it' side."

I knew of the cul-de-sac killing, as I had rolled on it and assisted another team investigating it. I was working another case, and they had asked for assistance. When I got there, there was a crowd of about a hundred people around the crime scene, and the crowd was becoming unruly. It was late at night, and we had to get some patrol cars out there to move the crowd back and protect the scene. I remembered talking to the victim's brother, Tyree Rankin, who was a transvestite. In fact, Tyree would call me about every six months to see if we had found out who had killed his brother. I would always tell him I didn't have the case, and he would tell me I was the only police officer he would talk to. He would always say that I understood him and the other cops didn't. If nothing else, maybe I would be able to give him an answer now. I knew the case had not been solved, but I was not aware of its status, and I would have to look it up. When we had sorted out the unsolved cases, it must have been put with the cases we felt had no leads, and it had been given a low priority.

"Is Billy still living in Jordan Downs?" I asked.

"He still lives in the same place he was living when he killed his old lady. He has got him another old lady that's living with him in there. She has a couple of kids and supports him with her welfare money. I don't know if Cle paid him for the Marcus shooting or not."

"Speaking of getting paid, here is the fifty dollars, and I owe you another fifty dollars. It's been two years since the Marcus thing went down, and from what you have told me, I don't have a case. I promise you I will not jam you with making my case for me. If I can't make a case without you, it will stay on the books as an unsolved case. Just your seeing Billy with a rifle, after the shots were fired, is not enough to make the case, anyhow."

Popsicle put the fifty dollars in his pocket, and we finished the beer. I then took him back to Will Rogers Park and dropped him off. I told him to get word to Bob at Bob's liquor store if he got to hurting and needed the other fifty dollars. I then drove to the station to put what he had told me in some kind of order. The first thing I did was pull the case from 1972, which was the killing of Billy Cunningham's common-law wife. As I suspected, he was brought in but was let go. There was a jacket on him in the case file that showed his record. He had an extensive juvenile record, and it showed the arrest for murder in 1966. He had done three years for that murder. I also found the murder book on the Joey Rankin case, from 1970. It was one of the cases we had pulled when we first started reviewing the unsolved cases, and, as I had suspected, we had disregarded it. Billy Cunningham was not mentioned in the case file. As I saw it, if Billy was good for the last three killings, he had killed in 1970, 1971, and 1972. Popsicle had always had good information in the past, and I did not have reason to doubt what he had told me was true. I knew that he had not told me about Billy being involved in the killings before because I hadn't asked him about them. A snitch does not volunteer information unless you ask them to.

The only way I could see to connect Billy to any of the three killings would be through the rifle on the Marcus case. I did not hold out hope of coming up with witnesses on any of the cases. The projects were the worst places to try and find witnesses. The people living in the projects had to live there, and they knew in order to survive they had to see no evil and speak no evil; doing evil was another story. It was also understandable that Billy was getting away with what he was doing, and I wasn't sure that there were other cases he was good for. I searched all our homicides that were unsolved, but did not find any others that fit into his realm of possibility. I was sure that he probably was good for some other assaults, but the end results would be the same. It was going to depend on getting that rifle, in his possession. I knew that talking to him would be like talking to a wall.

We crossed all our t's and dotted all our i's on the three cases and got nowhere with Billy Cunningham. We searched his house for the rifle and came up empty. We brought him in and arrested him on the Marcus/Adair case and interrogated him until the cows came home, and got nowhere. We had to let him go after forty-eight hours, and the cases remained unsolved. We felt sure he was our killer, but we could not prove it on any of the three cases.

Now let me jump ahead to show you how street justice works its ways and takes care of business, in some cases. In 1974 Billy Cunningham was found shot to death in Jordan Downs. He was found dead just outside his residence, in a cul-de-sac. His body was found in the curbside grass, and he had been shot several times. It appeared that a car had driven up to him, and the person inside the car had shot him and drove off. It was assumed that the suspect had lain in wait, and, when Billy came out of his house, they drove up and shot him. I was the homicide coordinator at the time and came in on the case with the team that caught the case. The investigation failed to turn up any suspects or a description of a car. After several days I decided it was time for me to meet with Popsicle again and pay him the fifty dollars I still owed him.

I found Popsicle at Bob's liquor store and picked him up, and we went to Will Rogers Park. It was late at night, and we would go unnoticed in the park. I opened up the conversation.

"I got your fifty dollars that I owe you, and I would like to use it for anything you might know about the shooting of Billy

Cunningham. Not that anyone is going to miss him, but the law applies to everyone equally—know what I mean?"

"You really want to know who shot that piece of shit? They ought to give him a medal instead of putting him in jail. Do us all a favor and let it go."

"You know I can't do that; if I could, I would. The only way to beat it is self-defense, and, as I see it, that's not an option on this one. Billy was not packing, and the killing has all the signs of a drive-by shooting."

"I think the shooter is safe; anyhow, you won't find a person to testify on this one nohow."

"All I want to know is what they are saying in the projects."

"OK, I'll tell you what the talk is, but I don't have a name. The talk is that Billy's first old lady, the one he killed, has a brother that was living down south. She also has a sister that lives in the Imperial Courts. It seems the brother came out here to visit the sister. It also seems he looked up Billy and took care of business. That's how I heard it."

"Where is he now; has he gone back down south?"

"The last I heard was that he was trying to get the money together to catch a bus and be gone."

"You let me know if that comes to pass. I need to hear from you if he starts to make the trip. Is he staying at the sister's house?"

"No, he's floating in and out. He doesn't want to bring the heat down on her. She has got some kids in her pad, and he doesn't want any trouble on them."

"Do you know what unit the sister lives in?"

"No, I don't."

"OK, then, thanks for the information; call me!"

I took Popsicle back to Bob's liquor store and went home. I asked myself if I really wanted to identify the brother and pick him up. What other choice did I have? I had the job of clearing homicides and not the job of picking and choosing which ones I would clear and which ones I wouldn't. If I couldn't clear a case because I couldn't identify a suspect, it was acceptable, but this case was not that way; this was a case where I had a lead on the suspect. I would give the team that was handling the case the lead tomorrow, and let the chips fall whereever.

The next day I met with the team that had the case and briefed them on what I had learned. We checked in the murder book on Billy's old lady's murder and found an address for her sister in Imperial Courts. As we were discussing the best way to approach her, I got a phone call. All the caller said was, "He's at the sisters house and is going to leave town tonight."

I told the team what the caller said, and they left the station to go out to the sister's house. After not hearing from them for a half hour, I drove out to the sister's house to check on what they were doing.

When I arrived I saw that a crowd of over a hundred people had gathered around the immediate area of the sister's house. My team was standing in front of the house with a Housing Authority officer. I went up to them and asked what was going on. They told me they had gotten to the house and knocked on the door, and no one would answer. They tried several times, and still no one came to the door. They then called the Housing Authority to come out there with a pass key and open the door. When he got there and knocked at the door, stating who he was, again no one came to the door. The Housing Authority officer would not unlock the door because he did not have the authority to invade the tenant's privacy.

"Look!" I said. "You can kick in the door on the basis of an emergency, to prevent an escape. Your entry would be justified based on probable cause to believe that your suspect is leaving town."

"We don't know that for a fact. All we have is a phone call telling us that," answered one of my team investigators. "We don't want to be wrong on this and have to subject ourselves to disciplinary action. Under current law we need a Ramey warrant to arrest a person in their house."

"Well, you got to do what you got to do. It's no sweat off me. If you want to pack it in and leave, that's what we will do."

They chose to leave, so that's what we did. Now was the brother inside? I guess we will never know, because we never caught up with him after that. The chance of taking him into custody, and maybe coming up with a gun or a confession, had passed. We eventually identified him but did not know where he had gone, nor did we have enough evidence to get a warrant. As far as I know, Billy Cunningham's case is still an unsolved case. I cleared the three cases—Adair, Rankin, and Billy's wife—by showing that the suspect was deceased.

• • •

I had only one other thing to do on these cases, and that was to drop a dime on Tyree Rankin.

"Hello, Tyree, it's Detective Reynolds. Good information has it that your brother was killed by a dude named Billy Cunningham. Last week Billy Cunningham was killed out there in Jordan Downs, just like your brother. What goes around, comes around. I know it's been four years now, but I hope you can find a closure out of this now."

"I had heard that it was Billy, but I didn't know if that was the truth for sure. I want to thank you for thinking of me, and I won't be bothering you any more. Good-bye and God bless."

Out of the big three—The Professor, Sugar, and Tookie—The Professor had the most book knowledge, but even though he grew up in the streets, he lacked in street knowledge. He looked like a professor, right down to the glasses. He was a tall and slim dude and was light in complexion, for a black man. What he lacked in bulk, he made up for in surrounding himself with an army of guns. As a lot of the Watts dudes had done, he had come up through the street gangs to get his piece of the narcotic pie. His narcotic trade was limited to parts of the west side, and, of the three, he was the weakest. Because of his intelligence with figures, he was able to maximize profits. He had kept his drug ring together for several years and did not make any attempts to enlarge his distribution into the other two areas of responsibility. That's why I was surprised when he was found shot to death in the subterranean garage of the apartment building he was living in, in 1973.

My subsequent investigation did not identify who had shot him, but it did come up with a probable reason or motive, and that pointed to an internal source. The Professor had turned to the finer things in life and overlooked his roots. He wanted to live the white man's life and, over the last year of his life, took to the Hollywood scene. His life became one of fast cars, fast white women, and the finer clubs and parties in Hollywood. All the profits from his narcotic trade were being spent in Hollywood. He would keep a couple of his bodyguards around on some of his jaunts, but the rest of his drug ring was suffering on payday. Then, to top it off, he started using his own product. As things go, he also was sharing his product with his newly found Hollywood friends. (Remind you of someone in New Jersey?) I remember I thought at the time that he should have stayed in his own end of LA, and Sam Cook should have stayed in Hollywood.

I worked the case, on and off, for a year and got no further with it. I felt sure that he had been killed because of his change in his lifestyle, but I could not come up with a suspect. I talked to all of his personal, from his lieutenants down to the street dealers, and after all of my shaking, rattling, and rolling, came up empty-handed. At the time of his death, I had gotten a photo album out of his apartment that had a history of his upbringing. He had taken group pictures of most of those who were working with him, and the home girls who hung out with them. There was also a photo album of his life in Hollywood, but I ignored that one. It was impressive, but I did not feel it would solve his death. I probably would have gotten rich selling it to the tabloids, though. As near as I could tell, his drug ring was still in place and business was as usual, not skipping a beat. How do they say that: "One day you are there working, and the next day you are gone and forgotten"?

It was 1974, and Tom and I were still working the unsolved cases. We had just finished up on the Billy Cunningham case and were in the office reviewing some new unsolved cases when our coordinator came over to talk to us.

"I just got notified by the patrol watch commander that they have a dead body out on Figueroa Street. The body is in a hotel and is in a bathtub. The patrol officers don't see any signs of trauma, but they want us to come out and look at the body. You are the only team in the office, and I would like you to go have a look-see."

Tom and I agreed to go out and take care of it, and we left the station after getting the address of the hotel. The hotel was located at 9203 South Figueroa, and, as we approached the hotel, we noticed it was a large building on the west side of the street. Neither Tom nor I had noticed the building before and were surprised at it size. The building was built with studio apartments opening to its interior. The building was one story and took up half the block. It had a large parking lot to the north of the building, where we parked.

As we entered the building, we noticed that there was a reception desk inside the front door and a long hallway running to the south. The hallway was *L*-shaped and had rooms off each side of it. We figured there were over forty rooms. To the north of the reception desk was a large room with closed doors. To the west, the inside of the building had a kitchen, dining area, laundry facilities, and other rooms with unidentifiable purposes. We were both impressed with the facility and the cleanliness of the building. We identified ourselves to the nurse who was at the reception desk, and she took us down the hallway to one of the rooms. The patrol officers were inside the room when we arrived. We asked the nurse if the deceased was being seen by a doctor, and she stated that he wasn't, and that she was not a nurse, either, she was just an aid. There were neither nurses nor doctors on the staff. The nurse then left us with the officers and returned to the desk.

The room was a studio-sized apartment, with a front room and a bathroom. The bed was a pull-down bed, and there was no kitchen. The officers told us the deceased was in the bathtub inside the bathroom. They stated they had received a radio call to the location. The nurse had told them that the deceased lived in the room and, when she had checked on him, after he had not shown up to eat, she had found him in the tub. She had checked his vital signs and found he was dead. She had called 911, at the direction of the director of the facility, and the ambulance had arrived and pronounced the deceased DOA. The officers had been present when the ambulance got there and had the ambulance slip on the call. We asked them if they had talked to the director, and they stated that they hadn't. We asked them to stand by while we went into the bathroom and examined the deceased.

We entered the bathroom and observed the deceased in the bathtub. He was sitting in the tub with his back resting against the back of the tub, and his legs extended out toward the front of the tub. He was unclothed and appeared to be asleep. There were no signs of injury to his person, and his overall appearance appeared to be unremarkable in nature, with one exception. He had old and new needle tracks on both of his arms. After discussing the situation, Tom and I decided to make the death a coroner's case. Since the deceased was not being treated by a doctor, who could sign a death certificate, we had no choice, even though we both felt the cause of death would turn out to be from natural causes or an overdose. We then told the officers we would handle the case, and that they could leave. We went back to the front desk and told the aid what we were going to do, and asked to use her phone to call the coroner.

While we were waiting on the coroner, we asked the aid what type of facility the building was. She told us it housed drug addicts and military veterans who were receiving either state aid or VA benefits. Their benefits offset their costs, and the state paid the cost of the employees through a grant. We asked how long the facility had been operating, and she told us she had been employed at the facility since it opened, and that had been over two years ago. She also stated the director had been the person who had opened the facility and hired her. We asked what was it that they actually did for their tenants and she stated; "Just give them a place to sleep and eat, no medical treatment."

We then asked her if we could see the director, and she made a phone call and then walked us to the large room to the north, with the closed double doors. She knocked on the doors and announced us, and we were asked to come in. I opened one of the doors, and Tom and I entered the room. I could not believe what I saw when I entered the room!

In front of me was the biggest desk I had ever seen. The desk was a good twenty feet to the north of the door, and there was one guy sitting at the desk and two others standing on either side of the desk. The two guys standing were dressed in full sets of army fatigues, complete with gun belts, weapons, combat boots, and lariats. The person behind the desk was dressed the same. What surprised me even more was that I recognized all three of the guys. The one sitting behind the desk was Marcus Anderson—remember him? The other two were two of The Professor's lieutenants, who I had talked to when I was working his case. Small world, isn't it! You never know who you might run into in the most unlikely places.

I had not met Marcus before, but I recognized him from the photos I had of him while I was working his case. I was sure he did not know me, but I knew the other two remembered me. I made eye contact with the two lieutenants and I felt that I had just solved The Professor's case. Marcus had not been able to replace Tookie, but he had been able to take over for The Professor. Plus, he was back running a scam on the government. He again had addicts coming to him, and this time was getting their disability money, and, in return for that taxpayer money, furnishing their narcotics.

He verified what I thought when he told me he was director Marcus Anderson and asked me what he could do for me. I told him that we were making a coroner's case out of the deceased death, and that he would be working with the coroner's office to take care of the paperwork and whatever else would be necessary to finalize the coroner's responsibilities, as well as his. I thought about saying more to him, but realized it wouldn't get me anywhere I wanted to go, so I decided to let dead dogs lie, and just left.

As Tom and I went to our car, I noticed a new Cadillac in the parking lot that had plates on it that read MARCS2. Now, what do you think the 2 meant? Did the 2 mean, like, replacing The Professor in the Big Three? At the time, you could have only six spaces on a license plate. Why hadn't Marcus used the six spaces to spell out his name, MARCUS? Are we having fun yet?

• • •

The year 1974 had been good to me. I graduated from college with a B.S. degree in Police Science, I had been promoted to the rank of Inv. III, and I had been put in charge of the homicide squad. I had also began working for Columbia Studios, and was working as a techional advisor for a series on TV called *Police Story*. The series used five of my cases over the next two years to produce five shows on TV. I had actors like Mickey Rooney, Dennis Weaver, Vincent Edwards, and Robert Culp playing me in the shows. I would use my vacation time and my days off to go to the sets and locations, when they were filming the shows, and advise the director and actors how to act as I would act in real life. Then I would go to the cuttings of the film to assist in what was to be cut in order to get the takes down to fit into an hour's show. I also got to go to the wrap parties after the filming was completed. I even helped write some of the teleplays for the shows. Because The Professor case was fresh in my mind, I did not allow the Hollywood scene to cause me to yield to its temptations, though, and I gave that up after the show was cancelled. I had been asked to move to another show, but I declined the offer.

• • •

In 1975 I caught the third case I promised to tell you about. I was handling the weekend on call with Jerry Rogers when we responded to the notification of a homicide on a Sunday morning at three thirty. The homicide consisted of a dead body in a car at the intersection of Manchester Boulevard and Orchard Street. The location was in the northwest corner of our division. We met each other at the station and responded to the scene at 4:15 a.m. Upon our arrival we noted that a patrol car had secured the scene and had a person in the backseat of their car. The victim's car was facing south and appeared to have stopped for a stop sign that was on Orchard Street, and was there to stop the southbound traffic. The patrol officers came to our car and briefed us as to what they had. The person in their car was the reporting party and had been driving south, on his way to work, when he came up behind the victim's car. The R/P (reporting party) had said it was around three in the morning and there wasn't any other traffic on Orchard Street at the time. He honked his horn, and the guy didn't move his car, so he pulled around the guy's car, and when he got alongside the car he saw the guy was shot. He then got scared and drove back home and called 911. The patrol officers also told us that when they had gotten to the scene, the victim's car was running, and they had shut it off and left the key in the ignition. The gearshift had been in Park, and the victim's feet were off of the pedals. The ambulance had arrived at the same time they did, and pronounced the victim DOA at 3:15 a.m. The victim had not been moved by either them or the ambulance crew.

Jerry went to the patrol car to talk to the R/P, and I went to the victim's car to examine the scene. We had instructed the patrol officers to get hold of the watch commander and have him contact the coroner and the photo lab, and have them respond to the scene.

When I got to the victim's car, I noted that all of the windows were up, with the exception of the driver's window, which was down. The victim was sitting behind the steering wheel and his hands were in his lap. His upper body was turned toward the driver's window, and his face was facing outward.

There was what appeared to be a gunshot wound to the center of his forehead. There was a minimum amount of bleeding from the wound, and the blood had dried. The victim's eyes were open, as was his mouth. The victim was a young black man, and he was neatly dressed. The inside of the car was very clean, and the car itself appeared to be well taken care of. Other than what appeared to be a GSW, I did not see any other wounds upon the deceased person. I decided to await the coroner's arrival before examining the victim, or his car, any further. I then examined the street around the victim's car and observed what appeared to be tire tracks, from a car that had peeled out from the location of the victim's car. The tracks originated at the victim's car and went south to the corner and then turned to the right, west on Manchester Blvd. It appeared that the burned rubber was too heavy for a tread to be identified, but the photo lab could give it a go. I searched for a possible spent casing, but did not locate any. My search of the entire area did not turn up any additional evidence.

Jerry joined me and told me he had let the witness go on to work, and that he hadn't come up with any other information. The witness did not know the victim, nor did he recognize the car. The witness had stated that the victim's car was running when he pulled up alongside it, and he was sure the victim was dead when he first saw him. I then walked Jerry through what I had done and again looked over the scene. Neither of us found any additional evidence. The coroner arrived and removed the deceased from the car. Further examination of the victim did not reveal any additional injuries, and the time of death was placed at sometime after two in the morning. We searched the victim's car and didn't find any new evidence in the car. The GSW was caused by a probable .38-caliber weapon, and there was no exit wound. The bullet would be in the victim's head, and I was in hopes of it being good for comparison.

The victim's driver's license showed him to be Aaron Day, Male, black, DOB-2-16-1954, twenty-one years old five feet ten inches tall, and 175 pounds. His residence address was 1234 West 96 Street, which was within a mile of where we were. He also had a student activity card for USC and money in his wallet. His wallet had been in his rear pants pocket, and we felt robbery was not a motive. He had an address book in this wallet also, and I took this after signing a receipt for the coroner. I also retained the driver's license in case we needed it for identification. The photo lab took all our photos, including a mug shot of the victim, and the tire tracks. I requested the coroner to notify us as soon as they identified the victim through prints, if the victim's prints were on file. Otherwise we were going to have to have a family member make the identification. I asked the patrol officers to impound the victim's car for us and to put a hold on it for prints. I didn't expect anything to come of it, but why not? We all then left the scene, and Jerry and I returned to the station.

At the station I ran our victim for a record, and we had him in our records division, and he had a jacket. He had only one arrest for joy riding, as a juvenile, when he was fifteen. At least the coroner would be able to identify him through his prints. One thing was for sure, though; our victim was not a gang member. At least he did not have a record that would indicate he was. I also checked his car for any wants or warrants, and there weren't any hits. It appeared as though our victim was not going to be a person sought out by someone seeking a little street justice. I went through his address book and came up with a dozen persons I could follow up on. I ran them all through our records and field interview cards and again struck out. Not only was our victim squeaky clean, all his friends were too. This might turn out to be a whodunit real fast. It was going to be a while before the coroner made the identification official, so Jerry and I went to breakfast at the Pantry and waited until the sun came up. We both knew our next move was going to be contacting our victim's family, and neither one of us were looking forward to doing that. At the Pantry we tried to put some reason to why our victim was shot.

"What do you think, Jerry, do you think our victim was on his way home, or what?"

"I would say that's a possibility. He was heading in that direction. It looks like he had stopped for the stop sign, and someone came up alongside his car. Then, for some reason, he either rolled down his window, or it was already down. It was cold out at the time, so I think he probably rolled it down. Either way he probably turned to talk to whoever it was. He had put his car in park, so it looks like he was talking to whoever it was. There were probably two persons in the other car too. If there was only a driver, that was a hell of a shot. Then our victim gets shot, and the suspects peeled out and drove off down Manchester."

"It sounds good to me! I'm thinking he knew the suspect or suspects, and it was not a drive-by shooting. If he had not felt comfortable, he would have driven off. If he did know them, it gives us a start. We will be able to work the case from the victim backwards and look for who wanted the victim dead. I don't think he expected to get shot. Whatever the suspect wanted with him, he didn't feel threatened by it at the time,

I'm guessing. After we talk to his parents, we will get started on his friends. I checked the addresses for them in the reverse-phone-numbers book and found five addresses. They are all around USC College, and the persons are probably classmates of his. His rap sheet showed that his parents lived at the same address he had on his driver's license, so he was probably still staying there. What do you think?"

"You are the college man; I was lucky to get out of high school. Are the friends going to be around on Sunday, or do they go home for the weekend?"

"My guess is they will be around early, sleeping off Saturday night. USC is kind of a confined campus, and the students don't venture far from the campus. The school sits right in the middle of a seedy neighborhood. If we strike out today, we can always get to them tomorrow while they are attending their classes."

"I vote for the campus first, and the parents second. It's now around eight in the morning and I would rather get a bunch of hungover students up than the parents."

"You got it. A few hours won't matter to the parents and maybe we will come up with something we can talk to the parents about.",

Our trip to the USC campus proved to be fruitless in our effort to identify a suspect, but it gave us some insight into the life of our victim. We woke up some unhappy campers, but when they learned our purpose, they cooperated with us and even came up with other persons who knew our victim. We were even able to hold a conference with six of his friends at a fraternity house. Over the next four hours, we had talked to a dozen persons, both male and female, who knew our victim.

The information we gathered was as follows:

1. Our victim did not have any known enemies and was well liked on campus.

2. The victim did not drink or use drugs, but had attended parties on campus, up until six months ago, when he had started to date a new girlfriend. The girlfriend's name was Vickie Barlow, and she was a student at the college. No one knew where she lived.

3. The victim lived at home and stayed over at one of his friend's apartment, on occasion.

4. The victim was last seen on Friday, on campus. He had not mentioned what his plans were for the weekend.

5. The new girlfriend was not known personally by any of the friends, and did not run with his crowd of friends, but he had fell head over heels for her and indicated to his friends that he had found his future wife. Several of the friends had seen him with the girlfriend on campus, and knew of her, but he did not share her presence with them.

6. The victim was pursuing a dental career.

7. None of the victim's friends were boyhood friends, and all of them had met him at the school.

We arrived at the victim's parent's house that afternoon and, after identifying ourselves, met with the two of them. We had contacted the coroner, and he had confirmed that the victim was in fact Aaron Day. The parents immediately asked us if something had happened to Aaron, and, after asking them to sit down, I told them that their son had been killed early that morning. They asked me what had happened, and I told them he had been shot while sitting in his car. When I told them where it had happened, they said he must have been on his way home because he always came home on Orchard Street. The victim's mother asked to be excused and left the room. She was taking the death of her son badly, and I asked her husband if he would call us later, when he felt it would be okay for us to come back and talk further. He said to give them a few hours and he would call me that night. We gave him our business cards and then left and went back to the station to complete our reports.

At the station I checked all available sources I had to identify Vickie Barlow, and came up with a big zero. She also appeared to be squeaky clean, without a record or any police contacts that I could find. I could not come up with an address on her and the phone book had too many Barlows, and none listed under Vickie. DMV records were closed on Sunday, so I couldn't check her for a driver's license. I decided to wait until Monday and locate her through the school. Maybe Aaron's parents would know where I could find her. I knew I was just going to have to let things happen as they might; sometimes good things happen when you let them come to you, as they may. Jerry had finished the reports and had notified prints to print the victim's car.

We had finished our reports, ate some barbecue, and were drinking coffee at the station when Aaron's father called and asked us to return to the house and talk to them. His wife had taken a sedative and would be OK, at least for a while. We got back to the victim's house around eight that evening, and were sitting in the kitchen with his father, when his wife joined us. She was a basket case but wanted to hear what we had to say. I started off the conversation: "When was the last time you saw your son?"

"He was here last night and left the house around eight, and said he was going to go to the school and see some friends. He often did that, you know, he is twenty-one and comes and goes a lot, but he always let's us know what he is doing," hhis mother replied.

"Did he mention who it was he was going to see?"

"No, but I'll bet it was his girlfriend. He has been seeing her a lot lately, I'm sure. He doesn't always tell us it's her he is off to see, but a mother knows these things."

"What do you know about his girlfriend?" Jerry asked.

"Not much," the mother replied. "Her name is Vickie Barlow, and he met her at the school about six months ago. He keeps her to himself, but I know he is quite taken by her. I have asked him to bring her by and he always says, in good time. I don't know where she lives but I know he goes by there now and then."

"Has he had any problems with anyone that would lead to what has happened?' I asked.

"None that we know of," the father answered. "He was a good boy and didn't get into trouble. We raised him right, and he was serious about his career path. He was going to be a dentist, and that's where his head was. I don't know where this girlfriend fit in, but he wouldn't let her distract him from his goal, I know that for a fact. We talked about that a lot and I know, even if they were having sex, he wouldn't let it interfere with his school. It must have been those gangs that thought he was someone else. You know, one of those drive by shootings. That's the only thing that makes sense to me."

"Where is Aaron now?" the mother asked.

I replied, "He is at the coroner's office, and I have the phone number for you. You can call the coroner any time and make arrangements with him to go there, or make any requests you might have. Also feel free to call me at any time; I might be able to help you, in any way I can. Has Aaron ever stayed out all night, or over a weekend?"

"He used to. He would stay with his friends at the school. But since he met Vickie, he hasn't done that. He has been coming home every night. Sometimes it's late, and we are already in bed. When I ask him what time he got in, he just says it was early morning. Sometimes I hear him come in, and it's usually around three in the morning," his mother replied.

"How often did he go out?" Jerry asked.

"Usually only on Friday and Saturday nights," his father answered. "Sometimes he goes out during the week, to attend something at the school. Like I told you, he takes his schooling seriously and was here studying during the week. He don't run those streets nohow! If he was seeing that girl, it's on weekends."

"Was Vickie with him when he was shot?"

"No one, that we know of, was with him when he was shot," I replied. "Did he call you last night after he left?"

"We didn't hear from him after he left," his father answered.

"I think we have been keeping both of you from finding closure to this. We don't want to overstay our welcome, so I think it best we leave. We can get together again when we have something to tell you about your son's death. I know you might need some quiet time, and we need to leave here and do what we have to do on your son's case."

"The only closure I will need is you coming back and telling us who killed our son," his father said.

Monday morning Jerry and I attended the autopsy and found that the victim had in fact been shot with a .38-caliber weapon, but the bullet had mushroomed out flat and was not good for comparison. The victim had died as a result of the single gunshot wound.

After the autopsy we went to USC and at the administration office we found the file on Vickie Barlow. The file showed that she was twenty-one years old and was majoring in accounting. She had listed her residence address as 6821 South Broadway, Apartment 3. We also got a phone number and car description for her out of the file. She was in her first year at the school and was attending daytime classes. We got a copy of her classes and decided to try and find her at one of her classes that afternoon. We ended up going to all of her classes, and she did not appear at any of them. We ran into one of Aaron's friends and found out that Vickie had been at the school that morning and had been trying to find Aaron, and she had been told about Aaron's death. This told us that she had not been aware of his death, but it didn't put us any closer to whoever had killed him. Our case was over forty hours old and we hadn't gotten any direction yet. At the time we knew our next move was locating Vickie, but we didn't feel she was going to be able to shed any light on who had killed Aaron.

I called Vickie's phone number and did not get an answer, and we then drove by her address. We located her address and found it to be a building that was tucked into a business district, close to the Muslim temple, where I had been assaulted years ago. The building consisted of four apartments, two up and two down. Her apartment was upstairs and to the south. We went up to the apartment, and no one answered the door. We then looked for her car. We discovered that there were carports to the rear of the building ,but her car was not in one of them, nor was it parked on the street. It was getting dark, so we decided to stake the apartment out and see if she showed up. We really didn't have anything better to do on the case. Around ten that night, we saw her drive up and park in the carport and go up and enter her apartment. We gave her about a half hour and then we went up and knocked on the door. She came to the door, after a few minutes, and reluctantly let us in, after we identified ourselves.

I noted that she was a very attractive girl and had the shape to go along with her looks. She had long hair, which she was wearing down at the time. She was wearing a robe and had it pulled tightly around her waist. She was picture-perfect, except she had been crying, and her eyes were puffy and bloodshot. It was obvious that she was very nervous and was not sure if she wanted us there or not. We all sat down in the front room of the apartment, and I noted, at the time, that the apartment was very nicely furnished. It was a large apartment, as the sizes of rooms go, with a large front room and kitchen. I could not see the bedroom or bath, but, judging by the location, I would expect them to be large rooms as well. I did not know what my best approach with her was going to be, so I took a frontal, direct approach, and showed her Aaron's driver's license and told her we were there to talk about him. I had also used Aaron's driver's license on campus to identify him. I had a photograph of him from the scene, but it showed the gunshot wound.

She stared at the driver's license for a few minutes, and tears started to run from her eyes. I could tell that she was trying to compose herself and talk to us about what she knew about her relationship with Aaron, but was not sure what to say. I decided to go in another direction.

"We were on campus earlier today looking for you, and we talked to some of Aaron's friends. We also were there yesterday, but we couldn't find you. We had to go to administration to find this place. All of Aaron's friends tell us you two were tight, and you might be able to shed some light on what had happened to him. That is the reason we are here: to learn what you can tell us about Aaron, nothing else."

Vickie looked at me and then at Jerry, took a deep breath, and began to tell her story. "I met Aaron on campus around six months ago. We started seeing each other on campus, and I liked being around him. We were both there to get our education and didn't care much for the college life outside of getting our education. We would go to some sports events, but didn't run around with his friends. I don't have friends at school, and only started to hang around there after I met Aaron. I tried to keep our relationship limited to seeing each other at school. Aaron lived with his parents, so he started wanting to come here, but I wouldn't let him, nor did I tell him where I lived. Then, about a month ago, he showed up here knocking on my door. I asked him how he had found out where I lived, and he told me he had followed me home from school."

"Do your parents live around here?" I asked.

"They live out in Inglewood."

"Do you see them much?"

"That's where I have been all day. I had to tell someone about Aaron and I don't have anyone else to talk to." Vickie then started to cry again, and I went into the kitchen and came back with a wet towel and gave it to her and let her get her composure back.

"What is it about Aaron that you had to tell your parents?" I asked.

Vickie wiped her face, took another deep breath, let it out, and started to talk to me again.

"That Aaron had been killed, and I was sure Sugar had killed him."

Jerry and I looked at each other, and we were both thinking the same thing. The only Sugar we knew was the Sugar that was one of the big three, and ran a dope ring. Could this be who she was talking about? If it was, we were going to have to be careful with Vickie.

"Tell me about Sugar and why you think he killed Aaron," I said. "What is Sugar's real name?"

"His name is Raymond Long, and I met him at a club about eighteen months ago. At the time I was working for a broker, and Sugar and I started seeing each other. After a while Sugar told me he wanted me to work for him, and that he would pay me to keep his books full time. He told me he loaned out money and needed someone to keep track of his money, and who owed him what. I took the job, and one thing led to another, and I ended up in this apartment and going to school, all paid for by Sugar. He wanted me to learn how to invest his money, and since I already knew a few things from my previous job, he thought I ought to go to school and learn more."

"Were you intimate with Sugar, and does he stay here?"

"No, it wasn't like that. He would stay over sometimes, and we would have sex. I guess he thought I was his girlfriend, but I knew he had other girls and lived somewhere else. He would come by and bring me his books, and I would work his accounts, and he would come by and pick them up when I was done. I would call him and let him know when I was done with them. He would come by himself, or send one of his friends by to pick up the books. There were only two of his friends who came by. He had brought them by and introduced them to me and told me I could give them the books if he couldn't come by. I kept his books here most of the time. I don't think he wanted to have the books at his place."

"Who were his friends?"

"One of them is David Thomas, and the other is Eric Watson. Sometimes Sugar comes by with them, and they all stay awhile and drink. Both of the friends have hit on me, but Sugar put an end to that fast, and has told me not to pick up on a boyfriend. I guess you could call me a kept woman, and that was OK, until Aaron came into my life. I always thought I would stay with Sugar until I got my education, and then I could get another job."

"How do you think Sugar makes his money? It doesn't look like it's only from making interest off of loans. Did it not cross your mind that he was dealing dope?"

"Yes, I thought about that, especially after working his books for a while. But it was no sweat off me; all I was doing was keeping the books. There is no law against that, is there?"

"No, you're right there, but now let's get back to why you think Sugar killed Aaron."

She started to cry again, and I had to wait for her to answer. While I was waiting, Jerry nodded, and I took it to mean that he was verifying that Raymond Long was the Sugar we thought he was.

"I'm probably responsible for Aaron getting killed! Sugar found out about me seeing Aaron and had told me to break it off and to get rid of him, and I didn't. I didn't want to tell Aaron about me and Sugar and just felt it would work itself out. I kept telling Sugar I would tell Aaron I couldn't see him any more, but I didn't do it. Sugar had told me if I didn't do it he would do it for me, but I didn't expect him to, and didn't think it would ever come to this. He told me Aaron was going to eventually interfere with his business, and he couldn't have that happen. I told him I would never let Aaron know what I did for him, and I thought he would let it slide."

"Did Aaron ever meet Sugar or his friends, that you know of?"

"Not that I know of. I tried to get Aaron to keep our relationship away from my apartment, but he kept coming by, and I couldn't stop him from just showing up. I knew that David and Eric kept an eye on me for Sugar and would drive by now and then. They wouldn't come up here because Sugar wouldn't have that, and they would've had to answer to him for it."

"OK, what is it that makes you think that Sugar killed Aaron?"

"Because he came by early on Sunday morning, and had David and Eric with him. He told me that I would not be seeing Aaron any more, that he had taken care of his problem with him. At the time I thought he had just talked to Aaron and told him not to come by any more. Then I went to school this morning and found out Aaron had been killed. They might have killed him, but I was the cause of it. I could have kept it from happening. I really liked Aaron and thought we had a future together."

"Did anyone say who killed Aaron and how?"

"No one said anything about killing Aaron. That's why I thought they had just scared him. I told my mother that I was going to come back home and give up my job with Sugar. I can't stay here any longer, and I don't know what is going to happen to me now."

"Are his books here now?"

"No, he took them with him this morning. I don't keep any records here, either. He is very careful about that, and don't leave me to keep anything besides the books. If he finds out I talked to you, he will flip out over it. What I told you I told you out of my heart, because I owe it to Aaron. I'll take my chances with Sugar."

We spent a little more time with Vickie, and I continued to question her about Aaron and Sugar but didn't get anything that would prove our case against Sugar. All we had was a statement he had made about her not seeing Aaron anymore, and that he had taken care of it. I wasn't sure if she had been told more about Aaron's death, but I was sure that she wasn't going to tell us, at least not now. I offered her protection, and she refused it and said she would feel safe at her mother's place. We were getting ready to leave when the front door opened and Sugar and two other persons walked into the apartment.

Sugar sat down next to Vickie, and the other two walked around through the apartment. After they returned and told

Sugar that no one else was in the apartment, he took Vickie's hand and asked her if she was alright, and she told him she was. All three of them gave the appearance of being ex cons, in that they were all buffed out and had prison tattoos showing on their arms. They all looked like they were in their late twenties, and they were all dressed in the latest fad clothing. All of them were assured of themselves and had the air of confidence about them. Sugar had processed hair and wore it long. He had dark skin and had a long face, and, in my opinion, was not handsome.

"Who are you, and what are you doing here?" he asked me.

"I am Reynolds, and this is my partner, Rogers. We are with LAPD homicide. Now that you know who we are, who are you guys, and what are you doing here? You answer that, and I'll tell you what we are doing here."

"I don't think we are going to tell you who we are or why we are here, no way. This is my place, and this is my woman, and I don't have to tell you anything in my own place."

"OK, I will make it simple for you. We are conducting a homicide investigation and are talking to Miss Barlow about a classmate of hers who was killed Sunday morning. She has told us she knows nothing about our victim being killed, and that she found out about it at school this morning. We have spent the last two days talking to all of his classmates and are finishing up with her. Now maybe I need to talk to you guys about the death of my victim. I probably don't need to, because you are not students, I assume. But on the other hand, you might know something; I really don't know. "What I do know is I don't know who you are, and you are impeding my investigation by not identifying yourselves, and I have the right to take you to my house and find out who you are. Now we can either do that here or we can do it there, your choice."

"OK, I can handle it. Eric, you and David show the man your ID and I'll show him mine—no harm, no foul. After you are satisfied who we are, I will be asking you to leave. You are really bothering Vickie, and she don't need that tonight. I can see that your news has had a negative effect on her."

We were shown their driver's licenses, and they were who we thought they were. We told Vickie we would not be bothering her any more, and that if she were to hear anything, to let us know. We then left the apartment and went back to the station.

At the station we ran the three suspects through records and found that they all three were on parole. We would be contacting the state parole office in the morning to find out who their parole officers were. It would not put us any closer to tying them to our homicide, but it might give us some rope for them to hang themselves with. As I thought earlier, they were all in their late twenties and had all done time for robbery.

"Did you notice how Sugar never asked us who had been killed?" Jerry asked me.

"He also didn't want us around there asking any question of him. I didn't feel he would tell us anything, and I didn't want him to see that Vickie had told us what she had. Hopefully he bought into what I said she had told us. I still think she knows more than what she is telling us. We will need to talk to her again, but I want to give it some time to cool down. We got other cases to work, so I'm thinking if we don't find something we can do, from their parole officers, we let it sit."

"I agree with that, for now. I got a murder trial starting this week, anyhow, and I will be tied up with that. It's not like we got a lot of leads to follow up on, know what I mean?"

"I think we are on the right track but doubt if our train is going to come in early, if at all."

The next day we found out that all three of our suspects had the same parole officer, and we met with him that afternoon. (Most police officers don't like parole or probation officers because they think the parole and probation officers protect their parolees or probationers. The truth of the matter is that they have more authority over their parolees and probationers than law enforcement does. They can go into their residences 24-7, without a warrant. I always like to be on good terms with them in order to pick up those suspects I am looking for through their parole or probation officer. I can go to their residences, with their officer, and arrest the suspect inside the residence. We can then search the residence under the authority of the parole or probation officer.) The parole officer stated that all three of our suspects were on summery parole, which meant that they checked in with him once a month. They did not have to come to his office to check in. Originally he had gone out and checked on them but had stopped doing that some time ago. He told us that all three were living in a secure apartment building in the Baldwin Hills. They all had apartments on the third floor. Eric's apartment was facing the elevator, and he could see who got off and on. David's apartment was at the end of the hallway, and he could see anyone coming down the hallway. Sugar's apartment was to the side and at the end of the hallway. The parole officer was sure Sugar was selling narcotics out of his apartment and packaging them there, but he gave up trying to catch him a long time ago. He also told us they were all high-school friends and had grown up together. They had got their start robbing illegal gambling games and supermarkets. They had been arrested together on a supermarket robbery and had caught five years and did three. Their parole was going to be over this year. The parole officer told us he would get us into Sugar's pad, but we should not expect to find him dirty. He was too smart for that, and would know we were coming as soon as we got off the elevator. He kept his Corvette in the garage, underneath the apartment building, and you needed an identification card that could be read at the gate to get into the garage. We thanked him for his information and told him we would get back with him later, and left.

Bottom line was, our train didn't come in at all. Matter of fact, it had a train wreck, and Sugar got his Christmas present. Vickie had moved back in with her parents, and I had been by there while Jerry was in court, and she would not or could not tell me any more on the case. Then, about two weeks later, I got a call from her, and she asked me to come by that night—she had something to tell me. I went over there around nine that night, and the ambulance was there when I got there. Vickie had committed suicide by taking an overdose of pills. The only thing her parents could tell me was that she had gotten a phone call and became very upset after the call. She would not tell them who had called, but they were sure it was Sugar. She also would not tell her parents what had been said to her, but she called me to come over. She then told them she was going to take a nap before I came over. They had gone in to wake her for my visit and found her not breathing and had called 911. They had never met Sugar and knew nothing about him, other than their daughter had worked for him.

We took down Sugar's pad, and it went down as his parole officer said it would: nothing incriminating came out of it. The case ended up in our unsolved case files, even though we felt sure that Sugar was good for it. We could not put the case on him and had to tell Aaron's father we couldn't get him the closure he was after. Another case of good lives lost to the evil of narcotics. But in this case, the victim had no idea of where his death had come from. He probably thought he was just going to help out a lost motorist.

77th Detective Division 1970. I am in the 3rd. row, 6th from the left side. Rex Simpson is next to me on the right side, and Art Sage is directly in front of Rex.

1972 77th Homicide Unit Front Row, Left to Right: Me, Jerry Rogers, Art Sage Back Row, right to Left: second person over Tom McGuine, fifth person over Rex Simpson.

Chapter 6

Major Crimes Division

January 1976–June 1978

In December of 1975, I had a phone call from a Lieutenant Henderson, who I had worked for a few years earlier, and it would change my career path. He informed me that the department was going to put together a new homicide unit, come the first of the year. The unit was going to consist of three teams of four homicide detectives and three lieutenants. He was going to be the first lieutenant to be assigned to the new unit, and he was looking throughout the department to pick up four homicide detectives. He stated that he could pick any detective that the chief of police approved of. He told me he was reporting directly to Chief of Police Gates, and my name had come up, and the chief and he would like me to transfer into the unit on the first of January, 1976. The other two teams would be formed later: the first of the two in April of 1976, and the second in August of 1976.

Lieutenant Henderson further informed me that the unit would be responsible for investigating any and all of the major crimes that would occur in the city in the future, with an emphasis on homicides. Another of the unit's responsibilities would be to escort all dignitaries who came to the city and handle any of their assassinations, should they occur. The teams would either operate as two-man teams or four-man teams, depending of the specific case. I would have a car to take home with me, and would be subject to being called in at any time. The unit was going to operate out of Parker Center, in downtown Los Angeles, and would have citywide jurisdiction. The unit's first cases would be taken from the Robbery / Homicide Division and would be followed by cases, as they occurred, anywhere in the city.

Lieutenant Henderson then told me that I was one of the first of four detectives selected, from all of the available detectives in the city, and it was the wishes of the chief that I accept the assignment. Of course, I could refuse, but it would be in my best interest not to do so, in that the assignment was coming directly from the office of the Chief of Police. Needless to say, I accepted the assignment.

I reported for duty at the office of the Major Crimes Division on the first of January, 1976. At the time I wondered if I had done the right thing. As far as my career was concerned, I knew I had, but as to my abilities to handle the assignment, I was apprehensive about my future there. I had left Watts once before and was glad to get back there. Would I regret it again? Besides, I couldn't figure out why the unit had been formed to begin with. Our department had always had a robbery / homicide division, since I had become a police officer. It was tasked with just what we were being tasked with doing, and that division was not going away. In fact, that division was even on the same floor, in Parker Center, that our division was on. Talk about bad blood! The first thing I learned after arriving at Parker Center was that friends there were few and far between. Everyone working for the Robbery/Homicide Division resented us and everyone associated with them did too. But I decided to give it my best shot and not worry about the politics of it, and just do the job that was expected of me. I had never been a person to try and figure out the politics involved in the decision-making side of the department, and just went with the flow, as long as I could work my cases outside of politics. In the next two years, I would find out that it would be impossible to do that at Major Crimes. As to why the Major Crimes Division was formed in the first place, I never did find that out.

• • •

Now I will tell you two war stories that will illustrate what I have just stated about crime and politics. One of the cases took twenty-seven years to bring to court, and the other one started and ended with the FBI. I will leave the truth of the matter in both of the cases to rest with the reader and tell the stories as I know them. As they say, truth is stranger than fiction.

The first case came to the attention of the Major Crimes Division, and me, shortly after I had been assigned to Major Crimes. Pacific Division, which had jurisdiction over the Los Angeles airport, was investigating a murder that had been reported at the airport parking garage. A body had been discovered in the trunk of a car parked in the garage. It was felt that the car and body had been at that location for over two weeks. The car had not caused any concern until garage attendants noticed a strong odor emitting from the car. This led to the discovery of the body. It was found, after an examination of the body, that the victim had been shot. The victim did not have any identification on his person. The original investigators, out of Pacific Division, ran the license plates of the car and found the car registered to a Michael Ariola. When they went to the residence of the parents of the victim, to have an identification of the victim made at the coroner's office, they discovered that the victim was the son of an Los Angeles councilman. After getting a positive identification of the victim, and verifying that the victim was in fact Michael Ariola, a councilman's son, the news media had a field day and reported his death in the papers and on the news broadcasts on television. As a result, the case was transferred into Major Crimes Division.

The case was one of the first new cases that was brought into our division. Other than the identification of the victim and that he had been shot with a .22-caliber weapon, the case came to us unsolved and without a suspect or witnesses. We would have to begin our investigation with the victim. We found out from the father that the victim was a college student at UCLA and owned two massage parlors in Hollywood. He had a partner by the name of Gary Utley in the ownership of the parlors. The father couldn't tell us anything about the partner other than that he was quite a bit older than his son and didn't seem to have any other interests or occupation outside of the parlors. The father knew that they did not get along very well, and that his son felt that he was being cheated by his partner. His partner always owed his son money. He had not paid his son the up-front money it had cost him to go into the partnership. His son had told him that he had taken Gary on as a partner because he appeared to be connected and always came up with girls to work at the parlors. His son didn't spend a lot of time at the parlors because of his school and was more of a silent partner, letting Gary run the daily operation of the parlors. Gary had been trying to buy his son out, but his son did not want to give up his interest in the parlors and would not sell out to Gary.

Our team was given the case to work. The team was made up of St. John, Kent, Weaver, and me. The four of us decided we would take on the parlors first off and see what would come out of it. We went to the two parlors at closing time, which was ten in the evening, and picked up all the girls who were working that night and took them to our office. We asked the girls the whereabouts of Gary Utley, and none of them knew where he was. There had been two girls working at one of the parlors and two girls working at the other. Two of the girls, one from each parlor, were acting as the manager of each respective parlor, and one of the managers was Gary Utley's girlfriend and shared an apartment with him. Her name was Cindy (nineteen years old), and the other manager was Kathy(twenty years old). The girl who had been working with Kathy was named Sally (eighteen years old) and the girl working with Cindy was Sandy (also eighteen years old). St. John chose to talk to Cindy, and his partner (Kent) chose to talk to Sandy. I chose to talk to Kathy, and my partner talked to Sally. It was decided to get initial statements from all the girls and then compare notes and see where it would take us. We all felt, at the time, that Gary was our only possible suspect, based on what we knew.

The girl I talked to was twenty years old and was a Native American from Seattle. She had been working at the parlors for just under a year and stated Gary had met her at the Greyhound bus station, and he had offered her the job. She had just arrived in LA from Seattle. She told me that Gary got all the girls who worked at the parlors that way. He would bring the girls, including her, to the parlors and let them stay there until they were able to rent apartments for themselves. Most of the girls got apartments together, and all had left their homes to try their luck in Hollywood. She would admit only to giving massages at the parlors and adamantly denied that any prostitution was going on inside the parlors, but did admit that some did occur outside of the parlors. Sometimes their clients at the parlors wanted more than a massage and would pay extra for sex, but they had to get a motel. If this occurred, the girls had to kick back a percent of the money to Gary. She was sure that Michael Ariola did not know about the prostitution, because he was not around that often, and Gary had instructed all the girls that it was his and their business, not Michael's. Kathy told me she kept two sets of books, one for Gary and one for the parlor. The book for Gary had the tricks turned in it and the names of the tricks, and the other book for the parlor had just the daily business. She told me there were another dozen girls who worked for Gary at the parlors. She also told me that she didn't work at the other parlor and didn't know what went on over there; only that Gary's girlfriend operated the parlor. She knew that Gary and Michael were partners, but believed Gary ran the parlor she worked at and that Michael ran the other parlor, even though Gary supplied the girls. After getting the background information, I got to the meat of the matter.

"Do you know when the last time it was that you saw Michael Ariola?"

"I think it was about two weeks ago. That's what I told his father too."

"What do you mean by that?"

"His father had been looking for him and said he hadn't been to school in over two weeks. I told his father I last saw him at the parlor about two weeks ago on a Saturday night. I told his father that he was at the parlor that night and had left the parlor with Gary. That was before I heard on the news that he had been killed and left at the airport."

"Does that surprise you?"

"Not really, since no one seemed to know where he was. What I didn't tell his father was, that night at the parlor, Gary told us that he and Michael were going out to make a big score and he was cutting Michael in on some big money. He told me that after that night Michael wouldn't be after him any more about the money."

"Did Gary tell you what the big score was?"

"No, he didn't, but Gary always talked like that. He always wanted everyone to know how connected he was. You know, the mafia and all that, like he was a hit man or something. I never believed much he said, because he never had much in the way of money. Michael was always after him to pay him what he owed him. If he was so connected, why didn't he have a nice car and dress in some nice clothes, and why was he always after us to make more money, so he would get more from us?"

"Did Gary say where they were going that night to make this big score?"

"No, he just left with Michael in Michael's car. Was Michael killed that night?"

"We don't know for sure when he was killed. Have you seen Gary during the last two weeks?"

"I see him all the time at the parlor. I had asked him if he had seen Michael, and he just said that Michael was probably out spending some of the money he made from that night they made their big score. Gary also told me he was going to buy Michael out of their partnership and that I probably wouldn't be seeing him anymore, anyhow. I wouldn't have thought anymore about it, but when Michael's dad called I thought something might have happened to him. I really don't trust Gary, and I don't believe much of what he says. If they scored that big, how come Gary isn't spending any money big-time? This was all before I heard Michael was killed. Then after I heard about what happened to Michael, I wandered if it had something to do with whatever it was they did that night."

"Do you think Gary is capable of killing Michael? Do you think he did?"

"Under the right conditions I think he could have, but, for my money, he would have to have the upper hand. He talks a lot about how bad he is, but I really think it's all talk. I think a real man would be no match for him. I do know Gary had a rifle that night. He had it at the parlor and told me if things got ugly, he would take care of business with the rifle. I asked him what the rifle was, and he said a .22. Then Michael and Gary went out to Michael's car and left. That's the last time I saw

Michael. Now Gary is saying he didn't have to buy Michael out, that someone had helped him out there."

"Have you ever seen Gary with any other buddies or running mates?"

"No, Gary is always by himself. The only person I see him with is his girlfriend, Sandy."

I decided to break the conversation off there and go out and see what the other detectives had come up with before taking her any further. When I came back to the office, I found that the other three detectives were there waiting for me. I got some coffee and joined them.

St. John was the senior detective, with over twenty years on the job. He had transferred into Major Crimes from Robbery/ Homicide Division and knew everyone working at Parker Center. It was said that he was the best homicide detective in the city. He was going to be the lead detective on the case. Next senior was my partner, Weaver. He also had over twenty years on the job and had transferred in from Wilshire Homicide. Then came Kent, who had transferred in from Central Homicide and had about the same time on the job as I did, but had worked homicide a year longer than I had. That made me the fourth fish in the barrel.

I started off the meeting by telling them what I had learned from Kathy. Weaver then told the group that Sally had said about the same as Kathy had said, in that she had last seen Michael with Gary at the parlor that Saturday night. She had not talked to them because she had been busy with customers. She also knew that Michael had been killed and did not know anything about the killing. Neither Cindy nor Sandy had any information to give to St. John or Kent. Both had refused to talk to the detectives and had only stated that they knew nothing about Michael's death.

St. John then told us that while he was waiting for us to get done, he had gotten a phone call from a person on the department that he knew who worked OCID (Organized Crime Intelligence Division). The person told him that they had gotten a call from one of their undercover operators, and he had given them information on our Ariola homicide to pass on to us. The undercover operator was in a bar called Co Co's that was a noted hangout for organized crime figures. Gary Utley came up to him and was drunk. The news had just given an account on Ariola's killing, and Utley told the undercover operator that he had been the one who had killed Ariola. He had said he had taken him up into the hills and shot him with a .22 rifle. He had put his body in the trunk of Ariola's car and left it at the airport. Utley also told the undercover operator that it was a contract hit, and he had been hired to do it. The friend then told St. John that the information was just being passed on and that they could not burn the undercover operator, who would never be identified or testify in court.

St. John then addressed our group. "Based on what we now know, it looks like we are dealing with organized crime here, and it probably has those parlors behind it. That's why we couldn't find Gary Utley tonight—he's sitting in a bar bragging about the killing. I know that bar, and it is always full of mafia people. Utley is probably just a hanger-on, but he might be the real thing and have done the job for the mob. I see this case going two directions, one being organized crime and the other being personal between Utley and Ariola. I say we get this Utley in here and try and get enough from him to nail him with this. Kent and I will work the organized crime angle.

Weaver, you and Reynolds work the personal angle; I'm sure we still have time to stake out the bar and pick him up when he comes out. We will work a stakeout and let him get home, if he goes home. That way it won't cause him to suspect anything from his being at the bar. If he doesn't go home, we will see where he goes and take him down there. We will take the bar, and you guys take his apartment. We will keep the girls here until we have him. We will use a tack frequency to talk to each other. What do you think?"

We all agreed and played it that way and were able to get him as he started to enter his apartment. We took him back to our office, and St. John and Kent interviewed him and got nowhere. He invoked his rights and demanded his attorney be called. While they were interviewing him, my partner and I took the girls home and I told Kathy, after I had dropped the other girls off, that I would be by to see her at the parlor that night, in that I wanted to see those books. I also wanted to look for the rifle, which I did not tell her. When we got back, we found out that St. John and Kent had left the office and were taking Utley back to his apartment. They had left us a note that simply stated, "Struck out."

When they got back, we all went out together to get some breakfast. It was almost dawn, and the city was waking up. We talked about the case at breakfast, and I suggested that my partner and I go to the college and see what we could learn there. I told them that I had told Kathy that I would be by the parlor that night, and that I thought that we should go by both parlors and look for a rifle. I also thought that it would be a good idea to get a search warrant for Utley's apartment in order to search for the rifle. As I saw it, the rifle would be one of the first things we would want to come up with, even though it had been over two weeks since the shooting, and I didn't feel Utley would give us permission to search his apartment. St. John agreed with me and said that he and Kent would get the warrant and go to the apartment while we were at the college. He also had some people he wanted to see about the case, and we needed to work in the two directions he had mentioned earlier. After eating we each went in our separate directions, and me and my partner headed out to UCLA, and St. John and Kent went for the warrant.

At the college we found out that Ariola belonged to a fraternity. After talking to several fraternity brothers, we found out that on the Friday before the Saturday we suspected he was killed, he had attempted to get someone to go with him on a trip, that Saturday. He had told them that he and his partner were going up to Moral Bay and off-load a boat that was bringing in a load of marijuana. He had said that he would cut anyone in on the deal if they would go with him and help them off-load the boat. No one had taken him up on his offer, and they had not seen him since. When they had heard of his death, they all felt that he had been killed as a result of that trip and were glad that they had not taken him up on his offer.

We went to the parlors that night and searched for the rifle and didn't find it. We had learned from our partners that they had gotten a warrant and served it and had also came up empty at Utley's apartment. I went through the books with Kathy, and she showed me the difference in them, and it was obvious that Gary was holding out on Michael. Not only was he making money on the side, he was doctoring the book he would show him by not including all the normal business that took place. Neither Kathy nor Sally could tell us anything more on Michael's death, but did tell us that Cindy knew a lot about it.

She had not told them anything, but had hinted around over the last two weeks about Gary looking out for their interests. Cindy was now in charge of the other parlor, and Gary was still the man at their parlor, but was not coming by as often as he had done before Michael's death.

The next day I was in the office and was the only one in at the time. It was around seven in the morning, and I was waiting for my partner to come in and was thinking about what we would do next on the Ariola case. I was to meet with St. John, and he was going to brief me on where they were at on the case. Little did I know at the time that the path I was going to take would take me away from the Ariola case and in a whole new direction, and it was about to start in a few minutes.

My lieutenant came in the office and asked me to go to the airport and pick up an FBI agent and take him out in the valley to meet some other agents. He stated that since I was the only one in at the time, he wanted me to do it for him. The chief had just told him to get someone out there immediately and meet the agent. The agent was coming in from DC, and the FBI didn't have any agents available to pick him up. The agent was a crime-scene expert and was coming out to draw up a crime scene for a case that was currently being tried in federal court, and the FBI needed it done for court that afternoon. I was to do whatever it took to assist them in getting it done. After I got the address to take the agent to, I looked up the directions to the location and left, went to the airport, picked up the agent, and took him to the location.

The agent would not talk to me on the way out to the location and stated only that I was to wait for him at the car when we got there. When we arrived I noted that the location was a single-story house with a guest house at the rear of the property. The agent joined other agents at the guest house, and I stayed with my car. I was standing and smoking a cigarette at the front of my car when I saw a guy come out of the guest house and head in my direction. The guy was dressed in street clothes, so I knew he was not an agent. He looked white as a sheet and appeared to be sick. He came up to me, and, as he approached my car, he leaned up against the front fender for support.

After taking a few deep breaths the guy started to talk to me. "Are you an FBI agent?"

"No, I'm a homicide detective and I work for LAPD."

I then identified myself with my badge and ID and told him I worked Major Crimes. He asked me if I solved murders, and I told him I did. I asked him his name, and he told me he was Craig Petzold.

"You look like you're going to throw up, Craig."

"I got sick inside that guest house. All those FBI agents in there are trying to have me say things that aren't true. I told them I had seen a dead body in there, and it made me sick to be back in there."

"Are they investigating a murder?"

"No, they are trying Ullo on loan-sharking charges. We are in court right now. I am testifying for them against Ullo, and I am committing perjury for them. I told the FBI about the murders, but they told me they weren't interested in them. They said murders were state offenses, and they want to convict Ullo of loan-sharking because it is a federal offense."

"Who is Ullo?"

"He is the guy that lives here. I have got myself in this too deep, and I just want out of it. I got a wife and kid to think of."

"Tell you what I'm going to do. Here is my business card with my phone number on it. After you are through with these FBI agents, you give me a call and I will meet up with you, and I will help you any way I can. As long as you haven't killed anyone, I can work with you."

"I haven't killed anyone, but I have been along when two persons were killed. I told this to the FBI, but they don't want to help me with that."

Our conversation was interrupted by several agents who had come up to us and asked Craig to come back into the guest house. They told me that they didn't need me any longer and that I could leave, and I did just that.

Later on that night, I got a call from Craig, and I arraigned to meet him at the Van Nuys police station. That meeting produced the following:

1. Joseph Ullo was being tried for loan-sharking in federal court by the FBI. Craig identified four agents involved in the case to me.

2. Craig Petzold was testifying against Ullo and making false statements, as was Robert Zander. Craig felt that Joseph Ullo was going to have him and Zander killed.

3. Craig Petzold was working for a guy by the name of Eugene Conner. Conner had a heating and air-conditioning business in the valley that was a front for an auto-theft ring. The business was used as a chop shop.

4. Robert Zander, Craig Petzold, and Eugene Conner had gone to Jack Molinas's house, and Eugene Conner had shot

and killed Molinas for Joseph Ullo. Jack Molinas had owed Ullo fifty thousand dollars and was killed for this reason.

5. Ullo had a mole working as a civilian worker for the LAPD. The mole had worked in the photo lab and had gotten copies of all the pictures taken at the Molinas homicide. The mole also works in the radio shop and had gotten crystals of all of the LAPD frequencies. That way, when they located a vehicle they wanted to steal, they would stake it out and monitor the police frequency. When they heard the police car in the area get a call and leave the area, they would take the vehicle they were staking out. The vehicle was taken to the chop shop, and all the numbers were switched over to a vehicle they had gotten from a junkyard that had been totaled out. The stolen vehicle was registered as the totaled-out vehicle, with a pink slip to go along with it. They were doing this with trucks, RVs, and cars. The vehicles were sold to buyers all over the country.

6. Vincent Calderazzo had been killed in Ullo's guest house by a guy named Johnny Kerns. (Craig thought that this was a phony name.) Craig and Robert Zander had taken the body out to the desert near Victorville and buried it. He was killed because Ullo felt that he was sent out to California from New York to kill him because he refused to pay back a loan from the Mob, aka Gigante.) Ullo had been tied in with the Vito Genovese family in N.Y. before coming to Calif.

7. Eugene Conner was in FBI custody, and they were keeping him out of state. He had tried to commit suicide by carbon monoxide poisoning while in their custody.

8. Robert Zander had a brother in Iowa who was selling the stolen vehicles back there. He would come out to Calif. and drive the vehicles back there. The brother also knew of the murders, having been told of them by Robert Zander.

Now I'm not saying what Craig told me was all the truth, and I'm not saying it was all lies. I am just saying it's what he told me.

The next morning I began to verify what I had been told by Craig. I found out that there was a murder of Jack Molinas and it was an unsolved case, being handled by Hollywood Homicide. There were no suspects identified, and it had gone down as described by Craig.

I contacted San Bernardino Sheriff's and found out that a body had been found, buried in the desert, when a camper's dog had uncovered it. The body had not been identified as of yet. (I gave them Vincent Calderazzo's identification and they identified the body through dental charts as being him.)

I went to federal court that morning and sat in on Joseph Ullo's trial and identified all of the FBI agents, Robert Zander, Ullo, and Ullo's attorney, Charles Gietz. Craig Petzold was testifying for the prosecution, and, after his testimony, the prosecution rested their case. It was a Friday, and the judge put the case over until the following Monday, for the defense to start their case then. (Craig had told me that he was going to be called as a defense witness as well, and that Charles Gietz was also going to enter false statements into the testimony.) Note: That weekend Charles Gietz went hiking in the San Bernardino Mountains and died as a result of a purported hiking accident. The trial was postponed, as a result, and was subsequently dismissed, for whatever reason. Again, I'm not saying I'm right or I'm wrong—I am just saying what I heard.

That weekend I took Craig Petzold into protective custody and put him and his family up in my favorite motel and had them baby sat by some of our detectives.

I had went to the FBI office to speak with the agents I had identified as being on the case, and who Craig had told me that he had told about the murders, and was told that they had been transferred out of the area and were unavailable for me to talk to. I even went to the attorney general's office to try and get them made available to me, and did not have any success in getting to talk to them.

I knew that I had to support what Craig had told me by finding someone else to back him up on his story. I found out that Eugene Conner was out of state and was hospitalized as a result of his suicide attempt. It appeared he was still in the custody of the FBI and I would have a hard time getting to him. That left Robert Zander, and I decided to work on him. Since Craig had told me that Zander was part of everything that had occurred, he was the logical choice.

In the meantime I went to the Auto Theft Division and gave them the information on the Conner auto-theft ring and the mole in the department. I told them about the chop shop and got them together with Craig to identify all the vehicles he and Zander had stolen. I asked them to build a case on Zander and his brother so I could use it to get Zander to admit to his part in the murders.

I then filled my lieutenant in on what I had done thus far, and the conflict I had with the FBI. I explained what direction I was taking on the case, and he told me he would take it to the chief of police and get approval for me to continue my investigation. I had to get approval to get the city to reimburse me for my cost of housing Craig and his family, and to continue to pay the motel cost. I also wanted to go back to Iowa and deal with Zander's brother. Then there would be the need to get to Eugene Conner, and that would go through the FBI. This case was getting bigger and more complicated as time went by, and time was again the most precious commodity I had. I wanted to have an auto-theft case on Zander and his brother, so I could get him into custody and work on him through his brother. Once I saw where that would go, I then wanted to see what he could tell me, and I would then sit down on him and Craig and build my cases on the two murders and go after Joseph Ullo. I also felt that I would eventually have to go back to New York and deal with the Manhattan Family, and Vincent "Chin" Gigante. My game plan was going to have to be approved by the chief and probably would have to pass the beaucratic political test. It sure was simpler to work my cases back in Watts than it was to work cases down here at Major Crimes. Down here politics was the name of the game.

I was given the approval of the chief of police to continue to work the case but was to advise his office of my every move, and the case would be reevaluated at every step. The cost of housing my informant would be covered presently, but would be turned over to the district attorney as soon as possible. I was instructed to go to the DA and brief him on the status of the case and work with his office on any steps I took in the future.

I then got together with a detective by the name of Carl Sims, from Auto Theft Division, and we sat down with Craig and identified five pickup trucks and three RVs that had been stolen and switched out and were back in Iowa. Zander's brother had found buyers for them back there and had picked them up in LA, from Eugene Conner, and delivered them to the buyers.

The next move was to get Zander into custody and see where that would take me. I got him and arrested him for auto theft, on a Friday night, so I would be able to hold him until Wednesday without filing any charges on him. This would give me time to go back to Iowa and carry out my game plan.

As I expected, Zander was not going to give up the murders without a deal. The deal I gave him was to not charge him with the murders and to not charge his brother with auto theft in exchange for his testimony against Eugene Conner, Joseph Ullo, and Johnny Kerns, as to their part in the murders. As I saw it, he could identify Conner as the shooter on Molinas, as he was present when he was shot, and could identify Ullo as the person who hired them to kill Molinas. He could also identify the shooter on Vincent Calderazzo as Johnny Kerns and identify Ullo as the person who ordered the hit. He could also identify Ullo as the person who got him to dispose of the body. He had also been present when Calderazzo was killed and could testify to Ullo being present when Johnny Kerns shot him, at the direction of Ullo. Zander then verified all this and said he would give it up for my deal, as long as he got assurance his brother would skate out of it. He also admitted that his brother knew about the murders. His brother had been out in LA picking up a truck when he had told him about the murders.

Once I got my deal with Zander, I set up an arraignment with him to have his brother call him, at the county jail, after I picked him up in Iowa. I agreed to have the call made from the family home and allow his father to be part of the conversation. Zander told me he had six brothers, and they were all state wrestling champions. He identified which brother I was after and gave me the name of Frank as being the name of the brother I was after. I made sure he couldn't make any calls from the county jail until after I called him from Iowa and assured him I would be releasing him after I got back, as long as things went as planned. I also told him I would place him into protective custody, as I had done with Craig. We shook hands on our deal, and I told him he would hear from me in a couple of days.

I briefed my lieutenant on my progress and explained that Carl Sims and I would need approval from the chief to go to Iowa. I told him that I now had two witnesses who could put the murders on Joseph Ullo, as the driving force behind them, and identify Eugene Conner as the shooter on Molinas and Johnny Kerns as the shooter on Calderazzo. I still had to identify Johnny Kerns. I .had to work on identifying the .22-caliber weapon used, and attaching it to both murders. I also had footprints to identify on the Molinas murder and had to look for trace evidence on both cases. I would need to go to both scenes and work with both sets of original detectives to tie the knots together. I also briefed the district attorney on my progress. I got the approval of the chief, and Carl Sims and I left that Saturday for a little town in Iowa. I had notified the sheriff of the county in Iowa that we were coming and what it was about.

We flew into Kansas City, Kansas, and rented a car and drove around seventy miles north into Iowa. As we were driving in Iowa, it seemed that there were only two paved roads, one north/south and the other east/west. The other roads were all dirt roads. Of course we weren't country boys, so we didn't know the feel of the land and were lost outside of the big city. We finally got to where we were going and met up with the local sheriff. I further explained our mission to him and assured him we would allow him to control how we would accomplish it. We first wanted to find Frank Zander and then locate the stolen vehicles. Once we had the stolen vehicles and Frank Zander in custody, we would be making a phone call and in all probability would not be arresting Frank Zander.

The local sheriff agreed on helping us and put out the word to his deputy's to look for Frank Zander, both at his house and on the road. The sheriff said that Frank lived with his parents on the family farm. It was well known that Frank picked up vehicles in LA from his brother, and sold them. Everyone, including the sheriff, thought it was on the up-and-up, and that his brother was a used car dealer in LA. The sheriff knew where some of the stolen vehicles were and knew what truck Frank was driving. It wasn't long before one of the deputy's spotted Frank driving his truck on one of the county roads, and another brother was with him. I went with the sheriff, and a deputy went with Sims, in our rented car, and we headed out to head Frank off at the pass.

Talk about Keystone Kops—that was us. The sheriff was on the car radio with his deputy who had first spotted Frank, and was attempting to block him in. All I could see was dust trails from the cars driving on the dirt roads out in the distance. I thought of Bonny and Clyde and pictured myself back in those days. Eventually the sheriff set up a perimeter with his four cars, including Sims and his car, and we boxed Frank and his brother into about a two-mile-square area. Frank left the road and was driving down the side of a field, and the sheriff said he was driving into a Farmer Brown's place. We turned into a long entrance road that led back to a farmhouse and barn, and, when we got back to the barn, we saw Frank's truck parked next to it. The truck was facing us and was parked tight against the barn. Frank and his brother were standing at the rear of the truck, and the truck was not running. The sheriff and I got out of our car, and the sheriff walked out to his left, and I got out and went to my right. We both drew down on the two of them, and the sheriff ordered them to put their hands on the tailgate of the truck. They did so, and the sheriff told me to approach the suspects while he covered them. I walked up to the front of the truck, and I had to go down the side of the truck between the truck and the barn. The truck was so tight against the barn that in order to get to the back of the truck, I had to duck under the rearview mirror. Before I did this, I looked at the two brothers and saw that they still had their hands on the tailgate of the truck and were watching me intently. I told myself to go for it and bent down and tucked myself under the mirror and came up on the other side. As I was coming up, all hell broke loose. A Germen shepherd that had been lying in the bed of the truck was spoken to by one of the brothers and came up out of the bed of the truck and attacked me. The dog was growling and clawing at me and snapping its teeth. The only thing that saved me was that the truck was so close to the barn that the dog couldn't get down to where I was, in that I had crouched down in between the truck and the barn. I hollered at the brothers to call off their dog or the dog would be dead in a matter of seconds, and, fortunately for the dog, they did. It almost goes without being said that my taking the two of them into custody didn't occur as tenderly as they would have liked.

I decided to take the brothers to their family home and talk to them about my purpose for being there rather than taking them to the sheriff's office. It was late in the afternoon, and I wanted to make the phone call to the county jail that night. Carl Sims had arrived at our location, so we put one brother with him and the deputy, and the sheriff and I took the other brother with us. The sheriff had them lock up their truck and leave it at the farm, and said they could pick it up later, if they cooperated with us. We then all left and drove over to the Zander's farm.

When we arrived we went inside the farmhouse and met with the brother's father and mother. We were taken into a large kitchen, and all of us sat down at a very large kitchen table. There were eight of us sitting around the table, and I could picture the parents and all of their sons sitting around that table. For my money this was a good family, and I was going to make it a point to keep it that way. At least I would have plenty of witnesses to whatever was going to be said by Frank Zander. I laid the whole thing out then, and told the parents that their sons, Robert and Frank, had gotten mixed up with the wrong people, and what they originally thought was fun and exciting had turned ugly fast. I explained that I had Robert in jail, and he was subject to being charged with murder, accessory to murder, auto theft, and accessory after the fact. I then told the family that I could charge Frank with auto theft— multiple counts—and transporting stolen vehicles across state lines, which would be federal crimes. I then informed the family of my deal with Robert and told them that I was interested in going after only the real bad guys on the murders. If Frank admitted to the auto thefts and helped the sheriff in recovering the stolen vehicles we knew were back there, and told me what he knew about the murders, I would not arrest him, and he would be staying at home when I went back to LA. Otherwise, I would be arresting him and taking him back with me. I also made it clear that if he cooperated with me, I would not be charging Robert with anything, and I would place Robert into a witness protection program until after the trials. I told Frank and his father that if they agreed to do what I wanted them to do, I would be making a phone call to the LA county jail, and they could talk to Robert and let him know what I was doing for them back here. I then asked the sheriff, deputy, and Carl Sims to step outside with me while I smoked. We all went outside and gave the family time to talk it over among themselves.

When we reentered the house, Frank and his father told me that they agreed to what I had offered, and that Frank would take us to the locations of all of the stolen vehicles and would tell his brother that I was not going to arrest him. Frank would also tell me everything he knew about the murders. I made the phone call to Robert and he, Frank, and their father talked it all over; and after they were done talking, Robert told me that he would give me a full statement when I got back to LA. All three of them then assured me that they knew that they had to cooperate with me or the deal was off.

We then spent the next two days recovering all of the vehicles that were back there and impounded them at the sheriff's impound lot. We picked up the five trucks, including Frank's, and the three RVs. Carl and I then caught a flight out of Kansas City, on Tuesday night, and headed home.

On the flight back, I got to thinking about the case and where I was at with it. I also got to thinking back to when I was a kid being raised up in Ohio by a stepfather who was Italian. I had done some checking up on Joseph Ullo and found out that he had a record in NY, and he had been a New York Mafia soldier in the Manhattan Mob, prior to coming to California in the early 1960s. My stepfather had a brother named Louie Grillo who had done the same thing at around the same time. Louie had left town because it was rumored he had killed someone while he was part of a Mafia family. Had Ullo done the same thing? It stands to reason that he had, or he would not have left New York. My stepfather also had a brother named John who was in New Mexico, and I had been told he was also Mafia. In fact, I had been told that he had four sons and one was a bail bondsman, one was a judge, one was an attorney, and one was a deputy sheriff. One of the sons was one of the four owners of the Stardust Hotel in Las Vegas, on paper only. I remembered that most of my friends growing up were Italian, and the Mafia was always present. I also hung out at the pool halls. I had had school buddies whose fathers had been killed in town for one reason or another. I had grown up going to all the Italian social clubs and got good at playing pool, Motto, and boccie ball. I worked in the steel mills every summer, after I turned sixteen. I would walk to work with my stepfather and back home every day. He constantly told me to stay away from who I was running with, because he knew their fathers, and they would only get me in trouble. My stepfather also had a part-time job as a cop in my hometown, and he was not part of the Mafia, and felt it had ruined his brother's life. I remembered that one of my best friends from the neighborhood, Al Zina, was Mafia and was in Phoenix, Arizona. Maybe I would go see him and find out if he knew anything about Joseph Ullo. Or I could go see Louie, who was now in Las Vegas. Man, I was really reaching now. It's crazy how thoughts come in and out of your head when you got nothing but time to think, like when you're on a plane and can't leave until you land. I even remembered going home to Ohio for a family reunion, after I had been on the police department for two years. All of my extended Italian family was there. They all asked my mother if she was afraid of something happening to me, now that I was a cop. She replied, "No, I'm glad he made that choice, because he was on the top of a fence, and if he had fallen off on the other side, I would be visiting him in jail." Getting back to the cases, I thought I was in pretty good shape. When I got back in LA, I would get Robert Zander released, and then I would sit down with Craig Petzold and Zander and really go over the details of the two killings and make sure I picked their brains dry. I was sure I had a lot more to learn from them, at least more than I already had. I had to identify Johnny Kerns (or whoever he was) fast; he would soon know what was going on and he would be in the wind. I also wanted to get custody of that mole inside of the department and twist him for what he could give me. I only had what Craig had told me, and the only thing I had verified was the two deaths. All of the rest of what he had told me could be bullshit. This trip had put me behind schedule, but it had been worth the time it had taken. Those were the last thoughts I remember, because I fell asleep and woke up landing in LA.

We went to the police sub station at the airport, I picked up my police car that I had left there, and I took Carl home and I went home and crashed. I woke up late on Wednesday morning and hurried into work, because I had to get to the county jail and release Robert Zander and take him to my motel, where I would meet up with Craig Petzold. I had to go to my office first and brief my lieutenant, so he could brief the chief. When I entered my office, it was around nine in the morning, and I was surprised to see all the detectives were in the office. They all looked up at me when I came into the office, but no one said anything to me as I entered. St. John just nodded his head at me and then buried his face in his paper work. My lieutenant then told me to grab my coffee cup, and that we were going to the cafeteria to get some coffee and have a cigarette. I told him I needed to make a phone call to the county jail and have them hold Robert Zander and to not release him until I got there, and he told me the call could wait. As we were walking out of the office, I could feel everyone's eyes on me, and I began to wonder what it was that I had done.

We got our coffee and sat down at a table and both lit up cigarettes. I entered into that silent period you experience when you feel like your parent is about to tell you they know about something you have done that you should not have done, and you know there is no way out of it. I started to go over all I had done on the case, searching for where I had screwed up, and finally said to myself, "He is about to tell you."

"Your case has been given to the FBI, and your informants have been turned over to them," my lieutenant told me. He continued, "As of now you are officially off of the case, and you are to write up a summation of everything you have done on the case, and it will be forwarded to them. You are to ask no questions about why this is being done and just move on to your next case, which I will be briefing you on. The Ariola case has been given to them as well, and you are not to do any work on that case either. It's like the two cases never existed. What I can tell you is that you haven't done anything wrong, and the cases haven't been given over to the FBI because of anything you did on them. It's just the way it is."

That was the last time I heard anything about the three murders. I went on and worked other cases and eventually forgot about the three murder cases. It would be years before I learned anything else about those cases, and I was never approached by the FBI, nor included in their investigation of the cases, in any manner. What I eventually learned about the cases I will share with you in the following article.

Break in the Hit-Team Hunt (*Time* Magazine Sept. 1977)

The Mafia's current version of Murder, Inc. is a squad of professional hit men armed with silencer-equipped, .22-cal. automatic pistols. Although they have accounted for at least 20 Mob executions over the past two years, mystified lawmen knew them only as the ".22-cal. hitters" (TIME, April 18). But now the FBI believes it has a big break in the case—and indeed one of the killers. Last week federal prosecutors in Los Angeles were preparing indictments against an underworld moneylender named Joseph Ullo, charging him with two of the .22-cal. slayings.

Ullo, 49, a short, wily onetime New York City hoodlum who moved west 14 years ago, had been arrested a week earlier on a convenient charge of loan-sharking, with bail set at $1 million. Federal officials believe that he murdered Jack Molinas, 43, a gambling figure and porn-film distributor who was found shot in the head in his Hollywood Hills home in August 1975. The other victim: Vincent Calderazzo, a New York Mafia soldier whose bones were discovered by hikers in a shallow desert grave near Victorville, Calif., in March. Both were killed with .22s.

Authorities have the testimony of three accomplices in the murders. They also have two .22-cal. weapons that one accomplice says were used in the killings; a gun fanatic, he could not bear to follow Ullo's orders to dispose of the pistols and instead stashed them in a safe. FBI agents found them there, along with seven other guns allegedly used by Ullo. The three witnesses told their stories last week at Ullo's bail hearing. Eugene Connor, 43, a man with an arrest record of car theft, said that he was Ullo's getaway driver on the night of the Molinas slaying. Reason for the hit, according to Connor: Molinas refused to pay a $50,000 <u>debt</u> to Ullo. Connor says he waited in the car while Ullo crouched behind a neighbor's <u>backyard fence</u>, waiting for Molinas to return home. Then, Connor has testified, Ullo dropped Molinas with a single shot; Connor heard the popping sound that is characteristic of a silencer-equipped .22.

The story behind the Calderazzo killing was apparently more complicated. Investigators say that it involved an old associate of Ullo's from his New York City days: Manhattan Mobster Vincent ("Chin") Gigante, a power in the Mob family once headed by Vito Genovese. Calderazzo worked in Gigante's gambling network. Following a 1976 FBI raid on his operation, Gigante suspected he had been betrayed by Calderazzo and ordered him to Los Angeles—ostensibly for his own protection.

Calderazzo's sojourn soon ended at Ullo's San Fernando Valley home. The FBI's two other witnesses, Robert Zander, 28, and Craig Petzold, 32, say that they were working at Ullo's place when they heard screams from a guesthouse. Minutes later, they said, Ullo summoned them to the house, where they saw Calderazzo's body. They testified that Ullo gave Zander a .22 automatic with instructions that it be delivered to Connor. Then the pair were ordered to dump Calderazzo's body in the desert, where it became fodder for scavenging animals. The FBI hopes to link Ullo with a third Mafia hit victim: Michael Ariola, a massage-parlor operator who was shot with a .22 in Los Angeles last year during a Mob takeover of such emporiums. His body was found in a car trunk at the Los Angeles airport. Just before his death, the FBI has learned, Ariola rejected an Ullo demand for a share of his massage-parlor revenue.

At his bail hearing, Ullo's bond was cut to $250,000, but he was told that if he managed to post the sum he would have to report to a U.S. marshal twice a day, every day. At week's end Ullo was still behind bars. That was surely a relief to Witnesses Connor, Zander and Petzold. All are in protective custody after alleged death threats by Ullo. They have more reason than most to remember that two victims of the .22-cal. hitters were FBI informants—and four others were potential prosecution witnesses.

Joseph Spencer Ullo (born 1929) was a New York mobster and suspected as one of the ".22 caliber hitters" hitmen during the 1970s. Born in New York, Ullo was suspected by NYPD detectives in connection to two unsolved homicides before moving to California in the early 1960s. Operating as a loan shark until his arrest in September 1977 on loansharking charges, prosecutors attempted to charge Ullo with the gangland slaying of gambler and pornography distributor Jack Molinas and Vincent Calderazzo, a New York mobster. Both men had been shot with a .22 caliber pistol (the same type of gun used in a series of gangland slayings) and, as Molinas had reportedly owed Ullo money, police suspected Ullo's involvement. Police also attempted to connect the murder of a Los Angeles massage parlor owner Michael Ariola, another victim of the ".22 caliber hitters", who resisted mobsters' attempts to take over his business. Despite the testimony of car thief <u>Eugene Connor</u>, who claimed he had driven the getaway car during one of the murders, Ullo was acquitted.

According to the testimony of <u>Frank Tieri</u> in 1980, several New York mafia leaders ordered Ullo's death in September 1976 after refusing to pay a loan. Ullo avoided these attempts on his life however; he was eventually sentenced to imprisonment for six years after <u>making false statements</u> during a federal investigation and released on January 21, 1983.(Found on Wikipedia(4-19-2011)

I also found other articles during my research that stated the following: Both Craig Petzold and Robert Zander were given one year suspended sentences for testifying. Eugene Conner received a life sentence and Joseph Ullo's jury acquitted him on a paucity of evidence

As to the Michael Ariola case, I got a call from a LAPD Detective Ito twenty-seven years after Ariola's murder, asking me to meet with him to discuss the case. It was in 2002 when Ito came to my house and brought the old file on the case. Ito told me that LAPD had just gotten a new chief, and Councilman Ariola, Michael's father, had approached the chief and asked him what had ever happened to his son's case. Of course the new chief (Williams) knew nothing about it, so he had instructed Robbery/Homicide Division to research it. They had found the folder on the case in the LAPD archives, and the case was still listed as unsolved and was showing that it had been transferred to the FBI for follow-up investigation. Ito stated that he had checked with the local FBI, and that they had no record of the case.

I went over the case with Ito and told him what I thought was the answer to solving the case. I explained to him that I felt that the killing of Michael Ariola had nothing to do with organized crime or Joseph Ullo. I felt that he had been killed by his partner, Gary Utley, over a dispute about where the money was going from the parlors. Gary Utley was spending all the profits and not putting anything back into the business. He also owed Michael a lot of money that Michael wanted paid back.

I told Ito that if I were him, I would start by looking up the four girls from the parlors and talk to them. I had felt, at the time, that they knew that Gary Utley had killed Michael and were not telling what they knew. Cindy was his nineteen-year-old girlfriend, at the time, and I was sure she knew the true story. I had not talked to her at the time, but felt sure that she could solve the case. I showed Ito where I had talked to Kathy, and that she was the last person to see Gary and Michael together. She also saw Gary with a .22-caliber rifle that night. I was sure that with all the time that had passed since the murder, the girls were not teenagers now, and they would not feel threatened by Gary and would tell Ito what he wanted to know. Then there was the undercover LA cop who heard Gary bragging about killing Michael. Surely he would be able to tell his story now and could back the girls up on whatever they knew. The rifle was a piece of the puzzle too, and it needed to be tracked down. Cindy would probably know something about that. The other two girls, Sally and Sandy, had never given any accounts of their knowledge of the murder either. And last but not least was the FBI. They might not be telling now what they knew, but it was for sure that they had worked the case back then. Ito left and told me he would keep in touch.

It was about six weeks later when I got a call from Ito, and he updated me on the case. He told me that he had found Cindy in Florida and that she fingered Gary on the murder. She also told him what had happened to the rifle he had used to shoot Michael—it was the rifle Kathy had told me about. Kathy had died in Oregon several years ago of an overdose, and I would probably have to testify after they arrested Gary. They had located Gary in Phoenix, Arizona, and he was driving a cab for a living. They still had not found Sally or Sandy, but the district attorney said they had enough for trial and had issued an arrest warrant for Gary, and they were leaving in a couple of days to arrest him.

It took another six weeks before I heard back from Ito. When he called, he told me they had finally got Gary back to the LA County Jail. He told me that when they had arrested Gary at his apartment and told him he was being arrested for the killing of Michael Ariola, Gary had a heart attack, right on the spot. They had just been able to transport him back to LA, as he had been in intensive care at a hospital in Phoenix. Ito told me he was expecting to go to trial in around two to three months, and he again would let me know. The next thing I heard was that the DA lost the case at a preliminary hearing in that he did not introduce enough evidence to support the probable cause to hold Gary for trial. I could not find out where the case went from there, and Ito has retired from the department. So much for that cold-case file. They say you win some and lose some, but I would have liked the chance to win these cases way back when, given the chance.

• • •

In 1977 and 1978, Los Angeles had a rapist in the south end of the city. He was committing rapes in three L.A. Divisions, (University, Newton, and Seventy-seventh) and in the county surrounding those divisions as well. Our lieutenant told my team we were to compile all of the cases we could attach to the rapist and develop a way of catching him. The chief was getting a lot of heat over the inability of the department to catch the rapist. The division detectives were unable to get a handle on the cases, and we had the ability to coordinate all of the cases and bring the sheriff's cases into our investigation as well.

We looked for a common denominator or MO that would separate the cases and developed a matrix chart to do this. What we found was that the suspect we wanted to go after was covering his victim's head with pillowcases when he was committing the rape. We found some cases where he would use something other than a pillowcase, but these cases still fit the plotting of the rapes on our chart. When we got done organizing all of the cases from the three divisions and the county, we ended up with over 150 cases that fit our profile of the rapist. Considering that rape is the least-reported crime, we knew we were after a very active rapist.. From where we started with cases in 1977 and ended with cases in 1978, we found that the rapist was averaging three rapes a week. There were also cases from 1976 that could fit his MO as well. We decided to call the rapist "The Pillowcase Rapist."

Our plotting on our matrix chart showed us the following patterns:

1. The rapist would work a specific area for a specific time period, from one to two months, and then he would move to another area and do the same thing. It appeared that he

would leave an area when he felt he was staying there too long and could be caught.

2. The rapist's victims were always unmarried woman who lived alone, or had small children in the house who would not be a threat to him.

3. The rapist committed the majority of his rapes in the early morning hours, between two and five o'clock.

4. The rapist always entered the victim's home through an unlocked door or open window. He never broke into a home.

5. The rapist would almost always use a pillowcase from the bed to cover the victim's head so she could not see him. If there was no pillowcase, he would use an item of the victim's clothes that were present in the bedroom.

6. The suspect never used physical force against the victims other than restraining them. Not one victim had to be treated for injuries other than the rape.

7. The rapist would always apologize to the victim, after the rape, and tell them he was sorry for what he had done to them. He would always tell them to not report the rape to the police, and if they did, they were to wait for a half hour after he left. In some cases he would put the victim in the bedroom closet.

8. The rapist victims were all under forty years in age.

9. The rapist was described as being a male, black, thirty-five to fifty years old, 140 to 160 pounds, slender build, and under six feet in height. Several victims had gotten a look at the suspect, but none of them felt they could identify him.

10. A car was never seen or heard leaving a location.

The normal way a rape case was reported was that a victim would call the police, and a patrol car would respond, and the victim would be taken to the hospital. At the hospital, virginal slides would be taken and a report would be completed. The report would be forwarded to the detectives, and they would pick up the investigation the following day. We decided to form a task force and form teams of two detectives, one being a policewoman, to respond to the location of a rape as soon as the rape was reported. We set a priority of the victim's head being covered with a pillowcase or other object. That way we would start working the case as soon as it was reported. We also brought twelve teams of the Metropolitan Squad into our task force. We used them as two-man teams, in uniform and in plain police cars, and had them flood an area and shake, rattle, and roll the alleys and out-of-the-way places. As soon as a rape was reported, they were to blanket the area of the occurrence and shake down anyone they found on the streets.

After examining the pattern of movement on the part of our suspect, and the last rape that had occurred, we felt that he was working in University Division. We put the Metro officers in that division, and had our detectives respond to any reported rape in that division. Two weeks after doing this, we caught our rapist. A rape occurred at four o'clock in the morning, the victim reported it, and our team arrived at the scene within twenty minutes of the rape. The victim had had a pillowcase placed over her head, and after the rape she had been placed in the bedroom closet. The suspect had apologized for the rape and told the victim not to call the police, and if she did to wait until a half hour had went by. The victim called the police as soon as the suspect left her house. After receiving this information from the victim, our team put out the information that it was felt that the suspect was the Pillowcase Rapist. As soon as the rape was reported, Metro flooded the area and picked up a suspect running down an alley, two blocks from the victim's house. The suspect fit our general description and was dressed in a post office employee's uniform.

It turned out that the suspect worked for the post office. (Reminded me of the burglar I had caught long ago.) He was a mail carrier who was moved around to fill in for vacations and when other carriers were sick. (That explained why he bounced around to different areas.) He would pick his victims by delivering mail to their houses and checking the house for unlocked doors or open windows. If the mail was addressed to a single woman, he would know that there wasn't a man at the house; or, to make sure, he would knock at the door and tell the woman that he was a new carrier and just wanted to verify her name, or things to that effect. He would also decide if the woman was to his liking this way. He was identified as Reginald Muldrew, male, black, forty-nine years old. He was convicted on four of the rapes and sentenced to twenty-five years in 1979. He served sixteen years and was released in 1995.

Another assignment we had at Major Crimes was escort duty for all VIPs who came into the city. We were to stay with them, 24/7, while they were within the city limits, and handle an assassination, or an assassination attempt, should it occur. Our chief felt that the department hadn't responded fast enough to the Bobby Kennedy assassination, and he wanted to make sure that we would be on top of any future occurrence. As a result, I was escorting President Ford in 1976 when he appeared at USC to give a speech. I knew at the time that there had been attempts on his life in San Francisco in 1975, so I stuck to him like glue. Of course Secret Service was there to protect him, as was our SWAT team, and I was there only to investigate his death—should an assassination take place—but I still didn't feel like I could leave him out of my sight. Fortunately nothing happened to him while he was in LA. I was standing in line to shake his hand when he boarded Air Force One at LAX. As I was shaking his hand, he spoke to me. "Do you think I made a good speech at the college?"

I answered, "Yes, Mr. President, I think it was a good speech."

The President then made the following statement. "I am sure glad you did not have to do your job!" He knew I was there to investigate his death, should it have occurred.

My answer was, "So am I."

With President G. Ford at LAX. My partner is shaking his hand, and I am to the right of my partner.

Chapter 7

Southeast Homicide O.I.C. (Officer in Charge)

July1978–April 1984

The department was opening a new station called Southeast, and it was going to cover the Watts area. Seventy-seventh Division was going to move north in its area and so was University, which was going to be called Southwest. The department was looking for a homicide coordinator and someone to pick the homicide detectives who were to work there, and also to help in the selection of the other detectives to work there. Even though all my coworkers and my lieutenants insisted I stay with the unit at Major Crimes, I felt I would have more time to share with my sons by leaving, and applied for the job. Besides, I would again be going home to Watts. I had by now gained the reputation as one of the best homicide investigators in the city, and even though I was getting the "big" cases to handle, I felt my calling was to go back to Watts, and to raise my boys, in that it was a time in their lives that I always knew was coming. My wife was divorcing me, and I had gotten custody of my two sons. It was a time when they needed a dad to teach them how to play baseball and to be there for them when they needed me to be there. My oldest boy, Rob, was eight years old and my youngest boy, Troy, was five. I felt that the move would be a no-brainer. At Major Crimes I could go to work and not go home for days, and I had to place my boys with babysitters who could "live with them" until I could get back home. By going to Southeast as a coordinator, I could pick and choose what cases I wanted to work and just supervise the others.

In July of 1978, I was selected from fifteen outstanding candidates for the position of Homicide Coordinator at the new Southeast Station. I then made the selection of the entire homicide squad. I also assisted in the selection of other key personnel, helped divide the division up into reporting areas, and assigned personnel to these areas. I established controls and procedures for the accountability of the homicide squad, and got to work solving homicides in Watts again. I was also assisted by a wonderful woman I met in August of 1978. I took her to work with me, on some of my cases, in order to show her what I did and to assure the both of us that a marriage would work out; as a result, she gave up her job in San Diego and moved in with me to take care of our children. This gave me the time I needed to work my job in the fashion I needed to in order to be successful at it. We were married on December 20th of 1980. She had custody of her son, who was eight years old at the time, and we set up a family in a home I had bought in Huntington Beach. As it turned out, we were a perfect match and raised our boys together, and at the same time I finished my career at Southeast solving Watts's homicides. I continued to work at Southeast until I retired in April of 1984. Our section was the busiest homicide squad in the city, year after year, and would handle between 130 and 150 homicides a year and carry the highest homicide clearance rate (71%–86%) every year I was there. In 1979 I was given four other detectives from the Crimes against Persons section to supervise, bringing my span of control to twelve detectives. I also took on my own cases to work, and for the rest of my career acted as such—a coordinator and a case-carrying detective. I became so successful that I earned the trust and support of my commanding officer to the extent that all homicide functions were left to my discretion and control. The following article appeared in *The Times* of London, England in 1981, in a Foreign Report:

Chief Justice Warren Burger says street crime is imposing "a reign of terror" on American cities.

"Like it or not, we are approaching the status of an impotent society whose capability of maintaining elementary security on the streets, in the schools, and for the homes of our people is in doubt." The concerns he voiced are probably nowhere more deeply felt than in Los Angeles, Ivor Davis reports:

Lieutenant Earl Rice, chief detective in one of Los Angeles's' worst crime area, drinks his coffee black and does not mince his words: "There's more chance of dying by murder down here than by accident or natural death."

His territory covers only 10 square miles and takes in a population of 107,000, mostly black and Mexican Americans, in south Los Angeles.

Lately, the increase in violent crimes has shocked residents in this city of three million people. Mr. Daryl Gates, the police chief, confirmed these fears last month by announcing that 1,021 people were murdered in the City of the Angels in 1980, an increase of 27% over 1979.

But at Lieutenant Rice's bureau they view the sudden hysteria over the rocketing murder rate with some cynicism.

"Every weekend here people are routinely murdered in the streets and nobody takes any notice," Detective Bob Reynolds, of the homicide squad, notes. "Rapes and murders are considered part of the lifestyle. There is a big double standard operating. The same homicides we have here daily are now appearing in west Los Angeles (a predominantly white affluent area)," he says.

South-east police headquarters is a red and grey brick fortress in the street of the black ghetto that resembles the aftermath of an air raid. Shops are boarded up, rubble strewn on empty lots, graffiti on walls, houses abandoned. Compared to the manicured tidiness of the rest of the city this is a wasteland. There are few people on the streets.

A recent *Los Angeles Times* poll reported that residents all over the city are worried more about crime than are people in other American cities. "They have an inordinate fear of it that cuts across socio-economic boundaries."

Yet the poll noted that few homes had actually been touched. Not so in the south-central section, which is a ghetto in the real sense of the word. The only way out is by private car or an inadequate bus system. Unemployment hovers around 20%: there are few local jobs because industry is loath to open new plants.

The jobless—and 40% of the area's young blacks are out of work—aimlessly hanging around the local housing estates or join street gangs. Schools do not attract top flight teachers and as a result the quality of education suffers.

Many residents live from welfare money and, in fact, police note that robberies increase on the first and fifteenth of each month, on "Mother's Day," as they bitterly term the welfare pay-days.

When Los Angeles's much publicized 300-man crime task force moved into the ghetto for several days, they made 558 arrests but mostly on minor offences.

"Most of the heavy guys just cooled it until the heat was off," one of the crime scene investigators remarked.

I spent a couple of days recently with division's murder squad. Detective Jim Deli is one of the eight-man homicide force trying to catch up with the backlog of murders. He has only been in the division a year but already has a caseload of 16 unsolved murders.

"We need twice the number of detectives to even make a dent in the cases," he says.

The station is a self-contained island of refuge. When officers leave they usually do so in twos and get into their cars immediately. They bring sandwiches for lunch to eat at their desks and seldom venture out to neighborhood restaurants.

Outside it is considered a war zone and the police appear battle-scarred and weary. The fatigue shows on their faces. They are remarkably frank and many are disgusted by the conditions they have to work under.

During the two days I spent with the detectives the pace was hectic. It was sheer murder and mayhem, with little sleuthing required. The count for 1981 stood at 11 murders in less than four weeks- a 57% increase over the same period last year.

A wife shot her husband after he threatened her with a knife. A shopkeeper (whose husband had been killed a few years earlier by an armed robber) was confronted by three armed teenagers. She beat them to the draw and pumped a bullet into one of them. The robbers fled dragging their bleeding companion to a car and then dumped the youth at the front door of the local hospital. He was dead before he reached the emergency ward.

The homicide detectives reserve some of their bitterest word for the court system. "We used to kick the door down if we thought a suspect was hiding and take him in," says Detective Reynolds, who has spent most of his 20 years working in homicide. "Not any more. Now we need a search warrant and that takes five hours to get. By that time he's long gone. And even if you do make an arrest by the time you get him to the DA (district attorney) it's the policeman who ends up on the hot seat. You get the third-degree like you're on trial.

"Whenever there's a gang shooting they want witnesses-so we get a guy who talks to us. We arrest a suspect and then the DA decides there is not enough evidence to hold him. Less than 24 hours later he is back on the streets and our witness is running scared. Try explaining a judicial decision like that to some kid in the ghetto who's terrified for his life."

They blame "soft" judges for the mounting street crime and complain that tough young street gang hoodlums are shipped off to holiday camp-like farms and released on parole too quickly.

They would like to see San Quentin's gas chamber back in business. "These people are not dummies," remarks Detective Reynolds, "all a murder suspect has to say is "I dropped some pills," or "I was drinking" and it's diminished capacity. He gets at worst seven years for murder—and in three he is paroled."

Some detectives bemoan decaying morality and falling social standards and feel they are fighting a losing battle. And they scoff at the police department's million dollar advertising campaign to refurbish the policeman's image.

To some, the troubles of the south-east division policeman might seem to have little to do with the rest of Los Angeles, being a function of a totally alien world. But more and more demarcation lines between the wastelands and the heart of one of the most affluent cities in the world is being blurred.

Ask those policemen in the division and they will tell you that the problems are nation-wide. Crime is out of control, they say, and they look to what they perceive as a tough new conservative President to do something about it.

• • •

I am putting this article here for a purpose, and that purpose is that it brought the local media's attention to Watts, and all of a sudden our murders became news and our cases were appearing on TV news and in the local papers. The *Los Angeles Times* and the *Herald Examiner* were printing our cases weekly, and the TV news channels were camped on my doorstep. I was being interviewed on our cases live by George Putnam of Channel Five News, almost weekly. It was as if overnight our cases became important and the city felt compassion for the victims of crime in the ghetto. The murders, rapes, robberies, and gang activity became the "BIG" cases and attracted just as much attention as the same types of crimes in the other parts of the city did. Our crimes were no longer just black on black crimes; they were crimes that were uncalled for and as important to try and eliminate as any other crimes in the city were. This in turn caused a lot of good people in Watts to feel that finally the city cared about them, and they lent us their support in cooperating with us by telling us what they knew about criminal activity. I was really proud of the fact that I had been part of bringing this change in attitude to Watts. The fact that my cases in Watts got as much attention as my cases had at Major Crimes made it worthwhile to come back to Watts and solve cases for the good people there.

Now I will get back to telling a couple of war stories from my days working at Southeast Homicide. I am going to tell you about two task forces I put together to coordinate two investigations. One of the investigations led to my being awarded the department's Police Meritorious Unit Citation in recognition of outstanding service, and the other led to the solving of a case twenty-seven years after the murder occurred. Both of these investigations received media attention weekly and remained the top stories in the news for weeks.

The first investigation began with the shooting death of Diego Calvario. On November 10, 1981, at around nine o'clock at night, Diego Calvario was driving his vehicle south on Central Avenue when he stopped his vehicle at Lanzit Avenue for the red tri-light signal. Also in the vehicle were his wife,

Balvina Calvario, and their four children. As Mr. Calvario waited for the signal to change, the vehicle was approached by four to six male suspects, fifteen to seventeen years old. The suspects surrounded and shattered the windows of the vehicle with rocks. Both Mr. and Mrs. Calvario were forcibly removed from the vehicle, and one of the suspects confronted Diego with a sawed-off rifle. As the entire family watched in horror, the suspect with the rifle shot and killed Diego as he stood outside the vehicle. Although robbery was the apparent motive, the suspects fled on foot without taking any property. The crime-scene investigation was conducted by me and one of my detectives. We learned from the deceased wife that her husband couldn't speak any English and had been trying to tell the suspects to just take his money and car and to let his family go. The wife stated that she could identify the suspects and would never forget their faces. She also stated that the suspects were on foot and didn't have a car.

The case received considerable press coverage and because of the personal concern of Los Angeles County Supervisor Kenneth Hahn, efforts were initiated to establish a reward for the suspect's arrest. Eventually a reward of five thousand dollars was raised.

On November 13, 1981, at around four in the afternoon, a gang-related shooting took place at Avalon Boulevard and Imperial Highway, in a gas station. Three victims were shot and were lying in and around the gas pumps at the location. Upon being notified at the station, I grabbed one of my homicide teams and immediately went to the location. When we arrived, we found that two of the victims had been transported to Martin Luther King Hospital, and one of the victims was still lying in the gas station. This victim lying in the gas station had died as a result of his gunshot wounds. Our investigation revealed that the three victims were members of a street gang out of Imperial Courts Housing Projects called the Imperial Courts Cripps. (The gang consisted of the old Bounty Hunters.) The suspects were on foot and had come into the gas station by way of running across Imperial Highway at the traffic signal. They had left the same way, and were last seen running down the railroad tracks at that location. This was the same way the suspects had run from the Calvario crime scene. It appeared that this shooting was not a drive-by shooting but was a run-by shooting.

After talking to witnesses at the scene, and the two victims at the hospital, we found the suspects to be four male black juveniles, between the ages of fifteen and seventeen. Three of the suspects were carrying handguns, and the other suspect was carrying a sawed-off .22-caliber rifle. The deceased victim had been shot with the rifle, and the other two victims had been shot with two of the three handguns. At the time, we felt that the suspects were the same suspects who had committed the Calvario homicide, based on their descriptions, their being on foot, and the direction they took leaving the crime scene, and the use of the .22-caliber rifle. (After getting the slugs from the two autopsies and comparing them, we verified that the same weapon was used to commit both homicides, and it had been a .22-caliber weapon.) This shooting also drove the media wild with their coverage.

After checking with my informants and having our gang unit check with their informants, we learned the identity of the four suspects and learned that they were all fifteen and sixteen years old. We also learned that they all lived in the Jordan Downs Housing Project and were all members of a new gang that had just formed up around a month prior to the two shootings. The gang had been on a crime spree since that time. The gang was made up of around twenty members of Jordan Downs's teenagers, and they had been wannabe gang members of the Cripps. They had decided to branch off and form their own gang and were calling themselves The Jordan Downs Cripps. We also found out that they were out gang-banging almost nightly, and were committing strong-arm robberies in and around the Jordan Downs Housing Project. They had also decided to declare war against the gangs in Imperial Courts in order to show off their muscle and gain status. One of their requirements, in order to be accepted into the gang, was that you had to be either fifteen or sixteen years old. Our informants knew some of the gang members, but not all of them. The word was that everyone was giving them a wide berth and was afraid of them. They would just as soon shoot you as look at you, and had shot other robbery victims. It was felt among our informants that the shootings gave them status among themselves.

I decided to form a mini task force in order to attack the problem and best control the investigation. The task force consisted of four detectives, four uniform police officers, and me. I had the detectives put together a matrix chart and plot the crimes on it. They went back a month and accounted for every robbery that had occurred in Southeast. They also went to the Firestone station of the LA County Sheriff's, which bordered Watts on the east, and gathered their reports around Jordan Downs. Within a month we had plotted over one hundred strong-arm robberies, of which half could be tied to our suspected gang. At the same time that I had my detectives doing this, I put my uniform officers out in plain cars to shake, rattle, and roll in the Jordan Downs Housing Project. Their orders were to shake down every person who was seen running with our four suspects and every teenager on the streets in and around Jordan Downs. If they observed a crime, they were to arrest the perpetrators, but all I wanted was their photographs to compile a mug book with. I wanted to be able to show this mug book to all of the victims of the crimes we were plotting, for identification of the suspects of those crimes.

During the following month, we kept constant pressure on Jordan Downs Housing Project. We worked day and night in the project, and when my detectives were not plotting crimes or getting identifications of suspects with the mug book, they were with me out in the project shaking down suspects, as were the uniform officers. Initially we found some suspects carrying guns, but once the word got out we were in the project, the suspects stopped packing guns. The crimes also tapered off during that month. I got the results I wanted, and we were able to identify twenty gang members and identify all of them as suspects in over fifty strong-arm robberies. We were also able to identify the four involved in the two homicides through Calvario's wife and the two surviving victims of the gas-station shooting. The investigation proved to be very complex and difficult, but in the end it proved to be fruitful.

On January 29, 1982, I formed a force of over one hundred police officers, made up of the entire Metropolitan Division, three divisional gang units, twenty Southeast patrol officers, and sixteen Southeast detectives. We served sixteen search warrants on locations in and around the Jordan Downs Housing Projects, simultaneously, at seven o'clock that morning. We apprehended seventeen suspects and confiscated twenty-one guns, along with four cars we had identified as belonging to four of the suspects. While we were impounding the cars, we heard someone crying inside the trunk of one of the cars, and when we forced open the trunk, we found a teenage Caucasian girl in the trunk. (The girl turned out to be a kidnapped victim who had been reported missing three days prior, out of another division. She had been gang-raped and physically assaulted and was near death. She survived her ordeal and identified her assaulters. We found out from the suspects that they had been arguing over whether or not they would just kill her, so she would not identify them, or ask for a ransom and then kill her. They also had decided to kidnap other girls for the same purpose they had her, and they were going to kill her and then ask for a ransom. She was to be killed that night and dumped off of a freeway ramp. (They had placed her in the trunk the night before we found her.)

After interrogating all the suspects, and getting admissions from them as to their parts in all of the various crimes, we were able to convict all seventeen of the suspects, and identify five additional suspects, who we also arrested and convicted. We solved over fifty strong-arm robberies, two murders, one kidnap/rape, and several assaults with intent to commit murder, which were based on several robbery victims who had been shot. We also had identifications of the suspects from a lot of the victims, after holding stand-up lineups. In all we had taken down a complete street gang that was just starting their crime spree and in all probability would have killed and raped again. The officers in my original task force, including myself, were commended for our responsiveness to instructions, professional behavior, and temperament under stress, which precluded any negative encounters during the service of the warrants.

As you might expect, the press was all over this, and I was on all the local TV news channels, and the papers carried it as front-page news. The investigation led to my being recommended for a Major Service Citation for my efforts as the Task Force O.I.C. I was presented the department's Police Meritorious Unit Citation at the Department's Fourth Annual Recognition Day ceremonies on February 16, 1983, by Chief of Police Daryl F. Gates.

• • •

Now let's move on into the second of the two investigations I said I was going to tell you about. The investigation started on March 9, 1983, between the hours of 2:30 p.m. and 3:30 p.m. The victim, Victoria Denise Brown, female Negro, eight years of age, was walking home from school on Anzac Avenue at Ninety-seventh Street, in Watts, when she was kidnapped by a male Latin, twenty-five to thirty years of age, driving an unknown manufactured blue van. On March 10, 1983, at 5:00 p. m., the victim's body was discovered lying in the trunk of an abandoned and stripped vehicle on East "Q" Street, Wilmington, some twenty miles from the kidnapping. I was assigned the case, upon the discovery of the body, and responded to the location of the body with a team of my detectives, to assume the investigation. I had been aware of the kidnapping the day before.

At the crime scene I had a criminalist from the department, and a coroner's criminalist, respond to the location to gather trace evidence from the victim's body, as well as the trunk of the car the body was in. The evidence removed from the deceased was collected by the coroner's criminalist and booked by the department criminalist for analysis. Nine pieces of foreign hair or fiber were removed from the deceased's body prior to removing clothing at the scene. (I was later informed that all of the hairs removed from the deceased's body were hers.)

On March 11 my supervisor asked me to form a small task force to investigate the crime and told me that the press was demanding information on the case. I was allowed to use eight detectives from my twelve detectives on the task force. During the course of the investigation, over 350 clues were received and organized for investigation. This case was not solved, but was subsequently transferred to Major Crimes because of the drain it took on Southeast homicide detectives and the need for them to work other cases. Major Crimes would have the ability to work the case without the interference of other cases. My supervisors said that it was because of my expertise and supervisory controls that the case was allowed to be taken up by another specialized department entity with very few transitional problems. The truth was, I was giving the case to detectives who I had worked with at Major Crimes and had established a good rapport with in the past, and they knew my working abilities and accepted the case as it was. The case was transferred to Major Crimes on April 6, after being worked on at Southeast for a little less than one month. I hated to give up the case, but it was the right decision in that we did not have the time the case was going to take to work properly. I am now going to show you how an unsolved case is written up in progress reports by including the report we made to Major Crimes when the case was transferred. The report won't contain all the information that was sent them, in that the 350 clues investigated aren't all written up in the progress report and are attached as attachments, as were our reports on these clues.

Unsolved Murder Investigation

Progress Report

Fact Sheet

Victim (s): Brown, Victoria Denise Case No 83-487 991 Coroner No. 83 3182

Date/ Time Occurred: 3-9-83 1430/1530 Hours

Location of Occurrence: 9532 S. Anzac St., Los Angeles—1600 block East "Q" Street, Wilmington

Cause of Death: Ligature Strangulation

Motive: Probable Sexual Gratification

Area of Occurrence: Southeast Area—Harbor Area

Detectives Assigned: Det.3 R Reynolds—Det.2M. Calagna—Det.2 P. Marshall—Det.2 M. Rhodes—Det.1 C. Merritt—Det.1 D. Parks—PLM.3 C Wilder

I. Brief Synopsis

On March 9, 1983, at approximately 1425/1430 hours, the victim, Victoria Denise Brown, female Negro, 8 years of age D.O.B. 9/7.74, was walking home from school southbound on Anzac Avenue. An unknown manufacture blue van proceeded northbound on Anzac Avenue from 97th Street and struck a red 1976 Cadillac DeVille, California License #1EXZ199, which was parked in front of 9612 S. Anzac Avenue. The blue van continued northbound on Anzac Avenue and stopped in front of 9532 S. Anzac Avenue.

A short time later, a male Latin, 25/30 years of age, 5-9/6-0″ tall, 130/150 lbs., brown wavy hair, wearing blue short-sleeve shirt with white stripe on sleeve and faded blue jeans, was observed standing on the grass parkway at the rear of the van, stretching. The victim approached the van and walked off southbound on Anzac Avenue. The victim returned to the passenger side of the van. The van left northbound on Anzac Avenue, and then turned right (eastbound) on 95th Street. The male Latin and the victim were not seen after the van left.

On March 10 1983, at 1700 hours, the victim's body was discovered lying in the trunk of an abandoned and stripped vehicle, which was parked in the 1600 block of East "Q" Street, Wilmington. The victim had been strangled with a piece of 16-gauge wire, and was sexually molested.

II. Notification of Detectives

On March 10, at 1810 hours, Det. III R. Reynolds, Det. II M. Calagna and Det.II M. Rhodes were telephonically notified at their respective residences, by Sgt. R. Grafton, Southeast Watch Commander, that the body of a female child had been discovered in the trunk of an abandoned vehicle, in the 1600 block of East "Q" Street, Wilmington, in Harbor Division. Sgt. Grafton further stated, the body was possibly that of the missing kidnap victim Victoria Denise Brown.

Detectives Reynolds, Calagna and Rhodes responded to Southeast Division, and were briefed by Detective III K. Brutsch Southeast Division Juvenile Coordinator. On 3-10-83, at 2030 hours, Sgt. Grafton telephonically notified PLM 3 C. Wilder, who responded to Southeast Division.

III Crime Scene Investigation

A. Exterior Characteristics of Crime Scene

Detectives Reynolds, Calagna, and Rhodes responded to the crime scene, arriving at 1955 hours. SID Criminalist and Coroner's Office Criminalist were notified and were requested to respond to the crime scene.

Detective Reynolds, Calagna, and Rhodes were met by Lt. W. Pruitt, Lt. M Markulis, and Detective L. Kallestad, who briefed them regarding the crime scene and evidence observed.

The crime scene is primarily an industrial area in the 1600 block East "Q" Street. The area was illuminated by single-glove mercury vapor overhead lamp standards and the department light truck, which is equipped with six large halogen lanterns. The 1600 block East "Q" Street is bounded by Drumm Street to the east and Blinn Street to the west. On the south side of the street there is an auto salvage yard that runs the entire length of the block. The north side of "Q" Street is a vacant lot and hillside that runs the distance of the block and beyond.

The crime scene was photographed by Department Photographer N Sauro, who arrived at 1855 hours. All evidence except that removed directly from the deceased was collected and booked by Department Criminalist W. Loomis. (Arrived 1950 hours.) Evidence removed from the deceased was collected by Coroner's Criminalist K Inman (arrived 2100 hours), and booked by Criminalist Loomis. Nine pieces of foreign hair or fiber were recovered from the deceased's body prior to removing clothing at the scene. The clothing of the deceased was removed at the scene by Criminalist Inman and booked by Criminalist Loomis.

Prior to arrival of Detectives Reynolds, Calagna, and Rhodes, the crime scene had been secured and searched by Officers J. Christ, D. Raymond, N. Healing, and Detective L. Kallestad. Any possible evidence observed was noted, but not touched, until it was collected by the Criminalists.

The abandoned vehicle in which the deceased was found was fingerprinted at the scene by S. Conrad (arrived 1850): however, no lifts were obtained.

Coroner's Investigator Butler arrived, and following collection of the evidence took custody of the body. The environmental temperature was 61 degrees at 2155 hours. The liver temperature was 69 degrees at 2200 hours. Investigator Butler estimated rigor mortis as 3+ in the legs and 2+ in the arms and breaking.

The crime scene was secured at 2230 hours.

B. Interior Characteristics of Crime Scene.

The crime scene was entirely outside.

C. Characteristics of the Dead Body.

The victim was lying in the trunk of an abandoned vehicle that was parked in the 1600 block of East "Q" Street in Wilmington. The vehicle was facing eastbound on the south side of "Q" Street. The deceased was lying in a supine position with her head pointed to the west. The torso was straight, bent at the waist, with the legs extending in a southerly direction. The right arm extended out from the shoulder, bent at the elbow, with the forearm and hand extending back toward the torso. The right hand was under the torso. The left arm extended down from the shoulder and along the torso.

The victim was dressed in a pink and lavender print skirt and vest and a pink blouse. The victim was wearing a white sock on the right foot. A piece of black wire was knotted and affixed to the victim's neck, as a ligature. Petechial hemorrhage was observed in both eyes. Numerous pieces of hair and fibbers were removed from the body. A greasy diaper was observed under the victim's skirt and over her vaginal area. The victim wasn't wearing any panties when found. The victim's liver temperature was 69 degrees at 2200 hours. The air temperature was 61 degrees at 2155 hours.

The victim appeared to have been placed into the trunk of the abandoned vehicle, in such a manner as to conceal her from view by placing her up under the left rear fender well.

D. Weapons

Ligature: Black insulated stranded electrical wiring, with three consecutive overhand knots. See DID reports for further information.

IV. Personnel at Crime Scene

See Crime Scene log, Form 3.11.4, for names, units, arrival and departure times, and duties of the personnel who responded to the crime scene. The Crime Scene Log is attached as Addendum #2.

V. Follow-Up Investigation

On March 9, 1983 at approximately 1430 hours, the victim, Victoria Denise Brown, female Negro, 8 years of age, was walking home from Graham Avenue Elementary School when she was kidnapped by a suspect in a blue van in front of 9532 S. Anzac Avenue. The van left the location northbound on Anzac and then turned eastbound on 95th Street.

The Los Angeles Police Department Complaint Board received the first telephone call at 1431 hours, advising that the victim had been kidnapped. The caller did not identify him/herself; however, it probably was someone in the Hays family (witness of suspect). A few minutes later the Complaint Board received a telephone call from Francis Brown concerning the victim's kidnapping.

A Command Post was established at the victim's mother's residence. The area was checked by uniform officers for possible witnesses. Lt. W. Pruitt was in charge of the Command Post. Detectives K. Brutsch and C. Wright assisted in the Command Post. (Refer to concerned follow-up investigation report.)

Communications Division broadcasted the victim's description along with the van description over the police radio.

On March 10, 1983, at 1700 hours, witness David Allen was walking in the 1600 block of East "Q" Street in Wilmington when he discovered the victim's body lying in the trunk of an abandoned vehicle. The Los Angeles Police Department was contacted, and Harbor Division patrol units were dispatched. Unit 5A25, Officers Romero and Copper, responded to the location. RA Unit 285, Attendant Jacobs, responded and pronounced death at 1713 hours. Lt. Markulis, Commanding Officer, Harbor Detectives, and Detective III L. Kallestad responded to the location. Both were aware of the kidnapping of victim Brown in Southeast Division. Lt. W. Pruitt was contacted and responded to the location. The victim was positively identified as victim Brown and Southeast detectives were notified and requested to respond to the location.

Detective R. Reynolds, M. Calagna, and M. Rhodes responded to the crime scene and completed the investigation. The Crime

Scene was secured at 2300 hours. The residential area, near the location of "Q" Street and Blinn Avenue in Wilmington, was canvased by uniform officers of Harbor Division and Southeast detectives. No information was obtained.

On March 11, 1983, Det. R. Reynolds formed a task force of 8 detectives to assume the investigation.

Detective M. Rhodes attended the autopsy, which was performed by Dr. Golden at the Los Angeles County Coroner's Office. During the autopsy, pieces of peaches and pears were discovered in the victim's stomach. Dr. Golden advised that the victim would have been dead no later than 3 hours after she had eaten the fruit.

Detective Rhodes contacted Mrs. Aquilino, Principal of Graham Avenue School, and determined that the victim had eaten fruit cocktail at 1230 hours on March 9, 1983, in the school cafeteria. This would place the time of death at no later than 1530 hours on March 1983.

On March 11, 1983, at 1530 hours, the case was reassigned to Detectives P. Marshall and C. Merritt.

Detective Marshall contacted SID Representative Wolfer and requested that a criminalist conduct an investigation of the red Cadillac that the suspect's vehicle struck just prior to the kidnapping. Criminalist Schwecke responded to 9612 Anzac Avenue. He checked the red Cadillac DeVille and determined that the mark on the driver's side was only the dulling of the wax built up on the vehicle. No paint transfer was observed on the Cadillac.

At approximately 1815 hours, Traffic Control Officer Smith called back to Detectives and advised them that he remembered that, at the time he checked the vehicle trunk, a blue

Chevrolet van, California license plate #72462-Z, was parked behind the red Cadillac.

The follow-up investigation revealed that this van belonged to Jessie James. Mr. James was contacted on March 12, 1983, and responded to Southeast Station. Detectives checked the van and discovered it to be white in color. The license plates were affixed to both the front and rear of the van and appeared to have been in place for some period of time. The interior of the vehicle was searched and no evidence was discovered. Mr. James admitted that he had been on Blinn Street on March 10, 1983, waiting for Pick Your Parts Auto Store to open. Detectives eliminated Mr. James as a suspect for the following reasons: Mr. James did not fit the suspect's physical description. Mr. James's vehicle was white in color, not blue. The victim had been killed on March 9, 1983, at approximately 1530 hours, and her body was placed in the trunk of the abandoned vehicle shortly after her death. T.C.O. Officer saw Mr. James's vehicle on Thursday, March 10, 1983, at approximately 1230 hours.

On March 11, 1983, at 1933 hours, Lt. E Henderson, Robbery-Homicide Division, conducted an interview of Harriett Hayes at Southeast Station. During this interview Harriett Hayes was hypnotized. She related a description of the suspect as a male Latin 25/30, 5-9/6-0, 130/150 lbs, thin, and wearing a blue short-sleeve shirt, blue faded jeans, with brown wavy hair that touched the top of the ears and was full in the back of the head.

The van was described as blue in color, with no windows on the driver's side. The back of the van had two doors, and at the top of each door was square window. No stickers or chrome were observed on the van. The van had a white bumper. A blue and gold California license plate was attached to either the center of the bumper or just below the bumper. No license plate holder was observed around the license plate itself.

Detectives had received a possible clue that several relatives had driven to the area where the victim's body was located. During their drive around the area, they located a blue van that was parked at 137 E. I Street, Wilmington. On March 12, 1983, Detectives Marshall and Merritt proceeded to the location and interviewed Jorge Garcia. He denied that the blue van had been at his place of business. Detectives observed two blue vans parked at the fire station parking lot that was behind the auto body shop. These were possible the vans that the relative had seen.

On March 14, 1983, Detectives interviewed George Freeman, an inmate at the County jail. He had called Southeast Detectives and indicated he had information concerning the victim's death. Detectives interviewed him and he wanted to know if the victim's father was driving a cream color or beige pickup truck, 1980/1981. Detectives stated no. He then advised Detectives that he had known about a Mexican who wanted a black dope dealer killed or beaten who lived in the Watts area. This incident did not appear to be connected to the Brown murder.

On March 15, 1983, Detectives located and interviewed Laura Baker and Nanette Gardner. Both stated that they were standing on the corner of 95th and Hickory on March 9, 1983, at approximately 1430 hours, when they observed a blue van driving at a high rate of speed eastbound on 95th Street. It is unknown if the van that these witnesses saw was the suspect's van.

On March 21, 1983, Detectives located and interviewed Mr. Leroy Richards. Mr. Richards saw the victim walking southbound on Anzac Avenue, south of 92nd Street. He further stated that he last saw her at approximately 95th Street and Anzac Avenue. His grandson was released from 92nd Street School, and he left. He puts the time as 1430 hours. Detectives transported him to 92nd Street School, where a teacher, Nancy Banton, viewed him. She stated that Mr. Richards was not the person she saw the victim talking with on the date the victim was kidnapped.

On March 17, 1983, Harbor Division patrol officer arrested Jon Jay Barrientos for 664/459 PC Burglary. Mr. Barrientos was driving a Ford van at the time of his arrest. On March 18, 1983, Detective Merritt interviewed Mr. Barrientos, who admitted an attempt burglary but had no knowledge of the murder. Detectives checked Mr. Barrientos's van and found that it was a 1970 Ford, green in color, with windows on the sides. Due to the van's description, the suspect and his van were eliminated.

On March 17, 1983, at 1530 hours, Detectives walked the neighborhood from Graham Avenue School to the victim's house on Anzac Avenue. Detectives also walked 95th Street, from Anzac Avenue to Alameda Avenue. A complete list of names of persons contacted and their statements are contained in the homicide folder under neighborhood statements. Also a map showing the areas canvassed are located under Section #16 Crime Scene Surveys.

On March 24, 1983, Detectives contacted Agent Brian Parry, from the Department of Corrections, and requested a list of all parolees who had recently been released to the Los Angeles area with a sex-crime background. As of this writing, this list is not completed.

On March 24, 1983, a composite was completed at Southeast Station by the police artist utilizing statements of witnesses Hayes, Harriett; Hays, Ruby; Baker, Laura; and Gardner, Nanette, of the suspect's van.

On March 24, 1983, Detectives met and interviewed Parole Agent Michael Paul, who is in charge of parolees in the Wilmington, Long Beach, area. Agent Paul was advised of the circumstances of the murder. Agent Paul stated he did not have any parolees who fit the physical description of the suspect. He stated he would attempt to solicit information from parolees in the area.

Detectives canvassed the Wilmington area in an attempt to locate any witnesses. This met with negative results. Detectives contacted the manager of the "Pick Your Parts" junkyard and learned that they had a security guard, who only stayed inside the business at nighttime. Detectives dropped off a copy of the composite to the manager and requested they talk to all of their employees and ask them to look for the van.

Detectives learned that the vehicle the victim's body was discovered in was a Long Beach stolen, DR#830-4966. The vehicle was reported stolen on 1-29-83 from the rear of 1343 Long Beach Blvd., Long Beach. Detectives interviewed the owner Sally Demetro, female white. She stated that she did not know anyone who lived or worked in the Wilmington area. She stated that she moved to Long Beach from Oakland, California approximately 6 months ago. She did not know if the vehicle had the original engine and transmission.

Detectives complied a list of computer printouts with male Mexicans who have blue vans registered to them, and who live in the Los Angeles area. These computer printouts were turned over to Robbery-Homicide Division.

A diaper with what appeared to be grease and foreign substances on it was recovered from the victim's person. This diaper appears to have been left by the suspect. As of this writing, Criminalist Loomis is conducting an analysis of the diaper. Stamped in ink on the diaper are the words "Service fold by Curity Diaper Service," Inventory Control #S/DS 76502. The Curity diapers are distributed throughout the United States. The serial number is placed on the diaper as a deterrent for theft. The number is not used for inventory purposes, and no record is kept as to where each number is distributed.

Detectives learned that this diaper is a commercial type and is not sold in the store. Local diaper services in the Long Beach–Wilmington area were contacted for possible uses of Curity diapers. Detectives learned that Tidy Didy and By-Dee services used Curity diapers in the Harbor area.

The following information was received from analysis of evidence by the crime lab. The swabs taken in the sexual assault kit were examined and the swabs from the anal and vaginal were positive for spermatozoa. These swabs ere further tested for "ABO" and PGM enzyme activity. No activity was detected in the ABO system. The PGM system was determined as type 1.

The ligature was checked and determined to be black plastic wire, 16 gage, with 19 strands of copper wire. This wire is extremely common and is the type used in ground wire in automobiles, and is also the type used in fixtures in buildings.

Items recovered from around the crime scene, i.e., bottles, beer cans, and electrical parts, were fingerprinted. No latent prints were developed from these items. The automobile from which the victim's body was recovered was dusted for prints: none were detected.

Hair and miscellaneous fibers removed from the victim's body were examined. The hairs were analyzed and compared to the victim's hairs. They were similar and probably came from the victim. Two other hairs recovered from the victim were animal hairs, resembling dog hairs.

All analyzed evidence reports are retained under Section 6 in the homicide book. A package of information was compiled with the crime information, victim's photograph, composite of the van, missing property, and known facts about the suspect and vehicle. These packages were distributed to the following police departments: South Gate P.D., Huntington Park P.D., Vernon P.D., Maywood P.D., Bell P.D., Long Beach P.D., L.A.P.D. Harbor Division, Firestone and Lynwood Sheriff Departments. As of this writing, no information has been developed from this crime information packages.

The following computer runs have been requested and received:

- All sex crimes and kidnaps in Reporting Districts 514, 515, 516, 517, 519, 525, and 529.

- A list of all registered sex offenders in the Los Angeles area

- All blue vans which were F.I.'d in the Harbor and S/E Divisions in the last year.

These computer printouts are retained in the Homicide book.

The following suspects or possible suspects have been interviewed and eliminated:

On March 16, 1983, Detectives Marshall and Merritt were advised that Firestone Sheriffs had an eyewitness at their station. Detectives responded and interviewed a Joseph Howard White Jr., Male/Negro D.O.B. 7-1-59. At the time of the interview, Mr. White was under the influence of PCP.

Mr. White indicated that on 3-9-83, at 1410 hours, he observed the victim, who was fleeing from a guy named "Jug" and his wife. "Jug" is described as a Male/Negro, 38/39 years of age, with jeri curl hair, 6-0 feet, 200 lbs., dark complexion, and walks with a cane. Mr. White indicated that the victim bumped into him, cutting her lip. He showed Detectives a spot of blood on his pants, which he explained was the victim's blood. He stated he told the victim it was OK to go with "Jug" and his wife. The victim entered "Jug's" blue van, which had a pink- or peach-colored stripe on the side. (The autopsy disclosed no injury to victim's lip.)

On March 18, 1983, Joseph White contacted Sgt. Ferguson, Southeast Area Patrol, and advised him that he had seen the victim and that he knew the suspects. He advised Sgt. Ferguson that the suspects were "Big-Headed Willie" and "Cochise." "Big-Headed Willie" was identified as Willie Thompson, D.O.B. 12-17-36.

On March 18, 1983, at 1100 hours, Detective Marshall observed Willie Thompson's van at 88th Street and Compton Avenue. The van was a 1972 Ford, California License 339898L. The van did not fit the description of the suspect's van because it had a roof rack on top, chrome ladder on the rear and the license plate in the rear door. Willie Thompson was observed to be a male/ Negro, 6-0 feet, 220 lbs., black natural and dark complexion.

On March 22, 1983, Willie Thompson was contacted concerning the victim's murder. He denied any involvement in the crime.

On March 23, 1983, SID Representative Blair Eckand administered a polygraph examination to Willie Thompson. Mr. Thompson ran truthful and was eliminated as a suspect.

Detectives learned that Joseph White was in the hospital for drug rehabilitation. On April 4, 1983, Detectives reinterviewed Joseph White. He stated that "Big-Headed Willie" and "Cochise" had killed the victim. Mr. White was transported to the area of 95th Street and Anzac where he described the crime and pointed out the location.

Mr. White submitted to a polygraph examination conducted by Dale Olsen. Mr. White showed deceptive on the polygraph concerning his personal involvement in the crime: however, Mr. Olsen stated that due to White's PCP use, he felt that Mr. White possibly had a "flashback" concerning his knowledge of the crime. Due to the changes in Mr. White's story and the fact that he did not fit the physical description of the suspect, Detectives have eliminated him as a suspect or witness in this crime.

On March 16, 1983, Detectives learned from Hazel Shelby, that the man, who lived at 1823 E. 89th Street, knew the victim. She also stated that this person had a friend who owned a blue van. She further stated that her brother, Lee Arthur Wilson, had driven the possible suspect to a store where he purchased two tea sets (child's toys). Hazel Shelby stated that someone had shot into the suspect's house on March 10, 1983, at about

10 p.m. Several shots were fired into the house. She stated that she had never seen an adult female inside the house and it appeared that he liked young children. The suspect's house had a real-estate sign posted outside.

Detectives checked with the manager of Realty World, who indicated the property was rented to a Reynaldo Boyso, male/Latin, 28/30 years if age. Detectives contacted Reynaldo Velix Jaimes, who stated he had seen the victim visiting next door on occasions. He stated he did not kill the victim and did not know who did.

On March 30, 1983, Mr. Jaines submitted to a polygraph examination concerning his involvement in the crime. Detective III Ramos, SID, Polygraph Section, advised Detectives that Mr. Jaimes was not involved in the murder. This suspect was eliminated, based upon this and other evidence known to Detectives.

On March 29, 1983, at approximately 1700 hours, Frank Joseph Macias, LA# 1189221M, was arrested in connection with a kidnap-rape which occurred in Newton Division. He is a registered sex offender. Detectives Marshall and Calagna interviewed Macias on March 30, 1983, in Newton Station. He denied any involvement in the murder of Victoria Brown and stated that he was at work on March 9, 1983, from 0900 hours to 1430 hours, at the Jolly Roger, Florence and Market Street, Inglewood.

Detectives contacted the main office of the Jolly Roger, at telephone number 546-0331. Detectives verified that Mr. Macias was in fact employed on March 9, 1983, from 0900 to 1430 hours. Detectives checked with employees of the Jolly Roger.

None had a blue van, and they had only seen Mr. Macias drive a Chevrolet, brown in color. This suspect was eliminated.

Starting on March 11, 1983, Detectives received twelve telephone clues from citizens in the area that Marvin Smith had killed the victim. Detective Calagna interviewed a witness, Stephen Jessie Cisneros, male/Latin, D.O.B. 3-28-51, who advised him that a friend named Johnny Lopez had received a confession from Smith.

Detectives located Marvin Smith and interviewed him on 3-15-83, at 1500 hours. Marvin Smith denied any involvement in the crime. SID Representative Blair Eckand administered a polygraph examination to him, concerning his involvement in the victim's murder. SID Representative Eckand advised Detectives that the results were in conclusive.

On March 16, 1983, Detectives verified that Marvin Smith was in Division 3, North Court, Huntington Park on March 9, 1983 until after 2 P.M. (1400 hours). He was picked up by his mother and transported home. This suspect was eliminated.

As of this writing, 17 clue books containing 26 clues per book, pertaining to possible vehicles and/or suspects, have been compiled. These books have been turned over to Robbery-Homicide Division Major Crime Investigative Section for their review.

VI. Evidence

Refer to Property Report attached as Addendum #5 for items recovered as evidence subsequent to this investigation.

Items No. 1 through 8 were recovered by Coroners Criminalist K. Inman, and given to Criminalist Loomis at the crime scene, and subsequently booked as evidence. Items no16 through 18 (paint samples) were recovered on 3-11-83, at 1520 hours from a red Cadillac, (License #1EXZ199), located at 9612 Anzac, by L.A.P.D. SID Criminalist E Schwecke and S. Scheverman, and subsequently booked as evidence.

Note: The above vehicle was allegedly struck by the suspect (s) vehicle.

Items No. 19 and 20 (hair samples) were removed by Detective C. Merritt (Southeast Homicide) form possible suspect Marvin Smith, at Southeast Division, on 3-15-83, at 1730 hours.

Items No. 21 through 25 (rape kit samples, etc.) were obtained from the Coroner's office on 3-16-83, by SID L. Gutierrez, and subsequently turned over to SID Criminalist W. Loomis.

Item No. 27 (blue denim pants) was recovered by Sgt. C West, Southeast Supervisor, from witness Joseph Howard White.

Item No. 28 (mother's hair sample) recovered on 3-29-83, by Detective P. Marshall from victim's mother while at St. Francis Hospital.

Item No. 29 (hair sample) recovered on 3-24-83, at 110 hours, from the trunk latch of the vehicle that victim was found in, by Detective P. Marshall.

Additional Information—The vehicle ('66 Chevrolet, 2 door, red) as well as evidence items No 2 through 4, and 7 were held for latent prints with negative results.

VII. Vehicles

Vehicle #1-Suspect's Vehicle—described as an older model work-type van, medium to dark blue in color: no windows on side: two doors on rear of van: with a square shaped window on upper portion of each door: White bumper on front and rear, with a probable California plate (yellow lettering with blue background) attached to rear bumper, at center, or below center of bumper. (N.F.D.)

Vehicle #2- The victim's body was discovered in the trunk of a stripped and abandoned stolen vehicle (1966 Chevrolet 2 door, red) license plates and vin plates missing. See vehicle report under Addendum #2 for further information.

VIII.   Victim Information

Victoria Denise Brown is a female Negro, 8 years old, 4-0 feet, 60 lbs, and born 9-7-74, in Los Angeles, California. Victoria was currently residing with her mother, Francis Brown, at 9622 S. Anzac Avenue, Los Angeles, California. The father, Ernest Brown is separated from the victim's mother, and resides in Coolidge, Arizona. The victim was in the third grade at the Graham Elementary School.

IX.   Suspect Information

The perpetrator of this homicide remains unidentified. The suspect is described as a male/Latin, 25/30 years, 5-9/6-0 feet, 130/150 lbs., brown wavy hair, wearing a blue shirt with a white vertical stripe on the sleeve, and faded blue jeans. (N.F.D.)

X.   Witness Information

See witness list, form 3.11.7 and the statements of the witnesses attached as Addendum #14.

XI.   Injury and Autopsy Information

On 3-11-83, at 0825 hours, Detective M. Rhodes attended the autopsy of the victim, Victoria Denise Brown, performed by Los Angeles County Coroner's Pathologist Dr. Irwin Golden. The wire ligature and victim's clothing were removed and held as evidence.

Dr. Golden note and recorded the following non-fatal injuries to the victim:

1. Pinpoint abrasion—right upper arm.

2. Bruises—left wrist and back of right elbow.

3. Impressions on waist—probably due to elastic waistband of skirt.

4. Abrasion—left elbow (small) 3/8 in. X ¼ in.

5. Vaginal abrasions—3 o'clock and 9 o'clock, (hymen intact).

6. Rectal tear—5 and 7 o'clock—dilated widely.

Dr. Golden indicated the preliminary cause of death was due to ligature strangulation, supported by the following medical observation:

1. Petichia—both eyes, skin of eyelids (upper and lower), and both cheeks.

2. Abrasion—1 inch X 3/8inch just below angle of jaw, (left side), caused by ligature.

3. Ligature mark—1/8 inch width

Dr. Golden examined victim's stomach contents and determined, by the existing content (peaches and pears), that the victim's death was within the maximum period of three hours of her last meal.

Detectives have ordered a Coroners Protocol which was unavailable at the time of this report.

XII Communications

A. Teletypes:

1. On 3-10-83, Detectives C. Wright and K. Brutsch (Southeast Juvenile), caused a teletype to be sent describing crime, outstanding suspect, and vehicle.

2. On 3-12-83, Detectives P. Marshall and C. Merritt (Southeast Homicide) caused a supplemental teletype to be sent describing the subsequent homicide information.

B. Press Releases:

1. On 3-9-83, Detectives Wright and Brutsch, Southeast Juvenile, gave information regarding original kidnapping.

2. On 3-11-83, Detectives Calagna and Rhodes gave information pertaining to the homicide.

3. On 3-11-83, Lt. W. Pruitt updated press release pertaining to the homicide.

4. On 3-14-83, Detectives Marshall and Merritt updated the press release.

5. On 3-29-83, Detectives Marshall and Calagna updated the press release.

6. On 3-31-383, Lt. W. Pruitt updated the press release.

C. Wanted Information:

1. On 3-30-83, Information Wanted Bulletin was complied and distributed to various Police Departments, Sheriff's Offices, and LAPD Division, possibly related to investigation.

2. Reward Bulletin ($5000.00) was distributed by Los Angeles City Unified School District.

D. Press Clipping:

1. On 3-10-83, *Los Angeles Times*

2. On 3-11-83, *Orange County Register*

3. On 3-11-83, *Los Angeles Times*

4. On 3-12-83, *Los Angeles Times*

5. On 3-15-83, Los Angeles Herald Examiner

E. Communication Tickets:

1. Original calls to Complaint Board (see Addendum #20)

Six-Month Progress Report

Change location of occurrence on Kidnap Report from 9532 Anzac Avenue to 9538 Anzac Avenue.

Change Reporting District on Death Report from 515 to 519.

On 3-9-83, the Kidnap-Murder of Victoria Brown was assigned to Southeast Detectives under the direction of Lieutenant William Pruitt.

On 4-6-83, Robbery-Homicide Division, Major Crime Investigation Section formally accepted the Brown Case after receiving a briefing from Detective III R. Reynolds of Southeast Detectives along with a completed thirty-day progress report. Due to the exorbitant amount of information that had been generated both from press released and from a $5000.00 reward offered by the Los Angeles Board of Education detectives found it necessary to employee the task force concept. Each piece of information was recorded on a LAPD Clue form and assigned a clue number.

Between the dates of 4-12-83 and 5-18-83, the following personnel were loaned to Major Crimes Investigation Section to assist with the investigation of clues: Detective J. Cota, Detective T. Moreno, Detective E. Peters, and Detective J. Rockwood.

To date detectives have assigned 471 clues of which 445 clues have been thoroughly investigated and closed.

Five of the twenty-six remaining clues are directed toward one suspect—James Warren Prescott. The allegations contained in the five clues indicate that Prescott bragged to his friends about killing Victoria Brown that he was observed driving southbound towards Wilmington the night of Brown's abduction, that he owns a blue van with damage to the passenger side and has changed the appearance of the van since Brown's abduction, and that Brown was seen in Prescott's van the same day of her abduction.

On 7-20-83, Prescott voluntarily came to PAB and submitted to a polygraph examination. The results of this examination were ruled inconclusive by polygraph personnel due to Prescott's admitted use of prescription drugs.

On 7-27-83, detectives scheduled a second polygraph examination for Prescott, but, after Prescott's arrival he indicated to detectives that he wished an attorney present during the examination. Prescott is currently represented by attorney Carl Jones, who has refused to allow Prescott to submit to an additional polygraph examination. On 7-26-83, detectives photographed and searched Prescott's van, with his permission. The follow-up by detectives regarding the damage to the passenger side of Prescott's van disclosed that he had been involved in a traffic accident with an RTD bus and that the damage had been reported approximately two months prior to Brown's abduction. Prescott volunteered that he replaced the rear doors of his van after the neighbors broke out the windows in an act of vandalism because they felt that he was responsible for Brown's death. Detectives have been unable to locate any witness who personally saw Brown in Prescott's company or who personally heard Prescott brag of killing Brown.

Detectives continue to investigate the possibility of Prescott's involvement in this matter. However, to date they have been unable to obtain tangible evidence pointing to Prescott as the killer of Brown. Detectives have personally contacted all neighboring police agencies in an attempt to find similar crimes, but have had negative results.

Detectives have reinterviewed all witnesses to the Brown abduction and on 4-15-83 released a police bulletin with nation-wide distribution updating the description of the suspect(s) and vehicle along with a composite drawing of the suspect's hairstyle and length.

Detectives continue to communicate with victim's mother and father. Victim's father has recently moved to Los Angeles from Coolidge, Arizona, and is living with his mother.

This investigation is to be carried Investigation Continued.

One Year Progress Report

The Victoria Brown case continues with the ongoing investigations of clues. To date, 476 clues have been called in, of which 450 have been investigated and closed.

Unsolved Murder Investigation

Progress Report

Fact Sheet

Victim: Brown, Victoria Denise

Date/Time Occurred: 3-9-83 1430/1530 Hours

Location of Occurrence: 9532 S. Anzac St., Los Angeles

1600 Block East "Q" Street, Wilmington

Cause of Death: Ligature Strangulation

Motive: Probable Sexual Gratification

Area of Occurrence: Southeast Area

Harbor Area

Detectives Assigned: Det.3 R. Reynolds, Det.3 M. Calagna, Det.3 P. Marshall, Det.2 H. Rhodes, Det.1 C. Merritt, Det.1 D. Parks, and PLM.3 C. Wilder, all of the Southeast Division.

Date of this Report: 4-12-83

Note:

The case remained an unsolved case until I was contacted by Major Crime's detectives in 2004. They informed me that the case had been picked up again as a cold case, and the trace evidence had again been submitted for reexamination and to be analyzed for DNA. It was found, at that time, that all the hair samples that I had had gathered from the victim were not all hers, as originally reported. DNA proved to be present in some of the hair samples, and that DNA was not the victim's. The DNA was assumed to be that of the suspect, and the detectives believed that they were going to be able to iden-tify a suspect. They wanted me to come to LA to testify to the recovering of the hair samples when they came up with a suspect.

I did not hear back from them and did not know the outcome of the case until I did some research for this book and found the following article.

California:

DNA evidence links a man imprisoned in Mexico for another girl's murder in 2005.une 16, 2010 | Andrew BlanksteinAn arrest warrant has been issued in the 1983 abduction and slaying of an 8-year-old Watts girl, the Los Angeles Police Department said Tuesday.Detectives with the department's cold-case homicide unit said prosecutors have filed murder charges against Luis Garcia Villalvazo, a Mexican citizen who is serving time in a Mexican jail for the unrelated killing of another girl.

In March 1983, Victoria Denise Brown was walking home from Graham Street Elementary School in the Florence-Firestone area of South Los Angeles when a blue van pulled up next to her.

She stopped to talk to someone in the van. Moments later, the van peeled away from the curb, and the girl had vanished.

Police conducted an extensive search, looking for any sign of her in storm drains, vacant lots and alleyways.

Twenty-six hours later in nearby Wilmington, Victoria's body was discovered inside the lidless trunk of an abandoned car in a gritty industrial corridor bordered by oil fields and auto wrecking yards.

Victoria, who had been snatched just half a block from her home in the 9600 block of Anzac Avenue, had been sexually assaulted and strangled. Authorities circulated leaflets that included a drawing of the van and a sketch of a Latino man 29 to 30 years old, 6 feet tall, 190 pounds with brown curly hair and a light complexion. The Los Angeles Unified School District offered a $5,000 reward for information leading to an arrest.

At times, the anguish almost overwhelmed Victoria's father, Ernest Brown. In an interview Tuesday, he said he thought of committing suicide, and turned to alcohol and other substances to try to dull the pain of his loss.

The mystery of who killed Victoria lingered for decades before time, technology and dogged detective work provided police with a suspect.

Det. Elizabeth Estupinian of the LAPD's cold-case homicide unit said DNA evidence from Victoria's case was analyzed in 2004, but it did not initially appear that there were enough genetic markers to upload to the national DNA database.

The detectives reexamined the evidence in 2009 and submitted it to a national DNA databank. In November, the genetic material collected from the crime scene indicated a genetic profile matching Garcia Villalvazo and would show up in one in every 2 trillion people.

Garcia Villalvazo is serving a 92-year prison sentence for the murder of 7-year-old Airis Estrella Pando in May 2005. He also was found guilty in the sexual assault of three other young girls in Juarez, Mexico, in 2004.

Garcia Villalvazo committed those crimes after having served 10 years, beginning in 1994, of a 19-year federal prison sentence in the United States after being convicted in Illinois of drug trafficking.

On Tuesday, the Los Angeles County district attorney's office filed a request to extradite Garcia Villalvazo under the treaty that exists between the United States and Mexico.

Estupinian and her partner, Det. Luis Rivera, said the lingering question is whether there were additional victims in the Los Angeles area. "You have to ask yourself about what he was doing from puberty to 43 years of age"—the year Victoria was killed—Estupinian said. "We have an obligation to see if there are other cases."

DNA—it gets some people out of jail and others into jail. I wander how many other "cold cases" I will be contacted about. Until the next time, I am still a homicide detective in my heart and my soul.

It was September of 1983, and I had just left my captain's office and was sitting at my desk drinking coffee and reflecting on what he had just told me. He was a new captain and had told me that some changes were going to be made in the division. I was to stop working on the homicide cases, in a "hands on" mode, and to start working more as a supervisor. He wanted me to make monthly rating reports on my homicide detectives and assure him that they were not violating any civil rights in their searches and seizures. If I found any violations, I was to report them to Internal Affairs. It seemed as though the department was more interested in making sure that the police were in compliance with civil rights than in solving cases. I agreed with the merit behind this, but on the other hand, why should a criminal have civil rights? I and my section had always complied with the court's rulings and always found new ways around court decisions to get the job done and not violate anyone's civil rights.

More and more the courts were allowing civil rights to become part of the trial. It did not matter if a person could be proven guilty or not; what mattered was that the police did not violate their rights during search and seizure or during questioning. When I went to court in the 1980s, I was on the stand proving I had not violated the defendant's rights more than I was proving the defendant committed the crime. If it was proven that I had violated the defendant's rights, he would go free, and I would be subject to an FBI investigation, and I could go to prison.

Was it worth it to continue to work for the department any longer? I had to fight the courts, fight the citizens, and now, fight the department. I had been taking the family up to the state of Washington on my vacations over the last several years, and we all liked it up there. I got to pursue my passion for fishing, and the kids got to experience all the outdoor activities that nature offered. I had been up there in August, and was offered a job working with the federal government at a submarine base.

That night I talked it over with the wife and kids, and we all thought it was time for me to leave the department. We wanted to get the boys out of Southern California before they were in high school and I knew it was time to put my family in front of my job. I loved my present wife dearly, and did not want to lose her, or the kids, because of my job. The next day I announced to my captain that I was retiring, and the next month I went to Washington. It took me six months of working both jobs to finally officially retire from the department (April 1984) and move my family to Washington state.

29 HELD, POLICEMAN
7/2/67 HURT AT 'LOVE-IN'

Twenty-nine persons were arrested, 17 illegally parked cars were impounded and a police officer was injured in the course of a "love-in" that attracted more than 4000 persons to Griffith Park Sunday.

Officer Robert E. Reynolds was cut on the right side when struck with a broken bottle during a sweeping police operation to clear the park's Crystal Springs area at 10 p.m. closing time.

Earlier in the day, 14 adults and 12 juveniles were arrested for possession of marijuana.

A man wearing only a loincloth was arrested for lewd conduct. Another was arrested on arson charges after setting a grass fire in the area. A man found carrying a billy club was arrested for violating the State Deadly Weapons Act.

About 10:30 p.m. two city fire companies extinguished a blaze in an automobile parked near the park's merry-go-round.

The love-in was the largest such gathering since Easter Sunday, when more than 6000 persons massed in Elysian Park without incident.

A traffic alert was broadcast about 5 p.m. when traffic became congested in the area. The Los Feliz Boulevard and Golden State Freeway entrances to the Park were closed briefly.

Gen. Rogers
Dies in Capital

WASHINGTON, July 1 (AP) — Retired Lt. Gen. Gordon B. Rogers, 65, former U.S. 7th Army Commander in Europe, died yesterday at Walter Reed Army Hospital.

"When your day ends
mine starts."

L. A. P. D. Homicide Detective
R. E. Reynolds
Det. Sgt.

145 W. 108 St.
L. A. Calif.

Phone
485-6910

February 6, 1983 receiving meritorious Unit Citation from Police Chief Gates.

July 2 1967, Article in LA Times newspaper.

My business card while working Southeast Homicide.

Flyer distributed to public on the Victoria Denise Brown kidnap, rape, and murder in 1983.

1982-Southeast Homicide Unit. I am the gambler with girls hand on shoulder.

Summarization: This has been my story of how life really was working patrol and working homicides on the streets of Watts in the 1960s, 1970s, and '80s. I hope in reading my war stories, you were able to stay with me as I did my job as it had to be done. Keep in mind that this was the way it happened and the way it was, as I lived it, being a cop in Watts.

Robert E. Reynolds

Robert E Reynolds Spent 24 years with the Los Angeles Police Department, seventeen years of the 24 were spent working homicide. He left the department to work for the Federal Government as a security specialist at the Trident Submarine Base in Silverdale, Washington. He worked at the base for 15 years. He also taught Criminal Justice classes at Olympic Junior College in Bremerton, Washington for 21 years. In his spare time he coached baseball for 27 years, from American Legion baseball to coaching at local high schools and at the junior college where he taught.

This is his first book.

Made in the USA
San Bernardino, CA
10 December 2012